MARITIME STRATEGY AND

Maritime Strategy and the Nuclear Age

Geoffrey Till

with contributions from
John Hattendorf, Richard Hill, Barry Hunt,
Peter Nailor, Bryan Ranft, Stephen Roskill
and Craig Symonds

Second Edition

MACMILLAN

© Geoffrey Till 1982, 1984

First edition 1982
Second edition 1984
Reprinted 1990

Published by
MACMILLAN ACADEMIC AND PROFESSIONAL LTD
London and Basingstoke
Companies and representatives
throughout the world

ISBN 0–333–36589–5 (hardcover)
ISBN 0–333–35968–2 (paperback)

Printed in Great Britain by
Antony Rowe Ltd
Chippenham, Wiltshire

Contents

Notes on the Contributors

JOHN HATTENDORF is a Professor of Strategy at the Naval War College, Newport, Rhode Island. He is co-editor of *The Writings of Stephen B. Luce* and has written a number of articles on the history of naval thought.

RICHARD HILL is a retired naval officer who has made a particular study of the international law of the sea and its application to and enforcement by maritime forces. He was an adviser to the United Kingdom delegation to the United Nations Law of the Sea Conference at Caracas in 1974.

BARRY HUNT is an Associate Professor of History at the Royal Military College of Canada. He has published several articles on British and Canadian naval history and co-edited *War Aims and Strategic Policy in the Great War 1914–18*. He has also written *Sailor – Scholar: Admiral Sir Herbert Richmond 1871–1946*.

PETER NAILOR is Professor of History and International Affairs at the Royal Naval College, Greenwich. He has written widely on maritime affairs and has just produced a major study of the Polaris programme.

BRYAN RANFT was until recently Visiting Professor in Maritime History at King's College, London. He has written widely on maritime affairs and has edited *Technical Change and British Naval Policy 1860–1939* as well as a recent edition of the works of Sir Julian Corbett.

STEPHEN ROSKILL's last major work was a study of Admiral Beatty. Among his many earlier works are *The War at Sea* (3 vols), *Naval Policy between the Wars* (2 vols), *Hankey: Man of Secrets* (3 vols) and *Churchill and the Admirals*.

CRAIG SYMONDS is a Professor of History at the US Naval Academy, Annapolis. His books include *Charleston Blockade* and *Navalists and anti-Navalists*, a reinterpretation of early US naval policy.

Preface

A few years ago, Neville Brown pointed out that there were schemes afoot to use cyclones to destroy enemy fleets and tidal waves to drown enemy bases. 'When naval communities pay attention to ideas as quaint as this', he remarked, 'it is a sign that they are lacking something. That something is good contemporary naval doctrine. Our seafarers have yet to complete their intellectual adjustment to the disappearance of the battleship and the approach of thermonuclear sufficiency. Books and articles on sea power still derive far too many of their judgements from the axioms of yesterday.'[1]

One aim of this book is to investigate whether this is really so. What *is* contemporary naval doctrine? Is it still as defective as Neville Brown claimed it was in 1964? Is it too closely wedded to the 'axioms of yesterday'? In any case, how different is – or should be – the naval present to the naval past? Because they affect every aspect of naval development, these questions are, and in fact always have been, crucial to seafarers and to those interested in their activities.

By a survey of the writings of the maritime strategists of the past, this book tries first of all to identify what those axioms of yesterday actually were, and then to see how well they stand up to modern conditions and the axioms of today. What follows is essentially a general *tour d'horizon*, aiming to raise issues of past and present that need thinking about. It is intended to be an aid to thought, not a purveyor of illusory conclusions about the universal truths of maritime strategy. But since the right answers to particular problems at particular times depend on the right questions being asked in the first place, this limited objective seems, to me at least, both necessary and worthwhile.

I would, first of all, like to thank my contributors, who are listed separately, for their hard work and general support. They should not, however, be regarded as responsible for, or necessarily agreeing with, views expressed in this book outside their own particular sections; nor should their views, or in fact any views expressed in this book, be taken necessarily to reflect official policy in this or any other country.

I would also like to record the very real help given me by the many naval officers with whom I have discussed these issues over the past few years. Although they are too numerous to name individually, they will know who they are and I hope will accept this general expression of my gratitude. I am particularly grateful to those who read and commented

on parts of the manuscript. More specifically, I would like to thank for
their help: Lt Cmdr Philip Bosscher of the Royal Netherlands Navy;
Major Donald F. Bittner of the USMC Command and Staff College,
Quantico, Virginia; Prof. Keith W. Bird of the University of
Bridgeport, Connecticut; Prof. Donald C. Daniel of the US Naval
Postgraduate School, Monterey, California; James M. McConnell of
the Center for Naval Analyses, Arlington, Virginia; Ray Kipling of the
Royal National Lifeboat Institution and the editorial staff of *Portcullis*,
the newspaper of HM Customs and Excise; Mr Alan Pearsall of the
National Maritime Museum, Greenwich; Contre-Amiral F. de Quey-
lar of the French Navy.

I have also made considerable demands on Judithe Blacklaw, Ian
Mitchell and Bob Durham in the library of the Royal Naval College
Greenwich, and on Kathy Mason, Secretary of the History Depart-
ment. I would like to thank them all for their efforts on my behalf.

Finally, I would like to thank my wife, Cherry, who has deciphered
the indecipherable, corrected the text, located quotations and laboured
mightily over the typewriter. This book is dedicated to her.

28 July 1980   GEOFFREY TILL

1 An Introduction

(a) The influence of sea power on history

Every so often a book appears which captures the spirit of the times, sells in its tens of thousands and educates a generation. Captain Alfred T. Mahan's *The Influence of Sea Power Upon History 1660–1783*, published in 1890, was just such a book.

Mahan, as a good American, was mainly interested in converting his own countrymen to his line of thought, but his book aroused enormous interest in Europe too, especially in Britain and Germany, and Japan. The Kaiser, in 1894, said, 'I am just now not reading but devouring Captain Mahan's book and am trying to learn it by heart. It is a first class work and classical in all points. It is on board all my ships and constantly quoted by my captains and officers.'[1]

Although he concentrated only on a quite restricted slice of history, Mahan expected and indeed encouraged his readers to use the insights this survey generated to take the larger view. He hoped they would recognise first how important the sea had been in the past and secondly how important it would continue to be in the future. Until then, he wrote, 'the profound determining influence of maritime strength on great issues' had been overlooked, because historians were 'unfamiliar with the conditions of the sea', generally having neither the interest nor the knowledge necessary. America would only prosper, however, if it came into the light and recognised the role of the sea in its past and future destiny.

This was the main burden of the argument put forward by all the 'navalists' who followed in Mahan's footsteps. They sought to persuade by showing how well nations did if they observed these eternal truths and how disastrously if they did not. Britain was often regarded as the model. De Lanessan, French Minister of Marine, wrote in 1901:

> From the end of the reign of Louis XIV she [England] became the greatest commercial country of the world: our colonies passed into her hands, her merchant-ships circled the globe in thousands and her fleet kept ours shut up in our harbours if it was not to be exposed to bloody and ruinous defeats:

and this was all because France had turned away from her maritime destiny in order to pursue calamitous continental adventures for reasons of 'personal ambitions, caste interests and the atavistic passions which again burnt in the hearts of our rulers'.[2]

Some seventy years later much the same message can be found in the writings of Admiral Sergei Gorshkov, Commander-in-Chief of the Soviet Navy. History showed, wrote Gorshkov, that Russia could not take her place among the great powers without a strong fleet. Whenever the 'influential satraps of Russian Czarism' neglected their naval forces, political degradation and military defeat followed.[3] Instead, sea power now offered the Soviet Union the capacity to exploit all the resources and possibilities offered by the oceans for the economic benefit of the country. Furthermore, a 'constantly developing and increasingly sophisticated Soviet Navy' would ward off aggression, guarantee the building of communism and protect the great gains won by the workers.[4]

Navalists evidently believed that sea power had three great gifts to bestow. First it was an effective means of acquiring colonies, dominating trade and becoming prosperous. A colony, wrote Mahan, was 'a foothold in a foreign land, a new outlet for what it [the colonial power] had to sell, a new sphere for its shipping, more employment for its people, more comfort and wealth for itself'.[5] In the view of Sir Julian Corbett sea power explained how it was 'that a small country [like Britain] with a weak army should have been able to gather to herself the most desirable regions of the earth, and to gather them at the expense of the greatest military powers . . .'[6] Prosperity and contentment followed inevitably.

From the fifteenth century onwards the Europeans spread their dominion eastwards, into the Indian Ocean, South East Asia and the China Seas. When the reasons for which they did it and how they did it are considered, it is easy to see why the navalists thought that sea power and prosperity advanced side by side. Europeans surged to the east to exploit the riches of Asia, and they went by sea because it meant they could outflank the Islamic dominance of the land routes. Even though a large proportion of the crew would probably die on each voyage, it was still easier, cheaper and safer to go by sea. They arrived at a time when the Asian communities were in a state of conservative decadence; they found that a few gun-ships could easily blow local warships out of the water and scatter the strongest of local fleets. With the Portuguese setting the pace the Europeans were able to straddle the Indian Ocean with a chain of naval bases, patrol it with their warships and dominate its most lucrative trade routes.[7]

In an age when the first Dutch 'clove ship' made a profit for its owners of 2500 per cent, it was not surprising that the Europeans should enter into a bitter competition with each other to exploit Asian resources and should seek to protect their investments by gradually taking over the land areas from which the sea trade came. Sea power was as helpful in this final stage of colonisation as it had been before. When the British acquired India in the eighteenth century, their sea power allowed them to bring their forces to the area, supply them and switch them from place to place as the occasion warranted. This capacity gave them resilience in adversity and was the condition of final victory.

Sea power's second great advantage, according to the navalists, was that it helped its possessor to keep what he held. De Lanessan said:

> If we wish to become a great commercial democracy, which will necessitate a great development of our mercantile marine and important progress in our Colonial Empire, we must possess a fleet of such a strength that no other power can dominate to our detriment the European waters on which our harbours are situated, or the oceans where our merchant ships circulate.[8]

Naval power was an effective means of deterring or defeating potential rivals. Without it, maritime trade would diminish and colonial empires would crumble.

Finally sea power, both of the military and non-military varieties, was claimed to be a decisive means of prevailing in conflict. 'It can scarcely be denied', claimed Mahan, 'that England's uncontrolled dominion of the seas, during almost the whole period chosen for our subject [1660-1793], was by long odds the chief among military factors that determined the final issue.'[9] It had also played, he thought, the vital role in the defeat of Napoleon.[10] In fact, as the official British historian of the Second World War at sea pointed out, the whole of history was full of occasions when a continental power

> won a series of resounding victories on land only to find itself brought up against a method of waging war with which its leaders could not grapple and of which they had no clear understanding. Maritime strategy, founded upon centuries of experience of the sea, brought our enemies to utter defeat.[11]

Not everyone was persuaded by these arguments about the benefits of sea power. It certainly did not seem to be the case that sea power was the only, or even an indisputable, royal road to prosperity and security. Some countries prospered that did not have it; others failed that did. The extent to which countries and empires derived their strength from the sea varied enormously. There were, thought Admiral Sir Herbert Richmond, some 'natural' sea powers like the Athenians, the Carthaginians, the Venetians, the Dutch and the British who had sea power thrust upon them by the necessities of geography. But there were others, like the Romans, the Ottoman Turks and the Spanish who achieved sea power by the conscious and calculated decision of their rulers.[12] There were even those, like the Aztecs, the Indians and the Chinese, who generally turned their backs on the sea, but who prospered nonetheless.

The Chinese Empire was a particularly interesting case. The Chinese certainly had the capacity for maritime enterprise; they used the cross-staff and the magnetic compass long before these were regular features in European ships. In the early fifteenth century, under the Ming dynasty, they sent Great Sea Expeditions into the Indian Ocean and elsewhere and they could reasonably be regarded as 'the strongest sea power in the world'.[13] But Chinese sea power was too artificial a creation to survive for long. This best example of it sprang, not from social, geographic or economic circumstances, but apparently from the political fancy of a court eunuch who wished to glorify the regime he adorned. Apart from the importation of a few exotic beasts and birds, his maritime endeavours had no appreciable impact on Chinese society. Thereafter, for the next 400 years, the Chinese authorities effectively avoided international trade and contacts, except for occasional concessions on a grace and favour basis to properly respectful foreigners. In the nineteenth and twentieth centuries the Chinese were the victims, not the exponents, of sea power.

Nevertheless, apart from this last period, their civilisation flourished even without the trappings of sea power. This, and other similar cases, seemed to show that there was no necessary correlation between natural sea power and prosperity – and, perhaps even if there was, the former was best seen as the result rather than the cause of the latter. The suspicion consequently arose that the navalists were perhaps making too much of the unique and probably unrepeatable experiences of a handful of West European states over a quite limited period in history. The benefits of sea power may certainly have been considerable in their particular circumstances but it was not clear that their experiences had any wider implications. The age of territorial acquisition by simple colonial conquest seemed to these unbelievers long past, and with it, presumably, some of the principal advantages of maritime endeavour. Perhaps the general utility of sea power was actually declining, from a peak rendered abnormally high by a set of circumstances that had now run their course?

Another set of sceptics criticised the navalists not so much for the relevance of the views they propounded for the future but for their unbalanced verdicts on the past. Even one of Mahan's generally admiring biographers admits that his subject sometimes exaggerated the decisiveness of sea power in conflict with land power.[14] In fact, on its own, sea power was rarely crucial in deciding great issues. The War of American Independence demonstrated that 'without allied reinforcements to divert or pin down enemy forces, the Royal Navy was not, and never had been, strong enough to ensure ultimate victory in a major conflict'.[15] With sea power England could certainly wield a degree of influence fundamentally disproportionate to her relative strength; she could ravage an enemy's maritime trade, damage economies and seize overseas territories. But, without continental allies and armies, it was hard for her to prevail in a considerable European conflict.[16] To defeat Napoleon, England needed more than mastery of the oceans.

The point was neatly made by Sir Julian Corbett. He wrote:

> Of late years the world has become so deeply impressed with the efficacy of sea power that we are inclined to forget how important it is of itself to decide a war against great continental states, how tedious is the pressure of naval action unless it be nicely co-ordinated with military and diplomatic pressure... 'We English,' wrote Nelson in the Gulf of Genoa, '... have to regret that we cannot always decide the fate of Empires on the sea'.[17]

Sea power has, in short, exerted a decisive influence on world affairs, although the extent of that influence is evidently a matter of debate. The issue is complicated by the fact that the degree of influence has advanced and receded, like the tides themselves, over particular periods of history. The manner of its influence has varied too; as conditions have changed, some benefits of sea power have disappeared but others have taken their place.

In the contemporary scene, the historical utility of sea power in the gaining and keeping of colonies would seem to be a wasted asset. It might, though, be more than replaced by the current advantages sea power has to offer for those wishing to maintain an invulnerable military deterrent, or for the many more anxious to enjoy their off-shore resources in security. The influence of sea power on world affairs has therefore varied both in extent and in type. Its philosophers, however, have argued that this influence has always been important, and, at least to some extent, have tried to explore why and how this has been so.

(b) The influence of history on sea power

Many of the philosophers of sea power argued not only that sea power had an important influence on history but also the reverse. History, or at least the study of it, could have significant effect on sea power because it showed not only how important sea power was, and is, but also how it should be handled. Some of them looked to history for revealed truth. 'A knowledge of naval history', wrote Admiral Sir Cyprian Bridge, was necessary 'not as a mere gratification of antiquarian prediliction, but as a record of the lessons of naval warfare'.[18] Others used history to test or illustrate ideas apparently generated independently. Either way, the study of naval history and the processes of strategic contemplation seemed to go hand in hand.

Although neither was exactly new at the end of the nineteenth century, they seemed it because previous generations had neglected them for so long. Naval history hardly existed except in the form of admiring tales of heroic deeds. Serious strategic or tactical contemplation in the world's leading navies was almost a contradiction in terms. Their eventual re-emergence was a long and difficult process. Lord Esher's celebrated letter of 1915 said:

> Julian Corbett writes one of the best books in our language upon political and military strategy. All sorts of lessons, some of inestimable value, may be gleaned from it. No-one, except perhaps Winston, who matters just now has ever read it. . . . Obviously history is written for schoolmasters and arm-chair strategists. Statesmen and warriors pick their way through the dusk.[19]

The long resistance of the forces of darkness derived, or derives, from a number of factors. There was, first of all, the view that such things did not need thinking about because they were all perfectly obvious. The story was told of one of Admiral Duncan's commanders at the battle of Camperdown in 1797 who was so bewildered by the stream of signals made to him by his Admiral that he swore soundly, threw his signal book to the deck in great disgust and simply ordered his Quartermaster to steer into the middle of the enemy's fleet. This, of course, was precisely what was needed. In just the same manner the guidance of established and familiar precedent, tempered with commonsense, would enable the efficient officer to see what needed to be done. The Royal Navy of the eighteenth century did not spend its time in strategic rumination, nor did it produce a body of general theory. Yet it evolved a system of doing what was necessary that worked, generally speaking.

Thinkers like Admiral Sir Herbert Richmond were wary of this approach, especially in periods which were not, unlike the eighteenth century, technologically static and studded with sufficient naval wars for senior officers to keep in practice. The Dardanelles and anti-U-boat campaigns of the First World War, he thought, were good examples of the regrettable tendency to repeat past errors or ignore past lessons. They also seemed to indicate that commonsense was too often absent to be relied upon as a substitute for learning.[20]

Differences in outlook and operating style between the academic and the service officers caused problems as well. The academic was often as much interested in the twistings and turnings of the journey as in the arrival. The sailor, beset with the press of urgent business, wanted answers. Never mind the arguments, ran the old illustrative adage, what are the conclusions? Worse still, there was often something distinctly Delphic about the musings of Clio. The lessons of history were frequently nothing like as clear cut and unambiguous as some of its practitioners claimed and most of the seamen wanted. They could be misunderstood, misapplied or downright misleading as conditions changed. Impatient of such apparently fruitless endeavours, many a pragmatic seaman preferred to stay in his concrete world of barnacles, rivets or transistors, leaving the pursuit of history and strategic contemplation to those who had the time for it. For such reasons, argued Richmond, naval material dominated naval thought, and the means dictated the ends.[21]

There were also the seductive arguments of graduates of what Richmond called the 'School of Experience'. The proper place for naval officers, they said, was at sea, for the navy needed seamen not bookworms. This was the place to learn about strategy and tactics; after the due number of years on the bridge, a mystical appreciation of what sea warfare was all about could be expected to descend on the head of the efficient naval officer, rather in the manner of the Holy Ghost. Such ideas led those who held them to look with a jaundiced eye on the products, the necessity and sometimes even the character of naval theorists. Mahan, for instance, was described in 1894 as, 'not a good officer' since his 'interests are entirely outside the service for which... he cares but little'.[22]

These attitudes tended to spill over into a scepticism about the worth of those institutions like the US Naval War College of Mahan and Admiral Stephen B. Luce.[23] Their aspirations were criticised for being over-inflated and apparently based on the assumption that the naval officer should be 'occupied in desk, book, lecture room, laboratory and workshop studies, though he might perhaps be permitted to go to sea occasionally as a necessary relaxation from the severe strain of his intellectual pursuits on shore'.[24]

This antipathy to the theoretical side of the naval profession was principally a feature of the British, Dutch and US Navies and did not apply to such others as the French, Russian or German Navies. Perhaps it was a function of the alleged pragmatism of the first three peoples; perhaps it was because there was less of a need to 'sell' the navy in these countries; perhaps it was because the 'military-aristocratic' strain was less pronounced a feature of their naval culture. But their neglect of theoretical study, however explained, did not seem to prevent their being generally successful – except, of course, against each other. Their experience, therefore, showed that theoretical study was not a condition of success.

Nevertheless, the argument of the naval thinkers remained. Thoughtful consideration of the nature of sea power and the lessons of history seemed to them the obvious place to start when a navy was being justified, designed or prepared for use. Generalised thinking based on historical analysis might be an imperfect instrument liable to misuse, unable to guarantee success, apt to raise more questions than answers, but it was still the best method there was. This view was the basic justification for their labours. Richmond concluded, 'It is in the pages of history that we find our stimulation and guidance.'[25]

(c) The principles of maritime strategy

One reason for scepticism about the worth of theoretical analysis was doubt as to whether there existed principles of naval strategy that really meant anything and were applicable in all times and places. Were there not too many variables in the equation for the universal verities to rise above the level of platitude? Maritime strategy does not operate in a vacuum but in the real world where logistics, political dissension, administrative inefficiency, health and so forth all have considerable impact on naval operations. In 1689 the English fleet was forced to retreat to Torbay with 2558 sick and 553 dead – the equivalent to the losses of a large battle. In the butts of beer 'great heapes of stuff was found not unlike to men's guts, which has alarmed seamen to a strange degree'. In this case, an unexpected breakdown in logistics had wrecked the fleet.[26] The weather, too, could determine events. Mahan wrote, 'Nelson . . . beat furiously against a west wind, while two hundred miles away the fleeing Villeneuve sped by Gibralter before an easterly gale. Land warfare knew vicissitudes enough, but there was no such perpetual disconcerting uncertainty as this.'[27] Very evidently, the argument went, the conditions of naval warfare were too complex, diverse and unpredictable for simple rules to govern them.

Even if such rules could be drawn up, closer examination would probably show that they were not universal at all, but specific to a particular time and place. The whole body of theory associated with Mahan has even been described as 'relevant only to the United States and Britain. It was not relevant to those states with neither the need nor the inclination to use the seas in such ambitious ways.'[28] The question of whether there was a basic, universal, philosophy of sea power was also the subject of considerable dissension in Russia just after the

Revolution, with Trotsky vainly warning against the dangers of trying to 'infer a new strategy by speculative methods from the revolutionary nature of the proletariat'. The Soviet New School certainly claimed that things were now quite different and that theoretical principles of naval warfare must henceforth be 'based on the Marxist Leninist methodology, in accord with the general line of the Communist Party'. The actual novelty of their approach is still a matter of controversy, but the whole issue lends some weight to the notion that the so-called principles of war are really little more than a camouflage for the pragmatic responses of particular countries to specific requirements at particular moments in time.[29]

The main reason, however, for scepticism about the existence of principles of maritime strategy has certainly been the widespread view that technological advances have changed everything, and continue to do so. A. C. Dewar wrote in 1904:

> Correct strategy will not be built up from the past. . . .The first prerequisite is a thorough grasp of the powers and limitations of the weapons, forces and instruments which we will have to use; then to evolve trial methods which can be beaten into practical shape by manoeuvres and constant practice. . . .The principles of strategy must be hammered out anew as instruments change.[30]

Reactions to this heresy have been mixed. Interestingly, Mahan believed that, since it reduced the level of uncertainty in naval operations, technological advance actually made strategic theory more, not less, possible.[31] Others, like Captain Roskill, acknowledge the extent to which the instruments of war have changed but still maintain that 'the old established principles governing their use do not seem to require modification'.[32] Even more draw a distinction between the effects of changes in materiel on tactics and on strategy. 'From time to time the superstructure of tactics has to be altered or wholly torn down' wrote Mahan, 'but the old foundations of strategy so far remain, as though laid upon a rock.'[33] The whole complex issue of the relationship between technology and the notional principles of war is one that constantly appears, as we shall see, in the development of naval theory.

The sum of all these objections is that the pursuit of universal truths about maritime strategy may be a pointless, even dangerous, activity. John Keegan wrote, 'It is a pity that these primitive maxims, with all their limitations and all the bad advice they proffer, should survive to contradict so much of the good sense that modern soldiers learn and talk.'[34] A belief in universal principles could be dangerous if it encourages the dogmatic and inflexible attitudes so harmful to the sea-officer, whose object, said Nelson, was 'to embrace the happy moment which now and then offers'.[35] It could dissuade the timorous from taking opportunities because to do so would seem to go against the rules. Occasionally a preoccupation with jargon and dogma confused rather than clarified thought. 'The Air Ministry are primarily concerned with the maintenance of the object which is invariably the prosecution of the offensive, the only means by which the ultimate victory is possible', wrote the Air Staff obscurely in 1936. 'All naval strategy is primarily defensively designed towards the maintenance of the fleet-in-being, whereas we aim to strike directly at the source of all enemy air power to accomplish the object by achieving the offensive aim.' If an adherence to the principles of war produced jargon and concepts which confused the mind and encouraged the writing of such strategic gibberish as this, it might perhaps be best to do without it. [36]

While they accepted that the so-called principles of war could be abused, misunderstood or even wrong on particular occasions, most naval writers still maintained that they existed. Naval strategy, claimed Mahan roundly, was based on fundamental truths which 'when correctly formulated, are rightly called principles; these truths, when ascertained, are in themselves unchangeable'. But it was important to see what these principles were. [37] They were not hard and fast rules or fine-cut precepts to be observed on every occasion. War was too chancy and uncertain a business for that. It ought to be said that not everyone agreed with this. Dr F. W. Lanchester's celebrated 'N Squared Law' of 1916 (the fighting strength of a force is in proportion to the product of the square of its numbers and the fighting value of its individual units) and, in a milder way, the work of operational researchers of the Second World War, were both based on the proposition that operations of war could be reduced to numbers and analysed scientifically. The result could be precise guidelines for action (laws?) which would make war much less chancy. [38]

This was, however, quite different from Mahan's view of what principles were. He wrote, 'The best of rules, when applied to it [the conduct of war] cannot be rigid, but must have that free play which distinguishes a principle from a mere rule'. War is not a science, but an art and 'it is for the skill of the artist in war rightly to apply the principles and rules in each case'. [39] The principles of war, therefore, are general guidelines derived from historical precedent and independent thought which focus attention on things which need thinking about. Their character, and their contents, could best be understood, not in the abstract, but in the solid world of historical example. And it was to search out these principles and examples that most of the naval writers took to be the primary justification for their work.

Virtually to a man they believed that an appreciation of such principles would 'facilitate the understanding of strategic questions'; allow one man to profit from the experience of others; give shape to the complexities of ship design. Even Nelson would have been better, especially in his earlier years, with a little more 'systematic ordering and training of . . . ideas.'[40] The identification of the principles of naval warfare, in other words, would provide direct and practical benefits. In the minds of most naval strategists, such principles would be of universal interest too. They were not simply the evanescent and specific product of their place and time. In dismissing the notion that there was something 'uniquely Japanese' about Japanese naval strategy in the Second World War, Bernard Brodie declared: 'No valid conception of sea power can vary according to the psychology or culture of different nations. A concept of sea power is either correct and conforms with the realities of war, or it is wrong.'[41] Most strategists would like to think Brodie was right.

(d) An anatomy of sea power

When the Soviet Navy wished to pass the *Kiev* through the Dardanelles, they called it an anti-submarine cruiser, rather than an aircraft carrier, because they did not wish to be seen breaking the Montreux Convention (which forbade the passage of this last class of vessel). In this case, they profited from the apparently surprising degree of latitude involved in the process of attaching labels to such obvious and visible things as warships.

There is even more latitude in the labelling of such constituents of maritime strategy as 'sea power', 'command of the sea' and the 'fleet-in-being'. This is because these are abstract concepts which cannot be touched or seen. Although the problem of recognising abstractions is not peculiar to maritime strategy, its exponents have evidently found difficulty in creating a common, consistent and unambiguous terminology for the less concrete aspects of their subject. The words they use may be the same but all too often they seem to refer to different things. The degree of consensus about the meanings of some of the phrases and concepts of maritime strategy is so low that it need hardly occasion remark when Admiral Gretton uses Richmond's definition of 'sea power' to describe 'maritime strategy'.[42] ('When *I* use a word,' said Alice to Humpty Dumpty, 'it means just what I choose it to mean and nothing more.')

Exact communication is rendered even more difficult by the fact that a writer may use the same term in different ways, sometimes from book to book, even occasionally from page to page. At other times the problem of recognition is aggravated by the fact that the same phenomenon is seen differently by people because of their particular circumstances of time and culture.

The results of this confusion are not good. It impedes the development of an agreed corpus of strategic theory. It is significant that so many writers of maritime strategy have to start off with an exercise in the 'naming of parts'. It shows, in current NATO jargon, that these are problems in inter-operability. One device often attempted is to invent new words and concepts in the hope that these will prove more illuminating. Sometimes all this appears to do is to make it more difficult for the previous generation of naval officers to interfere in the activities of the present one, and to replace old confusions with new ones. Vice Admiral William Crowe US Navy, Deputy Chief of Naval Operations, stated, with devastating candour, 'You are absolutely correct, we are victims of our syntax . . . some of the things we write in the Navy are not necessarily understandable'.[43] Much more serious than this, it is often claimed that faulty conceptualisation has led to disastrous errors in policy and operations.

It is, of course, much easier to describe the disease than to cure it. The best solution is probably that of Admiral Castex. He declared that he had a horror of Byzantine wranglings on the meanings of terms, and contented himself by outlining the problem and identifying the premises he would be using.[44] Sage counsel indeed.

Virtually all writers on maritime strategy have some conception of the elements or constituents of sea power. Mahan had six; geographical position, physical conformation, extent of territory, number of population, character of the people, and character of the government. He also spoke of the three inter-locking circles of sea power, an idea taken up by Richmond and Roskill who identify merchant shipping, overseas possessions or bases and the fighting instruments as the three materiel elements of sea power. 'Skilled men to wield the instruments' is often added. The German perspective of Admiral Wegener – fleet, position and a sea-orientated mentality (*seehaftes Denken*) – seems sufficiently similar for a synthesis of the bulk of the writings on the subject to be drawn up (Figure 1) and discussed later.[45]

These are all constituents of 'sea power' – probably the most obscure concept in the whole lexicon of maritime strategy. The phrase was coined by Mahan 'to compel attention and . . . to receive currency'.[46] This it certainly did, but unfortunately from that time, as Fred T. Jane noted, 'it has become a sort of occult term, eluding exact definition and perhaps meaning different things to different people'.[47] Perhaps wisely, Corbett tended to avoid it.

The cause of the difficulty is the word 'power', a slippery abstraction over which rivers of ink, sometimes augmented with a dash of vitriol, have been spilt by those involved in the study of international relations. Its derivative – sea power – can also be variously used sometimes as an abstraction differentiating it from land or air power. It may appear as a label for certain countries with great maritime strength. It can be taken to apply as well to the material instruments which a country uses to attain maritime objectives. Very often it is defined in terms of what it

SOURCES   ELEMENTS

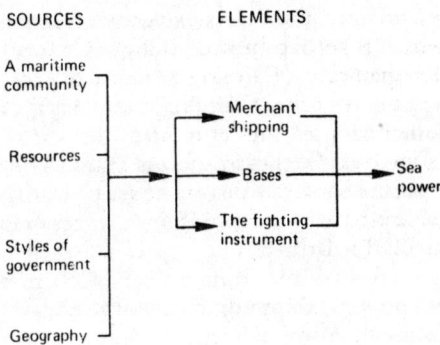

FIGURE 1   Seapower: sources and elements

enables a country to do. Richmond wrote, 'Sea power enables its possessor to send his troops and trade across those spaces of water which lie between nations and the objectives of their desires and to prevent his opponent from doing so'.[48] The ability to do this is usually regarded as a result of having the 'power to control movements at sea'.[49]

This tendency to equate sea power with the capacity to 'control' movement at sea may well be thought too restrictive a definition of the term. By linking the description of the nature of sea power to the successful accomplishment of its ultimate and most ambitious purpose, we exclude from the category too many countries who have been able to exert an important influence over events in peace and war by their maritime endeavours. It has been argued recently, for instance, that because of her adherence to continental ideas, 'Germany has never become a sea power'.[50] Although Germany was not a sea power in the sense that she put naval preparations at the top of her priorities, her maritime activities in both wars were more significant than this dismissive verdict seems to suggest.

It would seem better, in fact, to regard 'sea power' as a *relative*, not an absolute term. Countries may have degrees of sea power; they can exert influence in peace and in war by their activities at sea, to a greater or lesser extent. This is, at all events, how the phrase will be used from now on. It should perhaps also be emphasised that sea power – like power – is also relative to particular situations, and between particular countries. Richmond pointed out that 'no absolute comparisons can be made . . . Japan is stronger than America for a war in Northern Asia, but weaker for a war in the Caribbean'.[51] It is all a matter of degree, though the most successful of the contenders may be able to 'control' movement at sea so much that it becomes the dominant sea power.

This makes sea power a much less exclusive term than it sometimes appears to be, which is perhaps no bad thing, as it focuses attention on possibilities other than that of aiming at naval mastery – and also on instruments of sea power other than the purely naval ones. One of the reasons why Mahan adopted the term, after all, was to emphasise the role played by non-naval factors in success at sea. The possession of a large merchant marine confers a degree of sea power. And so, for that matter, may a shore-based air force. For such reasons as these some observers, particularly British ones, prefer to encompass all the possibilities in the label of 'maritime power'. Others prefer to divide this term into 'sea power' (shipping, bases – the non-military element) and 'sea force' (a navy). Admiral Wegener suggests that 'naval' be kept for war-orientated activities and 'maritime' for those of peace time.[52] At such a point, the absence of a consensus on terminology – and the problems it can cause – becomes painfully evident.

To attempt a synthesis once more, it seems possible to conclude that sea power consists of influence exerted by a mixture of military (mainly naval but with associated air and land) and non-military forces. A 'maritime strategy' will be taken to refer to the methods by which countries attempt to maintain or increase their sea power and how they try to use it to achieve desired objectives in peace and war.

(e) Constituents of a maritime strategy

At least to some degree, the immediate purpose of maritime strategy is to contest the control of the sea. The most direct method of doing this is to seek out the enemy's fighting forces and try to destroy them in some single massive encounter – or 'decisive battle'. The Peloponnesian War (431–405 BC) provides many illustrations of this and other concepts in maritime strategy, briefly summarised in Figure 2. The encounter at Arginussae (406 BC) certainly looks like a decisive battle. Three hundred warships were engaged.

> For this was the greatest sea fight that was ever fought by Grecians against Grecians that any history commemorates. And now at one instant, all the trumpets were commanded by the admirals to sound a charge, and the crews on both sides set up a great shout in their turn, one against another, and plying their oars with great heat and earnestness everyone strove who should be the first in making the onset. For there were many that by the long continuance of the war were well instructed for fights at sea, and the battle was very hot and obstinate on both sides, because the best and stoutest men were got together to fight in order to win or lose all at once. For none doubted but this battle would put an end to the war, whichever side so ever got the victory.[53]

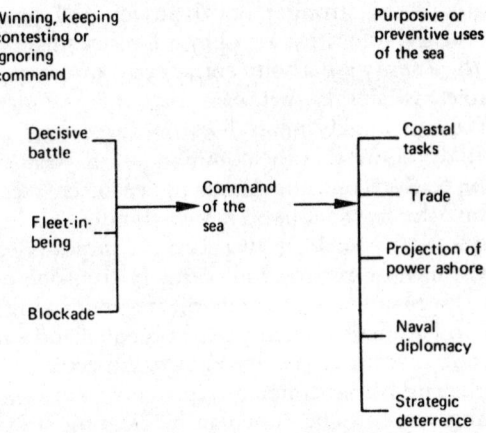

FIGURE 2   Constituents of a maritime strategy

The battle of Arginussae did not actually prove to be quite as decisive as the participants thought and the matter was only finally resolved in the following year after another battle. In fact, single decisive battles are very rare. The usual pattern is for a series of somewhat less-than-decisive battles to decide the issue cumulatively; the sequence of encounters between the Athenians and their enemies off the entrance to the harbour of Syracuse is a far more normal example of the 'decisive battle'.

In many cases, however, the weaker or possibly less ambitious side will not co-operate in the organisation of his own destruction. By a strategy of avoidance he may seek to keep most of his forces away from excessive danger. This caution need not mean a policy of total naval inactivity. By pursuing what has become known as a fleet-in-being strategy, even a weak naval force can confer significant strategic benefits upon its possessor. It may even be able to aspire to a certain capacity to control movement at sea. In the Peloponnesian War, both sides refused battle when a naval defensive seemed to offer more strategic benefits. Phrynichus said, 'There was no dishonour in Athenians retreating before an enemy's fleet when circumstances required'. Soon after this, however, the situation was reversed. The Athenians 'hoped to fight a decisive battle, but no one came out to meet them, and they returned to Samos'.[54] On both occasions the rival fleets seem to have adopted the 'active' variant of the fleet-in-being strategy, where the emphasis is on living to fight another day, rather than the passive which concentrates more on mere survival.

Confronted with an adversary pursuing either variant of the fleet-in-being strategy, the stronger naval power will probably seek to contain the enemy's fleet by a policy of blockade, which is either 'close' – off the enemy's harbour entrances – or 'distant' or 'open' – where the fleet is simply between the enemy and his possible objectives. This effectively neutralises his forces and prevents them from substantially contesting the command of the sea. In the course of the Expedition to Syracuse, the Athenian fleet attempted a blockading strategy against the Syracusans. They encountered all the difficulties that close-blockading squadrons usually do, compounded by the threat of other hostile naval forces behind them. Nicias, one of the Expedition's leaders, complained 'We have no means of drawing up our vessels and airing them because the enemy's fleet is equal and even superior in numbers to our own, and we are always expecting an attack from them'.[55] By the end of the campaign, in fact, it was a moot point who was blockading whom. The Athenian blockading strategy, in short, failed to give them the necessary control of sea movement which their Expedition required.

Being 'in command of the sea' simply means that a navy, in that happy state, can exert more control over the use of the sea than can any other. The degree of command varies greatly and is primarily illustrated by the extent to which it confers the capacity to use the sea for one's own purposes and prevent the enemy using it for his. Command of the sea is about the use of the sea, not its possession. Early in the Peloponnesian war the Athenian fleet did exercise considerable control of movement at sea. Their merchant fleet passed freely to and fro; they were able to act in support of allies and seize places like Melos: 'For we are masters of the sea, and you who are islanders, and insignificant islanders too, must not be allowed to escape us'.[56] The degree of their control was never absolute however for 'the Cretan Sea is a large place; and the masters of the sea will have more difficulty in overtaking vessels, which want to escape, than the pursued in escaping'.[57] Nicias, the half-hearted commander of the Expedition to Syracuse, doubted whether the Athenians had sufficient command to justify the enterprise in the first place. He pointed out, 'Our naval superiority must be overwhelming that we may not only be able to fight but may have no difficulty in bringing in supplies'.[58] In the event, his doubts were more than justified.

In the past, command of the sea was mainly exercised in activities connected with one of the two uses to which the sea could be put in wartime. These activities were directed either to using the sea oneself or to preventing the enemy from doing so. First of all, goods, men and supplies could be transported by sea and much maritime activity has been concerned with the protection or attack of the vessels engaged in this task. The whole pattern of Athenian maritime commerce was protected by their fleet and a network of naval bases in the Aegean and the Gulf of Corinth. In the Syracuse campaign, the Athenians proved to have insufficient command of the sea either to prevent reinforcement and supplies reaching their enemies or to guarantee the safe and timely arrival of their own. 'For they could no longer even introduce provisions with safety, but the Syracusan ships lay watching to prevent them, and they had to fight for the passage. General discouragement and dismay prevailed throughout the army.'[59]

The other principal use of the sea in time of war has been to project military power from the sea against the land by all means ranging from naval bombardment to the support of full-scale invasion. Attacking an enemy engaged in, or preparing for, such endeavours has also been an important and traditional part of maritime strategy. The whole expedition to Syracuse, of course, was an experiment in amphibious war involving several hundred ships and tens-of-thousands of troops. As they so often do in such operations, unexpected difficulties arose, the attack faltered, the invading troops got bogged down and were eventually defeated despite the arrival of fresh reinforcements and supplies. Not the least interesting part of this story was the suggestion made by Hermocrates that the Athenian assault could be deterred by a fleet operating from Southern Italy. This long-sighted advice (to which we shall return) was ignored; nevertheless the subsequent progress of the campaign on land was considerably affected by the Syracusans' increasing ability to interfere with the passage of Athenian supplies and reinforcements. The role of the sea in the defeat of land operations was as clearly demonstrated in this campaign as was its value in their support.

These have not, of course, been the only functions of navies in the past. Navies have had the task, to some degree, of protecting maritime resources, exercising jurisdiction and maintaining order in times of peace. With recent developments in maritime law and technology this 'coastal' task has much increased.

In the same way navies have always been used as direct instruments of a country's foreign policy and many of their activities in peace and war were more diplomatic than military in character. Shortly after the start of the Syracuse campaign, for instance, Nicias suggested that victory would come more quickly and easily if the fleet could be used in just such a way to deter intervention from the allies of Syracuse: 'They [the fleet] would then pass along the coast before the eyes of the other cities and display the visible power of Athens.'[60] In the nuclear age when the actual application of force has become increasingly hazardous, the relative importance of this 'naval diplomacy' role seems likely to increase.

Although it could perhaps be argued that operations in support of, or against, a country's sea-based nuclear deterrent forces could be regarded as a component of 'naval diplomacy' or 'projection' functions of navies (presumably as extreme versions of political persuasion or shore bombardment respectively) they seem, in fact, quite novel. Guidance on the problems and requirements of this last major concern of modern navies has obviously to be sought almost exclusively in the contemporary literature of maritime strategy.

2 A Review of the Literature

(a) Maritime strategy in the age of the galley

The ancient world does not seem to have produced a philosopher of sea power in the sense of someone who thought and wrote about maritime strategy as a whole. Of course, the general importance and military possibilities of power at sea were well realised; these ancient mariners very evidently knew what had to be done. But, as far as we can tell, none of them sought to generalise about the nature of warfare at sea or tried to uncover the principles by which it should be conducted.

Perhaps the nearest approach to it was that of Thucydides whose *History of the Peloponnesian War* has already provided us with illustrations of some of the main concepts of maritime strategy. Thucydides (c 460–404 BC) even had some naval experience himself. In 424 BC, he was given command of a fleet based at Thasos, but was dismissed for his subsequent failure to protect the city of Amphipolis. He wrote his *History* in the twenty years exile which followed this evidently unsuccessful foray into practical maritime strategy. But only on rare occasions, in his account of the long struggle between Athens and her enemies, did he, or the people whose views he represented, seek to generalise about the nature of warfare at sea as a whole.

Instead, he provided illustrations of the importance of maritime strength and the various uses to which it could be put. There was certainly no shortage of the kind of evidence needed to sustain general propositions about maritime strategy. From Thucydides' study of the expedition to Syracuse, for instance, Admiral Sir Reginald Custance was able to draw conclusions of some interest for the British of the late nineteenth and early twentieth centuries. He wrote, 'Athens was about to divert her armed forces, which were chiefly maritime, to the conquest of territory – that is to say, to a war on land, which is the business of an army'. This misuse of resources by a maritime Empire ended in a failure which illustrated the unwisdom of using the navy simply to supplement an inadequate army. The limits of sea power were evident too. Custance wrote, Athenian experience, 'shows that a navy is not of itself a menace to the independence of a continental power.'[1] In this and many other ways, it was as the sub-title of Custance's book stated, a case of modern theory and ancient practice.

Mahan too found his inspiration in the maritime experience of the

ancient world. Evidently it started in the library of the English Club at
Lima, Peru, where he read Mommsen's *History of Rome*. From this,
Mahan was impressed with the need to advance from the particular to
the general in order to explore the historical importance of control of
the sea.[2] Such was often the reaction to those who wrote about
maritime strategy in the ancient world for they mainly provided only
the evidence, leaving the conclusions to others.

(b) Maritime strategy in the age of sail

Martitime strength continued to be a source of prosperity in peace and
success in war throughout Europe's Dark and Middle Ages, but there
was little attempt at theorising about its importance and character or
how it should be employed. Naval warfare was largely a matter of
instinctive and unco-ordinated cross-ravaging of each other's coasts,
and sea-fights which were simply land battles fought at sea. Warships as
such hardly existed and there was little attempt at formulating or
executing a maritime strategy.

Contemporary leaders knew of course that events at sea were
important. One of the most celebrated testimonials to this was the
Libelle of Englyshe Policie, probably written about 1436 by Adam de
Moleyns, Bishope of the maritime See of Chichester. The Libelle
declares:

> For foure things our Noble sheweth to me
> King, Ship and Swerd and power of the sea
> Keep then the sea that is the wall of England,
> And then is England kept by Goddes own hand.

Nevertheless, technology, in the shape of the sailing warship armed
with cannon, was soon to force people to think about maritime tactics
and strategy in a much more ambitious way than this. One of the first
into the field was the Spaniard Alonso de Chaves who wrote his *Espejo
de Navagantes* (or *Seamen's Glass*) about 1530. De Chaves believed that
success would more likely attend the fleet that knew what it was doing,
and could be rationally directed to that end. He denied the view 'that at
sea it is not possible to order ships and tactics in this way, nor to arrange
beforehand so nicely for coming to the attack . . . and that therefore
there is no need to labour an order of battle since order cannot be kept'.
Accordingly, his was probably the first attempt to produce a definite
fighting formation and a set of tactical principles for sailing fleets.[3]

In England, writers like Sir Walter Raleigh and Sir Francis Bacon
were also taking tentative steps towards evolving a maritime strategy
for the age of sail. They, and other Elizabethans like Drake, Hawkins

and Sir William Monson, were practical men, not theorists. They were anxious to show, among other things, the solid advantages of a maritime rather than a continental strategy.

Hawkins wrote, 'In the continuance of this war I wish it to be ordered in this sort: that first we have as little to do in foreign countries as may be but of mere necessity, for that breedeth great charge and no profit at all'.[4] England should not waste her energies in fickle wars on land, as Athens had done against Syracuse, but should make the most of her maritime resources. 'He that commands the sea is at great liberty, and may take as much and as little of the war as he will,' wrote Sir Francis Bacon.[5] Control of the sea, in other words, conferred strategic initiative, offered the chance of great profit and limited liability if things went wrong.

The many advantages of naval mastery were perhaps best summarised by Mathew Sutcliffe in 1593:

The use of the Navy is great in peace, greater in wars. Thereby traffic and intercourse betwixt friends is maintained, victuals that go to the enemy are stopped, our wants of victuals, arms munitions, and other necessaries are supplied; the enemy's coast is spoiled, our own defended, the coast towns of the enemy's country that live upon the sea are brought to great extremities, our own maintained ... [without it] the trade of merchandise cannot be maintained ... [nor] the sea towns of the enemy be besieged, nor can be understand the enemy's proceedings, nor help or well defend our friends or ourselves.[6]

One of the two great maritime issues of the Elizabethan period was the urgent requirement to save the country from invasion. According to Raleigh it was unwise to rely merely on a defensive army resisting invasion at the point of impact. A sea-borne force would have so much more flexibility and mobility and could 'easily outrun the soldiers that coast them'. Instead, the English should remember that 'England is a country that can never be conquered while the sovereigns thereof have the command of the sea'.[7]

How should that command be contested and exercised? By waiting in the Channel or by a forward defensive at sea? Elizabeth's seamen argued vigorously for the second. Constant attacks on Spanish ports and shipping would oblige the enemy to divert their resources to defence 'to the infinite vexation, charge and discontent of [King Philip's] subjects.... The sequel of all these actions being duly considered, we may be confident that whilst we busy the Spaniards at home, they dare not think of invading England or Ireland.'[8] All too often though circumstances dictated the first, less satisfactory, approach.

The other great strategic task confronted by the Elizabethans was how best to strike at the roots of their enemy's prosperity. Drake proposed what was to become the orthodox route to success at sea: the seizure of a convenient base, then the achievement of naval mastery in Spanish waters and finally the complete extinction of the enemy's commerce. Others suggested a shorter more direct route to the acquisition of Spanish bullion. Perhaps an attack on the *flotas* at their assembly point of Carthagena or Havana?; or, as Hawkins suggested, by imposing a permanent naval blockade between the Azores and the Spanish coast with 'a sufficient company to distress anything that goeth through the sea'. If the Spaniards came out in strength to chase these ships away, the English, said Hawkins, should avoid a battle, keep their fleet in being 'hove daily in their sight and weary them and gain daily upon them'. Eventually the Spanish fleet would leave and the English could resume their blockading stations.[9]

Some of these ideas may certainly be thought misguided. Corbett, for instance, was extremely critical of Hawkins' idea of a cruiser blockade.[10] Also, deficiencies in the overall direction of the war, a shortage of funds and limitations in materiel meant there was, at this time, a considerable gap between conception and implementation. All too often the best laid plans were ruined by their principals behaving like a set of naval prima donnas. Nevertheless, the ideas of maritime strategy were beginning to emerge and be discussed.

The next step along the way was probably taken by the French. Although the Elizabethans – and their enemies and allies – clearly had effective ideas about the tactics of naval battle, their conception and execution were usually idiosyncratic in the extreme. Discipline and order in the handling of fleets and battles only really appeared with the development of 'the line' in the battles of the Dutch Wars of the following century. It was left principally to the French to explore the theoretical implications and consequences of this development.

There was, thought the author of what was probably the first rigorous study of naval tactics, an evident need for 'an art of naval evolutions'. Without it, he thought,

a fleet resembles a force of scavengers who do without order all that caprice inspires or chance suggests. Without it an Admiral can make only imperfect use of his fleet, whether it be to oppose the enemy in the proper way, or to cut his line, double on him, avoid him, bring him to action, or chase him; for all of these things require that the Admiral should be the moving spirit of his fleet, as the mind is of the various members of the body.[11]

The French realised, long before the British, that the sciences had to be pressed into the service of the navy, that naval officers had to be educated into their profession, even that ship design needed to be a matter of whole-time study. It is not surprising, therefore, that they took an early lead in supplying the need for a theory of fleet tactics.

Father Paul Hoste (1652–1700), one time chaplain to Admiral the Comte de Tourville and a Jesuit professor of mathematics, duly provided it. His *Traite des Evolutions Navales* (1691) and *L'Art des Armees Navales* (1697) were once described as 'the best work on Naval Tactics . . . ever published'.[12] Hoste reduced the chaos of naval battle to geometric form, codified such formations as 'la ligne de file' (line ahead), 'la ligne de front' (line abreast), 'la ligne de relevement' (line of bearing) and used these formations as the centrepiece of a system of fixed and constant conventions designed to turn the fleet into a single, controllable, disciplined unit.

The loss of initiative and ability to profit from unexpected opportunities that this formalism implied became clearer as the eighteenth century progressed, and French literature on naval tactics developed. Admiral the Vicomte Bigot de Morogues led the second wave with his *Tactique Navale* in 1763. He was followed by a good many other naval writers including the Vicomte de Grenier, *L'Art de la Guerre sur Mer* (1787) and Audibert Ramatuelle, *Cours Elementaire de Tactique Navale* (1802). It became clear that this theoretical grounding gave the French the edge tactically in their conflicts with the Royal Navy.[13]

The problem was made worse by the fact that the French evidently also had a different concept of the naval battle. To them, the sinking of enemy warships was not necessarily even the immediate aim of naval warfare. They had instead their 'ulterior objects'. Perhaps it was more important to lure the British away from some position or target, than to destroy their forces. Sometimes the French even passed up opportunities of attacking weaker, vulnerable British fleets rather than jeopardise the strategic purposes they had in mind.

This seemed contrary to the spirit of warfare at sea to many other naval writers. Indeed such a strategy of avoidance combined with a high level of tactical proficiency frequently baffled the British and produced a century of inconclusive skirmishes at sea. The tactical doctrine of the Royal Navy – with its excessive adherence to the notion of keeping to the line – made matters worse. It was to improve this situation that John Clerk of Elden (1728–1812), a retired merchant of Edinburgh, produced the first version of his *Essay on Naval Tactics* in 1782. Clerk, who had probably been no nearer the sea than Leith docks, analysed the problem, pointed out the superiorities of the French system and made his recommendations. He particularly advocated concentrating force against a portion of the enemy's line – a revolutionary suggestion at the time. He claimed the credit for Admiral Rodney's successful tactics in the Battle of the Saints in 1782 and certainly exercised much influence over British tactical thinking. It was, apparently, Nelson's favourite occupation to listen 'while the Chaplain read to him from Clerk of Elden's essay'.[14]

The pattern of naval battles in the Revolutionary and Napolenic Wars which followed was certainly much more to the British taste. But complacency had its inevitable consequence. The Royal Navy afterwards based such tactical and strategic doctrine as it had on the half-remembered and half-digested sayings of Nelson and effectively relapsed once more into the dark ages of naval thought.

(c) The Colomb brothers

For most of the next fifty years, the British Admiralty seemed almost deliberately bent on giving the impression that naval thought was a contradiction in terms. Its attention was largely concentrated on various imperial enterprises around the world and on the more practical consequences of the contemporary struggle between sail and steam. There was little real thinking about the future of maritime strategy.

All this doubtless played a part in the general loss of confidence in the navy that characterised much of the middle part of the nineteenth century. The basis of this feeling, though, was a sudden obsession with the danger of invasion and a widespread fear that the navy might be unable to do anything about it. Worries of this kind had a long ancestry. In 1628, for instance, Viscount Wimbledon had written about the problem of 'How the coasts of Your Maj'tes Kingedome may bee defended aginst any enemye, if in case your royall Navie should be otherwise employed or impeached'. This anxiety about what would happen if the navy for any reason could not defeat invasion led from time to time to expenditure on coastal defence. Most naval officers, however, were sceptical about the necessity for these panic measures. The sole justification that Lord St. Vincent could see for them was that they would 'calm the fears of the old ladies both in and out'.[15]

Nevertheless, these anxieties were greatly reinforced in 1844 when a French Admiral, the Prince de Joinville, wrote a truculent article in the *Revue des Deux Mondes* pointing out that the British fleet could be defeated in detail and, with the aid of steam, an invasion force could be rushed across the Channel in the darkness of one night. Against such a bolt from the blue, Britain would be powerless. For the rest of the century, the country was prone to bouts of panic about this. Richard Cobden identified three of these by 1862, and vainly pointed out the unreality on which they were based.[16] Steam, in Palmerston's view, had 'thrown a bridge across the Channel' and so justified the erection of various defensive monstrosities in red brick along the southern coast of England. Sometimes, as in 1888, money was sliced off the navy vote and re-allocated to coastal defence. There was also much controversy about the size of the home army and what size of invasion it should be prepared to guard the country against.

In all these ways, the traditional primacy of the navy in national regard was under serious threat. Among the first to come to the navy's rescue were the two brothers, Captain Sir John and Vice-Admiral Philip Colomb. Captain Sir John was the younger of the two being born in 1838 on the Isle of Man. After a short uneventful career in the Royal Marine Artillery, he retired in 1869 and spent the remaining forty years of his life writing about various aspects of Imperial Defence. The House of Commons had the frequent benefit of his views as he was a far from silent MP for some twenty years. These views first saw the light of day in an anonymous pamphlet called *The Protection of our Commerce and Distribution of our Naval Forces Considered* (1867). Some of his later articles were gathered together in *The Defence of Great and Greater Britain* (1880). He generally ignored politics, economics, history and complexities of that kind, preferring to drive his message home by simple and forceful logic and the accumulation of statistics. He was very much the pioneer, blazing a trail for others.

His brother Philip was an early collaborator. Born in 1832, he was the elder of the two but a full, varied and active life in the navy delayed his entry into the lists until 1873 when his *Slave Catching in the Indian Ocean* appeared. Although this was his first formal book, a batch of articles produced between 1871 and 1889 were published in *Essays on Naval Defence* (1896). This followed his successful *chef d'oeuvre*, *Naval Warfare* (1891). He retired from active service in 1886, but stayed on to become an instructor in naval tactics at the Royal Naval College, Greenwich, and produced a prestigious biography of Admiral Sir Ashley Cooper-Key in 1898. He died of a heart attack in the following year.

His approach was quite different from that of his younger brother; his was not just a functional interest in the best method of Imperial Defence, but a concern for the principles of naval warfare as a whole. He believed there was too little thought about maritime strategy and was sure he could discover its principles: 'The science of Naval Tactics still remains in an exceedingly vague and unsatisfactory state: but the Author is now, as ever, persuaded that there are no difficulties in putting it on an absolutely sound basis in peacetime.' It was necessary to have a guide that would help naval officers distinguish between the possible and the impossible, the prudent and the imprudent, the wise and the foolish. [17]

He was convinced that the best way to discover the truth about naval warfare was by a combination of inductive reasoning, experience and 'a pretty thorough investigation of its history.' His attitude to the past was not that of the disinterested historian, studying it for its own sake. He acted more in the manner of a highwayman, expecting the Muse of History to deliver the goods at the point of a pen. [18]

Nevertheless, his *Naval Warfare* of 1891, actually a collection of essays written earlier for the *Illustrated Naval and Military Magazine*, was the first historically based survey of the principles of maritime strategy, and was his most influential book. It was very long (Admiral Sir John Fisher with a typically atrocious pun called him 'a column and a half' from the length of his letters to the newspapers) and the reader was more bludgeoned than persuaded into agreement. The book analysed past struggles for command of the sea and identified the conditions under which attacks on territory succeeded or failed. It established general guidelines which recent wars seemed to confirm rather than deny, despite steam and other new inventions. There was, thought Colomb, 'no reason for believing' that these 'have modified the leading principles of naval warfare'.[19]

In *Naval Warfare* Colomb argued that real maritime strategy began with the Elizabethans for only then did ships develop the necessary sea-keeping qualities, and maritime endeavour became a really significant national activity. He analysed the development of the tactics of decisive battle, developed the notion of the fleet-in-being and identified the various types of blockade. Both the Colombs disagreed with the Royal Commission of 1859 which claimed that 'the efficient blockade of the enemy's ports had become well nigh impossible' and argued that command of the sea was still essential for all things.

Sir John argued that Imperial Defence was about the security of the homeland, its overseas possessions and the maintenance of the maritime communications between them. A maritime empire was at least as vulnerable to attacks on these communications as it was to the threat of invasion. The best defence against both, in any case, was command of the sea. His brother was the first to subject this elusive term to really systematic analysis. His conclusion was that it was fundamental to the success of all maritime enterprises.

Having command of the sea, in particular, was the best and indeed the only real safeguard against invasion on a large scale. An invasion would require such obvious preparation on the part of the enemy that no British fleet would allow itself to be decoyed away from the main theatre. It would be hazardous indeed for anyone to throw an invasion force across the Channel without first securing command of the sea. Pushing troop transports through waters swarming with enemy torpedo craft and submarines, thought Mr. Balfour (the Prime Minister) in 1905, would be simply 'the enterprise of a lunatic'. Of course a defending army on the British coastline was necessary, but its strength should be based on the assumption that the navy was the first line of defence and not on the desperate alternative that the navy did not exist.[20] Sir John's views on this were powerfully reinforced by the historically-based observations of his brother. Philip Colomb showed that some form the blockade had always been the main defence against invasion. Furthermore, in the whole period from 1690 onwards the supposition that a substantial invasion could be successfully mounted without first securing command of the sea had constantly showed itself to be a dangerous error.[21]

The real role of the army, thought Sir John, was to garrison bases at home and abroad, to defend India and to be used for expeditions overseas. Once the navy had secured command of the sea then the nation's main weapon of offence – the army – could be set for action. A small but highly-trained force striking out of the blue at a vital spot could, it was believed, produce a strategic effect out of all proportion to its size. The navy would provide the necessary maritime conditions for such enterprises and would act as the 'shield to guard'; the army, properly supported, would be the 'spear to strike'.[22]

Securing and exercising command of the sea were also the only ways of protecting the maritime communications so central to the safety of the Empire. It was the threat to these that most exercised the Colomb brothers (and most other maritime strategists) rather than the prospect of invasion. 'The Navy is the 1st, 2nd, 3rd, 4th, 5th... ad infinitum Line of Defence', proclaimed Admiral Sir John Fisher in 1904. 'If the Navy is not supreme, no army, however large, is of the slightest use. It is not *invasion* we have to fear if our Navy is beaten, it's *starvation!*'[23] This was Sir John Colomb's main message too:

> If the heart and citadel of the Empire is alone protected will it 'surprise us to hear' that, when the Empire is attacked, our enemy prefers cutting our unprotected communications and appropriating our undefended colonies and possessions, to a direct assault upon a 'small island bristling with bayonets.[24]

In fact, as the celebrated Three Admirals Report of 1888 showed, if this assault on Britain's ability to exercise command of the sea succeeded, then the enemy would probably not *need* to invade.

This was generally in line with Philip Colomb's view as well, but apart from a brief and rather unsatisfactory analysis of the relative merits of convoy,[25] the direct defence of trade does not figure largely in his work. The assumption is though, that with command of the sea, the country would be as secure from decisive attack on its trade as it would be from large-scale invasion.

Both the Colomb brothers had a considerable influence on their times. They set people thinking about maritime strategy and they did much to rescue the Navy from the intellectual stagnation into which it had fallen. Sir John's prestige perhaps faded a little towards to end; 'he probably feels', said one critic unkindly, 'like a small dog whose bone has been taken away by a bigger one'.[26] Philip Colomb's work was not restricted to the analysis of the particular problems of Imperial Defence and so was of more general interest. He probably had the greater impact on contemporaries, and on subsequent events, and this not least because he made naval history a respectable and relevant subject of enquiry for naval officers.

The ideas associated with the Colombs were also increasingly explored by others of their time. Sir John Laughton produced naval history; Sir William Laird Clowes focused the public's attention on their navy, its past and its future needs. Intellectual sailors like Admiral Sir Cyprian Bridge and Admiral Sir Reginald Custance wrote books, articles and gave lectures extolling the virtues of historical study and strategic contemplation. 'I hope,' said Bridge in 1874, 'that the study of it [naval tactics] will soon become the common pursuit of the many, rather than, as now, the special occupation of the few'. Custance, famous for his virulant dislike of Fisher, railed against the malign influence of the 'materiel school' who dismissed the past, neglected the study of tactics and strategy, and concentrated solely on the unthinking production of equipment. In 1907 though, he noted with some satisfaction that the 'historical school' were slowly forcing 'the materielists' back into their lair.[27]

Vice Admiral Philip Colomb in particular is certainly entitled to much of the credit for this. But in some ways he was robbed of much of his due glory by the fact that his *Naval Warfare* came out in 1891 at the same time as Mahan's *The Influence of Sea Power upon History*. Colomb told Mahan, with charm and considerable modesty, 'I think all our naval men regarded it as the Naval book of the age, and it has had a great effect in getting people to understand what they had never understood before'.[28] Colomb's work was a worthy essay in naval strategy, but Mahan's horizons were broader and, apparently, more generally appealing to the spirit of the times. For that reason, even in Britain, Colomb was mainly eclipsed by his rival from across the Atlantic.

(d) Alfred Thayer Mahan (by Craig Symonds)

In 1952, historian Margaret Sprout wrote of Alfred Thayer Mahan that 'no other single person has so directly and profoundly influenced the theory of sea power and naval strategy'.[29] On the surface there seems to be a great deal of evidence to support such a claim. Mahan's most famous work, *The Influence of Sea Power Upon History* (1890), still in print ninety years later, marked an important turning point in naval thinking in the United States and was enthusiastically received in much of the western world (and in the East as well: a Japanese translation appeared in 1897). But in fact, many of the arguments and conclusions proffered by Mahan in 1890 and attributed to him subsequently by historians, were common coin in the United States a decade earlier. The naval policy changes which occurred in the decade of the 1890s were more a product of changing national and international circumstances than of Mahan's rhetoric. His contribution was to provide justification for a naval expansion already well under way by providing it with a theoretical foundation. Mahan, in short, was not so much the prophet of sea power as he was a weathervane for a philosophical outlook whose time had come.[30]

More than one American naval thinker in the 1880s was becoming dissatisfied with the century-old tradition of coastal defence and commerce raiding that had served the United States so well in its earlier wars. Although as late as 1881, the majority report of an advisory board to Navy Secretary William H. Hunt urged that the United States build a large number of small, mostly wooden, sailing ships capable of threatening an enemy's commerce in time of war, but this was a last hurrah for the commerce-raiding school.[31] Only two years later, the United States Congress authorised construction of the first of a new breed of warships: the all-steel, steam-powered cruisers *Atlanta*, *Boston*, and *Chicago*, and the dispatch vessel *Dolphin*. Four ships do not make a navy, and, in fact, the official mission of these new ships was the same as that prescribed for the wooden vessels, but it was the first straw in a wind that would soon bring significant changes. Between 1885 and 1889, Congress authorised no less than 30 new warships, and on 30 November, 1889, Navy Secretary Benjamin Franklin Tracy delivered an annual report which called for a very ambitious programme of naval construction and the creation of Atlantic and Pacific battlefleets.[32]

Historians have offered several possible explanations for America's rather sudden interest in naval expansion. Certainly the decrepit vessels of the 'old navy' were a national embarrassment and needed replacement. Some historians have argued that the flag followed trade as an expanding capitalist economy required overseas protection from rivals. Whatever the motive, there is little doubt that tentative groupings for a new national naval policy were well underway by the mid-1880s before the appearance of Mahan's first 'Sea Power' volume. The shift in American naval policy was almost certainly due less to Mahan's arguments than to important changes in the national condition. Mahan recognised and cited these changes, but he cannot be credited for initiating them.

In the summer of 1883, while Congress debated approval of the three steel cruisers that would form the vanguard of the 'new navy', Mahan was seeing a manuscript through publication. It was his first historical effort, one which had little impact on either the profession or naval policy makers, but which nevertheless started him on his new career as an historian. It was entitled *The Gulf and Inland Waters* and was one of three volumes on the US Navy in the American Civil War commissioned by Charles Scribner's Sons. It was a workmanlike job and was fairly well received at the time. Soon Mahan felt the glow of authorship and determined to continue historical research and writing.

He came by this interest honestly. His father was Dennis Hart Mahan, whose classes on the art of war and military engineering were known to an entire generation of West Point cadets. Even though Mahan caused his father some disgruntlement by choosing to attend the Naval Academy at Annapolis rather than West Point the elder Mahan nevertheless influenced his son's historical and intellectual methodology. The father's interest in the strategic thinking of Henri Jomini impressed the younger Mahan with the importance of fitting things into an orderly system.

Young Mahan was not brilliant, but he did bring to his historical studies a mind that was orderly and systematic. Personally, he was somewhat prissy and was not particularly popular either as a midshipman or later as an officer. Moreover, and most startling in the character of a career naval officer, he did not like sea duty. He was prone to motion sickness and the fact that he often felt excluded from the camaraderie of junior officer hijinks by his own stuffiness, made him a morose, introspective, and altogether unhappy man at sea.[33]

Mahan therefore dreaded going back to sea in 1883 after completing his book on *The Gulf and Inland Waters*, but, as usual, the Navy Department had its way and he was dispatched to the leaky old *Wachusett* off the coast of Peru. Old, slow and prone to mechanical breakdowns, the *Wachusett* typified all that was bad about the 'old navy'. Before long, however, Mahan saw a hope of salvation from his purgatory in the person of Captain Stephen B. Luce, the founder, organiser, and first president of a new institution called the US Naval War College. Looking for the man who could do for naval strategy what Jomini had done for military strategy, Luce invited Mahan to become a lecturer at the new institution. Mahan, of course, was delighted. It was a ticket off the *Wachusett*, to shore duty, and an opportunity to pursue his historical studies. He responded with alacrity and enthusiasm. Almost immediately he embarked upon a serious reading programme in order to prepare himself for teaching.

Mahan later claimed that it was during a brief period of leave, in the English Library in Lima, Peru, that he was first struck by the insight which would later make him world famous. Reading Theodore Mommsen's *History of Rome*, he remarked at the fact that Hannibal, the Carthaginian general who invaded Italy in the second Punic War, had been forced to traverse the perimeter of the western Mediterranean rather than cross the narrow Sicilian channel because the Roman Navy commanded the seas. He was struck by the enormous impact which Roman sea power exerted simply by its existence. He wondered if perhaps sea power had an influence on historical events far beyond the immediate impact of battles won or lost.[34]

Mahan returned to the United States in August 1885, somewhat piqued that delays had prevented him from arriving in time to prepare adequately for his planned lecture series that fall. He therefore asked Luce for permission – soon granted – to spend a year in New York preparing himself. So it was that from October 1885 until August 1886, Mahan lived comfortably in New York City reading, writing, and thinking, and it was during this period that he gradually developed the ideas on sea power that would elicit such an enthusiastic response five years hence. By January 1886, though he had not yet delivered himself a single lecture on the subject, he had a fairly clear idea of what he wanted to do in his lecture series and the main thesis of *The Influence of Sea Power Upon History* had taken shape in his mind.

Mahan's approach was essentially historical in nature. Relying exclusively on published secondary sources, he sought to explain the uses of sea power in its broadest context, not by focusing on the particular tactics used in naval wars – though much of the subsequent book concerned such tactics – but on the purposes which navies had served. Since he was already an Anglophile, it required no great mental leap for him to seize upon the example of the Royal Navy in the period of its ascendance from 1660 to the end of the American Revolution. He discovered that British possession of the sea was the major determinant that allowed that nation to remain undefeated by its continental opponents. Mahan explained Britain's success by developing a simple deduction: greatness and strength are the product of wealth derived from trade; navies protect trade. The ability to produce a navy capable of maintaining this accumulated wealth was the result of certain characteristics that Britain possessed.

1. Geography (an insular power astride the sea lanes).
2. Physical conformation (the possession of useful ports and harbours).
3. Extent of territory (large enough to supply the necessary material wealth, but not so large as to be indefensible).
4. Population (large enough to man the ships).
5. Character of the people (seafaring).
6. Character of government (willing to support a progressive naval policy).

Although Mahan meant this list to be descriptive rather than prescriptive, the inference was unmistakable that any nation which possessed these characteristics shared the same opportunities for greatness.[35]

Mahan was acutely aware of the fact that for most of its history, the United States did not possess any of these characteristics. Its geographical isolation from Europe provided insularity, but also isolated it from the hub of western civilisation and commerce. Though possessed of many navigable inlets and fine harbours, the extent and richness of the territory was so enticing as to prevent the development of a dependence upon the sea. Though its people were of the finest stock (Mahan being somewhat of a racist as well) there were too few of them. And finally, and perhaps most important, the country lacked a sympathetic government.

But Mahan believed there was hope in the fact that these conditions were in the midst of change in the 1880s. The West was filling up, and though the total extent of national territory was no less, the elimination of an open frontier and the influx of European immigrants made the population less sparse. The expansion of trade with the Orient placed the United States in the midst, rather than on the periphery, of the world's trade routes (as a product of this development Mahan believed that the construction of an isthmian canal was a necessity). All that was needed was a government sympathetic to progressive naval policy and the United States could embark on the prescribed path to world power. Mahan complained quite specifically about the unwillingness of the United States government to nurture those institutions – maritime and naval – so essential to world power. His book was therefore a call for action to the government to build up the nation's sea power.[36]

Most American naval historians since then have sided with Mahan charging that the United States refrained so long from developing an assertive naval policy largely out of ignorance and that it was Alfred Thayer Mahan who finally pointed the way. But naval policy makers before 1890 had been fully conscious of the potential advantages of possessing a blue-water battleship navy. As early as 1799, Robert Goodloe Harper, a congressman from South Carolina, expounded the simple reasoning that lies at the root of Mahan's thesis:

> How has Britain been enabled . . . to maintain her own power, and to arrive at the present high pitch of consequence in the scale of nations? It was that navy, and the wealth which commerce, protected by it, poured into her lap, that enabled her to support, with glory, so unequal a contest, to call to her aid the military force of Germany, and thus to establish a counterpoise to the power of France.[37]

In just such terms – and using nearly the same words – Mahan described to an eager reading audience one hundred years later the essence of his sea power doctrines.

Prior to 1890, however, these arguments had fallen on deaf ears. Dubious legislators insisted that conditions different from those of eighteenth-century Britain applied to nineteenth-century America. What changed in the 1880s, then, was not the wisdom of naval policy makers, but the conditions in which the United States found itself. The recognition of the changes caused many opponents of naval expansion to drop their resistance and allow themselves to be carried along by the century-old arguments they had rejected in the past. Alfred Thayer Mahan's sea power volume, published at the cresting of this change in public mood, was perfectly timed to win accolades for its author, and provide a clear rationale for the new policy.

Though concerned primarily with strategy and policy, Mahan also wrote about navies in combat, believing that even though the character of naval vessels had changed dramatically since the age of sail, the same principles of naval combat remained unchanged 'as though laid upon a rock'.[38] In this area of thought, too, Mahan found reasons to reject America's traditional reliance on commerce raiding, dismissing it as the weakest form of naval warfare to be adopted only in the event that no other option existed. As proof, he pointed to the failure of French commerce raiding to deter the powerful British battleship squadrons which, concentrated in strength, and occupying the choke points of the world's commerce, succeeded in bringing France to its knees. Mahan asserted that the British experience illustrated certain immutable principles – fleet concentration; the importance of certain strategic locations, or bases; and effective communication to co-ordinate effort – all of which served to achieve the ultimate goal of naval forces: control of the seas: the ability to use the seas for oneself while denying them to the enemy. Such control could only be gained by possession of a battlefleet, the ultimate key to naval success. Once again, his conclusions were not entirely new, but his audience was newly receptive.

The Influence of Sea Power Upon History was an instant success, and its author an instant sage. Ironically, the book was far more popular in Europe than in America. Feted by European societies – even royalty – Mahan's head was turned by the critics who called him the new Copernicus. In fact, he was nothing of the kind. Mahan is assured of a place in the annals of naval history not because of the timelessness of his principles – indeed, the First World War would soon prove how ephemeral they were – but because his writing was so accurate a reflection of a movement current in fin de siecle America and Europe: a national assertiveness through sea power that eventually brought the United States into the world power balance, contributed to the Anglo–German naval race, and encouraged Japan in its rise to Empire. It would be absurd to claim that all this came about as a result of Mahan's writings. Indeed, with or without Mahan it is likely that events would have unfolded very much as they did. But Mahan is important to us now as the clearest representative of the philosophical rationale that lay beneath the two decades of naval competition. In short, Mahan's greatest significance is not as a strategist, or even as an historian, but as an historical actor.

(e) The Jeune Ecole

Mahan was clearly concerned with the central struggle for mastery of the sea, and with other general considerations of what the French called 'La Guerre Grande'. But such concerns were by no means restricted either to the books or to the policies of navalists in Britain and the United States, as might sometimes be supposed. Substitute Mahans appeared in virtually all countries with navies of any significance; they all had their opinions and emphases, but they all clearly officiated at the same shrine.

In Italy there was Professor G. Sechi, of the Naval Academy at La Spezzia. His *Elementi di Arte Militare Marittima* (2 vols, Leghorn 1903–6) was an orthodox treatment of maritime strategy, with a particular interest in combined operations and such practicalities of naval warfare as logistics, victualling and so on. G. J. W. Putman Cramer produced his *Inleidung tot de Maritime Strategie en Zeetactiek* in 1913 at Den Helder. Putman Cramer had ideas of his own but shared Mahan's general outlook; his book provided a comprehensive theory of maritime strategy but as such stands more or less alone in the naval literature of the Netherlands.[39]

Another pioneering effort along the same lines came from the Russian, Captain Berezin, in 1873.[40] Modern Japanese naval thought, on the other hand, really began with the work of the circle of officers associated with Akiyama Saneyuki (1868–1918). The Japanese made much use of American theory and practice but they qualified it with ideas drawn from their own maritime traditions. In particular they tended to stress the practical difficulties of securing complete command of the sea in the Pacific. Victory was also seen more as the consequence of the collapse of the enemy's will and the scattering of his forces rather than his physical annihilation. Nevertheless, in 1905, Akiyama played a central role in planning the Battle of Tsushima, one of the most complete examples of 'La Grande Guerre' there has ever been.[41]

Mahanist theories had a particular impact on Imperial Germany where they were carefully analysed in the *Marine Rundschau* from the mid-1890s, and echoed in the writings of Captain Alfred Stenzel and Admiral Carl Batsch, both of whom argued that only a battle fleet and decisive battle would properly safeguard Germany's maritime interests.[42] This was also substantially the message of Vice Admiral Baron Curt von Maltzahn, Professor of Strategy and Tactics and then head of the Naval Academy at Kiel from 1895–1905. In his *Naval Warfare*, von Maltzahn stressed the importance of the sea to Germany, 'and the reason for this is that all the great civilised countries have now become states that carry on a world-embracing commerce and are thus dependent upon maritime trade and the results of naval wars'.[43] Now even continental nations were 'becoming more and more exposed to the danger of damage by naval warfare'.[44]

However, in this book at least he rejected exaggerated notions of the efficacy of cruiser warfare. It had proved 'absolutely hopeless' against England after 1805 and was most likely to be effective when based on a secure command of the sea.[45] Instead 'the fight for the command of the sea in battle was the determining factor in naval warfare'. Since command of the sea was adaptable for all purposes – the defence of trade, for operations against the shore – 'the command of the sea is worth fighting for its own sake, and not in any one place or for any one end'. 'Battle', he thought, 'is the keystone of the whole system of naval warfare.'[46]

French naval thought owed a great deal to Admiral Jurien de la Graviere (1812–92). A prolific writer in maritime history, he was a clear and early advocate of 'La Grande Guerre'. The purpose of a navy, he wrote in 1874, was 'to occupy and maintain the great ocean highways. The occupation of the sea, even if it were only temporary, ought to have consequences of the very deepest importance, even in a purely continental war.'[47] He also doubted whether a predatory war on commerce would succeed unless command of the sea had first been gained through victorious encounters with the enemy.

In the next generation, these traditions were carried on by Admiral Gabriel Darrieus (1859–1931) and Rene Daveluy (1863–1938). Darrieus, a practical sailor with a pronounced interest in naval engineering, produced his *War on the Sea: Strategy and Tactics* in 1907 while teaching maritime strategy at the recently established Ecole Superieure de Marine. Admiral Daveluy wrote eight books on naval warfare, history and doctrine, his most famous works being *L'Esprit de la Guerre Navale* (1902) and *Strategie Navale* (1905). Daveluy and Darrieus were the best representatives of French naval thought before the First World War.

Both of them were good technical men, familiar with torpedoes and submarines, and so were in the best of positions to assess the impact these innovations might make on maritime strategy. They covered the same period as Mahan and Colomb, immersed themselves in historical detail and were determined to demonstrate the perpetual importance of sea power and to discover the abiding principles of warfare at sea. They argued that the best route to maritime victory was not by a war on commerce but by an offensive strategy and the decisive clash of arms. 'Destroy the enemy', said Daveluy, 'and you will have all the results at one time.'[48] Their message, essentially, was the same as Mahan's.

To some extent, though, their writings have to be seen as a defence of the faith against heretics. There were some who stubbornly refused to be converted by the arguments of Mahan, Colomb and the rest. In England, for example, there was Fred T. Jane (founder of Jane's

Fighting Ships). He thought sea power could be improvised as the occasion demanded, was sceptical about the existence of eternal principles of maritime strategy and did not believe that a navy necessarily needed command of the sea in order to conduct useful operations against the land or, more particularly, against commerce. Attacks on bases, he added, were more likely to have decisive results than attacks on fleets.[49] But the most celebrated alternative vision was that preached by the Jeune Ecole in France.

The immediate intellectual origins of this movement was Baron Richard Grivel's *De la Guerre Maritime* (1869). Grivel had been well schooled in the virtues of orthodox maritime endeavours, not least by his father who had produced a classic statement of them in 1837,[50] but he contended that these were inappropriate measures for France to take against Britain. Instead, he argued: 'Commercial war, the most economical for the poorest fleet, is at the same time the one most proper to restore peace, since it strikes directly . . . at the very source of the prosperity of the enemy'.[51] These ideals were expanded and publicised from 1874 onwards by Admiral Theophile Aube, the journalist Gabriel Charmes, Commander Paul Fontin and Lieutenant J. H. Vignot – these last two using the pseudonyms 'Commander Z' and 'H. Montechant' respectively. The influence of the school peaked in 1886 when Admiral Aube became Minister of Marine. He immediately suspended the battleship construction programme, built a naval base at Bizerta, boosted France's research and development efforts in submarines and began building cruisers and torpedo boats at a high rate. For a short space of a year and a half, the dream came true; the philosopher was king; ideas could really be put into practice.

These ideas were, however, by no means wholly new, especially in France. In 1706 Vauban wrote:

> If we were to be quit of the vanity of great fleets which can never suit our needs and to employ the ships of the navy partly on commerce warfare and partly in squadrons to support it, we should bring about the downfall of the English and the Dutch within about two or three years, in consequence of their great trade to all parts of the world.[52]

But in the last quarter of the nineteenth century technology appeared finally to confirm the promise of this approach. Torpedoes, mines, submarines, all seemed to make the battleship more vulnerable, and so to herald the end of the kind of maritime strategy that was based on big ships. 'Everywhere the dwarf has killed the giant', proclaimed Gabriel Charmes. 'Far-seeing naval men have long predicted that the most terrible danger threatening the ironclads in any future naval warfare will be when they are assaulted on several sides at once by a series of agile gunboats, difficult to hit.' An incidental benefit of this argument was that it provided a splendid means of attacking the naval and political establishment which seemed to depend on the continued dominance of the battleship as much in France as elsewhere. This gave the teachings of the Jeune Ecole a particular appeal for the young officers of the little ships.

If battleships were indeed this vulnerable then the whole concept of the command of the sea would be, said Admiral Aube 'an expression quite devoid of sense'. The British Navy would no longer be able to blockade the French into their harbours. Strong enemy naval forces would be so concerned with their own security that their offensive potentiality would be much reduced, while that of the smaller ships would be correspondingly increased. Admiral Aube planned to use torpedo boats against British ports, anchored merchant shipping and blockading squadrons in local waters. Cruisers would prey upon commerce on the great trade routes. A few coastal defence ships would protect the homeland.

Admiral Aube brushed aside the problem that the Declaration of Paris, made in 1856, had made attacking merchant ships illegal, and so politically hazardous. He expected his torpedo boats to 'send to the bottom cargo, crew, and passengers, not only without remorse but proud of the achievement. In every part of the ocean similar atrocities will be seen'.[53] The ends justified the means, and the advantage of such barbarous proceedings would outweigh all scruples.

It is important to note, however, that the Jeune Ecole did not expect to achieve their aim by starving Britain into submission. Said Admiral Réveillère, a writer with some sympathy for the Jeune Ecole, 'To suppose that we can sufficiently blockade the English coasts to reduce the country by famine by preventing the importation of food supplies ... is an idea which would never enter the head of a sane man'.[54] Instead, such a campaign would cause panic, a crisis in marine insurance and generally disturb the intricate patterns of British trade. It would strike directly at the shipping interests, the tradespeople and manufacturers who were the real masters of Britain. Their sufferings would force the government into peace.[55]

The parade of such views caused considerable controversy in France for nearly twenty years. Naval policy oscillated wildly as Ministers of Marine came and went (there were 31 between 1871 and 1902) and the whole era was one of much confusion. Other countries were affected too: people with similar ideas appeared elsewhere, such as Germany's Vice Admiral Viktor Valois, and, at the height of the craze, Austria, Russia and Germany all abandoned their battleship construction programmes. The British too were more worried about these ideas than they cared to admit.

Gradually, however, the influence of the Jeune Ecole began to wane, and the idea of a war on commerce slowly dropped out of favour in the French Navy; in 1901 battleship construction was finally resumed. This was partly for reasons which had nothing to do with the intellectual validity – or otherwise – of the ideas themselves. For one thing, as the strategic environment changed, Britain came to look much more like an ally and much less of an enemy. Anticipations of war against the British were so central to the conceptions of the Jeune Ecole that their collapse virtually demolished the whole argument as far as the French Navy was concerned. The domestic political climate changed too, especially after the Radical Minister Camille Pelletan's disastrous and hopeless attempt to purge the whole Navy of its conservatives. The establishment of the Ecole Superier de Marine also tended to steady opinions.

In this less sympathetic atmosphere some of the difficulties in the philosophy of the Jeune Ecole became more readily apparent. Their technical assumptions about the demise of the battleship and their claims about the effectiveness of the *guerre de course* seemed increasingly suspect. Was it not also true, asked one ex-Minister of Marine, J. L. de Lanessan, that a successful war on commerce required at least a degree of command of the sea, and so needed the ships and doctrines best suited to contesting it. 'The only times when it [corsair warfare] was really effective against our own enemies,' he wrote, 'was when our fleets were sufficiently strong to be able to dispute with our foes the mastery of the Channel or Mediterranean.'[56] The success of Confederate commerce raiders in the American Civil War was often used as evidence for the Jeune Ecole, but was it not true that the Northern commercial blockade, based on naval mastery, strangled trade while Southern corsairs like the *Alabama* merely harassed it?

But the real weakness of the Jeune Ecole was that the kind of navy it proposed would be virtually useless against any enemy except Britain. France might well have to go to war with Russia or Germany or Italy; she certainly had a global empire to expand and maintain. For all these purposes, she seemed to need a navy of substance, able to contest command of the sea, engage an enemy battlefleet and conduct operations against his coast. Even Grivel had admitted that for operations against any country but Britain, France would need the kind of navy able to defeat the enemy's battlefleet and so 'to acquire an influence and supremacy on the great roads of the sea, which will open the way for coastal and commercial warfare'.[57]

There were obviously great difficulties in the way of such radical new departures as the philosophy of the Jeune Ecole. Nevertheless, theirs was a bold and novel attempt to solve the historic problem of how best to use a self-evidently inferior navy against a predominant maritime power. Because many countries have found themselves in such a situation, the ideas developed by the Jeune Ecole have had considerable appeal at various times.

(f) Sir Julian Corbett (by Bryan Ranft)

Julian Corbett, who was born in 1854, gained a first class degree in law at Cambridge, was called to the Bar, but never seriously practised his profession. His comfortable private means enabled him to travel widely and later to concentrate on the writing of naval history. It was not until 1898 that his first major work, *Drake and the Tudor Navy*, appeared. By 1910 he had written four more authoritative works on British naval history, including what is probably his best historical book, *England in the Mediterranean* (1904), as well as editing three scholarly volumes of documents for the Navy Records Society. Amongst these, *Fighting Instructions 1530–1816* (1905) and *Signals and Instructions 1776–1794* (1908) are essential sources for the study of the evolution of sailing-ship warfare. The other strand in his career began in 1900 when he was invited to lecture at the Royal Naval War College at Greenwich. This connection with the contemporary navy was strengthened in the following year with the appearance of the first of many articles in periodicals in support of the reforms of Admiral Sir John Fisher, of whom he remained a constant, though not uncritical, associate. In 1914 Corbett, who had already begun an official history of the Russo-Japanese war, was appointed by the Committee of Imperial Defence to be the official naval historian of the naval war against Germany. He produced only the first three volumes before he died in 1922 and thus avoided the mortification of seeing, in 1923, the Admiralty insert in the last of these a disclaimer of accepting what they perceived as a 'tendency to minimise the importance of seeking battle and forcing it to a conclusion'. The origins of this attack probably lay in an over-simplified interpretation of strategic concepts which he had put forward in his lectures at Greenwich.

These had already been embodied in the work on which is based Corbett's claim to be an outstanding theorist of maritime war as well as an authoritative historian, *Some Principles of Maritime Strategy* (1911). Quite apart from its intrinsic merits the book derives additional importance from being the work of a man who had the ear of 'Jackie' Fisher, the architect of the ships and strategy with which Britain faced Germany's naval challenge in 1914, and who also for more than a decade had presented to senior naval officers his concepts of maritime strategy.

Corbett had derived from his historical research what he claimed to be permanent principles governing the conduct of maritime war, with which he challenged the preconceptions of his Greenwich audiences. Audiences whose main concern he knew was the ever increasing technological complexity of the ships and weapons they would use in war, and whose whole view of strategy centred on the conduct of fleet actions in which numerical superiority, skill in gunnery and the fighting spirit of the British sailor would annihilate the enemy and end the war at sea. To the great majority of these audiences, the past wars from which Corbett had derived his principles had no relevance to their professional tasks. The complete transformation of ships and weapons since Trafalgar had made 'the lessons of history' useless, except perhaps for an emotional recognition of 'the Nelson spirit', which was superficially identified with heroically aggressive tactics. Corbett did not claim that historical study would produce detailed rules for the future conduct of battles and campaigns. Its value lay in bringing to light the permanent characteristics of sea power and the specific nature of its contribution to national strategy; what it could achieve and what were its limitations. Equipped with these insights, the contemporary naval commander' would have a pattern of past experience; what had succeeded, what had failed, against which to assess his present situation and desirable course of action. He would be better equipped to argue rationally on matters of policy with military commanders and political leaders and so come to correct solutions to the problems of combined operations and grand strategy. Corbett's friendship with Fisher must have revealed to him how far this was from the confusion of Britain's pre-1914 defence planning.

His historical studies had convinced him that there was far more to naval warfare than the seeking out and destruction of the enemy's fleet. His *The Campaign of Trafalgar* (1910) had emphasised that not even that most decisive sea victory had prevented Napoleon becoming the master of Europe. The navy must learn to use its wide range of capabilities to bring pressures to bear on the enemy which would assist the work of the army and further the political objectives for which the war was being fought. In this context he stressed the importance of combined operations as being the most effective way for Britain to use her sea power in a European war.

There is no evidence that Corbett's views on these matters had any practical effect on British naval policy. The bulk of influential opinion remained obsessed with the centrality of the decisive fleet action. Failure to achive this in the First World War produced much bitterness and controversy in the post-war Royal Navy, and the Admiralty's disclaimer in Corbett's official history suggests a habit not unknown in that institution, the search for a scapegoat.

Corbett's overall view of war and strategy show a good grasp of the thought of Clausewitz and Jomini, and he is especially concerned to show how maritime strategy could add a new dimension to their essentially continental concepts. But he is no extremist. He defines maritime strategy as the principles governing a war in which the sea plays a substantial part, but constantly emphasises that sea power alone is not enough. Men live on land and it is there that the final decision must be sought. Success will only come from the achievement of the right balance and appropriate use of armies and navies. The most fruitful use of maritime power is in limited wars. Corbett had found that both Clausewitz and Jomini had indicated that wars might be fought for a limited object rather than the complete crushing of an enemy's will to resist, which was the characteristic of absolute war. Success in limited war demanded the ability to seize and hold a limited objective important enough to bring your enemy to the negotiating table. This was difficult to achieve for a nation relying on land power, but one with maritime superiority could, for example, seize a colonial possession far from its enemy's homeland, isolate and hold it by virtue of its command of the sea, until its political aims were achieved. Corbett claimed that this was the way in which Britain's empire had been created and its influence on continental Europe enhanced. There is much truth in this but he tends to underemphasise that major successes of this kind were unobtainable unless Britain had continental allies and directly supported them by contributing land forces to the continental campaign. The War of American Independence had been a catastrophic demonstration of Britain's weakness in fighting an entirely maritime war against a European alliance undistracted by defence of its land frontiers. Similarly, he tends to exaggerate the effect of sea power, in the form of actual or threatened landings from the sea, in forcing a continental enemy to weaken his forces on the central land front in order to meet them.

Command of the sea is the central concept in Corbett's thinking about maritime war and it is here that he makes an important distinction between land and sea warfare. In land war the objective is the seizure and holding of enemy territory, in naval war the objective is to gain and secure the use of the sea. Command of the sea is thus identified with the ability to use sea communications for military and civil purposes and to deny such use to the enemy. It was from this position that Corbett's thought moved towards what his critics thought to be a dangerous denigration of the importance of decisive fleet actions. This stemmed from his perceptive judgement that naval forces did not require the continuous concentration in mass demanded of armies when the main strength of their opponents remained massed and undefeated. Because of their mobility and flexibility naval forces could be detached to make use of the sea by, for example, attacking enemy sea communications or threatening his coasts, secure in the knowledge that they could reconcentrate on being warned of a likely attack by the opposing main fleet. Corbett did not, as his critics alleged, reject the classical doctrine that command of the sea could only be fully assured by the destruction of the enemy main fleet. What he did think, and the experience of the First World War was to show him to be right, was that it might prove difficult to bring about a fleet action. In such circumstances, he argued, utilising the flexibility of navies to put pressure on the enemy was the most likely way of compelling him to seek action, in self defence.

There is a seeming contradiction in Corbett's thought about landings from the sea. He dismissed the fears, common in his time, of a successful invasion of the United Kingdom on the grounds that technological change since 1815 was in favour of the defending forces, as long as they concentrated their attacks on the troop carrying vessels. Yet he also asserted that technological change had not diminished Britain's ability to launch military expeditions overseas, as long as their flanks were protected by her general superiority at sea. He seems to ignore the existence of mines, long range coastal artillery and torpedo boats, and, in a European war, the greater flexibility given to the defence by telegraphic communications, roads and railways. His one essential for success was close co-operation between military and naval commanders. He rejected the idea of a single overall commander on the grounds that no one man could be a master of both the military and naval arts.

A similar contradiction seems to emerge in his treatment of commerce warfare. Like Mahan he believed that attacks against seaborne trade were an indecisive and wasteful form of warfare which could never be decisive against a Britain with a large merchant marine and a navy able to ensure command of the sea. On the other hand he stressed the effect which British attacks on enemy shipping could have on her enemies' financial and industrial strength. The contradiction was resolved in his own mind by making a distinction between the complete blockade, which could be imposed by the nation having command of the sea, and the intermittent attacks on ships by individual raiders, which were all that an inferior naval opponent could offer. He did not foresee the advent of a new type of onslaught on merchant shipping which would make command of the sea's surface largely irrelevant. Corbett's study of past wars had convinced him that the heaviest losses of merchant ships had been in narrow waters rather than on the high seas. The abolition of privateering by the Declaration of Paris in 1856 had removed the major threat to Britain from such attacks, and made the task of defending seaborne trade much easier to handle. Technological change had also moved in favour of the defence. Steam merchant ships, unlike their sailing predecessors, were not tied to fixed routes and could be diverted from areas where raiders were suspected. The steam cruisers and auxiliary warships, which would be the attackers, would be limited by coal supplies in the range and duration of their operations. They would also be limited in the scale of their captures as they would not be able to provide engine- and boiler-room crews for their prizes. Corbett did consider the possibility of commerce raiders sinking their prizes but dismissed it on the grounds of the difficulty of finding accommodation for captured crews and passengers, and of the complete unacceptability of the alternative of sinking prizes with all hands.

He also rejected as misconceived the idea common in his day that the increased size of Britain's mercantile marine since the last major war meant that she would incur greater losses. Even if losses did not diminish as he expected, the proportionate loss would be less. He was equally opposed to another common argument, that the size of the Royal Navy should be decided by the size of the merchant service it had to protect.

As for tactical measures for trade defence, Corbett was well aware of the success of convoy in past wars but had strong doubts as to whether the system would be so effective under the new conditions. In days of rapid communication it would be impossible to keep convoy sailings secret and collections of steam-driven ships would be much easier to find at sea than their sailing precursors. The traditional drawbacks of convoys, economic losses through loss of time at sea and from overcrowding in ports, remained, as did the strategic dislocations involved in allocating considerable forces to their escort, and the likely attraction of enemy forces to such tempting targets. He admitted that the issue was far from clear and required re-examination, but the general bias of his arguments, as was that of the great bulk of British naval opinion of his day, was that the convoy system was no longer the most effective way of protecting merchant shipping. The preferred alternatives, which were used in 1914, were the stationing of cruisers at focal points where shipping concentrated and the deployment of offensive patrols in areas where raiders were expected.

He was equally in harmony with almost universal naval and political opinion in not foreseeing the unrestricted submarine warfare which was so nearly to prove fatal to Britain in 1917. But this must not be allowed to obscure the fact that virtually all his ideas about the inefficacy of cruiser warfare against Britain's trade were confirmed by the failure of the German surface raiders at the beginning of the war. He was equally correct in his forecast of Britain's ability to impose a crippling blockade on Germany by her general command of the sea.

Julian Corbett remains a naval historian of high reputation and a theorist whom no modern student of maritime war can afford to ignore.

(g) Admiral Sir Herbert Richmond (by Barry Hunt)

Admiral Richmond was best known to circles outside the Royal Navy through his historical studies of British maritime power. A second career as an historian at Cambridge, following his retirement from active service in 1931, firmly established him within the Colomb–Mahan–Corbett tradition of naval scholarship. Crucial to his intellectual development was his long service career in which, despite involvement in a constant struggle against professional prejudices and conservatism, he rose to the rank of Admiral. He was a rare hybrid: an experienced and highly competent officer endowed with an unusually active, analytical and perceptive mind.[58]

As leader of the so-called 'Young Turks' reform movement prior to and during the First World War, and as a teacher, defence critic and strategist, Richmond challenged the tenets of Admiralty orthodoxy and the dominance of materialist influences in the shaping of naval policy by emphasising the value of historical study as a means of spreading sound concepts of strategy and tactics. For him, the First World War revealed serious deficiencies in command and doctrine, in materiel and mentality as well as worrisome distortions of strategic perspective. The stark contrast between expectations and achievements was attributable in Richmond's view, to the failure to develop the Navy's intellectual apparatus and to the long neglect of the education of officers in the higher aspects of their profession.

Throughout his career, Richmond demonstrated a total commitment to reform. Through the combination of an outstanding intellect, an uncompromising personality and a deep grasp of historical realities, he challenged the cliches that passed for naval thought amongst his contemporaries. His influence was, however, limited significantly by defects in his personality – he was arrogant towards his superiors, impatient with less-gifted men, and was driven by a sense of scholarly integrity which often made him seem rigid; nevertheless, he provided the only impulse from within the Royal Navy's ranks for sustained, critical examination of a wide range of naval and national defence issues in the post-Fisher era.

In 1906, Admiral Sir John Fisher called Richmond to the Admiralty as his naval assistant. Like Jellicoe, Bacon, Oliver and other bright officers who had filled this position, Richmond had been singled out for rapid future progress. Two years later, aged 35, he was promoted to Captain and then to command of HMS Dreadnought, flagship of the Home Fleet and the first of Fisher's revolutionary all-big-gun battleships. But Richmond's enthusiasm for Fisher had clear limits and as he became associated with men who tried, unsuccessfully, to steer Fisher's reforming energies towards broader issues of general war planning and the creation of a modern naval staff, his enthusiasm turned to disenchantment.

At this time Julian Corbett became his close friend and confidant. It was he who encouraged the young captain's scholarly instincts and nurtured his growing interest in the wider problems of Empire defence and the need for extensive educational and organisational changes to ensure their systematic study. With Corbett's backing, Richmond undertook his first major historical work – a three-volume study *The Navy in the War of 1739–1748*. The book established his credentials as a historian of consequence and was later awarded the Royal United Services Institute's prestigious Chesney Gold Medal. The only other naval officer to be so honoured up to that point was Mahan. Writing this book proved to be an important formative experience in terms of Richmond's understanding of the major concepts of maritime strategy and in shaping his views on the role of a naval staff and the need for joint Admiralty–War Office planning for future war.

When he left *Dreadnought* he was relegated to command of second-class cruisers attached to the Torpedo School at Portsmouth. These next few years were important, however, for in addition to finishing his book and editing another for the Navy Records Society, he also lectured part time at the Naval War College. There he drew to himself some of the more thoughtful and similarly reform-minded students and instructors with whom he set about organising the Naval Society and its quarterly publication, *The Naval Review*.

Of all of Richmond's pre-war reform efforts, the *Review* was his most ambitious and enduring. Through it he hoped to spark an intellectual regeneration of the navy and to challenge the convention that matters of policy were the senior admirals' exclusive preserve. In his own words, his purpose was to 'stir up interest in what Kempenfelt called the "sublime" parts of our work – strategy, tactics, principles. ... What I hope to develop is the mental habit of reasoning things out, getting at the bottom of things, evolving principles and spreading interest in the higher side of our work.' To forestall official censure, it was decided to make the *Review* a 'private' journal with circulation restricted to members of the Society. Anonymity of authorship was also introduced to protect contributors and to encourage free discussion from all rank levels. Yet, despite a flourishing membership of over 1000 and the backing of Winston Churchill and Prince Louis of Battenberg (First Sea Lord), the *Review* still was viewed with suspicion by most senior officers. Censorship was imposed during the war until the mid-1920s when Beatty sensibly had it removed. The attempts to suppress the *Review* and those who had created it only strengthened their determination to persevere. During the war years, as public dissatisfaction with the Admiralty's handling of operations increased, the Naval Society became the framework around which Richmond and his friends concentrated their efforts to bring about changes, including their highly controversial liasons with Lloyd George that contributed to the decision to remove the Jellicoe regime in 1917.

The *Review* unquestionably set Richmond apart as a heretic to be watched with great care. As Assistant Director of Operations at the Admiralty (February 1913–May 1915) he also found himself caught between the cautious defensiveness of his service superiors on the one hand, and the unconstrained offensive obsessions of Winston Churchill on the other. It was Richmond's dangerous lot to expose most of the 'madness' in the First Lord's North Sea and Baltic schemes. In this he was probably too successful for when he also tried to dissuade Churchill from the navy-alone attack on the Dardanelles he was rusticated to a posting as Liaison Officer with the Italian Fleet. The irony in all this was that Richmond himself was a leading 'Easterner' who understood that a thoroughly planned and properly applied amphibious strategy in any number of places other than the Turkish straits could well have brought about many of the effects that Churchill wanted.

In 1917, under Beatty's protection, he once again began to take a more active role in influencing fleet planning and revising Grand Fleet Battle Orders. By this time, the war at sea had reached a crisis stage. Since Jutland, a state of seemingly inescapable stalemate had settled over the North Sea, but the German unrestricted U-boat offensive was alarmingly successful. Richmond tried to show how the Admiralty's preoccupation with maintaining the numerical superiority of the Grand Fleet was tying down flotilla resources and denying any possibilities of effective offensive measures against the enemy. He put forward his own proposals for limited offensives in the Mediterranean and Adriatic to draw off U-boats and for a more aggressive use of naval airpower against the High Sea Fleet under whose influence the U-boats sheltered.

Several of these schemes were impractical in the sense that deficiencies in the materiel and expertise on which they depended could not be made good overnight. They did involve risks; but not, it should be emphasised, to the squadrons of the Grand Fleet. On this score Richmond stood apart from Jellicoe's more extreme critics who argued that the primary objective of naval warfare should be to force a decisive fleet action. Richmond, in company with most naval professionals, countered that a deliberate push for unnecessary fleet actions was too risky; that unless the German's themselves offered battle, Britain's best course was to maintain strategic superiority in the North Sea, trusting to the long-term effects of the blockade, and to blunting the U-boats through convoying and realistic complementary offensives against their bases.

After the war, and with Beatty's appointment as First Sea Lord in November 1919, Richmond's prospects took a decided turn for the better. Promoted Rear Admiral, he was assigned to re-open the Senior Officers War Course at Greenwich. This was an important and rewarding post which allowed the full exercise of his considerable talents as a teacher and reasonable scope for serious educational innovation. Beatty's friendship also implied an opportunity for influencing postwar policy development generally and, although on many issues he differed radically from Beatty, his interventions did constitute some of the few occasions where originality and a deeper sense of perspective entered the postwar naval debate. Equally important, Greenwich allowed him to continue his own writing and to expand his contacts beyond the circle of the 'Young Turks' to the wider service and academic communities. He lectured at the RUSI, the Royal Institute of International Affairs, Cambridge and London Universities.

In 1926, after a period as Commander-in-Chief, East Indies, he was made the first Commandant of the new Imperial Defence College in London. Richmond played a considerable role in the creation of the IDC and in its subsequent progress on a course which made it, its successors and Commonwealth sister colleges, vital institutions for the higher discussion of national defence issues. As such, the foundation of the IDC is another important monument to Richmond's insight.

The IDC turned out to be Richmond's last active posting for when, in November 1929, he published two signed letters in *The Times* ('Smaller Navies' and 'The Capital Ship'), he embarked on his last confrontation with official policy that led to his enforced retirement two years later. For years he had opposed the Admiralty's faith in the future of big battleships. Prior to the 1921 Washington disarmament talks he had questioned Beatty's new battleship building programmes partly out of doubts as to the future impact of submarines and aircraft, and partly because the programmes took little account of the international economic realities upon which Britain's naval supremacy also rested. Maritime security defined solely in terms of battleship strengths had always, in his view, been an artificial measurement. During the Washington talks, in an anonymous *Times* letter, he had questioned the decision to limit capital ships to 35 000 tons and criticised the artificially high numerical ratios used to fix the size of navies. With another international conference about to assemble in London, he now openly challenged the ratios system, the doctrine of 'material parity', and called for a more rational approach which would fix national requirements on a qualitative basis that served strategic and tactical needs and defined tonnages for individual capital ships at very much lower limits (he suggested 10 000 tons). Whatever the theoretical merits of Richmond's 'small ship' suggestions, they clearly contradicted Admiralty thinking and could not be ignored. Instead of opening up public debate, they earned him a sharp reprimand and finally banishment.

Of course, retirement did not silence Richmond and he now entered what was in many ways the most rewarding phase of his life. He used his new freedom to finish his *The Navy in India, 1763–1783* and to write *Economy and Naval Security* (1931) which summarised his earlier disarmament and small ship arguments. That same year, he delivered the Lees Knowles Lectures at Cambridge, published in 1932 as *Imperial Defence and Capture at Sea in War*. In 1934, he returned to the theme of economy and collective security in *Sea Power and the Modern World*. Recognition of his scholarly contributions continued to grow with invitations to lecture in Europe and the United States. In 1934 he was appointed as Vere Harmsworth Professor of Imperial and Naval

History at Cambridge. Following this two-year appointment, he became Master of Downing College where he remained until his death in 1946. Throughout all these years, Richmond kept a close watch on contemporary defence developments, and wrote widely. In 1943 he delivered the Ford Lectures at Oxford, which were published in 1946 as *Statesmen and Sea Power*.

The catholicity of his interests and the intertwining of his influence as both reformer and scholar make it difficult to summarise his impact on contemporary policy development. His attempts to define a doctrine of war were never systematically developed and must be extrapolated from his writings. Generally he envisioned maritime communications linked by a network of bases whose defence was the joint responsibility of all services. Because it was maritime in focus, it raised criticisms that it downplayed the importance of the other two services. Although he was the only member of a RUSI audience to applaud Basil Liddell Hart's celebrated denunciation of Britain's 1914–18 continental commitment, he took pains to emphasise that the so-called 'maritime' and 'continental' strategic options had never been mutually exclusive; and under twentieth-century conditions their interdependence within an overall policy was even more essential. He was always wary of too heavy a reliance on strategic bombing and stressed the absolute priority of securing sea communications. Victory through the bombing of Germany alone, he feared, might be bought at the price of Britain's ruin as an oceanic-imperial power, a proposition which was an important example of his insistence on drawing distinctions between ends and means.

His achivements as a scholar were undoubtedly his most important and lasting. He completed and extended the earlier efforts of Mahan and Corbett by raising the general awareness of naval history's significance both as a distinct field of serious academic endeavour and also as a vitally important process in the education of officers. The fact that many of his books are now neglected may have something to do with his approach to history which was in some measure coloured by a determinism that seems dated by modern standards. Like Mahan, he did look to the past for 'timeless lessons'. This tendency was most pronounced in his more popular books where his purpose was to propagandise on behalf of a history-based doctrine to a largely untutored audience. Didactic in method and purpose, many of these were essentially tracts of their times and of lasting interest only as evidence of contemporary thinking and debate. His last two books, *Statesmen and Sea Power* and the unfinished *The Navy as an Instrument of Policy 1558–1727* (edited by E. A. Hughes, 1953), stand apart and have survived as his best remembered. In these broad surveys, he sought to explain to both political and military leaders their joint responsibilities for defining national objectives and for developing strategic policies to best serve them in peace and war.

But Richmond's principal purpose as a scholar was not to devise a universal theory of seapower. On this score he clearly parted company with Mahan's example. His major works, those upon which his credentials as a naval historian rested, were detailed specialised studies – *The Navy in the War of 1739–1748* (1920), *The Navy in India, 1763–1783* (1931), and the volumes edited for the Navy Records Society, *Papers Relating to the Loss of Minorca in 1756* (1913) and *The Spencer Papers*, volumes III and IV (1924). In these, his purpose was not to codify or systematise on the basis of some Jominian or other theoretical model, but simply to explain British maritime achievements in terms of specific personalities, circumstances and consciously developed national policies. In terms of research, reliance on primary sources and originality of interpretation, Richmond owed comparatively little to Mahan and a good deal more to his British forbears, especially Sir Julian Corbett. Always conscious of political, geographic and technological specificity, he challenged the more extreme 'blue water', navalist writers' preoccupation with the operations of the battle fleet in winning command of the sea. He went further to emphasise that sea power was always more complex and all-inclusive in its workings both in a direct military sense and as an instrument of diplomacy and economic power. Hence his own concern to explain such fundamental concepts as lines of communication and trade defence, blockade and belligerent rights, combined operations and alliance politics.

Richmond could not claim a direct line of his own disciples, nor have his writings ever occupied a place as high as Mahan's on staff college recommended reading lists. Perhaps the greatest measure of his influence is to be found in the works of a later generation of outstanding naval scholars such as Professor Arthur J. Marder and Captain Stephen Roskill, whose careers touched upon his in various ways. Richmond's mind and pen dominated the field after the First World War and extended the pioneering efforts of his own teachers to implant them more firmly into our general consciousness.

(h) Continental maritime strategy 1918–39

In France, the significance of the First World War for the future of maritime strategy was most thoroughly analysed by Admiral Raoul Castex. Castex had embarked on his literary career before the war with a series of works on such issues as the defence of Indo-China, but from 1929 he published his monumental five volume *Theories Strategiques*, arguably the most complete theoretical survey of maritime strategy to appear so far. Castex later presided over the Ecole de Guerre Maritime where, wrote Richmond admiringly, 'History was employed not as a record of facts to be remembered, but as a vehicle for studying situations and accustoming men to think for themselves'.[59] Castex's influence, though difficult to quantify spread widely outside France. A pupil of his, for instance, became first director of the Dutch Naval War College, then Chief of the Naval Staff and Navy Minister. Although he does not appear to have any discernible influence on the British and American navies, he was an important figure in the evolution of naval thought.

Like many other naval officers of his time, Castex was considerably exercised by the possible effect that technology, in the shape of submarines and aircraft, would have on the theory and practice of naval warfare. He did not, however, share the view that these new developments implied any diminution in the importance of large surface ships. Of course, the surface ships should now operate in a somewhat different way so as to make the most of these new weapons. Aerial superiority in particular had become a necessary condition of maritime supremacy.[60] Nevertheless, surface forces were still as important as they used to be.

The First World War had also shown that command of the surface of the sea was still vital for maritime success, although the degree and scope of that command might now be more limited in terms of time and space. Command of the sea was a relative, incomplete, imperfect concept: even the most absolute mastery of the oceans could not prevent an enemy appearing on these waters. Command of the sea really meant the control of surface maritime communications essential for any given purpose.[61]

This control was still the basic condition for successful attack on the enemy's coast or on his shipping. There was always the temptation to engage in these exciting enterprises before adequate command had been secured; this was a dangerous proceeding because the forces engaged would be very vulnerable to attack by the enemy's main fleet. In theory, therefore, command of the sea should be won before attacks were mounted against the enemy's trade or coast. In practice, though, necessities might arise which would demand the suspension of the theory; no theory, after all, was absolute.[62]

On the question of how this command of the sea was to be gained, Castex sounded at his most traditional. The essential element was *la force organisée* – the main concentration of the particular fighting forces of the time.[63] Although sometimes it might be necessary merely to neutralise, by some form of blockade, an enemy who refused to fight, every maritime strategy should aim at battle, immediate or deferred. To make the point he quoted Daveluy: 'to reduce the enemy to impotence, it is necessary to disarm him – that is, to destroy the organised forces which are the guarantee of his power'.[64]

Perhaps Castex's chief contribution to the maritime strategy of his time was that by so carefully and reasonably restating the ancient verities of Mahan and Colomb about the importance of command of the sea and the necessity for the destruction of the enemy's main forces in battle, he played a part in restoring navies' confidence in themselves. In the eyes of many, the First World War had shown both the impotence of two great battle-fleets locked in futile stalemate and also the beginnings of new forms of power at sea which challenged the primacy of the battleship. Castex argued that naval officers should not over-react to all this; the more things changed, the more they would be seen to stay the same.

All this was of very little help to the secondary naval power which could not realistically aspire to naval mastery because of its inherent inferiority at sea. How should the second-best naval power conduct itself so as to make the most of its limited assets? Castex argued, in fact, that the First World War had shown that useful things could be done with inferior forces if they were properly handled. Limited counter-offensives of various kinds might force a superior foe to disperse his forces and so render him vulnerable to defeat in detail. In some ways the new weaponry made limited offensives of this kind more potent. Aircraft, for example, could 'extend the possibility of a strategic offensive' for inferior navies, as their reconnaissance capacities would help them find worthwhile targets and avoid superior forces. Neverthe-less, Castex made the point that it was easier to develop the theory than to put it into practice.[65]

Castex was by no means the only maritime strategist at this time to explore the problem of what to do with the second-best fleet. In Russia, for example, the Soviet New School were proposing much more radical solutions. They rejected 'the theoretical legacy of the old Russian fleet and bourgeois theories' which they thought underpinned the classical theories of Professors Petrov and Gervais at the Voroshilov Naval War College. These prophets were denounced and fired, the faith discarded. Instead Soviet maritime strategy at the behest of the New School aimed principally at the efficient conduct of 'minor war' in coastal waters. Concerted action by submarine, mines and aircraft would protect the coastline against foreign incursions and provide the army with the best direct support possible in such straitened times. In true Marxist tradition, theory should be made to conform to economic, social and political realities. The extent to which the Russian Navy accepted these theories is a matter of some controversy; certainly by the late 1930s the construction of a big-gun, high-sea navy was once more underway.

In Germany, the most thorough examination of the problem was Vice Admiral Wolfgang Wegener's *Seestrategie des Weltkrieges* (1926), an extended memorandum produced as a short book in 1929. Wegener bitterly criticised the Commanders of the High Seas Fleet for playing a waiting game in the First World War, since this effectively gave all the advantages to the British. In Wegener's view, anything was better than a policy which resulted primarily in the German fleet, (the product of so much German effort, resources and pre-war anticipations) swinging uselessly at anchor in the Jade. Of course, the German fleet suffered from grave material and geographic disadvantages. Even so, the German Naval Command had not sufficiently grasped the point that there was no virtue in defending (however skilfully) a strategic position which was ultimately worthless.

Instead, said Wegener, a German Fleet should break out of its confinement. He said, 'The way to the Atlantic; that should have been our burning aim – to reach the Atlantic at all costs'. The German Navy should have launched a 'geographic offensive' up towards southern Norway (or possibly down towards Brest) and so been able to mount a real challenge to British naval supremacy. A move like this would have forced back the British blockade line and given the German Navy much more scope for offensive action. It might even have led to a decisive encounter with the British Grand Fleet on terms more favourable to the Germans than those which applied at Jutland.

Wegener's idea that an inferior fleet could still pursue the offensive and so become a strategically vital tool of a country which was at best only semi-oceanic naturally greatly appealed to his generation. His conceptions also clearly played a part in Germany's maritime strategy in the Second World War. Nevertheless, there were difficulties and ambiguities in his philosophy. Some of these were pointed out by Dr Herbert Rosinski, a contemporary of his, then working on a survey of naval theory at the German Naval Academy. Rosinski argued that Wegener made too much of geography and relative dispositions and not enough of the basic numerical inferiority of the German Navy. The weaker side was even more vulnerable at sea than it was on land: he later wrote, in the United States, 'in maritime warfare the side which loses the power to dispute the command is practically helpless against the attacks of its enemy and without any hope of changing that situation'.[66] In particular, it was not clear why a decisive encounter off Norway should be any more in Germany's favour than one fought in the middle of the North Sea. In short, although Wegener's reasoning seemed ingenious and appealing, it was fundamentally defective.

Other German writers of the period proposed a much more down-to-earth solution to their country's maritime dilemma. Why not abandon pursuit of command of the sea altogether – especially as this was a contest which Germany with all her territorial preoccupations could not hope to win? Why not rebuild the German Navy for a new war on commerce, rather than on the traditional lines which had so signally failed her in the past? 'In future' wrote one German admiral, 'the less one has to reckon with the clash of large battlefleets, as at

Jutland in 1916, the more trade warfare is going to become the main operative task of the strategy of naval war.'[67] Writers like Captain von Waldeyer-Hartz and Ernst Wilhelm Kruse argued that trade warfare would no longer be a subsidiary operation, but the main area of activity. The enemy's command of the sea should be accepted, his surface units avoided and his merchant shipping whole-heartedly attacked, by heavy surface ships, cruisers, submarines and aircraft.[68] 'Trade warfare,' wrote Waldeyer-Hartz, 'will be the dominant form of the naval warfare of tomorrow.'[69]

In fact these ideas did not win wide currency inside the German Navy until 1938 for only then did Britain (virtually the only target suitable for such a campaign) emerge as a likely naval enemy. Up to then, attention had been concentrated on the Baltic. Additionally, advocacy of cruiser warfare implied criticism of Tirpitz's pre-war naval policy and of the orthodox proclivities of his heirs and successors in the German Navy of the inter-war period. The future of the navy seemed to depend on its presenting a united front to rivals and detractors and so criticism, implied or overt, was muzzled wherever possible. As so often happens, the writing of history became a continuation of policy by other means.[70]

A perceptive but unassuming treatment of what could perhaps be called the orthodox British line on these and other maritime questions in modern conditions came out just before the Second World War, when Commander John Creswell published his *Naval Warfare: An Introductory Study* in 1938. Creswell, an evident believer in the power of history, intended his study to be of special benefit to junior naval officers: 'to put before them the lines of thought most likely to lead to sound strategy and tactics'.

Creswell argued that battlefleet supremacy still exerted as decisive an influence on naval warfare as ever. This supremacy would continue to be best established by winning victory in battle, on whose 'immense importance' and 'predominance over all other acts of warfare' he laid great stress. Neutralisation by blockade, although occasionally necessary, was a much less satisfactory way of gaining this maritime supremacy. He explored the possibilities available to a weaker navy and concluded that a defensive strategy had much scope if tackled in a skilful and enterprising way. Despite recent advances in submarine and aircraft, the battleship, he felt, remained the backbone of the battlefleet. He dealt fully with battle tactics, the defence and attack of trade, and the mounting of overseas expeditions.

Commander Russell Grenfell's *The Art of the Admiral* (1937) was another similar survey. Grenfell was an instructor at the Naval Staff College at Greenwich and was later to prove himself to be a more than competent naval historian. In this deceptively simple book, he covered much the same ground as Creswell, although his approach was a little more theoretical, and came basically to the same conclusions. A particularly interesting part of his survey, however, was his attempt to distinguish between the gaining of command of the sea by the destruction of the enemy, and the control of sea communications. The first was more than just the means to the latter, he thought; in many cases fighting for the sake of the moral ascendancy that actual victory gave was justified in circumstances where strict logic showed it to be unnecessary. His book, commented one reviewer, 'exudes the spirit of the offensive . . . if talking will do the trick our next opponents should stand no chance'.

The pursuit of the offensive was even more a theme of the lively and controversial writings of Captain Bernard Acworth (*Navies of Today and Tomorrow*, 1930; *The Restoration of England's Seapower*, 1935) Acworth was an arch-enemy of the school which put materiel before policy. He was hostile to the construction of large battleships, worried about the Navy's going over to oil, sceptical about the value of speed and the menace of aircraft, submarines and the torpedo: 'Perhaps the most vital need of the Navy today is to take up the torpedo by the gills, so to speak, and to look this pretentious bugbear squarely in the mouth'. Above all, he was opposed to what he termed the 'safety first' school of thought. Although Acworth's commentaries frequently verged on the libellous and his views on some aspects of technological advance were totally wrong, he makes very interesting reading. One critic observed, 'Those who can refrain from throwing the book across the room will still obtain considerable amusement and instruction, as well as mental exercise in sorting out grain from chaff'.[71]

Altogether, these three writers provide a fair cross-section of the assortment of ideas that the Royal Navy took with it to war shortly afterwards.

(i) Reactions to the Second World War

The lessons of the Second World War were analysed most thoroughly on the British side by Captain S. W. Roskill, the official historian of the Royal Navy at war. In his *The Strategy of Seapower*, Roskill made clear his belief in the value of history and in the necessity for naval thought. In his view, the Admiralty's handling of the U-boat menace showed that those who failed to absorb past lessons were often condemned to repeat past mistakes. It was important to think about these things before the necessity for immediate action arose.

The war had also provided a triumphant vindication of the potentiality of maritime power and of the wisdom of the British adherence to a maritime strategy. He defined a maritime strategy: 'as the means of bringing overwhelming forces to bear against the enemy in theatres of our own choice',[72] and showed its advantages in dealing with a continental foe. Sadly, these advantages, and what needed to be done to enjoy them, had not, in Roskill's view, been sufficiently well-remembered before the war. Throughout his many works, there runs a continuing skein of reasoned lament about Britain's almost habitual unpreparedness for war. Sometimes this is attributed to a passing infatuation with other 'continental' strategies, a reluctance to spend the necessary resources, inadequate inter-service co-operation and shortcomings in the navy's own policy and programmes.

Roskill argued that some unnecessary errors in the naval side of the Second World War could be attributed to the Admiralty's perverse adherence to outmoded doctrines and fallacious concepts. Prime amongst these was the tendency to pay too much attention to the requirements of a major battlefleet encounter at the expense of other less exciting but more useful naval activities, such as defending merchant shipping. The style of the decisive battle they pursued so ardently was wrongly perceived as well: in Captain Roskill's view, their tendency to see it primarily in terms of a prolonged duel between parallel lines of heavy gun ships paid too little attention to new naval developments in aircraft and submarine. A somewhat similar deficiency could be seen in the Admiralty's conduct of its war against the U-boat. There was too much stress on allegedly 'offensive' measures and not enough on the tried and tested method of convoy-and-escort.

Nevertheless, although the implementation of Britain's maritime strategy might occasionally have been faulty, Roskill showed that its potentialities were undiminished. Having established effective forms of maritime control, the Royal Navy was able to prosecute the war in a way which had a decisive impact on the final outcome, by its operations in the defence and attack of trade and in the mounting or prevention of overseas expeditions. He wrote:

> Though the exercise of maritime power in defence of trade is essential to the nation's war economy, and it alone can provide the conditions from which the final decisive offensive will be launched it is by exercising this same heritage in the despatch of great military expeditions overseas that a maritime strategy can be crowned by final victory.[73]

In short, despite all the pre-war claims of the advocates of air and continental landpower, the experience of the Second World War could be seen essentially as a vindication of the orthodoxies of sea power and maritime strategy. Fundamentally, this is also the message of the most thorough American reaction to the maritime implications of the war – Bernard Brodie's *Guide to Naval Strategy*. First published in 1942, as a 'Layman's Guide . . . ', Brodie's work soon became something of a naval classic and, in the words of the *New York Times*, 'required reading in naval academies'.

Brodie organised his analysis into themes and took a more 'theoretical' approach than did the pragmatic Roskill, who preferred the medium of a historical survey, organised chronologically. But though the methods were different, the substance of what they both said was similar. Brodie also believed in the command of the sea (and unlike Roskill, this is what he called it) and thought that it was acquired or asserted 'in a given area by offering to beat the strongest force which the enemy can place there'. A navy 'exercises its command by using its fighting supremacy to keep its own shipping moving and to stop that of the enemy'.[74] The ability to exercise this command was decisive because 'the belligerent who controls the sea that washes the enemy's domain exercises a power which is hardly known in land warfare'.[75] In such conditions sea power could carry out its most decisive functions of protecting the transfer of its own men and commodities and preventing the enemy from doing the same.[76]

The same sense of Neptune triumphant is strikingly evident in the first few pages of Admiral Chester W. Nimitz's celebrated report to the Secretary of the Navy in December 1947. Quoting a comment of 1657, Nimitz remarked that 'the purpose of achieving sea power and the recognised practice of applying pressure against an enemy whenever he can be reached by naval forces has not changed from that day to this'. He added: 'The basic objectives and principles of war do not change'.

He pointed out that the US Navy now possessed 'control of the sea more absolute than ever possessed by the British . . . so absolute that it is sometimes taken for granted'. This now undisputed 'control of the sea was achieved primarily through the employment of naval air–sea forces in the destruction of Japanese and German sea power'. Unlike Brodie, Nimitz paid little attention to the protection of trade, but believed, like him, that the new technology, far from limiting the power of navies, now gave it a much greater reach than ever it had before. Naval airpower, especially, 'provided naval forces with a striking weapon of vastly increased flexibility, range and power. The development and use of this weapon in World War II against both sea and land objectives is one of the great achievements in modern warfare'.

Naval airpower reached its height of perfection during the Pacific campaign. Nimitz concluded:

> In all these operations the employment of air–sea forces demonstrated the ability of the Navy to concentrate aircraft strength at any desired point in such numbers as to overwhelm the defence at the point of contact. These operations demonstrate the capability of naval carrier-based aviation to make use of the principles of mobility and concentration to a degree possessed by no other force.[77]

Nimitz's report went on to make substantial claims about the future employment of naval forces: it was in fact one of the first comprehensive attempts by the US Navy to list its missions and stake out its claim for defence resources in an age otherwise dominated by the advent of atomic weapons. The report's verdict on the Second World War has to be seen in this light, but all the same it shows that naval officers of this period were well satisfied with the performance and the importance of sea power up to then.

Nevertheless, times were changing and the advent of nuclear weapons in particular caused considerable perturbations amongst naval thinkers. European perspectives on these new problems can be gauged by looking at the works of Admiral P. Barjot of the French, Sir Peter Gretton of the British and Edward Wegener of the German navies.[78] All were clear about the past importance of sea power. Barjot sought to derive lessons from a long review of French naval history and put a particular stress on the relatively recent 'aeronavale' aspect of war at sea. Gretton made a bold attempt to produce a set of principles of maritime strategy from historical experience and then set about seeing the extent to which they would have to be modified to suit modern conditions. He went out of his way to stress the importance of the study of the past for this.[79]

Wegener specifically rejected the view that the naval theory of Mahan and Corbett about the exercise of sea-supremacy and the control of merchant shipping had become obsolete.[80] He used recent (and especially German) naval experience to illustrate an interesting discussion of terms. Sea power, he thought, comprised only two indispensable elements: fleet and strategic position. He distinguished between a strategic naval offensive (a determination to gain mastery at sea) and defensive (either being satisfied with the present balance or renouncing the concept altogether). Also, he suggested there was an important difference between mastery of the sea (the securing of which was a condition of its use) and control of the sea (activities associated with its exclusive use). 'Fighting at sea', he wrote, moreover, 'is only justified if the ultimate goal requires it.'[81] All this is very much in the familiar traditions of naval thinking.

Nevertheless, all three writers were very much aware of the possible impact of nuclear weapons on orthodox maritime operations. Barjot was the most sanguine of the three. He argued that the importance of the sea, especially for purposes of carriage, were growing, not diminishing. He thought surface navies would survive atomic attack, and could in any case bend these new developments to maritime ends. Both Gretton and Wegener, however, doubted whether the operation of the strategic deterrent at sea was really a naval function, although it was task carried out, for almost accidental reasons, by navies.[82] Gretton, moreover, did not believe that a significant maritime strategy was possible in a general nuclear war. In such a conflict, naval functions would largely be restricted to relief and rescue.

Wegener was not so sure of this, and discussed various naval activities in the 'post-atomic phase' of war, but nevertheless, devoted the bulk of his work to the analysis of the naval conflicts below this holocaustic level. To make the distinction clearer, he introduced the notion that naval strategy only related to attempts to control the sea in war time: maritime strategy on the other hand applied to 'non-war' situations.[83]

Even so, despite widespread doubt, dismay and confusion, Gretton and others remained convinced that navies would continue to have vital tasks to perform in limited conventional operations conducted in the shadow of the strategic nuclear stalemate. The destructiveness of nuclear weapons would inhibit their use, and so limited wars must become a possibility, given the present political turbulence of the world. Consequently, Gretton explored naval roles in cold-war situations, wars of intervention and 'grey wars' against sea communications. He argued that these roles requires an extensive set of orthodox maritime capacities and the continued application of most of the classical principles of maritime strategy.[84]

By and large, most modern naval writers have agreed with him. The question, therefore, becomes which principles and capacities to keep, which to alter and which to discard.

(j) American thinking on naval strategy, 1945–80 (by John B. Hattendorf)

In the thirty-five-year period following the end of the Second World War, there was no consensus on the theoretical basis of American thinking on naval strategy. Strategic thinking along the lines taken by Mahan, Corbett, and the other 'classical theorists' was faced with new perceptions which challenged the applicability of the older ideas. By 1980, there was no fundamental agreement among experienced practitioners or commentators which would allow the development of a comprehensive, theoretical approach to naval strategy which might replace the traditional works. Emphasis was placed on understanding certain areas of naval activity while others were neglected or disregarded. American writing on strategy was dominated by speculations and calculations on nuclear warfare, deterrence, and arguments over the composition and organisation of the armed forces. At the same time, students in several disciplines, raised issues which challenged several of the basic assumptions held by students of naval strategy and which remain unresolved.[85]

The very elusiveness of the term 'strategy' expressed a major symptom of the difficulty which strategists faced. In the late nineteenth century, the word had a specific meaning, but by the middle of the twentieth century, it came to have a variety of nuances which made it an extremely difficult word to define in a way which was readily acceptable. For some, strategy was a broad theoretical problem which involved the widest aspects of the nation in relation to its military power. At the other end of the spectrum there were those who dealt with strategy in terms of specific situations, technical abilities of ships and aircraft, quantitative analysis, and financial resources. For the strategist, the central problem of the period was a lack of cohesive thinking. Historian Russell F. Weigley characterised the period as one of 'American Strategy in Perplexity'. In 1977, Admiral T. H. Moorer and Alvin Cottrell wrote,

The United States remains without anything approximating a grand strategy. The instruments of military power inevitably become the first casualties of national indecision. Military power cannot be understood or defended unless it is harnessed to purpose – and purpose can only be defined in the context of comprehensive strategy.[86]

In practice armed forces and diplomacy were often treated separately rather than as directly related means to political ends. Although super-power rivalry provided a frame of references, strategy derives its meaning in the relation of the use of force to national goals, which must in turn be seen in the light of national perceptions, traditions, and ideology. The confusion surrounding this issue has been both a cause and a reflection of the lack of an acceptable theoretical base.

Theoretical issues became even more clouded in the political debates which arose in the late 1940s over the unification of the services, and almost every year over the Navy budget. It was seen also in the bureaucratic debates inside the Navy which involved various groups with vested interests in specific types of ships and weapons, and inside the Defense Department which involved the navy's position in relation to other services. These issues were essentially political, although strategic reasons were often used to obscure their actual political character.

To American naval men in 1945, the war against Japan seemed to have clearly justified the central theses put forward by Mahan a half-century earlier. The battles of Midway and Leyte Gulf seemed extraordinary proof of the idea that decisive victory in warfare was obtained through climatic battle between enemy fleets which resulted in command of the sea. This view tended to overlook the critical importance of the destruction of Japanese tankers and merchantmen by American submarines in a type of warfare which Mahan had believed was inconclusive. Nevertheless, Mahan was regarded as the guiding figure in naval theory. In the years immediately preceding the Second

World War, Harold and Margaret Sprout had extolled Mahan's virtues in their influential studies.[87]

During and after the war, a number of writers attempted to apply Mahan's theoretical ideas to the modern world. First and most important among these were Bernard Brodie.[88] Anthony E. Sokol made a similar attempt in *Seapower in the Nuclear Age* (1961) as did Admiral J. J. Clark and Captain Dwight H. Barnes in *Sea Power and Its Meaning* (1966). Among other writers, William Reitzel and B. M. Simpson, III, produced the best analytical syntheses of the scattered theoretical framework which Mahan produced in his historical commentaries.[89]

It became commonplace at the Naval War College to hear discussions and lectures on 'Mahan in the Nuclear Age'. Yet all of these valiant attempts to apply Mahan's ideas raised some fundamental questions. Most importantly, American historians had rejected Mahan's basic idea that principles for human action could be deduced from history in the way that scientists deduced laws from their observations. The validity of Mahan's method was questioned on this basis. Modern commentators tended to use historical analogy with greater precision than Mahan and with more attention to the factors which invited contrast as well as comparison to current situations.

Mahan's rejection of technology as irrelevant in establishing constant principles was equally challenged. In *The Sea in Modern Strategy* (1967), a book which was widely read in American naval circles, L. W. Martin argued that the strategic world of Mahan and Corbett was no longer relevant. Similar battle fleets no longer fought each other at sea; technological developments had altered the scene forever:

> In the second half of the century, developments in naval propulsion, in aircraft, missiles, explosives and techniques of computation, have overthrown completely the context in which fleet actions were the focus of strategy. Submarine, aircraft and missile have become the most dangerous enemies of the larger surface ships, while those ships find their prime targets on shore. Bombardment of the land, once one of the most humble naval tasks, has become a dominant concern of the larger navies – strategically with missiles launched from submarines, tactically with aircraft based at sea. The importance that guerrilla warfare has acquired as a result of strategic and political circumstances has required some navies to give greatly increased attention to inshore operations.[90]

Mahan's emphasis on the importance of a navy in his prescription for national greatness was similarly questioned. Some students saw this as an historical conclusion which was appropriate only to the history of Great Britain and to the age of sail. In an effort to replace the standard

American textbook narrative of battles, E. B. Potter and C. W. Nimitz's *Sea Power: A Naval History* (1960), Clark G. Reynolds made his *Command of the Sea* (1974) a survey of all naval history in the general terms which Mahan used. However, he differentiated between the strategic uses of three broad types of nations which used navies, maritime powers, continental powers and small powers.[91]

For years research in naval history had been based on Mahan's principles, but now historians inquired into the accuracy of his conclusions in explaining past events. In a book entitled *The Rise and Fall of British Naval Mastery* (1976), Paul M. Kennedy, an English historian, challenged Mahan's list of six conditions which gave Britain an affinity to sea power. Following a recent trend among historians to explain events in economic terms, Kennedy asserted that British naval power was directly related to her economic position. Moreover, he questioned the dominant position which Mahan gave to coastal states by pointing out that industrialism and improved transportation allowed great land powers to dominate maritime states. Finally, he stressed the need for balance between the army and navy in their strategic uses. This last point followed the general argument which Michael Howard had put forward in *The Continental Commitment* (1972) and *The British Way in Warfare: A Reappraisal* (1975).

Turning from broad, general studies of naval power, other historians examined smaller segments of history in their evaluation of Mahan. Geoffrey Symcox, an English born historian at the University of California, looked at the Nine Years War. In his book, *The Crisis of French Sea Power 1688–1697* (1974), Symcox showed the inaccuracy of Mahan's general conclusions by emphasising the successful use of *guerre de course*, the importance of a strategy of attrition as opposed to that of climatic and decisive engagement between battle fleets, and the importance of overall naval strength as decisive factors.

Looking at Mahan's emphasis on the primacy of battle from another perspective, Arthur J. Marder reflected on the effect which that concept had on the Royal Navy in the First World War. In the final chapter of his five volume work dealing with the period *From Dreadnought to Scapa Flow* (vol. 5, 1970), Marder pointed out that it had come from a misreading of history and its application resulted in a great deal of frustration and misdirection.

An US Air Force officer, John F. Guilmartin, Jr., argued in another study that Mahan's concepts were not applicable to all areas or situations. In his book, *Gunpowder and Galleys: Changing Technology and Mediterranean Warfare at Sea in the Sixteenth Century* (1964), Guilmartin showed that Mahan's ideas on control of the sea, the relationship between maritime trade and naval warfare, and the cause and effect relationship between naval battles and overall strategy did not explain the uses of sixteenth-century navies in the Mediterranean. In place of these ideas, Guilmartin stressed the amphibious nature of naval warfare in its direct relationship to battle ashore.

While some of Mahan's concepts were being tested and refuted in the process of being adapted to the modern world, historians began to emphasise Mahan's place in the context of his own times. Some viewed him within the context of American imperialism, as an advocate of 'navalism' and the elitist, racist and social Darwinist views which were dominant in his day while others saw him more broadly as part of a trend in the development of naval thought in the industrial age.

Mahan's work was the product of a particular person at a specific time in history whose ideas were somewhat inaccurately drawn from the examination of one peculiar set of historical circumstances. Despite doubts, refutations, and exceptions, Mahan's general framework survived in the United States and remained the standard against which an understanding of naval strategy was measured. As early as 1953, Rear Admiral John D. Hayes, a prolific writer on strategy and naval history, reached the tentative judgement which was to become the prevailing view by 1980: 'Until there comes another like him to dissect, analyze, and codify the experiences of our day, none of us can go wrong if we study Mahan's great historical works.'[92]

Mahan and Corbett had been concerned entirely with the conduct of war at sea. Not only had sea warfare changed, however, but the experience of the years after 1945 emphasised the uses of navies short of war. There was no book of theoretical writing on this aspect. In the pioneer effort in this field, the British diplomat James Cable attempted to categorise the uses of limited naval force short of war in *Gunboat Diplomacy* (1971). His efforts were refined by the analyst Edward N. Luttwak in his study, *The Political Uses of Sea Power* (1975). This in turn was broadened and refocused further by a study of naval functions in *Navies and Foreign Policy* (1977), by Ken Booth of the University College of Wales, Aberystwth.

The emphasis on the political use of naval force presented difficulty in measuring the relationship between adversaries who were competing in the naval area. In an important commentary on the Soviet–American naval competition, Admiral Turner, then Commander-in-Chief, Allied Forces Southern Europe, summarised three of the most important factors in analysing a naval balance: relative numbers, relative technical capabilities, and tempering political and moral factors.[93]

In the 1960s and 1970s, it became common for officials to discuss the navy's strategic role in terms of 'sea control' and 'power projection'. In 1976 Admiral Elmo R. Zumwalt illustrated this when he wrote in his memoirs that:

The industry and trade of the United States depended on ocean traffic in both directions and most if its important allies are on the far side of broad oceans as well. The economy of the United States requires that it have a large maritime capability. The political interests and commitments of the United States require that it be capable of having a large military influence overseas. Both of those exigencies, in turn, make a powerful US Navy imperative. Even more to the point, they define the double mission of the US Navy: to keep the seas open for commercial and military traffic of all kinds, which we call 'sea control', and to make it possible to apply military power overseas which we call 'projection'.[94]

A little earlier Zumwalt had categorised four missions for the navy: Strategic Deterrence, Power Projection, Sea Control, and Navy Presence. Unsatisfied with the statements which explained these terms, Admiral Stansfield Turner examined them in detail and provided a more thorough theoretical basis for them. In the process of doing this, he warned that such descriptions should not be rigid, but should be seen as descriptions of naval uses which were interdependent, overlapping, and changing in emphasis in relation to one another.[95]

The theoretical understanding of the navy's capabilities progressed along these lines. The older ideas had not been thoroughly reworked, but new ground had been broken with respect to peacetime uses. Despite this progress, there were repeated criticisms that this approach was too narrowly focused. As early as 1949, Rear Admiral C. R. Brown told the US Naval War College that what was needed was not a new Mahan, but 'brilliant strategists, not of land power, not of sea power, and not of air power, but able broad-gauged individuals who can view the whole picture of *military* strategy.'[96] A small group of individuals responded to this challenge. Among them was Herbert Rosinski, a refugee from Nazi Germany and former lecturer at the German Naval Staff College. Much of his earlier writing on naval affairs had been devoted to applying the ideas of Mahan and Corbett in their modern context. In 1955, however, he wrote 'New Thoughts on Strategy' at the Naval War College after discussions with Rear Admiral H. E. Eccles, Rear Admiral T. H. Robbins, Jr., and Vice Admiral Lynde McCormick. In this place, he attempted to develop a comprehensive definition of strategy by building on some of the major points expressed by Mahan, Clausewitz, and Corbett and by stressing the idea of strategy as control. 'Strategy' wrote Rosinski, 'is the comprehensive direction of power; tactics its immediate application'.[97]

These concepts along with Duncan S. Ballantine's view[98] that the economic aspects of war provide the bridge between the conceptualisation of a strategy and the practical limits to its application, were the foundation for the important work of Rear Admiral Henry E. Eccles. In his *Logistics in the National Defense* (1959), Eccles developed Mahan's views on lines of communication and bases and in *Military Concepts and*

Philosophy (1965), he postulated a comprehensive military theory. Using Reitzel's analysis of Mahan in *Military Power in a Free Society* (1979), he incorporated the distinction between maritime power, sea power, sea force, and sea control into his earlier ideas.

Rear Admiral Joseph C. Wylie took another approach and attempted to find a relationship among the various classical theories of land, sea, and air warfare. He found each to be valid within specific conditions, but diminishing in validity as each departed from the ideal. In response to this, Wylie sought to define the goal of a strategist as control of a war's centre of gravity for his own ends:

> The primary aim of the strategist in the conduct of war is some selected degree of control of the enemy for the strategist's own purpose; this is achieved by control of the pattern of war; and this control of the pattern of war is had by manipulation of the center of gravity of war to the advantage of the strategist and the disadvantage of the opponent.
>
> The successful strategist is the one who controls the nature and the placement and the timing and the weight of the centers of gravity of war, and who exploits the resulting control of the pattern of war towards his own ends. [99]

The reservations over the narrow focus of naval thinkers and the intellectual stagnation caused by the blind acceptance of 'strategic doctrine' gave rise to a broader approach in the education of officers at the US Naval War College. In 1972, Vice Admiral Stansfield Turner introduced a study of strategy through broadly based, historical case studies. Rejecting the use of established doctrine, definitions, and theory, the course was designed to bring out the basic elements of strategy and the general problem areas which are faced in strategic analysis. The historical case studies which ranged from the Peloponnesian War to the twentieth century were examined in the light of Carl von Clausewitz's theories, most notably his concept that military strategy is properly subordinated to policy objectives. This approach was one which was designed to explain basic considerations. It was argued:

> The strategic problem is essentially an intellectual problem. And before it can be addressed, it must be defined. And to define the problem, one starts with questions: What is the object? What are the means to achieve it? Are they available? What are the costs? The benefits? What are the hazards? What are the limitations? How will the public react? Are the proposed actions morally justifiable? What are the lessons of experience? How does the present differ from the past? [100]

Although this approach caused some hostile reaction within the US Navy, it was similar in some respects to the study of strategy which had been introduced at the Naval War College before the First World War and refined by Admiral William S. Sims in 1919.

The classical theorists assumed that the study of strategy was a logical process in which one could analyse a direct cause and effect relationship between naval capabilities and international affairs. Some of the issues which arose in this period were direct challenges to that assumption and remained unresolved in strategic theory.

Strategists were confronted by observers who contended that warfare could have no utility in the modern world. The issue was raised directly by the problem of nuclear weapons. It was a broad issue which can best be seen in the much wider context of the literature on nuclear weapons. In its narrow naval context, it can be illustrated by the strategy behind the submarine launched Polaris missile. This was a strategy of deterrence, based on a weapon that could be kept safe from attack. Oskar Morgenstern described the idea as early as 1959:

> The principal aim of shifting the weapons carrier, of putting it one moment here, the other there, below the water and in the air, is of course to hide it. . . . This is achieved by combining the properties of speed and depth of water with erratic movements, with randomization. Instead of deploying forces to carefully selected places, of giving their placement a pattern and formation such as fleets had to adopt by necessity even in the last war, probability alone should determine the geographical spot where the weapon carrier (submarine, floating missile base, seaplane) is next to appear. This is what the combination of nuclear propulsion of ships and sea-planes with nuclear weapons and solid fuel propulsion for missiles is making possible. Never before in warfare could a system be envisaged where mobile dispersal is combined with great power in each unit, the ability for all to act together from their dispersed points according to some previous plan, and be directed from a central point of command.[101]

The catastrophic implications of nuclear warfare, however, made some observers doubt that such weapons could ever be used, and from this they argued that the deterrent effect of nuclear weapons was of no value. Enthoven and Smith pointed this out when they wrote that:

> The trouble with this concept is faulty assumptions (for example, that civilian casualties and collateral damage can be kept to low levels); it ignores a basic lesson that the leaders of the US Government in all crises have learned – that when faced with the decision to start a nuclear war, almost any other alternative looked better; and it is too risky to serve as the foundation for a preferred strategy.[102]

Aside from nuclear warfare, civilian theorists such as Thomas C. Schelling began to apply the ideas of game theory to both nuclear and non-nuclear warfare. In his books *The Strategy of Conflict* (1960) and *Arms and Influence* (1966), Schelling argued that conflict was a bargaining situation. What was important to him was not the application of force, but the exploitation of potential force. This idea lay behind much of the theoretical work on the peacetime application of navies, but several influential serving officers advanced differing viewpoints. Rear Admiral J. C. Wylie wrote that, 'War for a nonaggressor nation is actually a nearly complete collapse of policy',[103] and Vice Admiral James B. Stockdale, objected particularly to the approach of systems analysts and game theorists. He wrote 'War in political theory may be perfectly rational, warfare in practice is most decidedly not'.[104]

Another serious problem was the difficulty in understanding the inter-relationship of technology and strategy. As early as 1948, some observers noted that strategic theory tended to collapse in the face of new technical innovations:

So much of the old has broken down and so much of the new has been added that there no longer exists an accepted closely-knit analysis of the whole of war and strategy. Instead, theories have tended to center around new technological developments which have given rise to more or less unconnected and very often contradictory doctrines like sprawling limbs without backbone or head.[105]

Using illustrative examples from naval history in his book, *Men, Machines and Modern Times* (1966), Elting E. Morrison drew some important conclusions about human reactions to technical change and Admiral Stansfield Turner applied some of these to the contemporary factors which prevented change and resisted the development of new ideas within the navy:

Unfortunately, the process of introducing change in Navies is more difficult for three reasons.

First, increasing specialization within the officer corps, resulting from the pressures of technology has accentuated tendencies to identify the interest of a special group with the interests of the Navy as a whole. Specific evidence of this is the subdivision of officers into three specialties; aviators, surface officers and submarine officers. . . .

The second element making change more difficult today is the temptation to use the burgeoning offerings of technology to temporize with what we have and avoid facing more difficult choices of replacing existing systems. . . .

Some of these are certainly worth the cost. Others are simply prolonging the life of dinosaurs. The problem is one of discriminating between space age gimmicks and changes that truly affect mission capability.

The third new impediment is the multiplication of actors with a legitimate interest in defense matters.[106]

The post-war period also brought an increased understanding of the governmental decision-making process in the formulation of strategy. Scholars working in this area pointed out the relationship between domestic and international politics. Graham Allison took the issue further in his *Essence of Decision* (1971). Demonstrating the influence of domestic politics and the interplay of bureaucratic pressure in policy decisions, Allison argued that the factors which determine action are more important than the goals which are sought.

In this way the traditional ideas on naval strategy appear to be narrowly defined and inapplicable to the full range of naval affairs. Fallacies were pointed out in the assumption that theory had direct practical applications. Furthermore, the impact of technology, with the problems of bureaucratic politics and decision making raised non-rationalistic factors which needed further consideration. Nuclear weapons raised the issue of the utility of warfare and a further extention of ideas in this area brought doubt to the assumption that war is a continuation of policy. Some suggested that the very conduct of war raised new and different objectives. These considerations were not resolved by American naval strategists in the thirty-five years which followed the Second World War. Americans found themselves generally perplexed by the problems of naval strategy. A clear and lucid consideration of the problem was prevented by a lack of semantic rigour in discussing the issues. By the end of the period, it was clear that terms relating to strategy were being used to serve two ends. On the one hand, they were used freely in a political discourse to achieve advantage in international politics, and at the same time, they were being used in a different manner to discuss the shape and use of military force. The two uses served to add to the existing confusion.[107] Professor R. E. Osgood wrote, 'Our concepts, and even our definitions ... are cloudy and misleading. We have not related them comprehensively or precisely to the richness of actual experience.'[108]

The lack of cohesion and consensus in American thinking about naval strategy is clearly evident. If progress is to be made in clarifying thought, it must be done with semantic rigour. Further work must include an understanding of the limitations as well as the rational and irrational factors involved in the full range of naval uses, both in peace and in war, in offence and in defence, and in terms of counter-action. Moreover, all of these factors must be related to the Navy's function as only one portion of the broad use of armed force in a comprehensive exercise to control an adversary.

(k) Admiral of the Fleet S. G. Gorshkov (by Bryan Ranft)

Admiral Gorshkov became commander-in-chief of the Soviet Navy in 1956 and presided over a radical transformation of its role and equipment. The essentially defensive tasks to which it had previously been confined have been replaced by a capacity to contribute substantially to the USSR's nuclear strategy as well as an ability to challenge its enemies' conventional naval forces throughout the world. In numbers of both submarines and major surface vessels the Soviet Navy is now superior to the United States. This does not mean that it is automatically superior in operational strength, but it has resulted in a significant shift in the balance of maritime power by ending the era in which the United States and its European allies could confidently use the seas without fear of effective challenge by the Soviet Navy. The increased strength of its navy has given the Soviet Union a new range of options in both war and peace which are particularly important because of the strategic and economic dependence upon the free use of the seas of its main rival, NATO.

Because of the obscurity of Soviet policy making it is impossible to be certain of how great Gorshkov's personal contribution has been. But, at the time of writing (1980), his continuing appointment, the apparent absence of any naval rival and the dominating role which he has played in publicising the importance of sea power to his country, all suggest that he deserves to be recognised as the chief architect of the modern Soviet Navy.

Sergei Gorshkov was born in the Ukraine in 1910 and commissioned into the navy in 1931. After earlier service in the Black Sea and Pacific Fleets, he commanded, in 1938, a squadron of destroyers, probably as a Captain, Second Rank. As such, he escaped Stalin's purges and presumably benefited from the disappearance of so many of his superiors. On the outbreak of the war with Germany he commanded a cruiser squadron in the Black Sea and distinguished himself in the combined operations unsuccessfully aimed at the holding of Odessa. As an unusually early promoted Rear Admiral in command of the Azov Flotilla he played a prominent part in December 1941 in the biggest Soviet combined operation of the whole war, the landing of some 40 000 troops at Kerch to relieve the pressure on Sevastopol. In the following year he was a member of the military council responsible for the defence of Novorosissk, which brought him into close association with the future Defence Minister, Grechko, then commanding the Forty-Seventh Army. The remainder of his war service was spent in support of land operations in the Crimea and finally in command of the Danube Flotilla assisting Marshal Malinovsky's armies as they drove Germany from the Balkans and the Ukraine. His wartime career was thus a personal example of the Soviet Navy's accepted role of support to the army, which he was later to transcend.

After the war his advancement was rapid. Following periods as chief-of-staff and, later, commander-in-chief of the Black Sea Fleet, he was, in 1955, appointed first deputy commander-in-chief of the Soviet Navy under Admiral Kuznetsov. At this time Khruschev was establishing his leadership in the Politbureau and was known to be an opponent of the big-ship navy which Kuznetsov had persuaded Stalin to plan. It was presumably on Khruschev's urging that Gorshkov succeeded Kuznetsov in 1956, in the belief that the new commander-in-chief's ideas on the future of the navy were compatible with his own. Equally important in enhancing Gorshkov's influence were his wartime connections with men now rising to the top of the political and military establishment; Malinovsky as first deputy minister of defence, Grechko soon to be commander-in-chief of the ground forces and Brezhnev increasingly important in the Party.

Until the 1960s Gorshkov's published speeches and policy statements echoed the traditional doctrine that the Soviet Navy's primary tasks were support of the army and the defence of the country's maritime frontiers. On the practical side, he launched the building programme for the first class of large missile-armed destroyers and thus ensured the prominence of surface ships in future naval expansion. Khruschev's fall in 1964 did not weaken Gorshkov's position and his promotion three years later to the rank of Admiral of the Fleet of the Soviet Union, giving him formal equality with the commanders-in-chief of Ground and Strategic Rocket Forces, was a public recognition of the increased significance of the navy. From this time onwards his published articles placed increasing stress on the navy's world-wide missions and its unique contributions to the country's nuclear strategy.

There is no evidence that Gorshkov has ever been politically active. He did not join the Communist Party until 1942 and, although he has been a member of every Party Congress since 1952, it was only in 1961 that he became a full member of the Central Committee.

The most fruitful way of understanding his thought and writings is to see them as the product of a professional naval officer, brought up to accept established Soviet views on internal politics, the international system and overall strategy and seeking to advance the navy's cause and influence within them.

Gorshkov's thoughts on the significance of sea power and the nature of the navies which exercise it are most systematically developed in two major works: a series of articles, under the general title of 'Navies in War and Peace', published in the naval journal *Morskoi Sbornik* during

1972–3, and a substantial book, *The Sea Power of the State*, which appeared in Russian in 1976 and in an authorised English translation, with a foreword by Gorshkov himself, in 1979. These are best approached as works of advocacy, designed to convince influential circles in the USSR of the advantages, indeed the necessity of the country's being strong at sea and of the continuing need to improve her maritime forces. His case is based on a selective use of history to show how Russia's world influence has grown or diminished with its naval strength. Today all great powers are maritime powers and Russia's major rivals aim to maintain a dominance at sea which is completely unacceptable. These general arguments are buttressed by one designed to impress on a predominantly land-oriented political and military hierarchy that recent technological changes, especially the application of nuclear science to maritime war, have revolutionised naval capabilities. Because of this they will in future play a major part in Russian global strategy, instead of the heavily restricted role in the continental strategy imposed by the country's geography. A secondary aim, more fully pursued in the later work, is to impress on naval officers the constant necessity to develop their strategic and tactical thinking in harmony with continuing technical developments and the necessity of effective training and the maintenance of high morale, so as to be always ready for war.

Inevitably for a man in Gorshkov's position, his professional arguments have to be supported by obeisance to Marxist–Leninist ideology and to the Communist Party under whose leadership the navy has grown to its present strength. But his analyses of the lessons of history, particularly of the naval elements of the two world wars, the impact of technological change on the evolution of maritime strategy and warfare, and of the contribution contemporary sea power can make to Russia's aspiration for equivalence with the United States, establish a strong claim for his writings to find a permanent place in the development of naval thought.

The first nine of the eleven articles comprising 'Navies in War and Peace' are mainly historical analyses of the significance of sea power up to 'The Great Patriotic War'. The historical interpretation is based on Marxist–Leninist doctrine supplemented by the strong Russian patriotism to be expected of a high ranking Soviet officer. Marx, Engels and Lenin are quoted to show their understanding of sea power as being both a prime mover in the historical development of nations and an essential component of a state's war-fighting capability. This political orthodoxy is matched by an unambiguous adherence to accepted Soviet overall military doctrine. No claim is made that navies have a predominant role in modern war or that maritime can be shown to be superior to continental strategy. Historical experience as well as the facts of the contemporary world are cited to support the central doctrine that although each armed service has a unique contribution to make, it is only one part of a larger whole. Success in war can only come from unity in strategic doctrine and operational command. Final victory only comes with the land forces' occupation of enemy territory.

The one unique claim made for naval forces is that they alone in peacetime can further the state's policies by demonstrating its strength and achievements far beyond its borders. World-wide voyages and port visits by naval vessels as well as the activities of an efficient merchant navy are highly effective ways of projecting and increasing influence. This ability to demonstrate power at sea is proclaimed to be of greater significance today because of the increasing importance of maritime resources. In addition to the sea's traditional role as a means of communication, its significance as a source of food, energy and raw materials is rapidly growing. History has shown that only those states with effective naval strength could take advantage of the sea's economic benefits. Countries which neglected their naval power or were defeated in war at sea had declined both politically and economically. This general emphasis on the peacetime roles of navies and the extensive development of it in the tenth article of the series, 'Navies as Instruments of Peacetime Imperialism', aroused a great deal of controversy in the West where some commentators saw it as signalling that the main role of the growing Soviet Navy was to be an instrument of a more adventurous and ideologically motivated foreign policy, especially in the Third World. Naval presence, and even the use of limited naval force, would be used to support regimes politically favourable to the USSR and to assist national revolutionary movements fighting against 'reactionary' governments.

Other Western experts were sceptical of this interpretation and saw the rise of Soviet naval power as being motivated at the other end of the spectrum of confrontation with capitalist imperialism by the threat offered to national territory from sea-based strategic nuclear weapons. The centrality of the defence of the homeland and its governmental system in all Soviet political and strategic thought and policy, make the second interpretation much the more likely. Gorshkov's stress on the political value of naval forces can best be seen as part of his continuous need to gain wider acceptance of his policies within his country's political institutions. The ability to intervene in the Third World would attract those concerned with establishing Russia's position as the champion of national liberation movements and the opponent of imperialist exploitation. His arguments on the necessary connection between naval power and the successful commercial use of the sea would appeal to a wide range of influential economic organisations and interests.

The primacy of the strategic task emerges strongly from the last article of the series, 'Some Problems in Mastering the World's Oceans', where Gorshkov gets to the heart of his thinking. He sees the USSR's status as a great power and her growing economic maritime interests as making it impossible for her to accept the long established sea superiority of the Western powers. In particular, the transformation of the oceans into launching pads for nuclear missiles capable of destroying the country's political and economic centres have made naval strength a matter of national survival. The central achievement to date has been the USSR's creation of its own submarine-based strategic nuclear capability which has faced the imperialists with the same dangers which they had imposed on Russia. Modern Soviet naval forces, Gorshkov claims, are not a slavish imitation of the US Navy, but specifically designed to meet the country's needs. Their main features have been to add the unique qualities of submarine-based weapons to the overall strategic posture and the equally important capability of challenging the enemy's maritime strategic nuclear forces.

The primacy of these tasks has resulted in the nuclear propelled submarine, armed with the latest weapons and electronic systems, being made the core of the Soviet fleet. Gorshkov is however adamant that historical study of the two world wars as well as objective scientific analysis of present circumstances have made it clear that submarine forces alone are not enough. They must have the support and co-operation of high-quality surface ships and aircraft if they are to fulfil their offensive and defensive strategic roles. Such additional forces will also of course have their intrinsic value because of their ability to carry out a wide range of tasks in both peace and war.

Despite his assertions to the contrary, this course of argument leads Gorshkov to make the case for a Soviet Navy in overall shape, if not in the characteristics of its components, resembling that of the United States. This tendency is further emphasised by his insistence that the effectiveness of naval forces is not primarily a matter of numbers and size of vessels but of the optimum combination of weapon platforms the weapons needed to fulfil all their prescribed tasks. This combination he describes as a balanced force, designed in accordance with objective mathematical and scientific analysis. Its operational characteristics will be based on constant readiness for combat because of the likelihood that in today's conditions the ability to fire the first salvo may well be decisive.

This concept of the balanced fleet is one of the central themes of *The Sea Power of the State*. That further advocacy of Gorshkov's ideas was needed is demonstrated by the very limited significance given to the navy in Marshal Grechko's *The Armed Forces of the Soviet Union*, which was reissued in 1976. That Gorshkov's second major publication was in some sense a counter to this is suggested by the far-greater claims it makes for the uniquely valuable qualities of the submarine-based missile system as compared with land-based rockets and, even more, by the assertion that a capability to fight the enemy's conventional naval forces is now an essential part of Soviet strategy. In addition to this message directed to the Soviet establishment, the appearance of an authorised English language edition of the book would seem to aim at offering to world opinion a reasoned exposition of why the USSR has increased her sea power and to convince readers that this has been defensive and beneficial to world peace and not the aggressive threat depicted by the imperialists.

Gorshkov's stronger advocacy of the importance of sea power stems from his view that the advent of SSBNs, with their ability to destroy the centres of enemy power has transformed naval forces from a secondary to a primary and decisive role in the general war strategy of the USSR. In addition to this they alone can further the country's interests in peacetime, a fact which also has great political significance as being the only effective barrier to the continuing attempts of the United States to use naval strength for aggressive purposes. Only the strength of the Soviet Navy can deny the US Navy the 'infamous position of strength' which it is the aim of the USSR to challenge in every constituent of national power. Having thus neatly based his claims for naval strength on the USSR's central foreign policy doctrine, Gorshkov scores another important debating point by denouncing those who unwittingly help the enemy by arguing the irrelevance of conventional naval forces in the nuclear age. For the USSR to accept this would give the imperialists the enormous advantage of unchallenged strategic mobility in peace and war. Tactically this advantage is based on the establishment of sea control. This is the main role of the US Navy and can only be denied by a Soviet Navy capable of dealing with the carriers and other conventional naval forces in which its rival is so strong. It is noteworthy that Gorshkov emphasises the increasing self-defence capability of surface forces and makes only a passing reference to the vulnerability of carriers.

This is significant as a lead-in to his detailed exposition of the shape of the ideal Soviet fleet. The nuclear submarine is still its main strike component, but its effective deployment depends on the availability of strong surface forces. These forces are also essential for combined operations, mine warfare and the defence of merchant shipping. Maritime aircraft are essential to anti-submarine warfare and attacks on merchant shipping. Although he frequently mentions the importance of sea lines of communication, there is nothing in this book to suggest that large-scale attacks on merchant shipping have high priority in his strategic thought.

The principles governing the nature and use of maritime forces are defined as 'Naval Art' and are arrived at by a combination of rational analysis and evaluation of experience, both of history and of new technology. Although it has the same aim as its military counterpart, the defeat of the enemy, 'Naval Art' has its own distinct principles because of the element in which it operates. Historically its main concern has been the defeat of the enemy's naval forces, 'Fleet against Fleet'. Today, in nuclear war, this would be subordinate to 'Fleet against Shore', based on the dual tasks of attacking the enemy's centres of power and defending its own territory from nuclear attacks. The more traditional form of naval warfare would still be of great importance in limited war, although new weapons have radically changed the nature of combat. Set fleet actions would be replaced by long range strike.

The concept of 'sea dominance' bulks large in 'Naval Art' and is described in terms which Julian Corbett would have approved. It is defined as the necessary pre-condition for the fleet's fulfilment of its strategic and tactical roles. It is thus not an end in itself but a means. Although complete dominance of all oceanic theatres would be desirable, it is unlikely to be achieved, especially at the beginning of a war. The immediate aim would be the dominance of specific sea areas needed for vital nuclear or conventional operations. For this to be achieved, balanced forces must be created in peace time.

This concept of the balanced fleet is developed at length and obviously is at the centre of Gorshkov's plans for the Soviet Navy's future. It simply means having the number and quality of vessels and aircraft needed to achieve all maritime aims, from those of strategic nuclear war to the peace time use of naval forces. Quantity and quality are of equal importance, as are a constant state of readiness, high standards of training and efficient means of command and control. The mix of forces needed to make up the balance must be constantly reviewed in the light of technological developments, and the state which decrees the political ends for which the navy is to be used must be prepared to face the vast expense involved.

Despite this strong demand for an increasing naval budget, Gorshkov restates the view that maritime forces must always be seen as part of a larger whole. Technological advance has made the close co-operation of all arms more necessary than ever before, but equally it has made those forces deploying nuclear weapons the most important. The SSBN is the ideal platform for them, and the fact that the Soviet Navy has now ended imperialist hopes of monopolising them by the creation of its own balanced fleet, is to Gorshkov the most significant development since the USSR first produced strategic nuclear missiles.

Such a claim puts Gorshkov high in the list of advocates of sea power. Whether he will achieve the naval forces to make it a reality is still a matter of dispute.

3 Sources and Elements

One thing on which virtually all writers on maritime strategy are agreed is that the constituents of sea power are many and varied. One recent listing summarises this very well. Says E. B. Potter:

> The elements of sea power are by no means limited to combat craft, weapons, and trained personnel but include the shore establishment, well-sited bases, commercial shipping, and advantageous international alignments. The capacity of a nation to exercise sea power is based also upon the character and number of its population, the character of its government, the soundness of its economy, its industrial efficiency, the development of its internal communications, the quality and number of its harbours, the extent of its coastline, and the location of its homeland, bases, and colonies with respect to sea communications.[1]

But, as we have seen, these same writers have all produced their own schemes for dividing these constituents into categories convenient for analysis and description. The consensus appears to be that there are sources of sea power (a maritime community; national resources; appropriate forms of government; geographical considerations) and that these lead on to the more immediate elements of sea power (merchant shipping; bases; fighting instruments). Over time, the form these constituents take and their importance relative to each other, may change considerably. All writers on maritime strategy agree, however, that the constituents depend on each other to a remarkable degree and must be assiduously fostered by the leaders of a country if they want to be strong at sea.

(a) A maritime community

Maritime strategists have often referred to the three interlocking rings of sea power, namely the navy, commerce and the colonies. The links between the first two were made clear by Lord Haversham, in a much quoted proposition:

> Your Fleet and your Trade have so near a relation and such mutual

influence on each other, they cannot well be separated; your trade is the mother and nurse of your seamen: your seamen are the life of your fleet: and your fleet is the security and protection of your trade: and both together are the wealth, strength, security and glory of Britain.'[2]

Mahan also put a strong emphasis on the interdependent fortunes of the navy and the merchant marine, and even came near to suggesting that the protection of shipping was the only legitimate reason for having a navy anyway.[3] In peacetime, navies helped establish orderly conditions in which trade could prosper, and in war they guarded merchant shipping from hostile attack. The more important commercial trade was to the well-being of the country, the more important the task of protecting it. In the case of great maritime powers, like the Dutch of the seventeenth century and the British subsequently, the requirement to protect trade was central to their survival and the maritime community very properly complained if they thought their interests were not being attended to. So, if a country had a substantial merchant marine, there was a *prima facie* case that it needed a navy to look after it.

Certainly a merchant marine was an important source of maritime power. One of the reasons why Mahan used the phrase sea power was his desire to call attention to the centrality of a strong commercial shipping industry, friendly ports overseas and foreign trade to maritime greatness. Maritime communications were considerably cheaper than any other, and it was economically important to make the best use of them both in peacetime and in war. The merchant marine itself could become a source of strategic and political influence through its capacity to transport men, equipment and goods around the world. In a sense, commercial shipping could also be a kind of advanced flotilla for the main fleet, gathering intelligence for it, opening up ports, keeping it supplied.

Certainly, if a country had a strong maritime community, it was easier for it to create or maintain an effective navy. If part of a properly diversified economy, commercial shipping could help supply basic financial resources. Its importance as a reservoir of seamen was well known, and this applied to the fishing industry too. Admiral Sir Charles Saunders declared in 1774, 'Give up your fishing and you lose your breed of seamen'. Merchant ships of all descriptions could be pressed into service as warships, a practice particularly common before technological advances (especially the advent of naval artillery, and later steam propulsion) caused the two types to diverge more fundamentally. Even so merchant and fishing vessels could still serve a multitude of directly military purposes as auxiliary cruisers, minesweepers or aircraft carriers. As though to complete the circle, warships could frequently be converted for civilian use once the war was over. Harbours, ports, repair and ship-building facilities and a general affinity with, and national consciousness of, the sea could facilitate the establishment of a significant navy. For such reasons, the tendency of maritime strategists to urge the careful nurturing of the mercantile marine become readily understandable.

Nevertheless, the extent of this cosy interconnection between naval and commercial sea power can be exaggerated. The two do not always rise and fall in due proportion, and there have been several instances of countries being well endowed with one kind of sea power but not the other.[4] Sometimes, moreover, the two may compete for the same resources. Finally, the protection of trade is far from being the only reason why countries need navies; navies would still be needed even if commerce vanished from the face of the oceans.

(b) Resources

As might be expected, the connections between sea power and economic potential are drawn most emphatically by maritime thinkers with a Marxist tinge. I. Grundinin wrote,

Changes in military affairs as the classics of Marxism–Leninism have scientifically proven, are conditioned by economic changes. The defence capability of a country and the combat might of its armed forces even in our time depend wholly on economic and moral-political factors. . . . These factors influence force levels, changes in tactics, operational art, and military strategy, as well as the organisation of the armed forces.[5]

Nowhere is the link between economic and maritime strength better illustrated, wrote Gorshkov, than in British naval history. A powerful economy, he argued, provided England with the strongest navy 'operating on the world ocean . . . [and so with] . . . the leading position among the capitalist countries . . . for almost two centuries'.[6]

Economic strength helps sea power in a range of ways. It provides money for defence, offers general support and gives a maritime nation resilience in adversity. Industrial expertise and ship-building skills are major factors in the number and quality of warships, obviously a key ingredient in naval success. 'A modern warship,' wrote Engels, 'is not only a product of major industry, but at the same time an example of it. . . . The country with the more developed major industry enjoys almost a monopoly on the construction of these ships.'[7] Economic prosperity also usually leads to effective shore support, an efficient, well-motivated personnel and a good operational performance.

However, the deterministic effect of the state of the economy can be exaggerated. The fact that Tsarist Russia, with her very limited industrial base, managed to produce some very good ships (like the world beating *Novik* class of destroyer) and was well up with the hunt in the development of new concepts (like fast battleships and aviation) shows that the relationship between the economy and the quality of warships is not a simple one. In fact, in some ways, the relationship was reversed: the Russian drive for good ships stimulated the process of industrialisation. Nevertheless, the foundations were insecure; it took Russia five and a half years to build a ship which the Germans and the British could complete in just over three. Building times revealed, as they always do, industrial vulnerabilities perhaps otherwise hidden. The First World War was to expose Russia's industrial weaknesses even more cruelly, a few years later on.

To take another example of this complex matter, the extent to which the inadequacy of Britain's maritime preparations for the Second World War can really be attributed to the twin evils of industrial decline and a parsimonious Treasury has been hotly debated. Some have blamed them almost exclusively; others have pointed to such things as unforced policy errors by the Admiralty.[8] While there are evidently no simple explanations, shortage of resources does seem to be linked to military inefficiency, even if the first is not a sufficient explanation of the second.

The particular resources which matter most also vary as time goes by. In the days when it took several thousand oak trees to make a first rate ship of the line, the connection between forestry and sea power was obvious. There was also a built-in time-lag in the process; the deficiencies in forestry management in Charles II's reign made themselves manifest in the third quarter of the eighteenth century and contributed to Britain's loss of the War of American Independence. The lesson was well learned by Admiral Collingwood who was given to wandering around the English countryside planting acorns so that the navy should never be short of its heart of oak again. Unfortunately, by the time the fruit of his labours was ready (about 1910) the particular resource that mattered had changed. It was now a question of coal, steel and iron – all the appurtenances of a modern industrial state. It was, above all, their strength in these that allowed 'new' maritime powers like Germany, the United States, Japan and, later, the Soviet Union to appear on the scene.

There was something of a benign circle at work here. A well-founded industrial economy provided the wherewithal for a strong navy. That navy then went out to secure or maintain overseas markets, bases and resources of ultimate benefit to the economy. Trade and the flag followed each other around the world in a complex way which ultimately defeats the task of trying to define exactly the order of their going.

The symbolic relationship between the economy and naval power is also revealed in the extent to which the first sets the objectives and sometimes even defines the strategy of the latter. In the age of the wooden ships, naval supplies (timber, especially for masts, hemp and so forth) often governed attitudes to places like the Baltic and North America. The conquest of Canada, wrote Admiral Sir Peter Warren in 1745, 'would give us the whole fishery, a valuable branch of trade and a flourishing nursery for seamen, upon whom the welfare and safety of our country so much depend'. It would also, he thought, be a good base for an assault on the sugar islands – a main source of France's European prosperity.[9] The connection between the state – and the requirements – of the economy and maritime strategy could hardly be made more clear. It seems reasonable to see the modern equivalent of this in present preoccupations with the securing of energy supplies and the areas from which they come.

(c) Styles of government

'It must be noted,' wrote Mahan, 'that particular forms of government with their accompanying institutions, and the character of rulers at one time or another, have exercised a very marked influence upon the development of sea power.'[10] The question of how many resources were to be devoted to maritime purposes was obviously fundamental, and Mahan thought the answer would depend largely on the complexion of the government making the decision. No great democrat, he believed that 'commercial, representative nations' would not prepare for war adequately, 'because the people in general will not give sufficient need to military necessities.'[11] People of Mahan's political persuasion tend to emphasise the military disadvantages of the democratic process: the apparent reluctance to spend money on defence; the close scrutiny given every military decision; the intrusion of 'irrelevant' ethical or political considerations into matters relating to the use of foreign bases, the supply of weapons and so forth. Of course, views from the other end of the ideological spectrum about the military propensities of capitalist states tend to be quite different. But the one thing these two perspectives have in common is that they both see a link between forms of government and readiness for war. Charting the connection between the two was a major preoccupation of Richmond in his historical surveys of the development of British sea power.

These surveys also show that, however willing they may be, governments are not equally able to translate maritime aspirations into an efficient navy of well-found ships, motivated personnel and high levels of operational skill. Inefficient governments produce inefficient navies and ineffective maritime strategies. The vicissitudes of the

Russian Navy over the last 150 years or so show how closely are tied the effectiveness of state and navy. But the situation of the Turkish Fleet in the early part of this century is perhaps one of the best examples of the way in which governmental decline limits naval possibilities. As the British naval attache in 1904 wrote:

> Of the ships that lie in the Golden Horn not one of them can go to sea, as the precaution is taken to remove some part of their machinery to ensure that they shall not leave their moorings without His Imperial Majesty's permission. The part thus removed is kept at the palace. . . . Along the north bank of the Golden Horn lies a line of ships — wooden and composite, iron-clad and torpedo-boat – all in various stages of decay. . . . The shore is strewn with wrecks, and on the jetties and all over the dockyard is a confused mass of boilers, engines, anchors, cranes etc., all rotten or rotting, and intermingled with heaps of refuse and pariah dogs. . . . The state of filth and dirt on board all these ships was indescribable. The guns, engines and boilers had not been touched for years . . . the decks rotten, with pools of muddy water lying every few yards.[12]

Sometimes this kind of decay can be attributed more specifically to the intrusion of political discord into the management of marine enterprises. The Royal Navy of the eighteenth century, for instance, was beset with political factions which impeded its efficiency; if one naval officer were to be roasted, it was said, another could surely be found to turn the spit. In times of great internal stress or revolution, this tendency can be very marked. Mahan frequently pointed out the bad effects that the Revolution had on the French Navy. Under the influence of the purification campaigns of such men as Jean-Bon St. Andre, officers whose 'civisme' was suspect were removed with scant regard for experience or skill. Crews degenerated into a disorderly rabble whose enthusiasm did not compensate for inadequate training and poor equipment. On the ill-prepared expedition to Ireland of 1796 said Mahan: 'Spars carried away, rigging parted, sails tore. Some ships had no spare sails'.[13] In such conditions, failure was inevitable.

Forms of government and political circumstances have a decisive impact not only on naval preparedness, but also on the way that navies are used. Aristocrats of the traditional kind, wrote de Lanessan, have a natural preference for continental, aggressive, army-based strategies; the commercial middle classes, on the other hand, will be more sympathetic to maritime pacific ones. There was certainly an element of this in the dispute between the Whigs and Tories of eighteenth century over the extent to which Britain should involve herself directly in war on the continent.[14] Both in Britain and in the Netherlands, the maritime community could also be expected to ask politically embarrassing questions, if they thought the navy's strategy was not paying enough regard to the safe and timely arrival of their great merchant convoys. In such ways as this, strategic conceptions can reflect the political values and interests of those ultimately responsible for them.

It has also often·proved difficult to reconcile political interests with effective command and control. In a very interesting passage about the downfall of the elder Pitt, Corbett indeed argued that the two were fundamentally opposed 'in a constitutional country'. Effective war direction seemed to require the accumulation of so much authority that it endangered constitutional propriety; military success and political health might well be mutually exclusive.[15] The tension between the two may be even greater in an age where the nature of the technology demands secrecy and fast reaction, rather than the lengthy and public deliberations of the kind associated with the normal political process.

In this and many other ways the efficiency of navies, both in their composition and their use, will normally be no greater than that of the society and government that produced them. To understand a country's maritime strategy, therefore, it is necessary to understand the nature of the regime it partially reflects.

(d) Geography and geopolitics

Maritime strategists usually lay great stress on the importance of geography for their subject. They make the point that geographical conditions have a good deal to do with the question of which countries are to become sea powers. Geography also helps shape maritime strategy both in terms of conception and of execution.

A country's urge to the sea, wrote Mahan for instance, will be the product of such geographical considerations as the conformation of the coast, the availability of harbours, the importance of rivers in internal communications and even of the relationship of soil fertility and the size of population. Proximity to important trade routes and a physical ability to get at profitable fishing grounds could be crucial too.

The rise of Dutch maritime power in the seventeenth century makes all this clear. The Dutch were well placed to dominate some of Europe's most important trade routes passing through the Channel: they had access to the Baltic and were close to key economic areas such as Flanders, Brabant and the Rhineland. Most of the Netherlands' centres of population were easily accessible by water and the Zuider Zee and a network of waterways 'behind the dunes' were important to her internal economy. Marine biology helped too; when the herring spawning grounds moved to the south of the North Sea (perhaps because of changes in the habits of the Gulf Stream) the Dutch were in a particularly good position to profit from it. In the off season, fishermen used their boats to transport cargo – and so facilitated Holland's entry into the highly lucrative international carrying trade. Even negative geographic factors pushed the Dutch in the same direction. Both the inability of her agriculture to support the population and her natural dependence on external supplies also drove the Dutch nation to the sea.

Although much of this once applied to the United States as well, Mahan mourned the fact that it no longer seemed to do so. As the interior was opened up, he wrote, its evident potential seduced America away from her original proper concern for the sea.[16] Mahan wanted to turn his country back to its maritime destiny. The fact that he felt he had to do so shows that considerations of maritime geography change as time passes, more than might seem to be the case at first sight.

Some aspects of marine geography are particularly mobile, like the patterns of the wind, water currents, short-term seasonal and long-term climactic changes. These not only influence countries to take to the sea in varying degrees, but also help shape what they do with their navies when they get there. The geography of the winds, for instance, in the days of sail, was the starting point for anyone planning military operations in the Indian Ocean.[17] In much the same way, the south-westerly winds prevailing around Britain had considerable strategic consequence, generally, acting to the permanent advantage of the Royal Navy, for a wind which blew them from their blockading stations would also shut the French into their ports, as Hawke reported in 1759: 'Their lordships may rest assured there is little foundation for the present alarms. While the wind is fair for the enemy's coming out, it is also favourable for our keeping them in, and while we are obliged to keep off, they cannot stir'.[18]

Weather conditions affect naval strategy and tactics and decide many of the parameters that ship designers have to observe. The importance of the weather to the success of such operations as the 'Channel Dash' of the *Scharnhorst* and *Gneisenau* in 1942 was so great that it led some weathermen to claim that they should have a final say in the planning of operations.[19] Certainly, argued Gorshkov, the need to know as much as possible about all conditions of maritime geography is such that it justifies the Soviet Navy in devoting considerable effort to oceanographic research. This view, in fact, echoed the historic practice of all the maritime nations.

Geography has effects on maritime operations which are more settled and predictable than this however. There is, for example, the matter of access to the high seas. Geographic conditions have focused maritime attention on particular areas which afford strategic access. The Danish Straits dominate entry to and exit from the Baltic and so have been the scene of continual conflict for centuries. Countries controlling such strategic locations reap considerable military advantage from their good fortune. Echoing Philip Colomb, Admiral Fisher proclaimed that, 'Five keys lock up the world: Singapore, the Cape, Alexandria, Gibraltar, Dover. These five keys belong to England,' he went on enthusiastically, 'and the five great Fleets of England will hold these keys.' With this advantage England should be able to dominate the maritime affairs of the world.[20]

Other countries have not been so well placed. Geography can, and has, confined some navies into local areas, excluded them from the high seas and so done much to confer command upon their enemies. Their maritime strategies, therefore, have been dominated by the urgent need to overcome the natural disadvantages of geography. This was true of Germany in both the world wars. It is even more so of the Soviet Union now.

The Russian Navy has always suffered from a considerable natural disadvantage in that the disposition of their coasts has frequently made it difficult for them to concentrate their naval forces or wield them as a cohesive whole. Gorshkov declared, 'The considerable difficulty for Russian sea power stemmed from her geographical position, which required having an independent fleet capable of ensuring the performance of missions confronting it in each of the [four] far-flung naval theatres'.[21] Only with the greatest difficulty and often with rather indifferent success, was Russia able to overcome this disadvantage by transferring forces from one fleet area to another. While there were occasional successes with this device (as in the case of the Mediterranean foray of Admiral Spiridov in 1769), there were also frequent disasters (particularly in the Russo–Japanese war of 1905).

Russia has by no means been the only country with this problem. The British possession of Gibraltar put Spain into the same category. At least until the Panama Canal was built, the United States had something of the same difficulty. France, too, in some ways: Cardinal Richelieu wrote, 'It would seem that nature wished to offer the Empire of the sea to France, by the advantageous situation of her coasts, which are equally well provided with excellent harbours, on the Atlantic and the Mediterranean'. But as France found in the eighteeenth century, this natural source of division could prove to be an embarrassment. It was difficult for the French to concentrate their fleets for some maritime endeavour (such as the invasion of Britain) especially when the Royal Navy sought to prevent it by a policy of blockade. Except in the case of overwhelming naval superiority, divided coasts in fact have proved more of a source of weakness than of strength.

Being an island, Britain has avoided this problem; she has also benefited in a more general way. Since the Channel protects the country from invasion, less attention need be paid to the maintenance of large military forces. With no land frontier to worry about, the British could concentrate their attention on the sea. This stood them in good stead even against such other maritime powers as France and the Netherlands

'History has conclusively demonstrated' concluded Mahan, 'the inability of a state with even a single continental frontier to compete in naval development with one that is insular, although of smaller population and resources.'

Geopolitics

Geographical considerations, therefore, clearly exert an important influence on maritime strategy. Some commentators, however, have gone much further than this to argue that geography actually *determines* strategy. Geography is the major factor in defeat or victory; it may even be, in one celebrated phrase, the pivot of history. But while navalists claim that geography makes sea power supreme, others of the geopolitical persuasion come to quite different conclusions. Sea power, they say, is a wasting asset and has entered into a period of irreversible decline: land power is about to come into is own. The elephant will defeat the whale.

Geopolitics has a long ancestry. Its ideas go back to German writers of the early nineteenth century, like Baron Dietrich von Bulow (*The Spirit of the New System of War* 1799), Karl Ritter and Friedich Ratzel. Academic respectability was conferred on,the school by the British geographer Sir Halford Mackinder in a famous lecture to the Royal Geographical Society in 1904. Mackinder argued that the natural superiority of land power would soon assert itself when the land-locked peoples of Eastern Europe and Asia at last came together to form the 'Eurasian Heartland'. They would reach out to incorporate the rest of Europe and Africa into 'the World Island' and would then dominate the rest of the world, as represented by the traditional maritime powers.[22] Of course, all this had a good deal of appeal for the ideologues of Nazi Germany: the particular apostle of this creed at that time was Karl Haushofer, whose writings did much to give the geopolitical school the cranky but slightly sinister connotations it still retains.

As far as the possibilities of maritime strategy were concerned, the geopolitical school argued that the 'world political potential of sea power had been in full retreat long before the rapidly increasing potential of land power, long before the first submarine had plunged below the surface and the first plane had taken to the air'.[23] They also believed that this process of relative decline would continue until the final triumph of the Heartland.

There were a number of reasons for this. First, the revolution in land transport (better roads and railways) meant that sea communications were much less important than they used to be. Once land transport was so bad that even a continental empire like the Austrian Hapsburg Empire depended on sea communications,[24] but now this was no longer the case. Since the maritime powers had derived their influence from their ability to control these communications, their importance would decline as well. Better still, with the decreasing effectiveness of the naval blockade, the main weapon of the maritime power, the Heartland would grow increasingly inaccessible to sea-based attack. Land powers could in fact now reverse the threat; with aircraft (and submarines) they could harrass the maritime powers own seaborne communications and bring about their ultimate downfall.

The other main reason for the relative growth of land power was its increasing ability to mobilise potentially overwhelming natural and human resources. George Kennan wrote, in 1966, 'Our problem is to prevent the gathering together of the military–industrial potential of the entire Eurasian land mass under a single power, threatening the interests of the insular and maritime portions of the globe'.[25]

In fact the last stage in what Castex called the 'eternal struggle of the sea against the land'[26] would be when the Heartland itself took to the sea, as Mackinder had warned it would. Just after the First World War he wrote, 'Must we not still reckon with the possibility that a large part of the Great Continent might some day be united under a single sway, and that an invincible sea power might be based upon it'.[27] Just as a dominant land power, Rome, took to the sea in order to defeat maritime Carthage, so might Rome's successors. Haushofer suggested it would be Nazi Germany; others, including Castex, wondered whether it might not be the Soviet Union. Both these states could use their armies to fight their way to the sea; they could absorb the maritime populations of the areas they enveloped; they could mobilise greatly superior resources. In the end, they might rule the world.

In short, the geopolitical school did not argue that geographical considerations had, or would, defeat sea power. What they said, instead, was that sea power would no longer be wielded exclusively or even primarily by the traditional maritime powers. They argued, also, that in the last analysis, the facts of geography meant that the resources of the land would be the more decisive for the future of the world. They challenged, in other words, the most basic assumptions of the maritime strategists.

(e) Shipping

Occasionally, maritime strategists have used the analogy of a boxer to explain the essential elements of sea power in time of war. Merchant shipping provides stamina and strength; bases the ability to move; the navy provides the power to hit. The capacity to use the sea as a medium of transportation is manifestly important, and this requires large numbers of ships 'adequate to feed our home population, to bring in the raw materials needed by our industries, to carry our exports overseas and to transport our armies and their multifarious supplies to the theatres where they are required to fight'.[28] Without this means of transportation the ability of maritime powers to influence events ashore would be severely restricted. It is obviously central to their capacity to fight and prosper.

(f) Bases

The seizure, retention, protection and use of naval bases has also been an important element of maritime strategy for centuries. Their possession is a significant attribute of sea power. Bases, such as those the Europeans strung across the Indian Ocean from the sixteenth century onwards, were needed for the erection and maintenance of overseas empires, and their loss signalled the loss of those empires. Said one colonial administrator, of Trincomalee, 'In the hands of a powerful enemy it might enable him to shake to the foundation, perhaps over turn and destroy, the whole fabric of our oriental opulence and dominion'.[29]

In wartime, bases were necessary for prolonged operations far from home. In Gorshkov's view, what was really remarkable about Admiral Spiridov's foray into the Mediterranean in 1769 was that it was 'an outstanding example of autonomous operations by a large naval formation completely cut off from its home ports.'[30] But the lack of bases meant that Spiridov could not consolidate his original success, so even this exception eventually proved the rule. The lesson was reinforced in the Second World War, where success was dependent on the seizure and use of naval bases in Europe, the Mediterranean and the Pacific. British naval operations suffered because not enough money had been spent on its bases at Scapa Flow, Malta, Gibraltar, Freetown, and so forth, in peacetime. The loss of Singapore had an even more dramatic impact on British naval possibilities. This disaster prompts questions about what would have been the impact of the loss of other such vital bases, as Gibraltar and Malta, on subsequent naval operations. Precise answers are impossible, but the consequences would clearly have been severe.

Naval bases range in degree of utility and importance from fleet anchorages at one end of the scale to main bases with supporting industrial establishments at the other. In varying degrees they support, and even make possible many forms of naval activity.[31] They provide a place of safety. Roskill wrote, 'If the bases are insecure the Fleet cannot possibly exercise its functions. It becomes homeless and harried and must wander in fear from one ill-protected anchorage to another.'[32] By supplying all necessities (food, shells, torpedoes) and by offering facilities for the repair of ships and the recuperation of personnel, they give naval forces endurance and make sustained operations possible.

Perhaps bases return some of the endurance that warships lost when they changed from sail to steam.

They also provide a marshalling place for convoys and give naval forces extra reach. Mahan said the US Navy needed bases in the outer oceans where shipping operated if it wanted to defend trade; otherwise the navy 'will be like land birds, unable to fly far from their own shores'.[33] The closer the bases were to the scene of action the better, since this would cut down the amount of time and endurance wasted in transit.

In some circumstances, however, the influence of bases on maritime strategy could be less beneficial. Philip Colomb, for instance, argued that smooth-water anchorages would meet more naval purposes than was generally assumed and warned against the undiscriminating creation of permanent bases. These, once acquired, tended 'to swell in assumed importance and real expense.' He added:

> We can never tell beforehand in war what points it will be necessary to occupy as naval bases, and . . . the making of provision which will tend to force ships to go for supply and repair to certain positions, whether they are places conveniently or not in regard to operations in hand, is a policy likely to end in some loss and much wasted expenditure.[34]

Permanent bases, then, could be expensive, in the wrong place and a constraint on naval action. They could also become a commitment and responsibility as well as (or instead of) a source of support. The Second World War showed that it was difficult and costly to defend bases such as Singapore. But without such defences, and without forces to operate from them, bases were more of a liability than an asset.

(g) The fighting instrument

The most obvious fighting instrument of naval power is the warship and the most important warship at any one time is the capital ship. For many years the battleship was the capital ship, the supreme expression of power at sea. In the Second World War its place was taken by the fleet carrier. Arguably the carrier itself has now been superceded – by the submarine. But capital ships are supported and complemented by a whole range of other warships and auxiliaries – without which they can not function.

Since the First World War, maritime air power has also been an important constituent of sea power. Initially, there was some resistance to this; partly from naval conservatives who doubted whether aircraft had anything to offer; partly from those of the world's air forces which believed in the Unity of the Air (the air was the air wherever it was, over sea or over land, and aerial warfare had its own preeminent and distinctive discipline and requirements) which made them unsympathetic to the idea of maritime air power.[35] But, as Richmond observed, aircraft could themselves be 'instruments of sea power; weapons employed at sea for the purpose of disputing the control of the sea, which is the object of sea power'.[36] In the Pacific campaign of 1941–5 maritime air power became arguably the most important of the many instruments of sea power.

This very diversity brings its own problems. Both for individual ships and for the overall size and shape of navies proper balances have to be struck between competing attributes and requirements. While ship designers need to allocate a ship's displacement between propulsion, armament and accomodation, those planning the shape of the navy as a whole have to decide priorities between the various tasks they think it will have to perform. The apparently ever-increasing rate of technological advance introduces another major source of complexity. Philosophers of sea power tend to think, however, that an acquaintance with the concepts of maritime strategy will help naval planners to pick their way more safely through this technological morass of competing confusions.

In fact, one of the most useful services maritime strategists usually claim to offer is that they show how technology can be a snare and a delusion. Richmond and his coterie, for instance, repeatedly warned their colleagues of the dangers of concentrating too much on the technological side of things. It is wrong, they said, to base assessments of naval strength merely on relative numbers of ships or the relative size of guns. Although this facile and misleading procedure is regularly nailed back into its coffin by men like Richmond, its powers of recuperation are evident;[37] doubtless the only real answer is a stake through the heart.

It is however equally misguided, declared Richmond, for one navy to base its construction programme simply on what it thought the adversary was likely to have. Indeed, wrote Captain Bernard Acworth in 1935, 'it seems to be a cardinal feature of Admiralty policy to build and maintain a class of vessels, not on its merits, but because the other fellow does'.[38] Finally, it was wrong, the anti-materialists thought, merely to build in the latest piece of equipment simply because it was the latest piece of equipment. A 16-inch gun was not *necessarily* better than a 15-inch one. Evidently modern navies have not yet shaken off this particular vice. Quite recently, for example, a prominent official in the United States Department of Defense claimed:

We shall not *in the future* indulge the present syndrome of incorporating into every system the most advanced technology as soon as it seems to be available or merely because it is advanced. We shall ask only for what we really need – the minimum necessary performance – and we shall match, wherever possible, proven technology to that essential, realistic need.[39]

As far as Richmond was concerned, the basic justification for naval construction was a clear conception of strategic needs. Otherwise, he wrote,

> It looks to me like beginning at the wrong end of the stick. No one says what we want to do and asks for stuff which will do it. It is *all* started from the material end, not the strategic. I say this is wrong. Our strategists (if we have any) should examine the situation. Where can we do most harm to the enemy?[40]

It was important to take things in this order, he believed, lest the tail be allowed to wag the dog.

The final danger of the obsession with the material was the 'pestilent idea . . . that the ship is everything, the man nothing; a desire to rely on steam and machinery; to think more of tonnage and horse-power, and thickness of armour – all excellent things in moderation – than the soul which gives life to the man'.[41] The quality, quantity, skill and motivation of its personnel is very evidently central to the strength of a navy. So much so, in fact, that such aspects of personnel management as the provision of fair conditions for the lower deck, and a promotion system not depending exclusively on 'a bloody war and a sickly season', are as vital to the navy's strength as the quality of the weapons it wields.

One of Mahan's least persuasive ideas about the elements of sea power was the importance he attached to 'national character'. This can no longer be regarded as a sufficient explanation: if salt does indeed flow in the veins of every true-born Englishman, it is necessary to know why. Presumably the reasons for the affinities with the sea, that certain peoples at certain times appear to have, are derived from such prosaic thing as their geographic, social, economic and political circumstances.

Just before the Armada sailed, for instance, its pessimistic commander reported:

> My health is bad, and from my small experience of the water I know that I am always seasick. . . . The expedition is on such a scale, and the object is of such high importance, that the person at the head of it ought to understand navigation and sea-fighting, and I know nothing of either. I have not one of those essential qualifications. . . . If you send me, depend upon it I shall have a bad account to render of my trust.[42]

This report is significant, not for what it tells us about Spanish character, but for what it implies about the system and the navy which chose and persisted with such a reluctant commander. In this, and in most ways, navies tend to reflect the strengths and weaknesses of the society that produced them.

Conclusion

It is evident that in identifying four sources (resources, forms of government, geography, a maritime community) and three elements (merchant shipping, bases, the fighting instrument) of sea power, a system has been described in which none of the components are static and all of them inter-act with one another. A change in one affects all the others. Political stability can encourage economic advance; this may produce novel methods of marine propulsion and so alter maritime geography. All of this can have a substantial impact on maritime strategy. An exploration of the sources and elements of sea power, therefore, warns us of the dangers and difficulties of trying to study the abstract principles of maritime strategy in isolation from the real world which produced them and which governs their application.

4 The Decisive Battle

(a) Introduction

In 1921, the British Government held an enquiry into the future of naval warfare in general and of battleships in particular. Among the witnesses called to give evidence before it there were several like Admiral S. S. Hall who believed that the day of the battleship was over; for evidence, he pointed to these vessels' relative inactivity and apparent uselessness in the First World War.

When it was his turn to give evidence, Richmond produced a scathing denunciation of Admiral Hall's views and a succinct summary of the orthodox concept of the value of decisive battle:

> Admiral Hall says that when the capital ship 'has been granted a battle and wins it . . . the main accomplishment of the purpose of our fleet, the protection of trade, has not even been commenced by anything it has done'. This statement displays ignorance of the most simple facts of the war. Much has been done by the destruction of the enemy's capital ships. Concentration of our own units is no longer necessary: in the past, battleships were set free to act as escorts; today it is the cruisers and destroyers. Your defending force is multiplied, your powers of exercising pressure by blockade are increased. If the enemy possesses overseas bases, your powers of affording escorts to expeditions sent to capture them are increased instead. The dangers of invasion are removed and ships and men and material are set free for protection of trade, or attack upon trade. The whole experience of war tells the same tale – a great victory is followed by a dispersion of the ships that had been concentrated . . . (for it).[1]

A battle was decisive then, not just for the immediate damage and loss the victor inflicted on the vanquished, but for what happened afterwards. A great victory could effectively confer upon the victor the ability to use the sea decisively for his own purposes and to prevent his enemy from doing the same. This explained in theory why such naval battles are fought; the practical matter of how they were fought depended on the strategic circumstances and the state of marine technology.

In the summer of 1770, a squadron of the Russian Baltic Fleet under the command of Admiral Gregory Spiridov and an Englishman, Admiral Sir John Elphinston, encountered a Turkish fleet at Chesme near the island of Chios off the coast of Asia Minor. The result was 'one of the most decisive engagements in naval history'. The Russians ambushed the Turks with fireships in an enclosed harbour, and said a contemporary account:

> A fleet consisting of 200 sail almost in one general blaze, presented a picture of distress and horror dreadfully sublime.
>   This description will convey but a faint idea of the catastrophe of the Turkish fleet. While the flames with utmost rapidity were spreading destruction of all sides, and ship blowing up after ship, with every soul on board that feared to trust the waves to swim to shore, the Russians kept pouring on them such showers of cannon balls, shells and small shot, that not one of the many thousands of their weeping friends on land, who saw their distress, dared venture to their relief.
>   Nothing now remained but united shrieks and unavailing cries, which, joined to the martial music and the loud triumphant shouts of the victors, served to swell alternately the various notes of joy or sorrow, that composed the solemn dirge of their departing glory.

Spiridov afterwards wrote enthusiastically, 'All honour to the all-Russian fleet. The enemy war... fleet was attacked, smashed, crushed, hurt, blown into the sky, sunk and reduced to ashes... and we ourselves became dominant over all the Archipelago'.

Elphinston wanted to use the command of the sea this victory afforded to seize the Dardanelles and attack Constantinople. Spiridov, however, thought otherwise, so a blockade was mounted instead and the Russian fleet launched a series of raids in the general area, even seizing Beirut at one point. In one of his many contemporary remarks masquerading as historical explanation, Gorshkov says, 'This detachment of the Russian fleet enhanced the authority of Russia in the international arena and attracted warm sympathy for the Russians from all the peoples of the Mediterranean.'[2] But although the execution of the actual battle could hardly have achieved a more decisive immediate result in terms of ships sunk and casualties inflicted, the Russians' very long and sorely stretched lines of communication and the absence of bases and substantial ground forces made it difficult for them to consolidate their success. The simple facts of geography robbed the Russians of some of the fruits of their success. This fact reinforces the conclusion that the decisiveness of a particular battle depends on much more than the losses inflicted.

But even when measured in these relatively simple terms, decisive battles are much rarer than might appear to be the case at first glance.

For one thing, it is almost impossible to conceive of either side being able to concentrate all, or even perhaps most, of its resources in one spot for one grand encounter. There will always be ships under construction or repair, in transit from one place to another, or away doing other things in other places. For this reason, even after a catastrophic defeat, the vanquished will often have plenty of naval resources left to fight with. The war at sea may continue, as in fact it did even after such famous victories as the defeat of the Spanish Armada and Trafalgar. One historian from the Royal Naval College, Greenwich, commented, 'Superficially, at any rate, the Battle of Trafalgar appears to have been one of the less important events of the war. Only a small part of Bonapart's naval forces were destroyed and only one-sixth of the total British ships of the line were actually engaged.'[3]

Decisive victories also seem to depend on some kind of significant superiority, whether it be in maritime geography, weaponry, operating skill or the number and quality of men and ships. Often the inferior side will have some inkling of this in advance and so will not co-operate in its own destruction. Instead, an encounter between the main fleets may be as strenuously avoided by the weaker as it is pursued by the stronger. For both these reasons, a sequence of battles which only become decisive when their results are added together is the more usual pattern. This is even frequently true in situations where both sides actively seek a decision, such as in, for instance, the Dutch Wars of the seventeenth century and the Pacific campaign of the Second World War.

(b) In the age of the galley

Fred T. Jane wrote:

> Ancient history does not record any characteristic guerre de course: the grand battle sufficed for the ancients' simple aspirations. Combatants of those days were fully persuaded of the advisability of that doctrine, of which Captain Mahan has been the modern apostle, that all sea dominion depends upon the issue of the grand battle. The Peloponnesians beaten by the Athenians, simply collected another fleet and tried again. Romans and Carthaginians almost always did the like. . . .[4]

There were many of these 'grand battles' in which the sole immediate objective of both sides was the achievement of naval mastery. Their individual character and outcome depended on a whole range of factors. The limited endurance and sea-keeping qualities of ancient warships meant these encounters usually took place in coastal waters: the ships tended to deploy in line abreast and the defending side would often try to secure its flanks against envelopment by anchoring them to the land. Battle tactics were usually variations on the several themes of ramming, boarding and longer range fighting with missiles of various kinds (javelins, arrows, rocks, Greek fire, pots of poisonous snakes). The selection of the precise mix of options depended on local circumstances. At Syracuse, for instance, the professional Athenian fleet tried to make the most of its greater level of maritime expertise by rowing quickly round to ram the enemy warships from the side. The Syracusans countered this by making sure the battle took place in the congested conditions of the Grand Harbour, which made such manoeuvres difficult. They knew the limits of their own expertise and so went to battle with heavy prows specially strengthened so they could ram the Athenians frontally. In their turn, the Athenians later abandoned nimble manoeuvre and opted instead for a boarding fight and so went to battle carrying more soldiers than usual. The Syracusans countered this by covering the prows of their ships with hides so that the Athenians grapnels would bounce off. Now, the Syracusans hoped to keep their distance and rely this time on long-range fire.

Altogether, a prolonged campaign like the Expedition to Syracuse might see a considerable variety of battle tactics, and so for that matter, might an individual battle. Victory often went to the side able to spring some such tactical or technological surprise on the opposition. A contemporary account of the battle between Demetrius and Ptolemy in 306 BC off Salamis shows that sea battles in such times were by no means plain and simple operations. Wrote Diodorus:

The fleets being deployed, the boatswains accordingly made the signal for prayers to the gods and the crews made the invocations aloud. The two fleets being then about 600 yards apart, Demetrius gave the signal to engage by hoisting a golden shield which was seen by all (and doubtless repeated by light craft in rear of the line). Ptolemy did the same and the two fleets closed quickly with each other, as the trumpets sounded the charge and the crews cheered. The engagement opened with archery and stones and darts from the catapults, and many were wounded during the approach. The contact was made, the rowers being incited by the boatswains to make their greatest exertions, and the men on deck fell on the enemy with spears. The first shock was violent, some ships had their oars swept from their sides and remained motionless with their soldiers out of action. Others, after striking, rowed astern to ram again and in the meantime the soldiers attacked each other hand to hand. Some captains struck their opponents broadside to broadside, and the ships being held in contact became so many fields of battle with the boarders leaping to the enemy's deck. In some cases these missed their footing and falling overboard were drowned, while others making good their foothold killed the enemy or drove them overboard. Many and varied were the fortunes of the ships. In one case a weaker crew was victorious owing to its higher deck and in another case the better crew lost because its decks were low. For luck has much to do in naval actions. On shore valour is pre-eminent, whereas at sea many accidents occur which bring ruin to those whose valour deserves success.[5]

Although galleys continued to be used into the eighteenth century, the last classic massed encounter of ram, missiles and boarding was the battle of Lepanto in 1571. Nevertheless, some of their traditions carried over to battles between fleets of sailing ships. Medieval sea warfare, for instance, was chiefly characterised by vicious encounters in coastal waters where the style of fighting exactly mirrored tactics on land. Sea battles such as that at Sluys in 1340 were simply land battles that took place on the water.

(c) In the age of sail

Corbett argued that the Royal Navy had always been convinced 'that by far the most drastic, economical and effective way of securing control is to destroy the enemy's means of interfering with it'. He, Colomb and Richmond all maintained that the idea of actively seeking a decision by battle on the high seas or by a preemptive strike on the enemy's coasts developed in the sixteenth century during England's struggle with Spain. The Elizabethan sailors (Drake above all perhaps) proposed such ventures as a means of seizing the initiative from the Spanish and striking them before their mobilisation was complete.[6]

Their aspirations were perhaps best exemplified in the instructions given to the later commander of the abortive 1627 expedition to Cadiz:

The chief intention of the voyage being the weakening and disabling of the enemy in his sea forces and trade, by taking and destroying his ships, galleys, frigates, and vessels of all sorts: by spoiling his provisions in his magazines and port towns, and by depriving him of seamen, marines and gunners . . . and by taking and possessing some place or places in the many of his dominions as may support and countenace our successive fleets.[7]

More often than not, however, such intentions proved to be little more than pious hopes. No country of that period really had the naval resources for sustained and ambitious projects of this kind. Too many naval commanders continued to regard war at sea as a commercial proposition to be undertaken or broken off according to the likely profit. Even Drake, during the pursuit of the Armada, broke away from his formation in the middle of the night causing some of his colleagues to heave to in confusion and others almost to blunder into the rear of the Spanish forces. Drake's object was the rich and crippled *Rosario* away to the south. Such insouciance was typical of the period and made the disciplined pursuit of decisive actions very difficult.

The idea of physically 'overthrowing' the enemy is more often associated with the Dutch wars of the seventeenth century. The Dutch and the British were comparable in skills, numbers and determination; they both aimed at command of the sea, and so at times the complete elimination of the enemy became the desired strategic outcome. For this reason, the wars were dotted with extremely grim and bloody battles and fleets began at last to be reduced to a disciplined order which they had not seen for many centuries. It is no coincidence that the deployment of warships in line ahead made its first real appearance at this time, when soldier/sailors like Monk, Deane and Blake breathed into the sea service, in Corbett's words, 'the high military spirit of the New Model Army.'

But even here the pursuit of command through decisive battle was, in practice, much qualified. The Dutch, for example, were plagued throughout by having divided aims, to seek decisive battle and to protect their trade: the British immediately compounded Tromp's difficulty by launching attacks on the Dutch merchant and fishing fleets. 'I could wish to be so fortunate', Tromp wrote, 'as to have only one of the two duties – to seek out the enemy or to give convoy; for to do both is attended by great difficulties.' But the pressure of the mercantile community for direct protection forced Tromp to try to live with his problem. Whenever the Dutch did concentrate on seeking a decision, they were beset with complaints from the 'murmuring community' of merchants upset about delays and losses to their ships.

Even when both sides did deploy numbers of, in Sir George Downing's phrase, 'very great ships and well man'd and gun'd, full of great animositie . . . [and] . . . earnestness to fight', the difficulties of finishing off the enemy and so enjoying the benefits of undisputed command proved very considerable. Often the vanquished fleet managed to slip away through fog, bad weather or a change of wind; on both sides, shortages of men and supplies, internal quarrels and an eagerness in their respective governments to economise by cutting back on naval expenditure, robbed the victors of the fruits of their success and allowed the vanquished to recover; on both sides, too, the struggle for command so exhausted the victor that he had not the energy to exercise it afterwards. 'This is all,' wrote Samuel Pepys in July 1666, 'only we keep the sea, which denotes a victory, or at least that we are not beaten; but no great matter to brag of, God knows.'[8]

In the following century, the Royal Navy faced a new adversary who studiously avoided decisive action. In the Dutch wars, the English had been beset by practical difficulties of execution: but now they confronted a substantial navy with very different ideas about the whole nature of war at sea. Their philosophy was summed up by one French writer: 'The French Navy has always preferred the glory of assuring or preserving a conquest to that more brilliant perhaps, but actually less real, of taking some ships, and therefore has approached more nearly the true end that has been proposed in war'.[9] In other words, French naval commanders had 'ulterior objects', a mission to accomplish, such as the protection of a convoy, or the support of a land operation, which took precedence over seeking out the enemy and destroying him in a decisive battle.

Thus the 1691 instructions to the recently victorious de Tourville:

it would be more important to capture this [the Smyrna merchant] fleet ... than to gain a second victory over the fleet of the enemy. His Majesty's intention is not that M. de Tourville should seek the enemy in the Channel. ... In the event of their putting to sea, and in superior force, his Majesty does not wish him to attack; on the contrary, he wishes to evade them.

Such ideas have been very widely condemned in the naval literature. 'Deadly instructions these', commented Richmond, for instance. 'They did more to destroy the French Navy than the English guns ever did.'[10]

According to their critics, this conscious relegation of the pursuit of command of the sea through decisive battle condemned the French to permanent inferiority. Even when they had the opportunity of inflicting heavy defeat on the British (such as off Minorca in 1756, Grenada 1779 and the Saints in 1782) they passed it up lest they endanger their mission. In a later period, de Lanessan argued against the whole idea. If the French aimed merely at avoiding battle, the enemy would still

be able to carry out offensive operations eminently damaging to France ... such as: a blockade of the naval ports, preventing our cruisers from slipping out, the destruction of our commercial harbours, the disembarkation of troops etc. etc. The very fast French squadron could, it is true, not be beaten; but it would not prevent France from being so.[11]

The Royal Navy's task during this period, therefore, was to force a weaker enemy to fight. This they attempted to do either by attacking an asset of such importance that the French would have to defend it (such as trade or colonies) or by trying to reach the French fleet in its harbours. There were schemes for combined expeditions: against Brest in 1694, and 1707; against Ferrol in 1741; against the Isle of Aix in 1758 because, thought Wolfe, it would force the enemy to sea and 'inevitably brings on a sea-fight which we ought by all means to aim at'; in 1799 there was another scheme against Brest and similar attempts against Den Helder, Ferrol and Cadiz. Generally though the results of such expeditions were disappointing.

When they were caught at sea, the French generally adopted a particular style of battle tactics most appropriate to their conceptions of war. Generally they preferred to stay to leeward of the British from where they could disengage more easily. They tended also to fire at their enemy's masts and rigging to slow him down so he could not easily follow them. High levels of tactical proficiency, partly derived from close attention to the works of Pere Hoste and Bigot de Morogues, made the French even more elusive when they wished to be. The difficulty was compounded by the excessive British adherence to the sanctity of 'the line'. [12]

It was obviously important to prevent the fleet collapsing into confusion (a danger which poor signalling systems exacerbated) and so the Royal Navy's Fighting Instructions encouraged its captains to stay rigidly in line ahead, until the fleet as a whole could be slowly manoeuvred into the best position to annihilate the enemy. The trouble with this notion was that it assumed that the intended victim would not sneak off in the meantime but wait about in patience and courtesy until the executioner had completed his cumbrous preparations. As Professor Lewis has shown, this formalism invariably produced ineffectual results: only when the line was deliberately or accidentally abandoned could clear cut victories be hoped for. [13]

But successful battle tactics demanded more than just a break with excessive formalism. It required, firstly, an energetic pursuit of victory. Nelson, in approved style, said 'Not blockade but battle is my aim. On the sea alone we hope to realise the hopes and expectations of our country.' Victory demanded high levels of operational skill, good ships and gunnery, effective intelligence, high morale. Rapidity of action, the achievement of surprise, flexibility, all could win the day. Victory also required stamina and determination enough for a vigorous and sustained pursuit after battle. 'Strenuous, unrelaxing pursuit is therefore as imperative after a battle as is courage during it', declared Mahan. [14]

This last point, however, is really a particular manifestation of that general principle of concentration the importance of which is stressed, in their various ways, by virtually all writers on maritime strategy. Custance wrote, 'It is a first principle in strategy to be as strong as possible at the decisive point'. [15] This did not mean necessarily having all one's forces in one place, but deployed with the same object in view, carefully co-ordinated and mutually supported. Even a divided fleet must be a cohesive whole. Eventually when the practicalities of war had been brought home to him, Mahan said, 'Such is concentration reasonably understood, not huddled together like a drove of sheep, but distributed with a regard to a common purpose, and linked together by the effectual energy of a single will'. Intelligent division, indeed, was central to the whole idea of concentration – a point developed by Corbett. 'Without division,' he declared, 'no strategical combinations are possible.' The whole of the Trafalgar campaign was a splendid example, he thought, of such elastic concentration. Best of all was the form of divided deployment which lured the enemy to destruction by its appearance of weakness.[16]

The corollary of all this was that the fleet must not try to do two things at once. Richmond described an example of what might happen when this golden rule was broken, which occurred during the Dutch wars. The British divided their fleet too soon after one success, before the Dutch, in fact, had been disabled. They sent part of the fleet off to protect trade in the Mediterranean; the remainder, now outnumbered by the recuperated Dutch, was in due course defeated. Thereafter, wrote Richmond, the British Navy learnt its lesson; from then on 'it focused its attention upon concentrating its forces on the enemy's main body.'[17]

In this Richmond entirely echoed Mahan who argued strongly that a wise naval commander would concentrate on destroying the main forces of the enemy before he tried to do anything else. Recent experience only seemed to him to confirm the wisdom of this policy. In their war with Russia in 1905, the Japanese appeared 'fully to have grasped, and to have acted upon, the principle that the one object of a navy is to control the sea; the direct corollary from which is that its objective is the enemy's navy – his organised force afloat'.[18] The Russians, perhaps contaminated by their notions of the Fortress Fleet (for which see later) flouted this rule and were defeated: the Japanese observed it, and, of course, won.

Concentration was also a principle to be well observed in the actual conduct of the battle itself. In Mahan's view, one secret of Nelson's success was that he was absolutely determined to bring about a decisive outcome. Another was that Nelson was no mere fighting blockhead given simply to charging at the enemy like a bull at a gate. Instead he aimed always at bringing the whole of his forces against a portion of the enemy. Since attacking the ends of the enemy line was in many ways like enveloping the flanks of an army, the ideal method of attack seemed to be a choice between a concentrated assault on the van or the rear of the enemy fleet. Generally the rear was better, as it would take the van longer to turn round to come to the rescue. At the Nile, Nelson even managed the celebrated 'double envelopment'; but whatever Nelson's particular choices at particular battles, his thinking was always (as the

Trafalgar despatch showed) dominated by what Mahan called the 'essential maxim of all intelligent warfare, which is so to engage as markedly to outnumber the enemy at a point of main collision'.[19] Hence Nelson's success; he won because he put into practice an age old rule.

As far as Mahan was concerned, naval warfare in the age of sail demonstrated the centrality of the decisive battle to the whole philosophy of war at sea. History showed, he thought, that:

> the assumption of a simple defensive in war is ruin. War, once declared, must be waged offensively, aggressively. The enemy must not be fended off, but smitten down. You may then spare him every exaction, relinquish every gain: but, till down, he must be struck incessantly and remorselessly.

At sea, the total destruction of the enemy's fleet was the best means of achieving control 'cutting off his communications with the rest of his possessions, drying up the sources of his wealth in commerce, and making possible a closure of his ports'.[20]

Nelson's plans for Trafalgar – and in particular his specific remark that 'my precise object [is] that of a close and decisive battle', won considerable approval from Mahan. Briefly to summarise him, Mahan argued that decisive battle was the surest means of destroying the enemy's main force; it could have a considerable moral and symbolic importance. He differentiated carefully (and this is a point that is sometimes lost sight of) between battles with decisive results, and sterile battles of no consequence, fought merely for the sake of winning them – such as the frigate actions of the war of 1812. These last, he said were 'scattered efforts, without relation either to one another or to any main body whatsoever, capable of affecting seriously the issues of war or, indeed, to any plan of operations worthy of the name'.[21]

The Battle of the Nile, on the other hand, was a decisive battle worthy of the name, for not only were many ships sunk and casualties inflicted but much of strategic consequence flowed from it. To illustrate its importance, Mahan quoted Jurien de la Gravière:

> The consequences of this battle were incalculable. Our navy never recovered from this terrible blow to its consideration and power. This was the combat which for two years delivered the Mediterranean to the English, and called thither the squadrons of Russia; which shut up our army in the midst of a rebellious population, and decided the Porte to declare against us; which put India out of the reach of our enterprise, and brought France within a hair's breadth of her ruin; for it rekindled the scarcely extinct war with Austria, and brought Suwarrow and the Austro–Russians to our very frontiers.[22]

Mahan thought the control of the sea was vital because it could, and often did, have such tremendous consequences as these. He also thought that only by achieving or threatening victory in a grand engagement could a navy effectively control the sea.

(d) In the twentieth century

Mahan fundamentally derived his views from a study of naval warfare in the age of sail but, by the time that these views had found their way into print, the world's navies had been engulfed in a rising flood of new technology. Propulsion, weaponry and protection were now all different, and there were many who supposed that principles of maritime strategy and concepts of battle would change too. At the least, there was a good deal of uncertainty about all these things.

To take the advent of steam, for instance, some believed that the sureness and independence of movement it afforded allowed the science of evolutions to be exact and geometric, making possible pretty manoeuvres in triangles, squares and parallel lines. Others thought steam would plunge the naval battle immediately into a ferocious and swirling confusion. Views were equally divided about the ram (the idea of which fleetingly and perversely reappeared after the Battle of Lissa in 1866), the breech-loading gun, the torpedo, the mine, the submarine and, eventually, the aircraft. These developments had a profound influence on the philosophy of ship design: they revolutionised the size and shape of the fleet, completely altering the way in which ships were classified and organised. Instead of the traditional three-fold division of ships-of-the-line, cruisers and frigates, there grew up an endless variety of specialised ships and also the almost metaphysical notion of 'the balanced fleet' – a formation in which all the diversity of modern naval warfare was adequately represented and efficiently co-ordinated.

Technological advance also had far reaching implications for the style of naval battle. For a while, notions of ships proceeding to battle in stately line ahead dropped out of favour; instead, some suggested that battle would degenerate into a melee, a vulgar brawl of smoke and confusion; others wanted squadrons to advance in line abreast to ram their enemies in a way which had not been seen in European waters for hundreds of years. In the event, the line ahead survived these assaults because it was the best way of using what was still the Navy's best weapon – the massed broadside.

Even so, the nature of naval battle in the age of steam was quite different in all material particulars from its predecessors of a century earlier. Jutland was not like Trafalgar. The circumstances, the range, the weaponry were all different. Even in something as basic as the approach to action, the conditions were quite dissimilar. At Trafalgar, the two fleets were in each other's sight at the break of day and they slowly approached each other at a rate of two knots until noon. 'The weather was clear and the sun shone on the sails of the enemy and their well-formed line. The British sailors admired the beauty and the splendour of the spectacle.' Nelson had hours in which to make his preparations and for much of the time, even when battle was joined, knew what was happening. At Jutland, the sailors saw their enemy, if at all, as smudges on a distant and murky horizon. The fleets approached each other at forty knots, and operated for the most part in considerable confusion. 'I wish someone would tell me who is firing,' complained Admiral Jellicoe, 'and what they are firing at.'[23]

If technological conditions were so different, what then could be the practical value of observations about the nature of battle which were derived from much earlier times? Sceptics concluded that there was very little point in analysing past battles and campaigns if the object of the exercise was to make the present, or the future, clearer. The historical school, however, stoutly defended the faith. Although material conditions were different, the principles were the same. Take the idea of concentrating the whole against a part, for example; Admiral Sir Cyprian Bridge maintained, 'As far as can be ascertained from history, every decisive victory at sea that has ever been won has been due to the observance of the above principle ... irrespective of modes of ship-propulsion, of armament and of protection'.[24] Examination of past battles was a good method of uncovering such principles – besides, what other guide was there?

There was, though, a deeper dispute about the nature of naval battle – and one in which the opposing forces were drawn up in a way which cut across the familiar lines of 'historians' versus 'materialists'. It was partly a dispute about the past but mainly about the present and future importance of naval battle, and all the activities associated with it. It was no more apparent than in the controversy about the Battle of Jutland. Was it decisive? What did it achieve? Should it have been fought at all?

First of all, there was, and is, an established opinion that Jutland *was* decisive. As one participant, Admiral Napier, commented: 'I think the papers ... must have been most depressing – but they only count losses, and score them up like a cricket match'.[25] The point was not so much the actual losses inflicted on either side during the battle but the strategic consequences that flowed from it. Gorshkov was quite clear about this. He argued that the Germans fought the battle so they could seize the initiative, destroy the British commercial blockade and impose their own. The British fought to stop them, succeeded and so ensured that Germany would eventually lose the war.[26]

Even so, according to Creswell and Grenfell, the battle could have been even more decisive. An undisputed victory might have opened the way into the Baltic, eased difficulties in dealing with German U-boats and could have had prodigious moral effects. 'In addition to the glamour of victory and the appeal it would have made to the imagination of the world, it would I believe, have convinced all nations that the final victory was bound to be with the Allies, and it might easily have shortened the war by a year.' Grenfell believed there to be *two* ultimate objects in naval warfare 'of which the destruction of the enemy's armed forces is one and the control of sea communications the other, both being closely interrelated'.[27] In the First World War, he argued, 'the Nelsonian tradition began to wear thinner and thinner. Men in authority began to ask whether after all there was any real need for a fleet action, since we had all we wanted without one'. The material object (control of sea communications) triumphed over the moral (the achievement of psychological ascendency). The British therefore did not do as well as they might have done; it was to be hoped that they would do better next time.

The same point was made by the '*Guerre à outrance*' school as represented by Admiral Sir Reginald Custance and Lord Sydenham of Combe. They even argued that Mahan himself had initially tended to elevate the secondary aim (descents on territory, the dislocation of trade) above the primary aim (the destruction of the hostile navy). Battle was the only means to provide the security these secondary objectives needed in order to succeed. This, argued Custance, was occasionally lost sight of by Mahan and Colomb, and frequently by the Admiralty, Admiral Jellicoe, even the official historian of the First World War. The Russian Navy had ignored it too, in their war with Japan, to their ultimate cost.

Custance qualified this a little by pointing out that there were other things that needed to be done at sea. He attacked Admiral Fisher's policy of scrapping older vessels in order to concentrate attention on the Dreadnought fleet. 'They seem to have pictured to themselves one particular sort of war in which great fleets and squadrons are alone to bear a part, whereas . . . there have been in the past various sorts of wars each having its pecularities and requiring special treatment.'[28] All the same, the Navy would not go far wrong if it focused its attention on the overriding necessity of seeking at every opportunity to annihilate the enemy's main forces.

Fisher's Dreadnought policy and its eventual consequences – the construction of bigger and bigger battleships – raised the ire of many in the inter-war period, Admiral Richmond among them, as we have seen. But this should not be taken to mean (as it sometimes was, and is) that the objectors were necessarily opposed to the idea of decisive battle. This was not the case, and to imagine that it was is to confuse their thinking on a particular style of battle (heavy gunships pounding each other into oblivion on parallel courses at long range) with their general ideas about the necessity of battle as a whole. They and other progressives of the period accused the Admiralty not of concentrating too much on battle, but on the wrong kind of battle.[29] 'The first and fundamental step towards gaining the command of the sea is always the destruction of the massed forces of the enemy,' stated Richmond.[30]

This was even more the view of Captain Bernard Acworth, another declared enemy of the *big* battleship. He declared:

> The main strategical lessons of the late war are not difficult to apprehend. It is clear that the primary mission of the British fleet, the mission for which its component parts should be definitely planned and constructed, is not, as is now almost universally preached, the patrolling of the trade routes for the protection of trade. Rather is it the decisive and overwhelming destruction, incapacitation or capture of the enemy's main fleet, an action which carries in its train certain automatic consequences of which the principal fruits are strategical initiative in the land campaign and the now comparatively simple business of trade defence, and the more effective blockade of the enemy's ports. If this is so, it is evident that the battleship is still, as always, the citadel of all effective sea power, a citadel from which all other classes of vessel derive their power to range the sea steadily and consistently.[31]

If one were to substitute some such more timeless concept as 'the capital ship' for 'battleship' in the last sentence, this could stand as a universal summary of the argument that decisive battle was the central business of naval warfare.

The other school of thought on decisive battle was, more or less, opposed to the simple adoption of this idea. They sought instead to introduce qualifications, objections and changes of emphasis in varying degree. 'The idea that naval strategy necessarily consists in gladiatorial combats between fleets is absurd', they said. Corbett wrote:

> By a strange misreading of history an idea had grown up that its [the battlefleet's] primary function is to seek out and destroy the enemy's main fleet. This view, being literary rather than historical, was nowhere adopted with more unction than in Germany, where there was no naval tradition to test its accuracy.[32]

In point of fact, many decisive battles of the past, such as Trafalgar, had not in the event been that decisive anyway, at least when measured in terms of its strategic consequences. Given the inherent difficulties of Fisher's plans for the Baltic and the natural geographic advantages of the British, moreover, what difference could even a clear-cut victory at Jutland have made? The author of the 1912 Naval Prize Essay wrote, 'If the German Navy were tomorrow obliterated from the earth no German citizen would by that fact be one penny piece the worse off; indeed he would be better off, since he would be relieved of the expense of maintaining the fleet.'[33]

In any case, 'pure' decisive battles were becoming rarer anyway, as Gorshkov pointed out with regard to the Second World War. 'Most of the combat clashes of the major forces in this war', he said, were 'associated with operations against the shore' (such as the carrier battles of the Pacific campaign) or 'to ensure transoceanic or sea communications' (sinking of the Bismarck, Battle of Matapan).[34]

In some circumstances, wrote Corbett, the possibility of decisive combat was slight because an inferior enemy would do his best to make it impossible. At sea, unlike on land, a weaker force could effectively be removed from the board (by putting it in an inviolable harbour); at sea, also, there was much more freedom to manoeuvre and it should therefore be difficult actually to find the victim. All this, he concluded, compelled us 'to handle the maxim of "seeking out the enemy's fleet" with caution'.[35]

In fact, subsidiary operations could be the best way of forcing battle on a reluctant enemy.

> our best minds cramp their strategical view by assuming unconsciously that the sole function of a fleet is to win battles at sea. That this is the supreme function of a fleet is certain, and it must never be lost sight of; but on the other hand it must not be forgotten that convenient opportunities of winning a battle do not always occur when they are wanted. The great dramatic moments of naval history have to be worked for and the first preoccupation of the fleet will almost always be to bring them about by interference with the enemy's military and diplomatic arrangements.[36]

In fact, in many cases decisive actions were not even necessary for the Royal Navy to enjoy 'complete control of the lines of passage and communication which our continued strategy required'. This was often the case, he maintained during the Seven Years War.[37]

For all these reasons, Corbett believed, it was necessary for commanders to strike a happy balance between the pursuit of the decisive action and the execution of apparently subsidiary tasks. It was possible to exaggerate the importance of general fleet actions. If navies 'deified the battle idea', they could expect penalties. He argued that the US Navy had committed this error during their war with Spain and by so doing had jeopardised their landings on Cuba.

In their war with the Russians, Corbett argued, the Japanese had demonstrated a much sounder approach. Admiral Togo was 'content, as the Americans should have been content, to have set up such a situation that the enemy must come and break it down if they were to affect the issue of the war'.[38] However, as has often been pointed out, nostalgic memories of the Battle of Tsushima had by the time of the Second World War seduced the Japanese into a fixation on the 'one decisive battle' idea, which led them to neglect the defensive aspects of naval war, to misuse the submarine and to pay too little regard to the necessities of protecting their own trade and supply lines and the possibilities of attacking their enemy's. Rather a similar case can be made out against the Royal Navy, in its conduct of both World Wars.

(e) Decisive battle and the Royal Navy (by Stephen Roskill)

In the 1890s Mahan argued that the *guerre de course* against shipping had never proved decisive and that 'fleet actions were the decisive thing'. Mahan's views accorded well with British naval thinking at that time, which was largely based on experience derived from the long wars against Revolutionary and Napoleonic France, and in particular on the 'decisive battles' fought by Nelson – whose influence permeated all aspects of naval planning and training. The worship of Nelson as the supreme exponent of the 'art of the admiral' had come to be regarded as incontrovertible gospel by which British naval policy should be guided in peacetime and applied in war; and so it remained until after the Second World War.

The cult of the hero in the nineteenth century was extremely potent. It was probably originated, or at any rate stimulated, by the series of lectures entitled 'On Heroes and Hero Worship', given by Thomas Carlyle in 1840, which ran through many editions in book form and was still in print in the World Classics series fifty years later. But Carlyle's views were extended and enlarged on by writers such as Thomas Babington Macaulay (1800–59) and Alfred Lord Tennyson (1809–92), and in the early twentieth century by Sir Henry Newbolt (1862–1938). In the Royal Navy several generations of young naval officers were suckled on Sir Geoffrey Callender's *Sea Kings of Britain* (3 vols, 1907–11) in which the Carlyle motif of hero-worship was applied with singular lack of discrimination to admirals from Drake and Hawkins to Nelson and Collingwood – and so, by implication, to the admirals of the day.

At the turn of the century the 'Decisive Battle' school had in this and other ways unquestionably asserted its ascendancy, and in all the naval building programmes of the next fifteen years battleships of ever increasing size and power were given priority. British governments did however remain anxious about the security of the nation's food supply, and in 1903 a Royal Commission was set up to investigate and report on the matter. The other issue which troubled British Ministers was the likelihood of invasion; for the Admiralty had no success in trying to convince them that as long as our naval power was intact the launching of a large invasion force across the North Sea invited disaster and was not a practical operation of war.

In 1899 Admiral Tirpitz enunciated his famous 'risk theory', which argued that the battle fleet he wanted to build would prove a deterrent to war and was not a threat to British sea power. Up to that time German naval policy had not aroused serious concern in London; but Tirpitz's purpose, combined with the Kaiser's irresponsible utterances, resulted in British attention being switched from France and Russia on to the country which appeared to be going to challenge our supremacy at sea. This began the building race which was later held largely responsible for the war. In 1905 the all big-gun ship *Dreadnought* was laid down by Fisher's Board of Admiralty; and she was completed in little more than a year. The chief effect of this innovation was to render all earlier battleships, in which Britain enjoyed overwhelming superiority, obsolete; and all naval powers embarked on building bigger and more powerful battle ships on the *Dreadnought* model. These developments emphasise the extent to which the 'Decisive Battle' school was dominant during the years leading to the outbreak of war in 1914. The creation of the Grand Fleet in the autumn of that year produced in its officers and men the confident expectation of another Trafalgar, which would, so they considered, bring the war to an early and satisfactory end.

But the German Navy only offered one chance for the Royal Navy to prove that the claims of the 'Decisive Battle' school were substantiated; and the Battle of Jutland (31 May 1916) was indecisive. The situation thus arose that the Grand Fleet, for all its mighty array of very powerful warships, was powerless to do much towards overcoming the crisis – except to lend some of its 100 destroyers to the forces concerned with commerce protection, and that only against the protests of the Commander-in-Chief. Despite the sense of frustration which this produced in the minds of successive Commanders-in-Chief (Sir John Jellicoe until November 1916 and thereafter Sir David Beatty) senior officers in Whitehall as well as in the fleet did not abandon the hope of a battle in which the defects and deficiencies revealed at Jutland had been remedied and so would produce a decisive result. The Kaiser and his advisers were however not disposed to risk their ships in such an encounter, but sought on many occasions to catch a proportion of the Grand Fleet with a superior force; which shows that the 'Decisive Battle' school was also influential in Germany.

As the underwater threat increased a large number of panaceas were tried – some of them quite ludicrous; but the plain truth was that the patrolled lanes on which such reliance had been placed before the war, had proved, in the words of Sir Julian Corbett no better than 'death traps'. By April 1917 losses of merchant shipping had become astronomical, a crisis of the first order had plainly arisen; and the Admiralty, with the pessimistic Jellicoe now First Sea Lord, found itself helpless. The story of how the escort-of-convoy strategy came to be introduced – at almost the eleventh hour – has often been told and need not be repeated here. The vital point to note is that by the end of the fateful year the submarine had been mastered and the gravest threat facing the Allies eliminated.

The cost in treasure and in lives of the first Atlantic Battle had been so great that one could justifiably expect that after the war the highest priority would be given to Defence of Shipping; but such was not the case. The development of the Asdic (Sonar in America) submarine detecting device produced a euphoric belief that the submarine would never again produce the threat of 1917; and the principles and practice of shipping defence again took only a low place in naval planning and strategy. After the First World War the accepted 'yardstick' for the measurement of naval strength was the tonnage and armament of capital ships. Early in the 1920s the Admiralty, where Beatty was now First Sea Lord, sought to restart capital ship building in order that Britain should not fall behind the growing power of the US Navy. The reaction against building such ships was however so strong that they were abandoned – for the time being. At the Washington Conference of 1921–2 it was only capital ships, aircraft carriers and cruisers, to which limitations of tonnage and of gun power were applied to the principal naval powers. Defence of shipping was only provided for by an amorphous 'Resolution' forbidding the employment of submarines as commerce raiders. At the Geneva Conference of 1927 and the First London Conference of 1930 it was the number, size and armament of cruisers which dominated the proceedings. Not until 1935 by which time the resurgence of German naval power under Hitler was plain, did British rearmament begin; and even then the emphasis was largely, though not entirely, placed on improved battleships, aircraft carriers and cruisers.

To any British naval officer who spent much of his service in between the wars at sea the continued dominance of the battleship and the 'Decisive Battle' school must seem as clear as it is surprising. Almost every fleet exercise of that period was planned to end with a battle between the giants; and the admiral who was held by the umpires to have 'won' it gained great esteem. Destroyers and submarines were disposed and employed to attack the other side's big ships; while the functions of carrier-borne aircraft were held to be reconnaissance, spotting for the battleships' gunfire, and using their torpedoes on a retreating enemy in order to slow him up and so allow the big ships to finish him off. Perhaps the best example of the continued dominance of the capital ship is to be found in the 'prolonged firing' which the recently modernised battleship *Warspite* was required to carry out in 1938 in order to test her new equipment. Admiral Sir Dudley Pound, the Commander-in-Chief, Mediterranean, took his whole fleet to sea and staged what can justly be described as a 'mini Jutland' off Malta. Indeed the study of that fight continued to take a prominent place in the Staff College and Tactical School throughout most of the uneasy peace; while amphibious warfare joined shipping defence as comparatively low priorities. The solitary voice raised against the building of more monsters was that of Admiral Sir Herbert Richmond; and very unpopular he made himself with the orthodox naval hierarchy.

In 1939 the dominance of the school which believed in a decisive battleship engagement was certainly less than it had been in 1914; but it had by no means been eliminated. It was the development of air power which finally proved it fallacious, and also forced the Royal Navy to abandon the centuries-old tactical principle of fighting in 'line of battle'. It also produced the necessity to give junior Flag Officers and Captains far wider freedom in the control of their own forces than had been the case under Jellicoe's very rigid 'Grand Fleet Battle Orders'; and the reason why that came to pass was that if centralised control was in force the ships would be sunk before the senior officer had got his intentions made clear. It was the British carrier-borne air attack on the Italian fleet in Taranto harbour on 11 November 1940, the Japanese attack on Pearl Harbour of December 1941, and the victory gained by carrier aircraft of the US Navy off Midway Island on 4 June 1942 which finally transformed the battleship into a useful but subsidiary weapon, which could be used to good effect for gun support purposes in combined operations.

As regards shipping defence far more preparatory work had been carried out by 1939 than had been the case before 1914. The escort-of-convoy strategy had been accepted in principle, though only reluctantly by the RAF, which was heavily conditioned by the gospel constantly pronounced by Air Chief Marshal Lord Trenchard and his disciples to the effect that the heavy bomber had become the dominant and decisive weapon, and that 'strategic bombing' of enemy installations and of his cities would produce victory. The naval building programme of 1935–40 did include quite a large number of small ships designed for escort purposes and for minesweeping; and the training of personnel in those skills had taken a place in the curriculum of the various establishments and schools. Moreover the use of convoy air escorts, which had proved their worth in 1917–18, was accepted – though it was not until 1943 that suitable aircraft became available to cover convoys over the whole North Atlantic.

In sum one can surely say that by 1945 it had been doubly proved that the primary function of maritime forces is best expressed – not by the abstract concepts of 'decisive battle', 'command of the sea' or 'control of sea communications' but by the concrete need to design and deploy them for Defence of Shipping. Once that has been accomplished all the other strategic purposes, such as overseas expeditions, were proved to be capable of fulfilment. But the dominance of the big ship and the 'decisive battle' was as enduring in the Royal Navy as the worship of tradition and the adulation of naval heroes – despite all the efforts of the Colomb brothers, Corbett, Richmond and others to teach that maritime war was an altogether more complex undertaking.

Although the complexities of the competing arguments do not lend themselves to simple resolution, several points seem to stand out. First, decisive battle evidently should not be regarded as the be all and end all of maritime strategy. Secondly, the requirements of the task of securing command through decisive battle and of exercising it through trade protection, amphibious operations and the like are frequently seen to conflict and this poses difficulties for those trying to allocate resources equitably between the two. Thirdly, no universal relative priorities have yet clearly emerged. Instead certain questions need to be asked of every situation: how likely is the battle and what would it take to defeat the enemy? How much would the pursuit of decisive action degrade the capacity to exercise command? How seriously could the enemy damage one's interests in the meantime? Obviously the answers to questions like these depend on particular circumstances of time and space, and so would the consequent priorities. Sometimes the pursuit of battle would be the chief priority, and sometimes it would not. As so often, the point was made by Corbett, this time in his description of Nelson's Mediterranean strategy in the Trafalgar campaign:

> No great captain ever grasped more fully the strategical importance of dealing with the enemy's main force, yet no one ever less suffered it to become an obsession; no one saw more clearly when it ceased to be the key of a situation, and fell to a position of secondary moment.[39]

5 Alternative Routes and Command of the Sea

(a) Introduction: The fleet-in-being strategy

The pursuit of victory in a decisive battle, or series of battles, is evidently the means of gaining command of the sea most advocated by orthodox maritime strategists, although, as we have seen, they do so in varying degree. It is a common assumption of their arguments that the fleet taking this obvious and straight-forward route to naval success needs to be stronger, or at least as strong, as the opposition – whether that strength is measured primarily in terms of number and quality of ships, operational skills or fighting spirit.

What of the fleet that knows it is inferior and cannot realistically hope to gain command of the sea by the normal method? In other words, what is one to do with a self-evidently second best navy? A succession of countries in conflict with the great maritime powers have faced the problem, but, as Castex remarked, it is by no means restricted to them. The strongest navy, as well, may be forced into a limited defensive in certain circumstances. The vulnerabilities created by the sheer size and spread of her maritime interests has even obliged England, he wrote, to adopt this policy on frequent occasions,[1] perhaps while pursuing a vigorous offensive elsewhere. At some stage or other, in short, all navies have had to deal with the problem of making the best use of limited assets.

The situation has usually been to adopt one of a number of related naval options loosely bundled together under the title of the 'fleet-in-being strategy'. They all proceed from the assumption that command of the sea is a relative and not absolute thing. Some of them actually aim to achieve a useful degree of command of the sea, but by a roundabout route avoiding a decision by battle. Many more represent the attempt by an inferior power to derive positive strategic benefit from its naval forces by doing something useful at sea, such as attacking the enemy's trade or his coasts, without aspiring to the eventual defeat of the other side's main forces. Others have the essentially negative aim of denying, perhaps by continuous harassment and evasion, a stronger enemy the capacity to enjoy fully the fruits of his superiority. Finally, there are campaigns which aim merely to ensure the continued survival of the weaker fleet.

These variants of the fleet-in-being strategy are different in degree, but not in kind. They range from the moderated offensive at one edge of the spectrum to passive defence at the other. They have been attempted on the high seas and in coastal waters, for long periods of time and for short. So varied are they, in fact, that it is not always evident that they can be contained within a single category in any very meaningful way. The main merit of so doing, however, is that it helps distinguish these strategies from the other, more orthodox, notions, which aim to 'obtain a decision' by central battle.

(b) The fleet-in-being and the defence of territory

One of the liveliest controversies in the evolution of maritime strategy has been about the value of an inferior fleet-in-being in the defence of territory against the hostile attentions of a stronger force. An early exponent of the idea was Hermocrates whose propositions were detailed in Thucydides' account of the Expedition to Syracuse. Hermocrates noted that the Athenian invasion fleet would have to sail to Sicily from Corcya on the island of Corfu: he argued that it would be very vulnerable to a flanking attack as it passed by the southern shores of Italy and so urged his compatriots to gather their ships at Tarentum and Cape Iapygia. When the Athenians found out about this move, Hermocrates argued, they would be in a cruel dilemma. If they left their stores and transports behind and came over to deal with the Syracusan fleet in battle, the Syracusans could refuse battle and then the Athenians would be in great trouble. 'Having come over with slender supplies and prepared for a naval engagement, they will not know what to do on these desolate coasts.' If, on the other hand, they came over regardless, with their invasion fleet, they would put themselves at a severe tactical disadvantage, compared to the Syracusans, who would be fresh, in good order and not encumbered with store ships, troops and transports. 'In my opinion,' concluded Hermocrates, 'the anticipation of these difficulties will hamper them to such a degree that they will never leave Corcyra.'[2] In fact, though, Hermocrates' pleas fell on deaf ears and his ingenious scheme was not put into effect.

Nor was the similar proposal of Admiral Lord Torrington, two thousand years later. The Torrington affair is of particular interest because in it was coined for the first time the phrase 'the fleet-in-being'; Philip Colomb's attempt to rehabilitate the reputation of Admiral Torrington also produced the first substantial exploration of the theory behind the concept. Briefly, the situation was that in the summer of 1690 the Royal Navy had been dispersed in several detachments, each of which was inferior to a large French force under the command of Admiral de Tourville, hovering menacingly off the Isle of Wight. The largest British force in the area was Admiral Torrington's fleet. On 26 June, Torrington reported that the French were in

> a strength that puts me beside the hopes of success, if we should fight, and really may not only endanger the losing of the fleet, but at least the quiet of our country too: for if we are beaten, they being absolute masters of the sea, will be at great liberty of doing many things they dare not attempt whilst we observe them.

For this reason, Torrington proposed to avoid the enemy fleet, until reinforcements eventually arrived from elsewhere. In the meantime,

> whilst we observe the French, they can make no attempt either on sea or shore, but with great disadvantage. . . . Most men were in fear that the French would invade; but I was always in another opinion: for I always said, that whilst we had a fleet in being, they would not dare to make an attempt.[3]

The Government, however, were not persuaded by this line of argument and Torrington was ordered into battle anyway. Possibly they misunderstood his intentions, thinking he meant to do no more than preserve his fleet from danger. At all events, the result was defeat at the Battle of Beachy Head on 30 June 1690. Court-martialled after this affair, Torrington was honourably acquitted but not employed at sea again.

Philip Colomb argued from all this that the French clearly did mean to invade and were deterred from doing so only by Torrington's fleet-in-being strategy. He went on to advance the general proposition that the mounting of attacks on hostile shores was so hazardous a proceeding that it was essential for the invader to secure command of the sea first. A defending fleet, even an inferior one, must not be allowed the chance of attacking the invader's transports and store ships; the invading fleet must never have to try to defend these transports and fight a decisive battle at the same time. For these reasons, the effective destruction of the enemy was a necessary preliminary to any combined expedition. Without it, no such expedition could safely take place.

> While descents on territory are common when there is no fleet-in-being, they are absent whenever there is a fleet capable of inter-fering . . . the mere neighbourhood of an inferior naval force which was free to attack was an absolute bar to any operations of the enemy against our shores.[4]

In such circumstances, as these, an inferior fleet, if coolly and correctly handled, could exert a strategic influence out of all proportion to its fighting power. In such a case it might well be wrong to seek a decision by battle. Torrington's strategy and Colomb's arguments, in this case, were treated sympathetically both by Corbett and by Richmond.[5]

Corbett, in fact, pointed out that there were other examples of the success of such a strategy in the Seven Years War (1756–63) – this time practised by the French against the English. Admiral Drucourt, Governor of Louisbourg, refused to let his fleet get involved in a battle with the Royal Navy, which the French would certainly have lost, and thus delayed the British assault and disrupted plans for forther operations in Canada. A little later, the cool resistance of the French prolonged the war over Quebec in the same kind of way. Corbett wrote, 'The success was due to their habitual skill in using the naval defensive, so as to dispute the control of passage and communication till the last moment'. Corbett argued that the whole war demonstrated the value of the naval defensive and 'how unwise and short-sighted it is to despise and ridicule' it, especially when the defending side could hope to benefit from a prolongation of the war. Perhaps this might be by a change of political or military circumstances and the consequent advent of new forces or new allies.

> In the long run and by itself the defensive cannot, of course, lead to a final attainment of the command of the sea. But it can prevent its attainment by the other side. . . . The real lesson of the war is . . . that we should note the supreme necessity and difficulty of crushing it down before it has time to operate its normal effect.[6]

The success of a fleet-in-being strategy depended, however, on its being conducted with verve and for reasons more ambitious than those of mere survival. Its requirements were summarised well by Captain Richard Kempenfelt in the War of American Independence:

> Much, I may say all, depends upon this fleet. 'Tis an inferior against a superior fleet. Therefore the greatest skill and address is requisite to counteract the designs of the enemy, to watch and seize the favourable opportunity for action, and to catch the advantage of making the effort at some or other feeble part of the enemy's line; or if such opportunities don't offer, to hover near the enemy, to keep him at bay, and to prevent his attempting anything but at risk and hazard; to command their attention, and to oblige them to think of nothing but being on their guard against your attack.

The point of this was that, with the intervention of the Spanish and the French, the Royal Navy was suddenly outnumbered and there seemed the possibility of invasion. The British attempted to prevent the concentration of French transports at Cherbourg and Le Havre, and hoped that their enemies, even with a greatly superior fleet, would not dare attempt to take over an invasion fleet without first defeating the Royal Navy. Accordingly, they hovered around menacingly, but avoided battle for weeks until the enemy, weakened by disease, problems of co-ordination and ineffectual manoeuvre, abandoned the whole enterprise. According to Corbett, this positive and effective policy was how the fleet-in-being strategy should most properly be understood: 'a naval defensive, keeping the fleet actively in being – not merely in existence, but in active and vigorous life'.[7]

Corbett argued strongly that the defensive was not the antithesis of the offensive, but its complement. A defensive in one place could make possible an offensive in another. Too many British admirals, he thought, failed to realise that there was something between attack and retreat. He wrote 'Their besetting strategical sin was failure to appreciate the power that lies in a well applied defensive.'[8] After all, in some circumstances, a fleet-in-being strategy could even serve 'offensive' purposes directly. In 1782, for example, it was an indispensable part of Admiral Barrington's successful campaign to capture one of the great French East India convoys. Altogether, argued Corbett, the fleet-in-being should not be confused with mere passivity.

Unfortunately all too often it was, sometimes by the navy practising it. The French Navy, for instance, gave the naval defensive a bad name by carrying it to extremes, by being too passive. In the eighteenth century, the French were generally the weaker side at sea: to compensate for this they developed their sense of the mission, the execution of some subsidiary task from which they would not be diverted even when some favourable opportunity for a local counter attack existed. Worse still, added Castex, passive defence frequently paralysed the spirit and caused such demoralisation that the French stayed on the defensive even when it was no longer necessary – as, for example, during the War of American Independece. For this reason, he went on, the passive defence must be avoided; there must be constant counter-attacks, and action against the enemy's coasts and communications; the enemy must be forced to disperse, creating thereby favourable opportunities for counter-attack. He admitted, though, that it was easier to enunciate the theory about this than to put it into practice.[9]

Mahan agreed that in some circumstances an active defence could achieve useful results, if it succeeded in forcing the enemy to divide his forces by threatening his vital interests and other strategic points. The aim should be to prevent the stronger enemy concentrating his forces.

Therefore the aim of the weaker party should be to keep the sea as much as possible; on no account to separate his battleships, but to hold them together, seeking by mobility, by frequent appearances, which unaided rumor always multiplies, to arouse the enemy's anxieties in many directions, so as to induce him to send off detachments; in brief, to occasion what Daveluy calls a 'displacement of forces' unfavourable to the opponent. If he made this mistake, either the individual detachments will be attacked one by one, or the main body, if unduly weakened.

Nevertheless, he clearly thought this a second-best strategy. He quoted Daveluy approvingly: 'The maritime defensive, from whatever point of view regarded, offers only disadvantages. It may be imposed; it never should be voluntarily adopted.' Its success seemed to depend on the stronger enemy making a mistake. It flew in the face of the basic truth that: 'The great end of a war fleet, . . .is not to chase, nor to fly, but to control the seas'.[10]

On the particular point of the role of the fleet-in-being in the defence of territory, Mahan maintained that this strategy would not work, and if it did work then it should not have. Hermocrates' advice was sound, and probably the best available in the circumstances; but, at the most, it would only have delayed an invasion. The Athenians would simply have concentrated their initial assault on Tarentum instead of Syracuse, destroyed the Sicilian fleet and gone on from there. England's safety in 1690, also, owed more to the ineptitude of de Tourville than it did to the far-sightedness of Torrington: the first should be blamed rather than the second praised. De Tourville should have followed up his victory at Beachy Head: instead he allowed himself to be diverted into a pointless raid on Teignmouth where he destroyed several harmless coastal vessels and carried off a few sheep. As Richmond pointed out in his turn, 'if Tourville had observed the great principle that tactical victory should always be followed up and consummated in relentless pursuit', the outcome might well have been fatal for the English.'[11]

Mahan was equally critical of the naval deployments adopted by the British during the War of American Independence: instead of concentrating against the main French ports, the Royal Navy adopted a defensive in home waters and tried to cover all vulnerable points in the Americas. As a result America was lost, and much of the West Indies and Minorca too; even the security of Gibraltar and Britain itself was in severe jeopardy. By no stretch of the imagination could the naval defensive be said to have covered itself in glory during this war. In home waters, it was the indecision of their enemies rather than the strategic insight of the British that had once more saved them from invasion. This indecision, of course, could be largely attributed to the defensive-mindedness of the French; and, in its turn, this was partly of their past experience at the hands of the battle-seeking British — or so Mahan maintained.[12]

Both Mahan and Castex argued that Colomb exaggerated the *extent* to which an invader needed command of the sea before launching his attack and so overestimated the ability of the fleet-in-being (which sought to limit the degree of that command) to deter such attempts. History provided scores of examples of an invader resolute enough to believe that 'war cannot be made without running risks' and willing to invade with an enemy fleet still in existence. In 1719, the Russian fleet launched a whole series of large raids and landings in the Baltic, virtually ignoring the Swedish fleet-in-being. In 1758, wrote Castex, the British went ahead with their landings at St Malo and Cherbourg, despite Conflans' fleet at Brest 'vaguely maintaining the role of the fleet-in-being'.

Colomb retaliated by pointing out that in the Spanish–American War of 1898, in whose strategic execution Mahan was personally involved, the mere existence of an inferior Spanish squadron under Cervera had much disrupted American landings on Cuba. The principle of the fleet-in-being, he argued, received 'extraordinary and unexpected confirmation' in Mahan's own war.[13] Mahan dismissed this as an abberation; Cervera's squadron may have had this effect, but probably it should not have done.

Certainly in more recent times there were many examples of landings taking place in an at least partially disputed sea. In the war of 1905, the Japanese went ahead with their landings in the Yellow Sea despite sombre warnings in *The Times* that they should not, while the Russian Fleet still existed. In 1914, the French and British shipped their troops to Europe despite the Austrian and German fleets respectively.[14] Amphibious landings in the Second World War, in fact, *usually* took place in the presence of hostile maritime forces, especially submarines and light craft. In one instance, the German invasion of Norway, they even took place in the presence of a *superior* enemy fleet. In truth, there seem to be at least as many exceptions to Colomb's rule as there were confirmations. In these circumstances it would hardly appear to be a rule at all.

(c) The fleet-in-being and the German Navy

Scepticism about the value of an inferior fleet in defence against invasion need not be extended to the concept of the fleet-in-being as a whole. To most naval strategists the phrase 'fleet-in-being' stood for more than it did in Colomb's restrictive sense. It represented, according to J. R. Thursfield, for instance, 'a Fleet strategically at large, not itself in command of the sea, but strong enough to deny that command to its adversary by strategic and tactical dispositions adapted to the circumstances of the case'. The range of possibilities such a strategy offered was well exemplified by German naval experience in both the world wars. The superiority of the British Grand Fleet to the German High Seas Fleet in the First World War was such that even the most aggressive German commanders were loath to accept battle except in the most favourable circumstances. The gap between the two was even greater in the Second World War, and the German naval command was correspondingly yet more cautious. Even so, an inferior fleet was found to confer important strategic benefits in both conflicts.

In peacetime, the mere existence of a first class but outnumbered fleet could be politically and strategically important. Its possible deterrent function was outlined in the celebrated 'Risk Theory', first openly stated in Admiral Tirpitz's *Naval Law* of 1900. The notion was that the German fleet should be strong enough to threaten the superior British fleet with such damage that Britain would feel dangerously exposed to further threats from elsewhere. Knowing their long-term strategic consequences, Britain would therefore be deterred from using her naval superiority to pursue policies inimical to German interests. Germany wanted 'a sea force which will compel a sea power of the first rank to think twice before attacking our coasts'. In fact, the policy did not work; the British were so alarmed by the German (naval) threat that they took steps to settle their differences with the Russians and French, and the 'other threats' Tirpitz relied on consequently disappeared. Even so, the Risk Theory was an interesting attempt to use an inferior fleet as an indirect political defence of what apparently could not be safeguarded by direct military means. [15]

When the war came, the German Admiralty's intention was to use their fleet actively – while avoiding a central confrontation. In varying degree, the Germans tried to force the British to disperse so they could, by a series of local ambushes on isolated detachments of the Grand Fleet, whittle away their enemy's superiority, until it was reduced to a level where the High Seas Fleet could deal with the Grand Fleet as a whole. According to Admiral Scheer and the German Naval Staff:

> The Fleet must strike when the circumstances are favourable; it must, therefore, seek battle with the English Fleet only when a state of equality has been achieved by the methods of guerilla warfare. . . . The Fleet must therefore hold back and avoid actions which might lead to heavy losses. This does not, however, prevent favourable opportunities being made use of to damage the enemy. [16]

Opportunities for this process of preliminary 'equalisation' should occur in plenty since the British would presumably be closely blockading the German Bight.

As Gorshkov pointed out, 'the implementation of this concept would have permitted Germany to operate freely on the seas, and then strangle

England with a naval blockade.' In other words, this active fleet-in-being strategy might eventually provide the conditions in which Germany would be able to assume a working command of the sea. (The Japanese fleet of the inter-war period intended to use much the same strategy against a superior United States fleet, advancing westwards across the Pacific.)

Unfortunately for the Germans, however, this policy did not work either. The British did not closely blockade the Bight after all; ambushes proved difficult to arrange and did not always have the desired result; differential construction rates tended to widen the gap between the two. Eventually, after the disappointing Battle of Jutland, the policy was effectively abandoned. Not surprisingly, the construction of the Risk Fleet and their hopelessly disadvantaged attempt to challenge British naval supremacy in this way is often attacked as a costly error. Should they, perhaps, have gone for a submarine and cruiser war instead?

In the Second World War the German fleet was in no position even to attempt such an ambitious policy. Instead, Admiral Raeder tried to make the most of his limited assets by a more passive version of the fleet-in-being strategy, one reminiscent of French practices of the eighteenth century.

> Enemy naval forces, even if inferior in strength, are only to be attacked if this should be necessary to achieve the main objective. Frequent changes in the operational area will provide uncertainty and delays in the sailing of the enemy's shipping, even if no material success is achieved. The temporary disappearance of German warships in remote areas will add to the enemy's confusion. [17]

The difference between these two versions of the strategy was only a matter of degree, and the benefits they conferred varied in degree as well. In both wars, the mere existence of significant naval forces anchored superior British naval forces in the North Sea area and affected Britain's naval dispositions and possibilities throughout the world. The *Tirpitz* in its Norwegian fjord forced the British to protect each convoy to Russia in strength and exerted a nuisance value out of all proportion to its actual capacity. Churchill summed it up well: 'It exercises a vague general fear and menaces all points at once. It appears and disappears causing immediate reactions and perturbations in the other side'. [18]

The containment of these forces required the presence of British ships that could otherwise be away doing something else. For instance, in the First World War, claimed Scheer, 'the English Fleet stayed far north and did not dare to attack our coast and stamp out the U-boat danger at its source'. Escorts that might have been valuable in the battle of the Atlantic had to be kept in the North Sea; decisive action against submarines (such as effective minefields off the German coast) could not be taken. And all this was thanks to the German fleet-in-being. In the Second World War, Raeder's plans were to tie the British down with a small fleet of older battleships in the North Sea area and then exploit their dependence on overseas supplies with attacks by U-boats, cruiser raiding groups and task groups.

Raeder's Z Plan, in fact, showed the connection there could be between the strategies of the fleet-in-being and *guerre de course*, with both providing the conditions in which the other could prosper. As Bacon pointed out, of the First World War, successful trade attacks might have forced the British into diverting some of their naval forces into direct trade protection and so made the Grand Fleet more vulnerable to sudden ambush.[19] Taken together the two strategies could have, and to a certain extent did, force sufficient strategic dispersal on the British to deny them the full rewards of their naval superiority.

There was enough of this in the First World War to lead critics to ask: 'What went wrong?' Acworth, at least, had no doubt of the answer; the British themselves had been contaminated by the defensive heresy, even though, since they had the stronger fleet, there was much less excuse for them than there was for the Germans: 'A fleet-in-being, a fleet of great material superiority, was to be regarded as an acceptable substitute for a decisive victory at sea... safety first became, perhaps for the first time in England's maritime history, a naval doctrine of war'.[20] Instead, thought Acworth, the British skulked about, over-reacted to the menace of torpedoes and mines and ignored their own traditions. For this reason the German Navy's defensive campaign was more successful than it should have been.

It is difficult to generalise about the success of the fleet-in-being strategy. Success does not depend on who is offensive and who defensive – but on who has, keeps and exploits the strategic initiative. This is by no means the exclusive preserve of the strongest fleet or of the side most ardently seeking a decision by battle. Success does seem to require certain minimum conditions of relative strength and geography, particularly sufficient room to manoeuvre and hide; it also depends in large measure on the strategic situation elsewhere. For all these reasons, it is hard to see how Admiral Sir James Somerville, despatched to the Indian Ocean to practice a kind of fleet-in-being strategy against the Japanese in 1942, could really have been expected to exert the degree of strategic influence Churchill hoped for.

Somerville's own offensive-mindedness, however, would probably have been a considerable asset in less unequal conditions for, in the past, the more actively the fleet-in-being strategy was practised, the better were its strategic results. It is of course true, as Castex remarked, that however vigorously the naval offensive is pursued, the weaker side is not usually able to 'throw off the yoke and transform the situation'. The side with command of the sea has more chance of having the last word.[21] Even so, an active fleet-in-being strategy would seem to offer the outnumbered fleet better prospects than either complete passivity or the kind of naval death-ride against a superior foe that the High Seas Fleet was rumoured to have been contemplating in 1918.

(d) The fleet blockade: General introduction

If an outnumbered fleet pursued some variant of the fleet-in-being strategy, its stronger opponent usually responded with a fleet blockade of some kind. Maritime strategists were at frequent pains to point out that the objectives of the fleet blockade were military and so it ought not to be confused with an economic blockade, the intention of which was to cut off the enemy's trade, or deny him essential supplies. The distinction remained even though the same ships could be executing both types of blockade at the same place and the same time.

The general military object of the fleet blockade was to prevent the enemy interfering in a substantial way with the blockading navy's capacity to use the sea as it wished. If the enemy was thus neutralised, the blockading navy would effectively be in command of the sea behind the blockade line; and surplus ships not actually involved in the blockading operation would be able to exercise that command.

As far as Mahan was concerned, the true station of the British fleet in the French Revolutionary Wars 'was before the hostile ports and as close to them as may be'. This was the first and main line of defence of Britain's maritime interests, and the most direct route to the attack of the enemy's. Mahan went on:

> As in all military campaigns, the front of operations of a powerful fleet should be pushed as far towards the enemy as is consistent with the mutual support of the various detachments, and with secure communication with their base. By so doing, not only are the great national interests placed more remote from the alarms of war, but the use of the region behind the front of operations, in this case the sea, is secured to the power that can afford to maintain its fighting line close to the enemy's positions.

Since this one fleet disposition would offer an effective indirect defence of all the blockading navy's maritime interests, Mahan argued, it was a much more economic proceeding than trying to defend those interests directly, as he thought the Royal Navy had mistakenly tried to do in the War of American Independence. Instead, the British should have concentrated at the decisive point – off the enemy's main fleet bases. He therefore approved of the way the British Admiralty seemed to be approaching the coming war with Germany. 'The British fleet is concentrated in the North Sea', he wrote. 'There it defends all British interests, the British islands, British commerce and the colonies; and, offensively, commands Germany's commercial sea routes.'[22]

The institution of a fleet blockade was an effective strategy towards these ends for a number of reasons. One of the most obvious was that it enabled the blockading navy always to know where its enemy was – the most fundamental of advantages. So imporant was this, thought Colomb, that it justified the kind of blockade which 'had no power of keeping the enemy in port, nor of fighting him if he came out'. Instead, such a force could observe what was happening and report back. This is what Collingwood did, with great effect, off Cadiz before the Battle of Trafalgar.[23]

But the precise way in which the blockade worked, and the nature and scale of the strategic benefits it conferred, depended largely on what kind of blockade it was. Maritime strategists usually distinguished between the 'close blockade' and the 'open' or 'distant blockade'. Captain Roskill wrote:

> If we keep the fleet more or less permanently off the enemy base, the blockade is said to be of the 'close' type: but if it watches enemy activities from a distance, cruising periodically off the base and exerting only a general control over the local waters, it is said to be of the 'open' type.[24]

The difference between the two was a matter of degree and indicated by a number of things in addition to the blockading squadron's proximity to the enemy base: one indication was often thought to be whether these squadrons replenished on station; another, pointed out by Corbett, was the degree of 'certainty of immediate contact' when the enemy came out. Both kinds, though, had their advantages and disadvantages.

(e) The fleet blockade: distant and close

The system of blockade most usually adopted by the Royal Navy throughout the eighteenth century was the distant blockade. To economise in ships and men, the Royal Navy in blockading the French naval base at Brest, for instance, would keep its main forces back at Torbay – or even Spithead – and rely on its light forces off the French coast to let it know when the French came out.

This procedure had several advantages. First of all, it avoided the extreme wear and tear of a close blockade. One reason, said Colomb, why Lord Howe decided on a distant blockade of Brest in 1800 was that he 'thought that in a blockading squadron off Brest there was a continuous process of deterioration going on, that both men and ships became gradually worn out, and that the force inside became more and more competent to beat the outside force as the time went on'.[25] The maritime strategists also stressed the necessity of supporting bases nearby, for forces engaged in the exhausting business of blockade; obviously the nearer to its own bases the blockading squadrons were able to operate, the better.

If the object of the exercise was not so much to stop the enemy coming out but to encourage him to do so that he could be beaten in battle, then a distant blockade was probably better than a close one. Richmond made the point that tight blockades rarely forced an enemy to sea.

> In no case in all the many wars at sea in which an enemy has been forced to keep under the shelter of the defences of his ports has a blockade forced him to sea to fight. Neither Spain, Holland, France or Germany, suffer though they did from pressure at sea, sent their fleets to sea to fight the superior forces which were the cause of that pressure.[26]

The idea of the distant blockade – or what Colomb called a masking operation – was, on the other hand, to tempt the enemy out with the prospect of success. Thus, in the Seven Years War, argued Corbett, Admiral Boscawen changed from close to distant blockade in order to lure his adversary, Admiral la Clue, to destruction. 'A decision was wanted, and open blockade was the best way to secure one.' The result was the Battle of Lagos of 1759.[27] The most celebrated exponent of the distant blockade, though, is often said to be Nelson himself. 'Not [close] blockade but battle is my aim. On the sea alone we hope to realise the hopes and expectations of our country', he wrote. 'My system is the very contrary of [close] blockading. Every opportunity has been offered the enemy to put to sea.' Thus when Nelson arrived, with his full force, near Cadiz in 1805 October, said Colomb:

> he was so far from blockading the Franco–Spanish fleet that he purposely kept his own ships out of view, in order if possible to deceive the enemy into a belief that his numbers were smaller than they actually were; but he kept close watch on Cadiz by an inshore squadron and repeating ships, so as to have the earliest intelligence of the enemy's movements.[28]

If the object of the blockade was to seal the enemy into his ports, then a distant blockade was a risky enterprise since it inevitably gave a determined enemy more chances to slip out. If the destruction of the enemy's main forces was the aim, however, it was the better device of the two. Because of this, added Corbett, with considerable insight, close and distant blockade conferred different degrees, and perhaps different kinds, of command of the sea. For a short time, he declared, close blockade

> would serve to keep the enemy in and the sea clear for covering or preventing a definite oversea operation – that is, for a temporary and local command. For permanent command it must always be doubtful whether it can compare with an open blockade conducted from a good interior position by a fleet that can retain its speed and fitness for action, without the demoralisation of absolute inactivity. [29]

But at least for short periods of time, the Royal Navy was occasionally able to mount a close blockading operation, the object of which was to stifle movement in and out of the enemy's naval bases, or in Colomb's phrase, to seal up the enemy's ports so that 'nothing floating should either leave or enter them'. The immediate consequence of a close blockade was, as Napoleon complained, that they could not put a cockle boat to sea without its being pounced on by English men-of-war. Hawke instituted such a blockade off Brest in 1758–9.

Its strategic consequences were very plain. To a large extent it inhibited the French from interfering with all kinds of British maritime operations: particularly it greatly reduced their ability to attack British trade. Of course, isolated raiders could be expected to wriggle through the tightest blockade. For that reason it was always necessary to have direct maritime defences, further back. Nevertheless, a close blockade would considerably reduce the scale of threat, and, thought Mahan, was the basic requirement for the successful defence of trade.

In Mahan's view, close blockading really proved its worth in a way more fundamental than this. The Royal Navy had often been in conflict with an adversary whose naval assets were dispersed between several bases or countries because of the geographical or political circumstances of the time. Not infrequently the combined total of those naval assets was equal or superior to Britain's. There was, therefore, an urgent need to prevent the enemy concentrating his forces. Without that essential preliminary concentration, the enemy would not be able to mount significant operations against British colonies or the British themselves.

> The strength of the British strategy lay not in hermetically sealing any one port, but in effectually preventing a great combination from all the ports. It was essential to Bonaparte not merely that his scattered squadrons should, one at a time and another at another, escape to sea,

but that they should do so at periods so ordered, and by routes so determined, as to ensure a rapid concentration at a particualr point. Against this the British provided by the old and sound usage of interior positions and lines.

And this they did by their policy of close blockade, 'not in the vain hope that no squadron could ever, by any means, slip out, but with the reasonable probability that at no one period could so many escape as to form a combination threatening the Empire with a crushing disaster'.[30]

Unless the French were willing to challenge the blockade directly – and to seek a decision by battle – their only hope was an illusory one based on evasion. Perhaps the French might be able to lure the British away, and then sneak over an invasion force before they came back? But so long as the British by a process of blockade kept their eyes fixed firmly on the main issue – the whereabouts and intentions of the French fleet – Mahan thought there was no chance of this.

In a justly famous passage, Mahan celebrated the effectiveness of this policy:

> Never in the history of blockades has there been excelled, if ever equalled, the close locking of Brest by Admiral Cornwallis, both winter and summer, between the outbreak of war and the Battle of Trafalgar. . . . They were dull, weary, eventless months, those months of watching and waiting of the big ships before the French arsenals. Purposeless they surely seemed to many, but they saved England. The world has never seen a more impressive demonstration of the influence of sea power upon its history. Those far distant, storm-beaten ships; upon which the Grand Army never looked, stood between it and the dominion of the world.[31]

Despite its obvious advantages, however, Corbett still considered the prolonged close blockade was fundamentally a weak form of war: it was extremely exhausting; it required a large superiority in ship numbers (somewhere between 25 and 33 per cent) and a considerable reserve for relief on station; it was very demanding on personnel and support services. To give just one example, the kind of cumulative wear and tear (particularly underwater fouling) that was the inevitable product of prolonged periods at sea meant that a blockading warship became increasingly slower and so less able to deal with a French ship fresh from the dockyards. For such reasons as these, close blockades not infrequently broke down under the strain, or were not instituted in the first place. Thus Pepys recorded Sir William Coventry as:

> disliking our staying with the fleet on the Dutch coast, believing that the Dutch will come out in fourteen days, and then we with our

unready fleet, by reason of some of the ships being maimed, shall be in a bad condition to fight them on their own coast.[32]

Perhaps to institute a close blockade was even to play into the hands of a navy pursuing a policy of masterly inactivity in its own harbours. For, by such a policy, the inferior fleet could inflict steady damage on, and occupy the attention of, more ships (ships-of-line and 'cruisers', the latter always in short supply anyway) than it could hope to incapacitate otherwise. By this means, an outnumbered fleet could 'contain' a superior opponent and enforce upon him 'a disproportionate expenditure of force, to the detriment of his power to take offensive action and to defend his trade.'[33] A close blockade, in other words, might give a passive fleet-in-being strategy more strategic effectiveness than it deserved.

According to some observers the relative disadvantages of the close blockade actually increased as naval warfare moved into the age of steam and beyond. Coal burning ships did not have the capacity for almost indefinite cruising as did their predecessors. The task of on-station replenishment became even more difficult than it was already. Being now independent of the wind the fleet inside could choose its time to wriggle through or challenge the blockading squadrons with much greater freedom than was possible before. Above all, perhaps, the advent of torpedoes, mines, submarines and eventually aircraft meant that the blockading squadrons would be increasingly liable to painful and possibly dangerous levels of attrition from shore. As we have seen, the Jeune Ecole were convinced that their torpedo boats would make effective blockade impossible.

In the Royal Navy there was a considerable reluctance to accept the demise of the close blockade. Steam, it was sometimes argued, might make the blockade more stringent than it was in days when lee-shores mattered: it might also make raiders and squadrons more difficult to find, if they *did* get out. Both Mahan and Corbett stoutly defended the broad principles of close blockade, but admitted that new developments would 'place a far greater strain on blockaders, and compel them to keep at much greater distance'. The close blockade would become more distant in practical effect if not in intention. By the beginning of the twentieth century, this fact had been accepted by the British Admiralty.

As a result, in the First World War, the British blockaded the North Sea rather than the High Seas Fleet and failed to appear off the German Bight, as the Germans expected them to, and hoped they would, so they could be cumulatively 'equalised'. The southern half of the North Sea became a kind of naval no man's land.

If the Germans chose to cruise about in this area, they took the chance of being cut off and engaged by the British forces, whose policy it was to leave their bases from time to time for what Sir John Jellicoe in the Jutland Despatch described as 'periodic sweeps through the North Sea'.... Thus for the old policy of close blockade was substituted a new one, that of leaving the enemy a large field in which he might be tempted to manoeuvre: and it had this value, that should be yield to the temptation, an opportunity must sooner or later be afforded to the British Fleet of cutting him off and bringing him to action. Meantime he was cut off from any large adventure far afield. He would have to fight for freedom.... Thus no naval battle could be expected unless... the weaker wished to fight, or was cornered, or surprised.[34]

Like most other distant blockades, the British fleet blockade of the First World War was partly intended to lure its adversary out to destruction on the high seas. In this it failed. At least it substantially succeeded in its other great purpose, the protection of maritime interests 'behind the line'. The German surface navy was effectively neutralised. It could not operate outside the North Sea, and so British interests in the oceans beyond were substantially secured from significant surface attack. One Professor of History at Greenwich wrote in ringing tones:

The battleships of Britain served the North Sea as double-barred doors serve a house. So long as Admiral Jellicoe and the Dover patrol held firm, the German fleet in all its tremendous strength was literally locked out of the world. The Hohenzollern dreadnoughts could not place themselves upon a single trade route, could not touch the outer hem of a single oversea Dominion, could not interfere with the imports on which the British Isles depended, could not stem the swelling stream of warriors who came from every land and clime to save the cause of civilisation.[35]

But, all the same, neutralisation by distant blockade did not provide total protection. The enemy surface fleet could still operate, however gingerly, inside the North Sea, sometimes with embarrassing effects for the British. Probably more to the point, German submarines could still slip out in sufficient numbers to attack British shipping behind the line with near devastating consequences. It was because they were conscious of the imperfections of the type of blockade then in operation that so many senior British naval officers of the period strove so hard to achieve a central decisive victory over the German Fleet at sea. And it was because they knew that, bad as it was, the naval situation could be so much worse, that the German Navy strove to avoid it.

Authorities on both sides thought such a victory for the British fleet could well pave the way for a blockade tight enough to seal the U-boats safely into their lairs. But others, again on both sides, were more sceptical about such aspirations. In the strategic circumstances then prevailing, they argued, and with the advent of the submarine, mine and aircraft, it would surely make better sense to concentrate resources on the direct defence (or attack) of British shipping instead.

Many of these trends continued into the Second World War. Blockading operations became even more closely integrated into, and indistinguishable from, the rest of the fleet's activities. They became more multi-dimensional too, with maritime air power in particular playing an increasingly important role in the detection and destruction (potential or actual) of naval forces on both sides of the blockade line. Finally, technology and strategic circumstances conspired to give blockaded navies (mainly the German and Italian fleets) more freedom and more sea room than they had before. But even though the practice may have had such difficulties as these, the purpose of blockade remained essentially the same. In this war, as in many of its predecessors, blockade provided the dominant navy with the best means of containing an inferior, though potentially dangerous, enemy, and so improved its chanceces of being able to use the sea in relative security. But, as always, it offered a degree of protection less complete than the wholesale destruction of the enemy's main forces would have done.

(f) Command of the sea: General introduction

Corbett declared,

> Command of the sea means nothing but the control of sea communications... and when we say that the primary object of our battlefleets must always be the destruction of the battlefleets of the enemy, what we really mean is that the primary function of our battlefleets is to seize and prevent the enemy from seizing the main lines of communication.

If this was command of the sea, what was the point of having it? According to most naval strategists, the answer was clear: command of the sea was worth striving for because of what it made possible. Command of the sea could be decisive not for its own sake but for what it might lead to.

Its possible advantages were summed up by Admiral Sir Cyprian Bridge:

> It enables the nation which possesses it to attack its foes where it pleases and where they seem to be most vulnerable. At the same time

it gives its possessor security against serious counter-attacks, and affords to his maritime commerce the most efficient protection that can be devised. It is, in fact, the main object of naval warfare.[36]

The trouble with such apparently reasonable descriptions as these is that they often conceal important differences of emphasis and interpretation. The phrase has sometimes been used, more or less, as a synonym for 'maritime greatness', as a descriptive attribute of a country which does indeed appear to 'rule the waves'. But since this encourages absolutist interpretations of 'command', it is probably better to avoid such hyperbole and use the phrase strictly and narrowly as a label for a strategic concept of warfare at sea. Another distinction that certainly needs to be borne in mind is that between winning command and exercising it. Corbett wrote, 'No principle of naval warfare is so much ignored in ordinary discussion, as that you cannot command the sea with a battlefleet'. The battlefleet could never he numerous or ubiquitous enough to exercise command and control the lines of passage: that was the job of 'the flotilla and its supporting cruisers and intermediate ships'. By destroying or neutralising the enemy, the battlefleet won the command which only these other naval forces could exercise.[37]

The difference between these two was made clear by Russell Grenfell: all the small ships exercising command, patrolling focal and terminal trade areas, escorting convoys and military transports, patrolling to intercept enemy commerce and so forth made up what he called the Control Fleet. The gaining and maintenance of command was the work of the Battle Fleet, under whose cover the Control Fleet operated. The point of emphasising the difference between these two functions was that they had different requirements in warships, tactical procedure and so on. Only with a properly 'balanced fleet' could a navy hope to perform both functions.

All too often there was excecessive peacetime concentration on the Battle Fleet and too little on the Control Fleet. As we have seen, the Royal Navy of Admiral Jellicoe has been widely accused of getting the balance wrong in this way during the First World War: for instance, while the Grand Fleet swept majestically to and fro across the North Sea, German submarines nearly strangled British commerce in the oceans behind it – or so at least the argument goes. It was also forgotten that the task of exercising command could be even more demanding than that of winning it, as the British found in the Second World War.[38] The consequent switch in priorities could be seen in the Royal Navy's wartime construction programme after this discovery: battleships and aircraft carriers would have to wait, convoy escorts and landing ships came first. In substantial wars, both kinds of fleet have evidently been essential and the success of one has depended on the success of the other.

Another source of confusion, and sometimes mistaken policy, has been the extent to which command of the sea is regarded as an exclusive and absolute concept. There are those who seem to think of command as being of all the sea for all purposes. 'There is no such thing as partial or incomplete command of the sea', declared Clarke and Thursfield. 'It is either absolute, or it does not exist.' There are ambiguities in Rosinski's views on this matter, but he too was plainly of the absolutist persuasion: a divided command of the same stretch of water was 'no "command" at all. . . . At sea there is no halfway house between victory and defeat.'[39]

Mahan has also been accused of thinking that 'Command of the sea ... was an exclusive thing: it could not be shared, and was applicable to one nation at a time'.[40] Mahan sometimes suffers from having written more than most people are prepared to read, and there is much scope for valid but differing interpretations of what he said on this and other matters. However, on frequent occasions he made it clear that he believed that command of the sea, a phrase incidentally which he hardly used, was essentially a relative not an absolute thing. And so did most other maritime strategists. Corbett often used the phrase 'a working command', which makes the point exactly.

The most obvious of the relativities of command is that of time, the length of time during which one navy could be said to be the master of the seas. Command of the seas could often prove a fleeting thing, no sooner won than gone. Mahan declared, 'It is evident that the sea in the past has not been so exclusively dominated, even by Great Britain at her greatest, that a contest for control may not take the form of a succession of campaigns marked by ups and downs'.[41] Sometimes, though, it could last 'for the duration' – as it did for the British and the French in the Crimean War.

Almost inevitably, command of the sea was also relative in terms of place. It could be local, or general, or somewhere between the two. 'The absence of overall command,' wrote Brodie, 'is especially likely to be the rule where the areas in dispute are vast and the bases of the opposing forces widely removed from each other. Such a situation is almost inevitable in the broad reaches of the Pacific.'[42] That ocean was so huge no-one could expect to be in command of all of it at one time until the very end of the conflict. The French Navy is often said to have practised a strategy aiming at combining the relativities of time and place in a particularly ingenious way. They hoped to lure away the British fleet for long enough to sneak an invasion over to England. In 1804 Napoleon wrote, 'Let us be masters of the Straits for six hours and we shall be masters of the World'. However limited, such command might be all that was necessary.

Lastly, command might be limited in extent – that is in the degree to which it allows one side to dictate events at sea. Mahan was quite clear that 'however great the inequality of naval strength' the weaker party always had at least some opportunities to sail about the sea, 'make harassing descents upon unprotected points ... enter blockaded harbours'.[43] Control was not absolute. It could relate merely to the conduct of operations within particular dimensions of maritime war: air, surface and sub-surface. Very possibly a different balance of command might apply in one dimension than in another; since the German Navy was so much more successful in contesting command by its underwater activities than it was on the surface, this description fits both world wars to some extent. Similarly, command might apply mainly to particular types of ship and the kind of tasks they performed. During the First World War, Admiral Bacon observed, 'even in the North Sea we had command of the sea only so far as battleships were concerned: the enemy still had the power of using battle cruisers, fleet light cruisers, destroyers and submarines offensively'. However tight their blockade, the British still needed direct defences of shipping and coastline behind the line.[44]

For all these reasons, even 'permanent and general' command of the sea could never be absolute in practice. The adversary would always have at least some maritime possibilities, but perhaps not of the kind that would have a substantial impact on the outcome of the war. In Castex's phrase, command of the sea was 'relative, incomplete, imperfect'. Perhaps it would be better to aim at establishing not a general command of the sea but fluid and temporary zones of control whenever, 'we desire to use ... [a] ... particular stretch of salt water for our own purposes'.[45]

In view of all this, it is sometimes suggested we should actually avoid the phrase 'command of the sea' in the first place. The concept is evidently misleading in some respects: it implies something more absolutist in theory than in practice, as we have seen. To the unwary, it may give such false impressions as that, if one side loses command, then the other side will necessarily gain it. More to the point, perhaps, the hazy ideas produced by this impression might actually encourage strategic error. By trying to achieve as absolute a degree of command as possible a navy might multiply its enemies (by menacing neutrals – a point emphasised by Corbett)[46] or might neglect the requirements of exercising that command (by concentrating too much on the Battle and too little on the Control Fleets). Strategic contemplation has various purposes. It may help explain past experience; it may help prepare for the future. Either way, with half-digested thought and woolly labels it could do more harm than good.

For this reason, some writers have preferred to avoid using abstract labels at all, but this makes it difficult to generalise and without generalisation there can be no theory. Others have replaced 'command of the sea' with alternative terms such as 'the control of communications', the 'dominion of the sea', 'maritime control' or 'naval mastery' – all of which suffer from their own imprecisions and generally imply much the same thing anyway. But, concluded Bernard Brodie, reasonably: 'So long as one bears in mind that "command" is always relative and means simply a marked ascendancy in the contest for control, one might as well continue to use a phrase which has so ancient and honourable a tradition'.[47]

(g) Achieving command of the sea: A summary

Of the three methods of winning or maintaining command (decisive battle, the fleet-in-being and blockade) the first is generally reckoned to be the main, quickest and most economical – at least for the stronger naval power. It was certainly quicker and surer than the fleet-in-being strategy, and it had the important advantage over blockade that once it had succeeded the ships so employed could be dispersed to help exercise command. Also the vastness and tracklessness of the ocean made it more difficult to pin an enemy down than on land and so multiplied the advantages of defeating him once and for all when he was located.

According to some commentators, indeed, the destruction of the enemy's main naval forces was so important an objective that it became an end in itself, as we have seen. Command of the sea was somehow more than merely the control of maritime communications. The *guerre à outrance* school complained of

> the strategic heresy started by Mahan and recanted in one of his last volumes, to wit, that sea power derived from and had as its object, the protection of sea communications: thus obliterating the whole of the real purpose of sea power, namely the destruction or neutralisation of any force that could threaten these communications.[48]

Such an emphasis on the pursuit of the decisive battle as the main means of securing command of the sea has been criticised on various grounds. First the effects of major fleet engagements were all too often, in Gorshkov's words 'no more than operational' with little discernible strategic consequence for the war as a whole.[49] Secondly, overconcentrating on the requirements of the fleet versus fleet engagement is often held to be responsible for a damaging neglect of those of the more hum-drum business of protecting commerce or preparing for operations against the enemy's coast. Thirdly, actually getting a decisive battle could prove too difficult, if the enemy chose to resort to some form of the fleet-in-being strategy. Finally, in some geo-strategic circumstances the maintenance of command might be more important than the defeat of the enemy's main fleet, a consideration making Admiral Jellicoe justifiably wary of running risks at Jutland.

The fleet-in-being strategy, as we have seen, was the sensible response of a weaker navy to its own inferiority. In its most active form, it could lead in theory to an initially inferior fleet eventually triumphing over a stronger opponent and so securing ascendancy at sea. This kind of success is very rare, however. More usually, fleet-in-being strategists seek merely to deny command to the enemy, or diminish his possibilities of enjoying it. In 1942 Brodie remarked, 'Our own Navy had given the world a lesson on what an inferior fleet can accomplish in the immense spaces of the Pacific if shrewdly and aggressively handled'. By 1944, a succession of disastrous defeats had reversed the situation and forced the Japanese Navy into a fleet-in-being strategy which was capable of 'exercising considerable influence on our moves. While it existed, we could not afford to extend ourselves too rapidly.'

The German fleet was another interesting case: it had no hope of surface ascendancy but its efforts could have been of signal value to its allies. 'In detaining a good number of British battleships... the Germans did give a magnificent opportunity to the Italian fleet in the Mediterranean, but the Italians muffed it completely. The only belligerent really aided by the existence of heavy German and Italian ships was Japan.'[50]

The usual response to this strategy was blockade, as we have seen. A fleet of adequate strength, suitably disposed geographically, could block an enemy from the seas and so provide the cover under which other forces further back actually exercise command. It often proved a long and tiring process, much less satisfying to the countless crews engaged upon it than some grand encounter on the high seas. Nevertheless, its object was the same, and its success rate probably better. In any case it often led to battle, as we have seen.

(h) Command as a means to an end

To most maritime strategists, command is no more than a means to an end. Corbett declared

> It never has been and never can be, the end in itself. Yet, obvious as this is, it is constantly lost sight of in naval policy. We forget what really happened in the old wars: we blind ourselves by looking only on the dramatic moments of naval history; we come unconsciously to assume that the defeat of the enemy's fleets solves all problems.[51]

and of course, it does not.

Writing of the Dutch Wars, Philip Colomb also stressed the

instrumental nature of command of the sea. 'It is incomprehensible that the whole naval force of each side should have gathered against the other again and again and simply fought for the mastery, unless something was to follow when it was gained.'[52] Both sides had enormous maritime interests to protect or expand and the dourness of their wars was by no means coincidental. The more important are the ends it serves, the more ferocious will be the struggle for command.

The value of command of the sea lay not in any fact of its physical conquest or possession – an idea which only makes sense in land warfare – but in the use to which it could be put. One recent commentator has noted, 'Maritime strategy is about the use of the sea and if one can achieve "command" then one can use the sea for one's own purposes and prevent the enemy from using it for his'.[53] The use it could be put to depended on circumstances. At one level, it could serve as the basis for the creation of a colonial empire, as it did the Portuguese in the sixteenth century and the Dutch and English thereafter.

Its more narrowly strategic consequences were made clear in the Pacific war when, in Richmond's words, the Japanese

> with an unopposed command of the sea owing to the absence of British sea forces, the disablement of the United States Fleet at Pearl Harbour, and the allied losses of Malaya and in the Java Sea, could move her military forces freely ... against the British, Dutch and American possessions in the Pacific.

But then in a series of battles the Allies broke and destroyed Japanese sea power, making her eventual defeat inevitable.

> The allies, with their now complete command of the sea, threatened Japan with three measures: invasion of the home islands, bombardment from the air and the sea of her factories and cities, and blockade, cutting off both those food-supplies she could draw from the mainland and the fisheries round her coasts. 'With our sea power making possible the use of all our other resources,' said Admiral Nimitz, 'we gave Japan the choice of surrender or slow but certain death'.[54]

Before we go on to consider these 'uses', however, three qualifications should perhaps be entered against this vision of command of the sea. First, it is neither limitless nor all-powerful. In some cases, as during the Norway campaign of the Second World War, for instance, its potency against air and land superiority could prove to be restricted. In this case, the northwards push of German forces and the spreading influence of their air force drove the British into the sea and harried them even there, the surface supremacy of the Royal Navy notwithstanding. The ability to command the sea may often depend on supremacy on land, rather than the other way about.

Secondly, there is the matter of sequence. The ordering of this and most other books on maritime strategy may suggest that there is a natural order to events in naval warfare. First, a navy must concentrate in order by battle or blockade to achieve command; then, having done so, it may disperse to exercise it. In point of fact, though, the matter is rarely so neat and tidy. As Corbett noticed, 'extraneous necessities intrude themselves which make it inevitable that operations for exercising command should accompany as well as follow operations for securing command'.[55] It was a 'difficult and disputed' matter, declared Mahan, whether in combined operations 'the fleet and the convoy should sail together, or the convoy held till control of the sea is decided'. It was unwise to make 'sweeping dogmatic assertions': far better to weigh up the particulars of the individual case. How much risk was permissable: how near and mighty the enemy fleet: how important the objective? Any decision on precedence must depend on such things as these.

Gorshkov agreed with this: 'Combat actions the aim of which is to secure dominance at sea in selected areas or in particular directions, may either precede the solution by the fleet of the main tasks or be conducted simultaneously'. Most of the decisive actions of the Second World War, he pointed out, were associated with and a part of some larger enterprise against sea communications or the enemy's coastline: thus, the Battle of Cape Matapan, the sinking of the *Bismarck*, the battles in the Coral Sea, off Midway, the Philippine Sea, Leyte Gulf and so on. He also believed this to be a growing trend as we shall see.[56]

This leads on to the third qualification, the question of the actual necessity of command of the sea for maritime endeavour. The orthodox view is that countries which restrict themselves to operations directly in defence or attack of land and trade, and shun the larger struggle for command – such as the French of the eighteenth century, or the German and Russian Baltic and Black Sea fleets of the Second World War[57] – usually fail, or at least do not do as well as they might. So, the question arises: to what extent does success in the four main kinds of maritime enterprise (the mounting of assaults against the land; or their defeat; the protection of shipping; or its attack) depend on command as yielded by the destruction or neutralisation of the enemy's main forces?

Starting with the first of these sea uses, most maritime strategists agreed that command of the sea was necessary to a country intending to mount a substantial operation against the enemy's coastline. The argument was made most fully by Philip Colomb. He maintained that unless a navy maintained maritime control, it could only conduct what he called 'cross-ravaging' – the practice common in the medieval wars of England and France of exchanging coastal raids on a tit-for-tat basis, which however rewarding for the people doing it, were still pointless strategically. In his view, it was the Elizabethans who first realised the necessity for command of the sea and had the kind of ships to make it feasible. He wrote:

> The control of the sea or what I shall now and hereafter call by its established title, the 'Command of the Sea', was henceforth to be understood as the aim of naval war. A power striving for anything else, such as evasions, or surprises of ports or territories, or merely defensive guardings of commerce, accepted the position of inferior and beaten naval power, and could never hope, so long as she maintained that attitude, of seriously damaging her opponent.[58]

Command was needed for substantial expenditions overseas. The scale of the enterprise and its chances of success depended on the extent of command enjoyed. For this purpose, the sea could not be neutral. The French, maintained Colomb, repeatedly failed to recognise this and sought by a sequence of ingenious schemes (such as that of Choiseul during the Seven Years War) to win a modicum of command by luring the Royal Navy away from the Channel. Even more unwisely, he said, they occasionally tried to do both things at once: win command and land troops at the same time. Military operations with two such diverse and conflicting objectives were bound to fail, he thought. Were he alive at the time, Colomb would undoubtedly have regarded the Japanese strategy at the Coral Sea and Midway as two good illustrations of the principle. This kind of double purpose operation could only work if the invader was so overwhelmingly superior that he could devote half his fleet to each task and still be reasonably confident of victory, whichever half the enemy attacked. But his ability to do this would probably mean he, in fact, already had substantial command.

It was because of the hazards of conducting such operations without this comforting superiority that Colomb put so much faith into the fleet-in-being strategy, as we have seen. The Battle of Lissa in 1866, he thought, was a dreadful warning of what might happen to those who left even a weak fleet intact while proceeding on an invasion. In this case the Austrians had a force at Pola and

> it was an absolute necessity to paralyse its action if the capture of the Island of Lissa was to be accomplished. If neither Medina-Sidonia [commander of the Spanish Armada, who also tried to do two things at once] nor Persano [commander of the Italian force] had naval force enough for the double operation of paralysing the defending naval force, and covering the landing at the same time, and yet attempted to pursue the descent, they each courted the fate they met and fully deserved it.[59]

Generally, most maritime strategists have agreed with this line of argument. For instance Mahan concluded, 'As a rule a major operation of war across sea should not be attempted unless naval superiority for an adequate period is probable'.[60] But it perhaps deserves emphasising that Mahan is not here talking of 'absolute' command, but of 'working' command very possibly limited in time, space and extent. The point was reinforced by Corbett. The notion 'that you cannot move a battalion oversea, till you have entirely overthrown your enemy's fleet', he declared was a ridiculous one which 'deserves gibbeting'. The extent of the command required depended on the ambitiousness and difficulty of the enterprise being envisaged.

The German invasion of Norway in 1940 was an interesting experiment in seeing how little command might be enough. The Germans clearly exercised a fair degree of control in the narrow waters of the Skaggerak, but this was much less certain the further north they went. Admiral Raeder pinned his faith on the achievement of complete surprise and on being able to counter any subsequent allied reaction with German air power – an advantage which other such schemers as Napoleon and the Prince de Joinville did not have. Nevertheless, the whole enterprise was extremely dangerous and, as Raeder openly admitted, 'contrary to all principles in the theory of naval warfare', as it would be carried out in the teeth of British naval supremacy.[62] Most maritime strategists would probably have agreed with him. Corbett, for instance, remained sceptical about 'the possibility of securing temporary local command by surprise' attributing it to a 'blindness . . . to the essential differences between land and sea strategy'.[63] The consensus seems to be that where the extent of required command is ambiguous, it is better to err on the side of safety since amphibious operations are particularly vulnerable to counter-attack.

As we have already seen, this very fact of vulnerability was the main reason why Colomb pinned so much faith to his original version of the fleet-in-being strategy. But although many strategists concluded that he exaggerated the deterrent effect of an inferior fleet – largely because he overestimated the degree of command the invader needed – most agreed that the best and surest means of defending teritory against invasion was to deny an enemy the necessary command, preferably while retaining it oneself. 'The fear of actual invasion', noted Clarke and Thursfield, 'is a pure chimera so long as our fleets are able to protect us.'[64] While the advent of air power seemed increasingly likely to usurp from navies this traditional protective function, this in no way implied that the strategic principle was outmoded, but merely that it might be put into effect by different kinds of forces. In fact, as we shall see, the 'fortress fleet' idea challenged orthodoxy much more substantially than this.

Turning now to the question of the necessity of command for the attack or defence of shipping, Colomb evidently thought the link between the precondition and the use of that command was looser than it was for operations against the land. He made the point that 'the forces proper for gaining command of the sea might be quite useless for protecting commerce'. Commerce was so difficult to defend that attacks on it 'have, historically, had little or no connection with the condition of the sea in the matter of command'.

Nevertheless in his discussion of the Dutch Wars, Colomb sketched out what was to become the orthodox view of the connection between command and the defence (or attack) of trade. He noted:

> There might be simply a series of great battles at sea, in which the element of merchant ships was absent, one fleet attacking in the hope of mastering it merely as a means to an end; the end being a free sea for the commerce of the winner, and the power of capturing, destroying, or simply hindering the flow of the commerce of the loser.[65]

The Dutch Wars seemed to show that command was important to the successful protection of trade. The Dutch often found themselves trying to do both tasks at once, while at least in theory the securing and maintenance of command should take precedence. The British too occasionally got the balance wrong. After the fight off the Kentish Knock in September 1652, for instance, wrote Roskill, the British committed the 'serious error of detaching a considerable part of the fleet to the Mediterranean – on trade protection duties – so allowing the Dutch to regain command of our home waters.'[66] Only when command was safely and permanently secured could forces be dispersed to exercise it in direct commerce protection. Increasingly, the forces exercising command were actually different from those winning it. But even in this case, the success of commerce protection squadrons usually depended critically on the cover provided by the main forces.

More surprisingly, perhaps, a working command is often considered just as central to the successful attack of the enemy's commerce. Mahan, in his most magisterial fashion, wrote:

> It is not the taking of individual ships or convoys, be they few or many that strikes down the money power of a nation: it is the possession of that overbearing power on the sea that drives the enemy's flag from it, or allows it to appear only as a fugitive; and which, by controlling the great common, closes the highways by which commerce moves to and fro from the enemy's shores. This overbearing power can only be exercised by great navies.[67]

This view was accepted by many, even in the France of the Jeune Ecole. For example, de Lanessan wrote:

In the opinion of most of our officers, if we have not battleship squadrons, or if our squadrons are not strong enough to dispute with the enemy the mastery of the sea which wash our coasts, we shall in all likelihood be obliged to give up all idea of carrying on a corsair warfare[68]

However, as we shall shortly see, there have always been the sceptics, unwilling to accept that the destruction or containment of the enemy's main forces is in fact a precondition of a successful assault on his shipping.

Now, having looked briefly at what the maritime strategists have had to say about how command was to be achieved, and what in general terms was the point of so doing, we should turn to the question of the way in which they thought it should be exercised.

6 The Exercise of Command

(a) Operations against the shore

The ability to mount or defeat operations against the shore is one of the two main ways in which command is exercised and the sea used. This form of sea use suffers from the absence of a consistent vocabulary in maritime strategy. Competing words and definitions jostle with each other to attract support: amphibious warfare, combined operations, land–sea operations, the projection of power ashore, overseas raids and invasions, attacks on territory from the sea. These all have strengths and weaknesses, but none have won universal acclaim. Probably in this case, th/)ugh, the consequence is not so bad as it is with 'sea power' or 'the command of the sea'. Even though the name is in dispute, there is broad agreement about what it stands for. Like Shakespeare's rose, it smells the same, more or less, whatever we call it.

Operations against the shore are generally taken to range from substantial invasions to conquer territory, at one end of the scale, to minor nuisance raids and naval bombardments, at the other. They vary considerably in terms of purpose, effort and impact on the outcome of the war.

The use of the sea in the physical conquest of the land was the most ambitious of all these possibilities since, as Gorshkov wrote, 'the goals of a war were achieved mostly by taking over the territory of the enemy.' He went on:

> Successful operations of a fleet against the shore brought a better result than the operations of fleet against fleet. In the first case the fleet solved a direct 'territorial' task, whereas in the second, victory over the enemy's fleet merely created the pre-requisites for the later solution of territorial tasks.

Or, as Brodie put it more succinctly, 'naval operations are important primarily because of their influence on land campaigns'. In other words, since wars are fundamentally about territory, the ability to launch operations against the land should be regarded as the general culmination of the naval art.[1]

By this means only, could navies act to consolidate gains already made at sea. When, in the early nineteenth century, the Russian fleet intervened to help the Greeks against the Turks, they rapidly discovered that their inability to land sufficient troops much reduced the value of their generally successful naval activity. Their experience demonstrated that, to be decisive, naval power usually needed to go ashore. Once there, its influence on subsequent events could be central to the outcome of the war.

This case was made out most forcefully by Fleet Admiral Chester Nimitz, US Navy, in his 1947 Report to the Secretary of the Navy:

The final objective in war is the destruction of the enemy's capacity and will to fight, and thereby force him to accept the imposition of the victor's will. This submission has been accomplished in the past by pressure in and from each of the elements of the land and sea, and during World War I and II, in and from the air as well. The optimum of pressure is exerted through that absolute control obtained by actual physical occupation. This optimum is obtainable only on land where physical occupation can be consolidated and maintained. Experience proves that while invasion in some form – of adjacent sea areas, covering air spaces, or enemy territory itself – is essential to obtain decisions in war, it is sometimes unnecessary to prosecute invasion to the extent of occupying a nation's capital or other vital centres. Sufficient of his land, sea, or air territory must be invaded, however, to establish the destructive potential of the victor and to engender in the enemy that hopelessness that precedes submission. The reduction of Japan is a case in point.

This was, however, more than a good many maritime, and even more continental, strategists were willing to accept. The geopolitical school had argued that sea power would be unable to defeat land power, even if it did try to come ashore. The British failure in the American War of Independence showed how difficult it was for one country, however strong at sea, to defeat another, large and distant one, much of whose territory was impervious to the workings of sea power. And this without continental allies and in the face of a hostile maritime coalition.[2] The same lesson could be drawn from British experience after the defeat of the Armada in 1588 and the Battle of Trafalgar in 1805. In both cases, the effects of glorious victories at sea were rapidly dissipated by the turn of strategic events on shore. Only by dint of great and co-operative effort with her allies was Britain able to defeat Napoleon: naval mastery and amphibious operations were not enough. In the earlier case of the war against Spain, the task of translating naval victory into strategic victory was wholly beyond England's power, with allies or without.

Many strategists, even those of the maritime persuasion, thought these difficulties more likely to increase than to diminish. Writing in 1934 for example, Richmond declared:

> An invasion by sea of a great modern military state may be dismissed as impracticable, even if there were no opposition at sea. The number of men which can be transported would never be sufficient to conduct an invasion in the face of the opposition of the military forces of any modern power.[3]

If this was true, then war-winning operations against the shore would be even less common in the future than they were in the past.

They could still be crucial, however, but at a lower level. In Gorshkov's view, the Second World War demonstrated 'that in a struggle even against a continental adversary an important role is played by the Navy'. He added: 'our naval science came to the conclusion that the outcome of the war would be decided on land, and therefore the Navy would have to carry out missions in the war stemming from the missions of the ground forces'.[4] This was true for the navies of both sides on the Eastern Front. Naval forces were expected to provide fire support, put ashore landing parties, defeat the opposition's sea and river forces, get troops across water barriers, transport military supplies and interfere with the enemy's communications. These tasks were by no means new. They were a classic part of every land campaign which initially depended on a sea-borne assault or which had a maritime front. Wellington is said to have declared of the Peninsular campaign, 'If anyone wishes to know the history of this war I will tell them it is our maritime superiority which gives me the power of maintaining my army, while the enemy are unable to do so'.[5] This kind of contribution could be vital and, thought Gorshkov, justified having a substantial navy even in war against a continental neighbour.

Assaults from the sea could also have a profound strategic influence by virtue of their diversionary potentiality. This possibility was explored most thoroughly by Corbett in his account of the Seven Years War. He was particularly interested in raids and in what he called 'eccentric attacks' whose size and intention reflected a diversionary purpose. They were 'a method of disturbing our enemy's plans and strengthening the hands of our allies and our own position'.[6] They were not true invasions aiming at the permanent conquest and retention of large slices of territory. These last were grand affairs involving large numbers of men – somewhere in excess of 50 000 – and more difficult to execute since they lost 'the advantage of rapidity, secrecy and surprise . . . and become . . . tainted with the inherent weaknesses of a true attack'.[7]

Instead, the object of the exercise was 'the containing power that lies in combined expeditions, and of the disturbing influence which a fleet properly used can exercise upon Continental strategy'. By continually threatening raids up and down the French Atlantic coast the Royal Navy, argued Corbett, forced the French to station large bodies of troops in the vulnerable areas and so considerably hampered their campaigns in Westphalia against Frederick the Great. Even the ill-managed Rochefort affair of 1757 caused the flower of the French army to march west and not east.[8] In fact there is some doubt whether this strategy did have the diversionary effect Pitt expected and Corbett claimed, but the idea was a familiar one before and after this time. A sequence of such raids caused Napoleon, then heavily engaged in his Austrian campaign, much aggravation: 'With 30 000 men in transports at the Downs, the English can paralyse 300 000 of my army, and that will reduce us to the rank of a second-class power'.[9] By such means as this a sea power like Britain could wield a strategic influence out of all proportion to the size of its army.

The maritime school proposed, however, that this kind of flexibility could be turned to even better account if the operations were directed not at vulnerable points on the continental coastline but at the enemy's most lucrative colonies and bases overseas. Henry Dundas, Secretary of War said in March 1801, 'I consider offensive tactics against the colonial possessions of our enemies as the first object to be attended to in almost every war in which Great Britain can be engaged'.[10] Such a campaign could serve a variety of purposes. It could help spread Britain's own empire, especially at a time when her most serious rivals were locked in mortal combat in the continent of Europe. This policy, declared Brodie 'explains how England, always a small country with weak armies, gained at the expense of the great military powers opposing her, an empire containing some of the most desirable regions of the earth'.[11]

More to the point as far as actually winning the war was concerned, it would deprive the enemy of considerable revenue – obviously a significant part of his war making capacity – and of useful bases for his navy and privateers. The strategic utility of these operations was a matter of controversy then and since. Mahan was sympathetic to them, Richmond was not. 'We can now see', wrote Richmond, 'that they did not produce the expected results on the course of the war as a whole and that the same efforts of the combined services extended in one or other of the European fronts would have been more profitable.'[12] All the same, such amphibious operations remained a prominent feature of European wars throughout the colonial period.

They served also a number of other more minor purposes. Sometimes they were mounted in order largely to seize places that would serve as bargaining counters at the subsequent peace negotiations. Sometimes they were mounted to boost the morale of the perpetrator and depress that of the victim. Coastal bombardments often came into this category too. While some had as their objective the systematic destruction of key points, others were short raiding bombardments done for the sake of being objectionable.

Lastly, amphibious operations have often been mounted for naval purposes; to seize, destroy or disable an enemy's naval base, or stop him getting one. During the eighteenth century, their larger purpose was occasionally to force an adversary (usually France) into such preparations for land warfare that it could offer less of a maritime threat. Said the Duke of Newcastle: 'France will outdo us at sea when they have nothing to fear on land. I have always maintained that our marine should protect our alliances on the Continent, and so, by diverting the expense of France, enable us to maintain our superiority at sea'.[13] Finally, as Corbett pointed out, an operation of this kind could sometimes be a way of forcing a reluctant enemy out to sea. General Wolfe (of Quebec fame) wrote of such a scheme and Corbett commented:

> The idea was absolutely sound. As a strategical device it is so obvious, so powerful, and so exactly suited to our peculiar resources, that the only wonder is it has so seldom been put in force. How many occasions could be counted when we have been baffled by our enemy assuming a naval defensive, and how seldom have we adopted clearly and resolutely this simple means of seeking out the enemy's fleet and destroying it.[14]

The British had such hopes in various of their schemes for the attacks on the German coast in the early part of the First World War, and so in a modified way, did the Germans with their East-Coast raids.

Whatever their purpose, operations against the shore were difficult to mount successfully and the maritime strategists had much advice to offer on this. They required at least, what Corbett described as, 'reasonable naval preponderance' in the relevant area. Roskill declared, 'It is plain that the establishment of an adequate and effective zone of maritime control in the approaches to and the coastal waters off the disembarcation area is an absolute pre-requisite for success in this type of operation'.[15]

The task of navies was to 'cover' the force against hostile interception from the enemy main fleet as it crossed the sea.[16] This cover would be 'full' if protection were the first priority; if not the cover might be merely 'general'. The 'squadron in charge of transports' would protect the force from more local and minor attack. It was generally thought to be absolutely essential to keep these two functions separate; the covering fleet had to be left free for independent naval action. Admiral Persano's dreadful fate at the Battle of Lissa was an object lesson of what happened to those who disregarded this rule. When the Austrians arrived, wrote Corbett, 'Persano was unable to disentangle a sufficient force in time to meet attack, and having no compact squadron fit for independent naval action, he was decisively defeated by the inferior enemy'.[17]

High levels of training and preparation were necessary for the task of shipping the Army over, disembarking them, offering military support and keeping them supplied. The lesson appeared to be that neither the skills nor the equipment for this specialised and demanding task could be improvised at the drop of a hat. This of course was equally true of the military side of the operation. Forethought was supremely necessary, declared Richmond: 'For want of thinking ahead, expeditions have suffered and sometimes failed because the necessary means were lacking – bombarding vessels to assist the landings, adequate shipping to carry the army, properly designed landing craft, maps and charts of the localities, knowledge of the climate'.[18]

It was particularly important that the expedition be free from the 'corrupting blight' of inter-service frictions. The army and navy should operate, thought Corbett, as 'two lobes of one brain, each self-contained and instinct with its own life and law, yet inseparable from the other: neither moving except by joint and unified impulse'. Above all, perhaps, 'the object they desire to obtain shall be clear in the minds both of those who order and those who command the operation.'[19]

Nations would only be able to indulge in amphibious warfare if they had secure home frontiers, declared Mahan. Bases near the scene of operations were essential too, he thought.[20] Surprise and speed of operation were particularly important as well, because the attacker would inevitably be dangerously exposed if the enemy knew where he meant to come ashore and was able to rush in reinforcements earlier. The Navy could help here. By demonstrations in various other places and a policy of calculated deception, it could keep the enemy in suspense until the very last moment. It could also help the army avoid strong points. All in all, secrecy, forethought and clarity of purpose were vital.

The requirements of success could sometimes be seen most clearly in their absence. Many of them, thought Richmond, were all too evident in the Dardanelles campaign of 1915:

Wrecked upon the rock of opposition to diversionary action. . . . Every principle that had governed the old strategists in the use of the forces of the country and of the tacticians who employed them was reversed. Continental campaigns took the place of diversionary amphibian operations, ships were expected to attack and overcome forts, secrecy was cast to the winds, for swift execution was substituted slow assembly. The enemy was given both warning of the attack and time to make his dispositions to repel it. . . . An operation which should have been 'amphibious' from the start was begun, against all teaching of experience, as a purely naval one; and the results were disastrous.[21]

The bitter experience of the Dardanelles campaign, together with a tendency to ignore the very successful German assault on Oesel and some other islands in the Baltic in 1917, fuelled general expectations of difficulty about amphibious warfare as the Second World War approached. It was widely believed that the advent of submarines, mines and aircraft had greatly increased the hazards of this type of operation. This was especially true the bigger the operations were. The internal combustion engine and much improved land communications seemed also likely to strengthen the hand of the defender vis-à-vis his assailant.

For all that, as Brodie observed, 'the Second World War has seen a succession of sea-borne invasions on such a scale as the world has never before witnessed'.[22] Gorshkov put it into figures: he arrived at a grand total of 600 landings in the war, or an average of one every three days. And what is more, nearly all of them were successful.

They came in two varieties – large scale invasions of major strategic significance like Norway, the Japanese operations in the Philippines and the East Indies, the landings in the Mediterranean area, Normandy and the great sequence of landing operations in the Pacific campaign. There were also the countless operations at what Gorshkov called the tactical operational level, such as those for instance on the Eastern front. Cumulatively, this and other forms of naval support exerted much influence on events. Admiral Ruge declared, 'The exercise of sea power in the closed Black Sea and the Sea of Azov had a considerable effect on the operations on land and may have saved the Soviets from complete defeat'.[23]

Amphibious warfare exceeded pre-war expectations for a variety of reasons. The strategic circumstances of the war, which separated many of the adversaries by expanses of water, obviously had much to do with it. Also the new technology of naval assault seemed to enable the sea-borne attacker to pose a much more substantial threat than ever before to the land defender, and that not least because of the advent of air power. Admiral Nimitz reported:

The development between World Wars I and II of naval aviation provided naval forces with a striking weapon of vastly increased flexibility, range and power. It spearheaded our Pacific attack. First, it swept the sea of all naval opposition. Then it became the initial striking weapon in the capture of Guam, Saipan and Iwo Jima. . . . In all these operations the employment of air–sea forces demonstrated the ability of the Navy to concentrate aircraft strength at any desired point in such numbers as to overwhelm the defence at the point of contact. These operations demonstrate the capability of naval carrier-based aviation to make use of the principles of mobility and concentration to a degree possessed by no other force.[24]

(b) Defence against invasion

The respective roles of the army and the navy in the defence of the country against invasion were the subject of a long and heated debate in nineteenth-century Britain, the process and outcome of which debate have already been touched on.[25] In brief, the army argued that there was a fundamental unreliability about the possibilities of naval defence which meant that the country needed strong defences behind the shore line. General Lord Wolseley commented in 1896,

> I know of nothing that is more liable to disaster and danger than anything that floats on the water. We often find in peace and in the calmest weather our best ironclads running into each other. We find great storms dispersing and almost destroying some of the finest fleets that ever sailed. Therefore, it is essentially necessary that it should always have a powerful Army, at least sufficiently strong to defend our own shores.[26]

The Royal Navy, of course, rejected all this. A strong fleet, they thought and had always thought, should so dominate the sea around the country that all but the smallest raids would certainly be intercepted and destroyed. Lord St. Vincent declared, ninety years earlier, 'I do not say the French cannot come, I only say they cannot come by sea.'[27]

Maritime strategists proposed what was in effect a whole system of naval defence. The maintenance of command (either by a restless pursuit of decisive victory or by blockade) was the first line against invasion. In the case of Britain, no enemy would even try to send invasion forces through waters commanded by the defending fleet. If the enemy fleet had command, on the other hand, they would not need to invade. An enemy in this happy position could bring Britain to submission far more quickly by an attack on her shipping. In the nature of things, therefore, argued Corbett, an invasion of this country could only take place over an essentially uncommanded sea. In this case, a fleet-in-being strategy might be of some use, as we have seen. Generally, though, the maintenance of high-level command would defend the country, or any of its overseas possessions, from assault by deterring the adversary from launching it in the first place.

In many cases the best way of doing this would be by a series of the kind of spoiling attacks launched by Drake before the sailing of the Armada. Drake urged this policy as a means of putting into her Majesty and her people courage and boldness not to fear any invasion in her own country, but to seek God's enemies and her Majesty's where they may be found.... With fifty sail of shipping we shall do more good upon their own coasts than a great many more will do here at home; and the sooner we are gone the better we shall be able to impeach them.[28]

Hence the very successful raid on Cadiz in 1587.

This forward and active policy stood in strong contrast to the views of those advocating what became known as the 'fortress fleet' strategy. These ideas have had a frequent currency, especially in countries with weaker naval forces, such as Italy and the United States in nineteenth century and the Soviet Union after the Revolution. These alternative ideas were best explored by the Soviet New School in the late 1920s and onwards. The war task of the navy was defined thus by Chief Commissar Mucklevitch in 1930:

In war, the fleet would accompany the army during its advance and it would not be guided in its activities by lessons drawn from the study of the Battle of Jutland, because it would not seek to solve its problems by an open sea encounter with the enemy's fleet, but would carry on a 'small war' relying on minefields, submarines and naval aircraft.

Russian naval strength, in other words, should not be concentrated in a few large units, but diffused amongst a host of minor ones. The resultant 'mosquito fleet' could mount an ever more intensive and ferocious attack on an enemy invasion fleet the closer it approached the shores of Russia. Aided by modern technology, the Soviet New School hoped to conduct their war at sea on lines quite novel in maritime strategy. 'Down with doctrines of the command of the sea!'[29] concluded one of their mentors, A. P. Alexandrov, in rousing fashion.

Orthodox strategists were very scathing about this kind of thinking. Lord St. Vincent said in 1805, 'Our great reliance is on the vigilance and activity of our cruisers at sea any reduction in the number of which by applying them to guard our ports, inlets and beaches would in my judgement tend to our destruction'. For this reason, he objected to plans to produce a large defensive flotilla of gunboats and small coastal craft and to back them up with 'sea-fencibles' on shore.[30] Mahan was equally critical of this whittling away of the navy. He wrote:

The navy's proper office in offensive action, results as certainly in battleships as the defensive idea does in small vessels. Every proposal to use a navy as an instrument of pure passive defence is found faulty upon particular examination... the effectual function of the fleet is to take the offensive.[31]

If the enemy was nevertheless able and willing to persist in sending an invasion fleet over an uncommanded sea, he had two choices. He could either put all his forces together, battlefleet and transports, and fight his way through, if necessary; or he could split the two up and use his battlefleet to lure the British away and then send his transports over in their absence.

In either case, it was the task of the Royal Navy to hinder the 'quiet passage to England' of the enemy and the maritime strategists had much advice to offer on how to do it. Discovering the enemy's intentions was an obvious advantage – hence the necessity for close observation (perhaps by blockade). Corbett recommended holding back the attack until the enemy was 'hopelessly committed to an operation beyond his strength'. This might produce better results than a precipitate offensive.[32] Certainly, he declared, 'whether the expedition that threatens us be small or of invasion strength, the cardinal rule has always been that the transports and not the escort must be the primary objective of the fleet'.[33] Altogether, Corbett believed that the speed of modern intelligence and an increased capacity to catch and overwhelm an invasion convoy and escorts made the chances of successful interception at sea at least as good as they were before. And yet, in both world wars the majority of invasions succeeded in reaching their objectives safely: only a few were even partially intercepted at sea (Crete 1941, Coral Sea and Midway, for instance). Arguably, though, the fear that they would be intercepted, especially with the advent of air power, led to many other amphibious enterprises not being undertaken in the first place.

Most maritime strategists agreed, however, that some invasion forces might get through, especially if they were only small ones. For this reason, it was necessary to have a third and final line of naval defence, just off the coast. Admiral Pellew, in the period before Trafalgar, said,

> I see a triple naval bulwark composed of one fleet acting on the enemy's coast, of another consisting of heavier ships stationed in the Downs ready to act at a moment's notice, and a third close to the beach capable of destroying any part of the enemy's flotilla that should escape the vigilance of the other two branches of our defence'.[34]

The army would have an important place in this third line as well.

Of course, the navy's task was by no means over if the enemy did, after all, effect a landing and consolidate himself. In this case, by harassing his maritime communications, the navy would hinder his every movement, or even oblige him to withdraw. Richmond noted an example of this: 'Korea, when invaded by Hideyoshi in 1592, was saved by investment of the Japanese army, the Korean navy cutting off its communications and investing it, forcing it thereby to evacuate the country'.[35] Orthodox maritime strategists believed that the obvious implication of all this was that the Navy should be regarded as the 'wooden walls of England' – the prime means of defence for this or any other maritime nation.

(c) The attack of maritime communications

Activities against, or in support of, the ability to use the sea as a means of transportation of men and goods have always been a considerable feature of naval conflict. In both world wars, assault on the enemy's merchant shipping took its place in a spectrum of activities which ranged from disruptive pre-emption of vital raw materials, at one end of the scale, to strategic bombing at the other. Although, like all these related activities, the attack of maritime communications was primarily intended to damage the enemy's war economy, it also often took a more direct part in the support of military operations on shore. The Russian campaign to interfere with the German army's sea-borne logistics had an obvious and intentional effect on the progress of the war on the Eastern Front.

Tidy distinctions between indirect economic and direct military operations were also blurred by the fact that amphibious operations have frequently had 'economic' objectives, as in the case of the British assault on the French West Indies in the eighteenth century and the German invasion of Norway in 1940. Since, as one commentator has noted recently, 'the military and commercial uses of the sea form a continuum'[36], elaborate distinctions between various kinds of 'sea use' frequently appear artificial and unhelpful. For this reason, attack on maritime communications will be taken to cover activities ranging from the imposition of a commercial blockade, at one extreme, to the disruption of an army's maritime supply lines, at the other.

A *guerre de course*, on the other hand, was directed just at the enemy's shipping. Its advocates pointed out that wars were frequently about trade anyway. 'What matter this or that reason?' demanded General-at-Sea, George Monk. 'What we want is more of the trade which the Dutch now have.' In the case of the Dutch wars, therefore, attacking the enemy's merchant shipping seemed to make obvious and practical sense.

Furthermore, it seemed a particularly logical course for the weaker naval side to adopt. So much so, in fact, that Corbett argued: 'A plan of war which has the destruction of trade for its primary object implies in the party using it an inferiority at sea. Had he superiority, his object would be to convert that superiority to a working command by battle or blockade'.[37] As Fred T. Jane pointed out, by accepting conventional operations, the weaker side would be forced into 'inevitable and rapid defeat, whereas by a *guerre de course* it prolongs operations very considerably and knows that before going under it will do some damage'. A few years later on, Germany's Admiral Hipper echoed these sentiments exactly with his notion that 'carrying out of cruiser war with the battle cruisers of the Atlantic remains the one way in which our High Seas fighting ships can damage the enemy and thereby justify their existence'.[38]

One of the most celebrated examples of the *guerre de course* began in 1693 with a French attack on a huge outgoing Smyrna convoy. The French Navy adopted this policy when their defeat at the Battle of the Hogue had ruined their chances of securing sufficient command of the sea to invade England. (This pattern of a defeat on the high seas leading to an *increased* threat to the security of the victor's merchant shipping is surprisingly common). Raiding squadrons of cruisers and privateers operating out of such ports as Dunkirk inflicted great damage on English shipping. Such exponents of the *guerre de course* as the redoubtable Jean Bart, Forbin, DuGuay-Trouin (and later Surcouf) established something of a tradition in the French Navy. Their ideas subsequently found expression in the philosophy of the Jeune Ecole, and were also taken up in some guise or other by a number of weaker navies such as the Russian Navy of the nineteenth century and the German Navy of the twentieth century.

The object of the exercise was usually the inflicting of damage rather than economic ruin. Apart from the physical destruction of intrinsically valuable cargoes, attacks on merchant shipping would push up marine insurance and freight costs. It might force its victim to cut back on certain commercial activities, allowing neutrals to take over his place and so injuring his long-term trading prospects. Altogether, a *guerre de course* would diminish the revenue and credit available for running the war. Since these were, in Mahan's term, the 'sinews of war', such an attack could be of considerable strategic significance. This was certainly the aspiration of the British in their attacks on the bullion convoys of the Spanish in the sixteenth century and of the French in the seventeenth and eighteenth centuries. Richmond wrote:

It was the convinced opinion that the stoppage of the treasure from the New World would serve effectively to cripple the power of the Bourbon allies to conduct the war... contemporary opinion ... both in England and France undoubtedly regarded the silver and gold as the essential raw materials of war.[39]

However, technological advance seemed to make the maritime nations more dependent on overseas supplies than once they were, and so more vulnerable to an assault on their maritime communications. At the same time the advent of aircraft and the submarine increased the lethality of the attack. Not merely economic damage, but ruin and starvation could then be a realistic aspiration for the practitioners of the *guerre de course*. Such was the object of the German campaign against the British in both world wars and of the US Navy against Japan in the second.

Maritime strategists of a more orthodox persuasion have usually been very sceptical about these claims. Corbett criticised Hawkins' ideas of such a war against Spain as a notion 'so often proved fatal and so often reborn as a new strategical discovery that a naval war may be conducted on economical principles and a great power be brought to its knees by preying on its commerce without first getting command of the sea'. Mahan was equally unimpressed by the efforts of the commerce destroyers in the Dutch wars. Unless properly supported, the cruiser 'can only dash out hurriedly, a short distance from home, and its blows, though painful, cannot be fatal'. Interestingly, Raoul Castex was particularly scathing about the ideas of the Jeune Ecole, his own countrymen. He believed that the *guerre de course* needed the support of the *guerre militaire* to effect a decision. Employed by itself, an offensive directed against communications and commerce would fail. The submarine warfare on commerce of 1914–18 failed because the support of a surface force was wanting. The master of the surface would always dominate essential surface communications: an offensive by submarines would not overcome that preponderance unless it was accompanied by surface action to dispute command. Gorshkov made exactly the same point of the German submarine campaign of the Second World War.[40]

Among the reasons for scepticism about the possibilities of the *guerre de course* was the idea that it would have to be unacceptably barbaric in execution in order to succeed, especially in the age of the submarine. De Lanessan declared:

These people forget to what reprisals the country would expose itself! Where are the commanders of our cruisers, destroyers etc. who would, except under the most imperative orders, do such dreadful work? Where is the Minister with so little regard for the honour and interest of his country who would give such orders?[41]

More to the point, possibly, sceptics argued that the maritime resources of a great sea power were so enormous that only the most sustained campaign against them could hope to succeed. And a substantial campaign most certainly needed the support of a substantial battlefleet.

> Where the revenues and industries of a country can be concentrated into a few treasure ships, like the flota of Spanish galleons, the sinew of war may perhaps be cut at a stroke; but when its wealth is scattered in thousands of going and coming ships, when the roots of the system spread far and wide, and strike deep, it can stand many a cruel shock and lose many a goodly bough without the life being touched. Only by military command of the sea by prolonged control of the strategic centres of commerce, can such an attack be fatal; and such control can be wrung from a powerful navy only by fighting and overcoming it.

So wrote Mahan, and Corbett agreed with this.[42]

It was no coincidence, the argument continued, that the more the *guerre de course* was supported by the conventional operations of naval war the more it tended to succeed. One reason why the *guerre de course* did so well after the Battle of La Hogue was because the fleet-in-being strategy pursued by the French at the same time prevented the British from protecting their convoys adequately against squadrons of commerce raiders.

It seemed to follow on from this that conventional naval operations in fact offered the best hope of success in the campaign to cut the other side's maritime communications. This aim was best achieved, thought Mahan, by 'the possession of that overbearing power on the sea which drives the enemy's flag from [the sea], or allows it to appear only as a fugitive'.[43] After all, it was Cromwell's main fleet, not his commerce raiders, which destroyed Dutch trade and made grass grow in the streets of Amsterdam.

The imposition of a commercial blockade was the supremely effective way of destroying the enemy's maritime commerce. Wrote Mahan, in one of his most celebrated passages:

> Amid all the pomp and circumstance of the war which for ten years to come desolated the Continent, amid all the tramping to and fro over Europe of the French armies and their auxiliary legions, there went on unceasingly that noiseless pressure upon the vitals of France, that compulsion, whose silence, when once noted, becomes to the observer the most striking and awful mark of the working of Sea Power.[44]

The British commercial blockade, argued its proponents, could devastate the enemy's war economy because, in Richmond's phrase, it strikes at the root, where sporadic warfare hacks only at the branches.[45] Although a most effective form of war, commercial blockade was generally held to be far more humane than mere plundering. For both these reasons the sea powers must be allowed to keep their traditional rights to interfere with the enemy's shipping in this way. The maritime strategists were anxious that their governments, alarmed about the *guerre de course*, might agree to make *all* forms of trade attack illegal. Because it did not attract attention in the same way as did dramatic battles on the high sea, there was a tendency for politicians and electorates to lose sight of the importance of commercial blockade. In fact, by following this policy, said Corbett, 'we exercise the highest form of injuring [the enemy] which the command of the sea can give us'.[46]

It was implied in their arguments that commercial blockades of the kind waged by the British against Napoleon actually did do decisive harm to the enemy's war economy. Historically, this is a difficult point to decide. There was no doubt that the British blockade of the First World War, for example, was one of the most effective of its kind. Bernard Acworth wrote, 'The expulsion from the sea of every German merchant vessel for four years provides perhaps the most striking demonstration of sea power that has ever been presented to the world'.[47] Germany's import and export trade with the outside world was choked: by 1918 it had fallen to one seventh of what it had been in 1913. There were severe internal shortages which naval writers had little hesitation in ascribing to the effects of the blockade. Russel Grenfell wrote, 'A German is said to have remarked that Germany collapsed, not because Germans were weary of eating rats, but because they could no longer put up with rat substitute'.[48] Social distress, disorders, military collapse and eventual defeat followed with awful inexorability. The Germans themselves at the time certainly had little doubt that the British blockade was a principal agency of their woes.

It is difficult to check the validity of these views because the effects of blockade in the First World War were so entangled with other things. The shortage of food in Germany, for example, so often ascribed to the activities of the Royal Navy, was due as much to the neglect of agriculture caused by the flow of men to the trenches. The effectiveness of commercial blockade was plainly a matter of degree, depending on a number of factors: the extent to which the country was dependent on external supplies; the ability to provide home-produced substitutes; the attitude of neutrals; its access to other land areas; the extent to which the blockade could exploit geography; the length of the conflict. When the circumstances were right, as they were for the 1914–18 campaign against Germany and even more for the equivalent campaign against Japan in the Second World War, the commercial blockade could indeed become an effective contribution to victory. Even so, the fact that Germany was able to launch a mass offensive in the spring of 1918 which nearly succeeded indicated that great as its effects were, they fell short of being decisive. The prospects were considerably worse for a blockade against Germany in the Second World War – an indication of the extent to which a land power could make itself impervious to the attentions of a sea power.

So far in this section, the attack on maritime communications has been treated as an end in itself, but naval writers of all persuasions have pointed out that it could be a means to other desirable ends. Attacking the enemy's trade could, for instance, be a means of defending one's own. It could also be a precondition, as Corbett noted, for a maritime power's ability to fight a limited war in distant places; such battle-grounds had to be isolated so the enemy could not turn the scales by sending in troop reinforcements. It could, of course, be a means of achieving battle with a reluctant adversary; 'such pressure', wrote Corbett, 'might be the only means of forcing the decision we seek'.[49] In some circumstances a *guerre de course* might be the only means of producing a sufficient 'displacement of forces' for a weaker navy ever to have a hope of defeating a stronger one. 'Commerce destroying', thought de Lanessan, could be 'a strategic means to compel our rivals to disperse their ships over the world, so as to lessen the difference in strength which exists between their forces and ours in European waters'.[50] Some such ideas certainly animated various leaders of Germany's navy a few years later.

Of course, the value of these strategic devices ultimately depended on the success of the other naval activities they led to. But, although they were indirect and conditional, the possible strategic consequences of attack on the enemy's maritime communications could be at least as great as those deriving from any direct tally of ships sunk and cargoes lost.

(d) The defence of maritime communications

It was entirely appropriate that Mahan, who named his pet dog after the great Swiss strategist Jomini, should believe like him that 'communications dominate war'. An ability to use the sea as a means of transportation was, he thought, 'the very root of a nation's vigour'. Although he modified his views a little later, he believed that 'the necessity of a navy . . . springs, therefore, from the existence of a peaceful shipping, and disappears with it'. As far as Mahan and most other naval writers were concerned, the attack and defence of maritime communications lay at the heart of maritime strategy.[51]

Because it was arguably the most important function of naval power, it generated a great deal of discussion, especially at times when new technology or new philosophies – such as that propounded by the Jeune Ecole – threatened to turn all established ideas and techniques upside down. The controversy about competing methods of trade protection was particularly bitter and spotted a good many otherwise unblemished reputations.

Sir John Colomb is generally applauded for raising the importance of protecting Britain's maritime communications in the first place; he is also vilified for introducing with his 'Imperial water roads' the pernicious notion of the sea lane. Mahan certainly, and even Richmond to an extent, are often accused of underestimating the importance of trade protection relative to other tasks. Even Corbett, that model of calm good sense, strayed from the straight and narrow with his ambiguous rejection of the idea of convoy, and is therefore held responsible, at least to some degree, for the capital British errors in trade protection of the First World War.[52] All in all, trade protection seems almost as dangerous and difficult a business to write about in peacetime as it is to carry out in war.

Sometimes, though, critics forget, in their enthusiam, that the protection of maritime communications was a multi-dimensional activity. There was no single solution to the problem, and few simple answers. Time and again it has been found necessary to adopt a number of complementary defensive strategies and the maritime strategists have all recognised this to be the case. The general validity of their arguments and the various differences between them are essentially matters of degree and emphasis. They stand out from each other only in that they advocate different mixtures of the same ingredients.

Mahan, for instance, has been criticised for the relative stress that he put on command of the sea as the essential recondition for the successful defence of maritime communications. In brief, his argument was that the degree of control that followed a victory in battle, or the successful imposition of an effective blockade, would prevent most raiders getting out anyway and would also provide essential cover for the flotillas protecting commerce against the relatively few that did. In the view of a later generation (Richmond, Castex and Rosinski) the First World War showed just how true this proposition was.

The point was made by Richmond to a committee of enquiry on battleship construction in 1921:

> The small craft acting as escorts, patrols or hunting were able to operate freely . . . solely by virtue of the cover afforded by the Grand Fleet. If an earthquake had closed the mouth of Scapa Flow and the fleet had been shut up inside, there would have been nothing to prevent heavy German ships in company with lighter vessels from going out to sea and sweeping away all the small vessels that constituted the defence of trade.

Rosinski agreed; with the High Seas Fleet safely blockaded, convoy escorts had only to deal with the submarines that found their way out of the North Sea. Their task would have been impossible had they had to guard against significant surface attack as well. The trials and tribulations of the Scandinavian convoys, which had to sail in front of the blockade line, were a dreadful indication of what would have happened more widely had it not been for the general cover offered by the Grand Fleet. German submarines would also have been much more effective than they were, had their navy secured command.[53]

A working command was also the precondition for the device of dealing with raiders at sea by attacking their bases. As Richmond observed, this policy (usually described in such bucolic metaphors as 'stopping the earths' or 'stamping out nests') was a traditional feature of British trade protection. It was so much more effective than the mounting of general patrols in open waters. 'Those who advocate the small cruisers on patrol,' wrote Fred T. Jane, 'are really no more logical than he who would suggest that instead of destroying the nest, individual hornets should be slain on the wing.'[54] Of course, nest stamping was much easier with a preliminary command of the sea.

All this being so, there was a natural order in naval proceedings, it seemed. Sir John Colomb declared:

The primary business of our war fleet is to destroy, capture or contain in ports, the enemy's warships. Until the work is done, all thought of applying the navy to the direct protection of commerce must be abandoned. To what extent our shipping and commerce may suffer in the interval between the outbreak of war and the completion of the Navy's real business, will depend upon previous arrangements made for, and carried out by, our Mercantile Marine itself.

A rather similar point was made by Richmond in connection with Tromp's operational priorities in the first Dutch war:

Was the previous experience to be repeated and the fleet again to have the dual service of fighting the enemy and protecting a merchant fleet? Tromp and the greater seamen were in no doubt that one thing should be done at a time. The merchantmen should 'lie still and not stir outward or homeward while the English are strong at sea but expect [wait] till our ships first go to encounter the English and either beat them or drive them into their harbours, which being done our merchantmen may then securely go and come with small convoys'. This doctrine of trade defence could hardly be better summarised.[55]

In fact, circumstances forced Admiral Tromp to use his 80 men-of-war to escort a 200-ship merchant convoy. For a whole set of reasons, the theoretical order of events has had to be much amended in practice.

Often the damage done to trade was too high simply to be ignored until the fleet's 'main Work' was completed. An elusive enemy was frequently able to postpone battle for far too long or even cancel it altogether. Blockades (especially of the distant variety) usually proved unable to stop large numbers of commerce raiders sneaking past.

In these circumstances, an over-rigid adherence to the necessities of command could, and did, make it more difficult to strike the required balance between direct and indirect measures of trade defence. Since naval resources (ships, men, time on station) were finite, there was inevitably rivalry between these two kinds of response to trade attack – as the frequent complaints of Nelson and Jellicoe about shortages of flotilla craft indicated. An over emphasis on the needs of securing command, therefore, could easily mean not enough emphasis on the difficult business of exercising it.

The point was also made that advocates of the orthodox approach sometimes not only exaggerated the effectiveness of command in trade protection but also, in a curious way, set their sights too high and aimed at a level of command that was unneccessarily ambitious and expensive. As Admiral Gretton argued, the Mediterranean campaign of 1941–3 demonstrated that wide and permanent areas of control were welcome but not essential. The Mediterranean was a disputed sea, but both sides were able to use it. They funneled through convoys as needed, their tracks crossing each other at right angles, 'fortunately without collision', Gretton added drily. This showed that it was only strictly necessary to maintain temporary control of a moving zone 'of water in which the ships float, as well as the air above and the depths below'.[56] Anything more than that was vanity, and did not warrant taking flotilla craft away from direct trade protection tasks.

Hardly less controversial than this was the emphasis given the idea of patrolled sea lanes, hunting groups and protected focal areas. The idea was that maritime communications should best be controlled by warships patrolling 'the ocean paths which connect one part of an extensive empire with another, which sea-borne commerce must traverse, and along which belligerent expeditions must proceed'. This kind of maritime highway patrol would be supplemented by hunting groups intent on 'the dogging, hunting down, and destruction of every enemy cruiser. The dogging to continue, if necessary, to the world's end'.[57] Patrolling and hunting would concentrate particularly on terminal areas for as Corbett said: 'Where the carcase is, there will the eagles be gathered together!' Raiders would find their targets more easily here than on the high seas and that is where they, in their turn, should be sought. As the battle for each focal point was won, and command extended outwards, there would gradually be built up a chain of sanctuaries straddling the world.

Critics of this scheme, however, pointed out that in the twentieth century it simply did not work. Dispersing potential convoy escorts in hunting or patrolling groups achieved little in the way of ships saved or submarines lost. It was often wearisome in the extreme and frequently disastrously costly – as the loss of the carrier *Courageous* and the near-miss on the *Ark Royal* in the early days of the Second World War demonstrated. It also meant countless missed opportunities of saving merchant ships and sinking submarines where the real action was – with the convoys.

Although the practice resembled nothing so much as slamming shut the doors of one empty stable after another, it proved amazingly resilient. It was the standard procedure for most of the First World War and it led to such episodes as the celebrated second Battle of Portland in September 1916 when three U-boats operated in the waters between Beachy Head and the Eddystone Light, an area dominated by the great naval bases at Portsmouth, Portland and Plymouth. Forty-nine destroyers, forty-eight torpedo boats, seven Q-ships and several hundred armed auxiliaries creamed the seas white with their furious activity; the air above was loud with the patrols of numerous aircraft. And yet, the U-boats sank thirty merchant ships in one week and escaped unscathed. The hunting group fallacy reappeared in the next war. The British only really abandoned it in 1941; and the US Navy only followed suit after less than two dozen U-boats in the Western Atlantic had sunk one million tons of shipping in six months.[58]

There were two main reasons for this perversity. First there was the idea that hunting groups and patrols were 'offensive' and therefore 'better', a habit of mind that doubtless derived from a misreading of history, and from an imperfect understanding of the meaning of some of Nelson's more ear-catching sayings.

More seriously there was also the view that trade protection was essentially a matter of strategically defending sea highways and focal areas, in the same kind of way as an army did a road. The two problems were actually rather different. The sea, unlike the land, had no intrinsic value and so need neither be possessed nor guarded. All that mattered was what passed over it. As Admiral Gretton remarked, 'it is *ships* which must be protected, not lines drawn across charts',[59] and the deployment of flotilla craft should reflect this basic fact. Instead of guarding sea routes, therefore, one should escort merchant ships as they passed along them.

The origin of this misconception, according to its critics, was largely semantic. Sir John Colomb with his his 'Imperial water roads' had some responsibility for this, and so did Mahan, especially through his description of the sea as 'a wide common over which men may pass in all directions, but on which some well-worn paths show that controlling reasons have led them to choose certain lines of travel rather than others'.[60] As an illustrative analogy, reference to the paths, roads or highways of the sea – or the celebrated 'sea lanes' – probably does little harm. But as an operational concept, it brings disaster. Naval officers with such concepts had best be exorcised. The harm these phrases do explains why many naval writers prefer to avoid abstractions like maritime communications and talk about the 'protection of shipping' instead.[61]

One unfortunate result of this hunting attitude of mind was a predisposition to be unsympathetic to the traditional convoy-and-escort concept of trade protection. These doubts were bolstered from other directions as well. Ship time lost in the assembly of convoys, and the rush at ports when several hundred merchantmen arrived at once was commercially expensive: it often paid for 'runners' to break away early so as to reach port before the rest of the convoy arrived. There were also considerable doubts about whether the merchantmen had either the skill or the discipline to keep their station in convoy. 'They behaved as all convoys that ever I saw,' said Nelson, 'shamefully ill; parting company every day.'[62]

It was widely believed that all this was even more true in the steam age, when interference with the peacetime movement of shipping was costly in the extreme, when the smoke of many funnels would reveal the presence of convoys to all and sundry and when individual ships with wireless and a wider choice of routes could hide so much more easily. In 1911 Corbett wrote, 'It now becomes doubtful whether the additional security which convoys afforded is sufficient to outweigh their economical drawbacks and their liability to cause strategical disturbance.'[63]

For such reasons there was always a temptation to abandon convoy-and-escort when the slightest excuse offered, or to modify its operation. In 1940, for instance, ships sailing at up to 14.9 knots were organised into convoy but faster ships were allowed to proceed independently. Towards the end of that year, this limit was reduced so there would be more independents – increasing delivery rates thereby; the experiment failed dismally. Precautions were relaxed too in 1943 in the Indian Ocean, with the same results. Roskill wrote, 'It seems incredible that the hardly learned lessons of the Atlantic battle were thus regarded as inapplicable to the Indian Ocean: and that the old heresy of the hunting group should have been revived at this late date and in defiance of so much previous experience'.[64]

Continuous changes in maritime technology and commercial practice not withstanding, convoy-and-escort has in fact remained – despite hunting, patrolling, the arming of merchantmen, evasive routing, Q-ships, and the like, all of which have their place – the best and principal means of trade protection for centuries. Even in terms of hard economy convoy has always made sense. This is shown by the fact that differential rates for marine insurance (another vital dimension of the trade protection task) were usually offered convoy ships and 'runners'. Market forces also pushed merchant ships into convoy.

Not only the desirability of convoy but even its tactics have remained substantially the same. In 1794, for instance, these were described in the following terms:

> To take the requisite case of a large fleet, there should be in the convoy a number of frigates, which are to be distributed ahead, astern and on the wings of the fleet, which is always to be kept in the order of convoy on three, four, five or six columns, according to the number it may be composed of: some other frigates are also to be sent on the look-out, in order to be informed of what passes at a certain distance, and warned in good time of the enemy's approach. . . . The men of war are to hold themselves in order of convoy a little ahead and to windward of the weather column of the fleet; because, in that position, they will be able with promptitude to attend wherever their presence may be necessary.
>
> . . . The degree of progress which the whole fleet will make will be regulated by that of the worst-going ships, which, however, are to be abandoned when found to cause too great a loss of time; for, sometimes, it is better to risk a small loss than to expose the whole by delay.[65]

If some references to air escort and intelligence were included, this would be a more than recognisable description of the tactics of Atlantic convoy in the Second World War.

Convoy made sense for two basic reasons. First, it offered the individual merchantmen the greatest mathematical chance of escaping detection and attack altogether – even if they were totally unescorted. Grenfell wrote:

> If we assume a ship to be visible at sea from ten miles away a vessel on the ocean will be represented by a visibility circle of ten miles radius, which visibility circle will move along with the ship as she alters her position. If, say, twenty-five ships are pursuing separate tracks through an area out of sight of each other, they will present twenty-five separate ten-mile visibility circles moving through the area. Those twenty-five ships, if formed in convoy will, however, present a visibility circle of little more than one ship; perhaps one of twelve miles radius. . . . It can . . . be seen that the chances of a convoy being sighted by hostile warships are very much smaller than of a similar number of ships sailing separately.[66]

Even if a raider did spot a large convoy, most of the ships would be able to escape, while it was dealing with an unfortunate one or two of their number. This argument also demonstrates the falsity of the proposition raised from time to time that convoys could not be organised because there were too few escorts to look after them, and also puts into its proper perspective the notion that large convoys placed too many eggs in one basket.

Secondly, convoy conversely also offered the best chance of finding, destroying and neutralising commerce raiders. It was, as Mahan pointed out, the best way of 'wisely applying the principle of concentration of effort to the protection of commerce'. He went on:

In fact, as the small proportionate loss inflicted by scattered cruisers appears to indicate the inclusiveness of that mode of warfare, so the result of the convoy system, in this and other instances, warrants the inference that, when properly systematised and applied, it will have more success as a defensive measure than hunting for individual marauders – a process which, even when most thoroughly planned, still resembles looking for a needle in a haystack.[67]

Later on, Richmond pointed out that Mahan derived this view merely from the experience of sailing-ship warfare, but it was eternally right nonetheless. 'Instruments alter, principles remain: a fact which those who so loosely talk of the new weapons – the submarine, the aircraft, and the mine – having "revolutionised" warfare would be wise to bear in mind.'[68] This remark is of interest in view of the widespread notion that, however interesting the experience of the past, 'It's all different now'.

7 A New Environment for Navies?

Maritime strategy has never been determined in a vacuum but always in a real world of constantly changing conditions. The works of the great naval writers like Mahan and Corbett can be seen, in fact, as a record of the way in which maritime strategy has adapted to those changes. But the extent of environmental change occasionally seemed to require something more drastic than mere adaptation; it seemed to call for some concepts to be totally discarded and others brought in to replace them. In modern conditions, the wisdom of past masters of the naval art might therefore be misleading, irrevelant or even downright dangerous, at least as a guide to present and future policy. This view has never been more widely held than it is now. Primarily it is a reaction to changes seen over the past generation or so in the political, economic, legal and technological environment of maritime strategy. The next step, therefore, must be briefly to consider these changes.

(a) The political environment (by Peter Nailor)

It is not so very long ago that applied force − which in its naval guise has so often been called 'gunboat diplomacy' − was a major instrument of foreign policy. This salience did not so much reflect a world that was inherently violent, as an international system composed of a smaller number of states than we have now, controlling or dominating a much larger number of dependencies, and having a range of military power which for the most part was traditional in its forms and purposes. The alternative methods of passing information, making threats or demonstrations, or inviting negotiation were relatively few in number; communications were less sure, less quick and in their public mode reached a much smaller audience; political and economic interdependence was less well developed and less complex; international conferences and organisations were less commonplace, and intelligence networks less pervasive. Subversion was less extensive, sport was less important, ballet companies stayed at home and neither the Eurovision song contest nor Radio Cairo existed. By comparison with the range of direct and indirect methods of influencing allies, adversaries and other

163

states which exists today, the international vocabulary of action was relatively limited; and the need to use it was relatively restricted to the mere handful of states who were in effect the managers of the system. The use, or the threat of the use, of force was a practical and legitimate tool of statecraft in a world where no one state was so powerful that its pretensions were incontestable.

But now, with all the changes in method that exist, and all the alternatives to military force that can be deployed, it seems that the utility, as well as the salience of applied force may have declined. Some of the most important reasons for this arise within domestic environments. The execution of an active foreign policy intention is affected by the confidence (and popularity, in democratic states) with which the objective of the intention is laid out. And confidence in turn is affected by the nature of the activity. Thus, in postwar Britain, it was more difficult for governments to take forceful initiatives in the period when it was a major objective of policy to concentrate British attention upon the European area and to relinquish mainland bases East of Suez. It was a period in which British power was on the decline; and there was very little doubt about the difficulties that faced Britain in trying to continue to find the resources that would have been needed 'to send a gun-boat'. In something of the same way, the post-Vietnam depression created, for a time, a similar disinclination on the part of the United States.

From some points of view, there was no logical reason why this should be so; foreign policy, like other state interests, is carried on at a number of levels, and particular interests may need to be supported even when the specific activity is not, in a general way, consonant with the drift of policy. But however carefully general principles may be articulated, the style of foreign policy is reactive; even the most powerful states cannot control the international environment and there is a general need to be able to respond to developments which may be unwelcome, and even unforeseen. What was more important however was the mood of the time: post-imperial nausea was debilitating and, for whatever reason, overseas adventuring was less popular. The costs had been counted, and found to be distasteful either because they were high, or because they were now rather more evident than before. This was particularly the case for the diplomacy of applied force, which attracted some criticism because, although its costs were fairly explicit, the benefits which accrued were indeterminate.

The fact of the matter was that a series of local bases in various parts of the world had provided an opportunity to engage in 'gunboat diplomacy', meeting a practical need for short response time, logistic support and so on, but which were difficult to attribute, in terms of cost. Naval forces were based on port X, not to be on call to deal with unforeseen emergencies, but because port X was (or had in the past been) important for some other purpose. If port X was no longer available for any reason, and a response to an unforeseen emergency still had to be made, it became more difficult to decide how to make an appropriate response from a distant, metropolitan base. It was not only more difficult to arrange, in the tactical sense, but also more costly still and more difficult politically: because the act of 'sending a gunboat' 5000 miles, to support an interest, seems to demonstrate a higher level of political determination than to send one 500 miles. It is the same sort of difference, qualitatively, that exists between having a local village constable who can, by his proximity, perhaps contain a brawl in a public house, and having to send a vanload of police from county headquarters. You send a vanload, because by the time they get to the scene of the brawl, it may have become a riot. You may not need to use them all, but you must face the possibility; because to commit an inadequate force which is overwhelmed is, in every sense, unaccept-able. Speed of response may in fact be a key factor, analytically in terms of deterrence, and politically in terms of the need to control events; and the perception of Western states that they were less-well able than in the past to provide themselves with reliable local bases undoubtedly contributed to the feeling that, because the application of implicit force was now more difficult to undertake effectively it was *therefore* somehow less useful. This feeling, however, was at odds with the contemporaneous growth of anxiety about the spread of Soviet naval activity. If 'gunboat diplomacy' really was not so useful, in helping to influence the hearts, minds and policies of other governments, why then should we be concerned if the Soviet Union began to dissipate its resources in so pointless a game?

The answer, of course, is complicated. Part of the United Kingdom case, at least, was related to the changing nature of the game. A British presence had been widely spread because of the fact of possession of widely spread colonies, and of the need to safeguard British interests and trading communications. But with the decline of empire and although it might well be desirable to offer to support the stability of a post-colonial regime by a defence treaty, it was also probably desirable not to maintain resident forces. The achievement of political freedom has to be manifested; even if political, social and economic ties remain close with the new state, the former colonial power – if it intends that the new regime should be reasonably independent – cannot continue to protect obtrusively. The *ethos* of struggle, so salient a part of many independence experiences, and so fundamental to the ideology of some independence movements, precludes too close co-operation with former proprietors. Actual practice varies: but the rhetoric has domi-nated the culture, to which most of the former colonial powers have, however unwillingly, come to subscribe.

This change in the functional ability of major states to use force in international disputes has been supported by the development of other policies and attitudes which affect the international community. The UNO provides both a forum and a set of norms about how international disputes should be contained. Attempts through arms control proposals to regulate military competition, and to limit the methods by which wars are waged, have also contributed something to our attitudes about the desirability of using force, actual or implied. The fact that wars still occur and that types of international behaviour vary widely do not, in one sense, affect the expectation that all states should conform to the highest possible standards; indeed, gross violations of these expectations are condemned by international opinion, however they may be justified by the needs, and explanations, of their perpetrators. The policies of even the most powerful states are, in a general way, constrained by these developments: not least in the sense that, if they need to use force instead of limiting themselves to the threat to use force, the choice must be a deliberate and – from their own perspective at least – justifiable decision; which may nevertheless attract disapproval and even retribution.

The super-powers are at least as much affected by these developments as other states. Indeed, one could argue that because the formality which has come to regulate their adversarial relationship in certain crucial areas has, as it were, spilled over to affect other issues, they have to be especially careful about what they do, and how they do it. Any show of force has a relevance to their bilateral concerns, partly because they are both, properly, sensitive to the possibility of miscalculation and partly because they both claim to have global sets of interests. Some of these interests are unlikely to spark off direct competition; but many could.

What is interesting here is the extent to which any clash of super-power interest has to be viewed as a separate type of activity, calling into play the concepts related to 'crisis management' rather than the 'rules of the game' in naval diplomacy for example as Dismukes and McConnell have called it. If that were indeed the case, then the calculations about what to do would be very complicated, right from the start. It is still open to one or other of them to back away from a direct and competitive response, but, if the challenge is accepted, a super-power competition in applied force is, *ex hypothesi* an activity in which the values and consequences can become of a significantly different order of intensity, unrelated perhaps to the intrinsic characteristics of the originating incident. The game changes, from chess to bridge; and the bid is doubled, and perhaps redoubled, even before the cards begin to be played.

(b) International law and maritime operations

(i) Before 1945 (by Bryan Ranft)
Attempts to diminish the loss of life and property in maritime war originated in the dual nature of the element. For belligerents the sea is a battle ground, for neutrals it is, in Mahan's terms, a wide common over which passes the trade essential to the well being of mankind. This duality has brought about a conflict not only between belligerents and neutrals but sometimes also between the trading interests of a country engaged in war and their own government. Such conflicts have been so important as to produce continuing attempts to resolve them by international agreement embodied in national and international law, designed to restrict naval activity destructive of civilian life and property.

These attempts have concentrated on searches for ways to establish the immunity of merchant ships, their crews and cargoes from the hazards of war. Some have seen these attempts as being based on humanitarianism. Others have regarded them as being designed to further the economic interests of neutrals. Governments of strong naval powers such as Britain, have seen them as unacceptable plans to deprive them of one of the most valuable fruits of sea power, the ability to bring economic pressure to bear on enemies of greater populations and resources. The attempts have centred on five main questions:

1. Is it possible for belligerents to agree to limit their maritime operations to naval vessels and to allow all merchant shipping to pass unscathed?
2. If such complete immunity is not possible, would it be practicable to limit attacks and seizures to those ships and cargoes directly contributing to an enemy's war effort?
3. If enemy merchant ships are to be subject to attack and capture, are any neutral cargoes they are carrying liable to seizure?
4. What is to be the position of neutral ships trading with an enemy? Are they to be as immune as neutral territory or can they be stopped, searched, and the offending goods seized?
5. Can there be circumstances in which a belligerent can legitimately claim that, in order to ensure national survival, he must cut off his enemy from all sea borne supplies to the extent of sinking all merchant ships, neutrals included, approaching enemy shores?

Technological developments in naval equipment during the twentieth century led to another set of problems. Acceptable rules on the treatment of intercepted merchant ships and their passengers and crews in the days when the only available weapons were relatively short-range guns, would invite the annihilation of the intercepting warship at the hands of submarines or aircraft; or, putting the problem in another way, if technical development has provided a belligerent with a weapons system, such as the submarine and its torpedoes, which cannot be effectively used against merchant shipping if it obeys the rules established before its introduction, can that nation be under an obligation to continue to accept such rules at the cost of diminishing its offensive power and putting its submarines and their crews at serious risk? From this situation there emerged the wider problems faced by Germany in particular during the world wars. Even if unrestricted attacks on merchant shipping inevitably leading to loss of civilian lives, including neutrals, are militarily justifiable, how can this be balanced against the equally inevitable moral denunciation and, even worse, the possibility of neutrals being won over to your enemy's side?

Technological development in the nineteenth and twentieth centuries changed not only the nature of combat at sea but also the very nature of war itself. It became no longer possible to think of it as involving only professional fighting men. Economic and industrial resources and their manpower were as important as the armed services and thus, arguably, legitimate objects of attack. The legal and moral dilemmas arising from this development assumed their most dramatic form in the aerial bombardments of industrial areas in the Second World War, but the fact that some countries, Britain chief among them, became literally dependent on merchant shipping for national survival, provided another possible justification for unrestricted maritime war aimed at destroying essential supplies, including food for industrial workers. Britain herself, as a maritime and strong naval power, saw the value of imposing a sea-based economic blockade on her enemies. Because of her geographical position and naval strength she was able to impose it, not without friction with neutrals, but certainly without arousing the violent international indignation and eventual strengthening of her enemies which was the outcome of Germany's unrestricted submarine campaigns.

A major positive step towards clarifying some of the uncertainties of the previous centuries was taken in 1856 with the adherence of most of the major maritime and industrial nations to the Declaration of Paris, at the end of the Crimean War. The terms of the Declaration were generally in favour of increasing the freedom of seaborne trade in war time. Privateering was abolished. This not only removed a practice open to abuse, which at times amounted to the condoning of piracy, but also deprived states unwilling or unable to maintain a large regular navy, of what had been a valuable weapon to use against their enemies' merchant shipping. This was a great gain for Britain whose trade in earlier wars had suffered so grievously at the hands of French privateers, even after she had gained complete supremacy over the French fleet. The United States however was so opposed to the abolition of privateering that she refused to sign the Declaration although, since her foundation, she had always been in the lead in pressing for the advantages to neutrals embodied in its other provisions. Her argument was that this abolition was solely to the advantage of the strong naval powers who, in future, would be under less pressure to provide escorts for their merchant shipping and so would have more resources available for offensive operations.

The second and third provisions of the Declaration clarified two long disputed points. In future, belligerents' goods carried under a neutral flag would be exempt from seizure unless they were contraband of war, and neutral goods in a belligerent's ship would be similarly exempt. No definition of contraband was arrived at and this was to lead to future disagreements. The fourth provision was that in future blockade, to be binding on neutrals, had to be effective. This removed an age old neutral grievance against general declarations of blockade, such as those made by Britain against France in the Napoleonic wars, which made any of their ships trading with France liable to seizure and condemnation in an English prize court. The term 'effective' was not defined and this too led to later disagreements.

The Declaration of Paris left unsatisfied those states, the United States among them, who wished to go further in limiting the effect of war on maritime trade by exempting from seizure all private, as distinct from government owned, cargoes, provided they were not contraband. This in turn demanded detailed international agreement on what constituted contraband, a problem which produced extreme disagreements. Those naval powers most concerned with belligerent rights wanted to see as wide a defintion as possible, including food. Their opponents wanted contraband to be confined to munitions and other articles of direct military application. This was the position of the United States, whose delegations at the Hague Conferences of 1899 and 1907 took the lead in pressing for the total immunity of private cargoes and a highly restrictive definition of contraband. They had no success then but, in 1909, the Declaration of London went a long way towards establishing their desired definitions of contraband.

Surprisingly enough, the then British government, reversing the policies of all its predecessors, supported this new move. The Declaration laid down three categories of goods. Absolute contraband included those cargoes which had only a warlike use. Conditional contraband consisted of goods which had both civil and military uses, and which were liable to seizure only if it could be estalished that they were destined for the latter. Finally there were 'free goods' which were not contraband at all. The new Declaration tried to complete the work of Paris by defining a blockade as being 'effective' only when naval vessels were present to enforce it. The detailed lists of the various categories of contraband and free goods were extremely widely drawn and, if accepted, would have virtually destroyed Britain's traditional policy of using her naval strength to weaken her enemy's economy, and it is not surprising that the Liberal governments's acceptance of the Declaration was thrown out by the House of Lords. When war came in 1914, Britain successfully resisted pressures from neutrals, led by the United States, to abide by the Declaration and gradually established, using heavy pressure on European neutrals, measures designed to cut off Germany from all seaborne supplies, measures incidentally accepted by the United States when she became a belligerent.

In both world wars Germany used these measures as a justification for waging unrestricted submarine warfare as an exercise of the recognised right of reprisal. The sinking of merchant ships in war was not a new concept. It had been theoretically advocated by the French Jeune Ecole and was not without some foundation in maritime law. It was only the sinking without warning by torpedo which was entirely novel. The right of a belligerent warship to stop and search merchant ships suspected of carrying contraband, or of being blockade breakers, was well founded in international law and custom. If the search confirmed the suspicion, the intercepted ships had normally to be taken into port for prize court adjudication. But it was also accepted that if circumstances, such as the weather or the proximity of enemy warships, precluded this, she could be sunk after provision had been made for the safety of crew and passengers. This applied only to enemy merchant ships, not neutrals. It was similarly accepted that a ship which refused to submit to search, or which attacked the intercepting warship, could herself be attacked and, if necessary, sunk. Another justification put forward by Germany was that merchant ships which were armed and equipped with radio had lost their non-combatant status, as they did when sailing in an escorted convoy.

Between the world wars Britain, mindful of the way in which she had been brought to the brink of defeat by the submarine, constantly sought for its abolition by international agreement. Failing in this, she had to be content with the limitations in submarine operations against merchant ships imposed at the Washington Conference of 1921–2, the London Conference of 1930 and the Submarine Protocol of 1936. This last was ratified by all the major naval powers including Germany and, by 1939, over forty states had accepted it. The total effect of these limitations was to make it obligatory for submarines to behave in exactly the same way as surface warships. Merchant vessels were to be stopped and visited, and were not to be attacked unless they had refused to stop after clear warning. They were not to be sunk without the safety of passengers and crews being provided for, and for this, leaving them in ships' boats in the open sea was not enough.

The German Prize Regulations of 1939 accepted these restraints but unrestricted attacks began very early in the war. Again the justification of legitimate reprisal was used but the underlying reasons were pragmatic rather than legal. Once the threat of invasion and air bombardment had failed to drive Britain out of the war, attacks on her shipping were the only powerful weapon Germany had against her. At the more specific naval level, the advent of effective maritime aircraft and radar had made it suicidal for submarines to spend the time on the surface required for stopping and search. Allied submarines in both the European and Far Eastern theatres acted under the same compulsion; an argument successfully used in the defence of Admirals Raeder and Doenitz at the Nuremberg war trials.

It would seem that legal attempts to restrict war at sea were of no avail when they were seen as obstacles to victory or to the effective use of new technology.

(ii) After 1945 (by Richard Hill)

To judge how international law has affected maritime operations since 1945, it is necessary first to note three factors which have had a major effect on law at sea. First, the growth of modern technology has introduced many new uses of the sea, its bed and its subsoil; and it has broadened the scope and capacity of many traditional uses such as fishing. The sea is now viewed as a source of numerous exploitable resources, particularly in offshore areas. Secondly, the advent to the international scene of something like one hundred new states, most of them with emphatic ideas on sovereignty and no prejudgments in favour of established international law, has meant that the customary international law of the sea evolved over the last milennium and to an extent codified in the 1958 Geneva Conventions is under challenge from more or less radically new ideas. Finally there is the supposition that to make war – or indeed to use force – is a bad action, justifiable only in exceptional circumstances. This supposition is enshrined in the United Nations Charter. The notion, of course, predated 1945: but it never carried such force, nor was it so explicitly codified, before then.

All these developments, and their outcomes in international law, interact. But since the first two affect the international law of the sea in general, and therefore the objectives and environment of maritime operations, while the last affects mainly the law regarding the conduct of operations, they will be addressed in that order.

The Law of the Sea, even in its prime function of allotting and defining jurisdiction and rights, has since 1945 been in a state of rapid development because of the influences already noted. The trend has overwhelmingly been in the direction of increased coastal state jurisdiction and resource enjoyment in the maritime zones off its shores. Particular aspects include the rapid evolution of a principle of sovereign rights over seabed and subsoil resources out to the edge of the continental margin; the recognition of the special interest, and subsequently of certain prescriptive rights, of a coastal state in the fisheries off its shores; the extension by the majority of states of their territorial sea beyond the commonly recognised limit, in 1945, of three miles; challenges to rights of passage, particularly by foreign warships, in coastal and archipelagic waters; and sensitivity by coastal states to vessel-source pollution leading, in some cases, to wide-ranging unilateral legislation. The 1958 Geneva Conventions were a milestone on this path; some parts of the law, as it were, rested awhile there but others marched straight on.

The law may in the early 1980s be further codified in a generally agreed convention whose elements have been discussed in the United Nations Law of the Sea Conference since 1974. The assessment which follows is based on the latest documents before that Conference. The law is likely to provide for a territorial sea up to twelve miles broad, for an exclusive economic zone up to 200 miles from the coast, for some rights of exploration and exploitation over continental margins beyond that limit, and for some form of international authority to manage the exploitation of resources on the deep sea bed. In the territorial sea, the coastal state has sovereignty; in its continental margin beyond the economic zone, it has sovereign rights and related jurisdiction only over seabed and subsoil resources.

These coastal-state jurisdictions and rights are balanced by the rights of other sea users. These include, in the territorial sea, a right of innocent passage which the coastal state may not permanently hamper, although it may make all necessary provision for good order including, for example, establishing sea lanes and traffic separation schemes; in the exclusive economic zone, a freedom of navigation and overflight in all areas except safety zones round oil rigs or similar structures; and beyond that, full high-seas freedoms of navigation, overflight and fishing. Freedom to lay cables and pipelines, having due regard to other sea users, is likely to exist in the exclusive economic zone and beyond it to seaward.

International Straits are generally accepted as a special case where, because of the access they afford from one sea area to another, the right of transit needs special safeguards but where, also, the sensitivities of coastal states may be much involved. An acknowledged legal right to a twelve mile territorial sea would make a large number of international straits indisputably territorial in character, and this had led to the evolution of a proposed regime of transit passage under which users would have a non-suspendable freedom of navigation and overflight, though the coastal state could prescribe certain measures to ensure good order.

The Law of the Sea, as it has developed and will continue to develop, affects maritime operations in two ways. First, its increasing complexities and the pattern of claim and counterclaim that it throws up will inevitably provide sources of conflict, perhaps also pretexts for conflict. The root causes of dispute will, no doubt, be trade, resources, strategic positions; but the focus of dispute will be the Law. Secondly, it may affect the movements and operations of maritime forces in time of peace or tension.

Examples of both effects in the history of maritime operations are easy to find. In the British experience, the three so-called Cod Wars against Iceland in 1958, 1972 and 1975 are striking examples of a law-based confrontation over disputed resources; that these are not unique can quickly be judged from any analysis of post-1945 history. In controversies over the movements of maritime forces, there is again a notable British example in the Corfu Channel incident of 1947, when two destroyers were mined and 44 men of the Royal Navy lost their lives in the assertion of the right of innocent passage through international straits. The subsequent case before the International Court of Justice, and that Court's judgment, became a foundation of International Law concerning such passage. But although the Corfu Channel case is the most dramatic example of such assertions of right, it is again by no means unique.

There can be little question that both effects will go on being felt in the future. The text before the Law of the Sea Conference in 1980 ran to over 300 Articles; and length does not, in this case, lead to clarity. It is certain that there will be variations in interpretation, and disputes will not all be solved by the adoption of a text. They will be about the nature, as well as the extent, of rights; merchant and fishing vessels, as well as seabed installations, will be affected. International machinery to settle disputes is likely to be neither adequate nor universally recognised; the nations' record of submission to the Judgments both of the International Court of Justice, and of other tribunals, is lamentable. Operations to maintain a legal claim to rights or resources are, therefore, unlikely to decrease in frequency, and as resources become scarcer the stakes may be even more attractive, with a resultant increase in intensity of conflicts.

So far as the effect on the routine movement and activities of maritime forces is concerned, the evolution of the law so far has permitted reasonable access for ships, aircraft and submarines to all the oceans of the world. Some 'enclosed seas', mainly those claimed by the Soviet Union, have probably been allowed to go by default. In general, however, maritime forces have not only gone where they needed to, but have carried out the exercises and activities necessary to their efficient operation. If the development of the Law of the Sea is in the direction described, this will probably hold. For example, there will be a right of innocent passage for warships in the territorial sea of other states (though they will not be able to conduct, say, firing exercises there and aircraft will have no right of overflight); there will be freedom of navigation and overflight for the purpose of transit in international straits; there will be freedom of navigation and overflight, with only the qualification of 'due regard for the rights and duties of the coastal state', in the exclusive economic zone. Submarines will be allowed to submerge wherever freedom of navigation and overflight is allowed. It may, of course, be that some coastal states will dispute the rights of warships and aircraft to do these things; such claims may be based more, in future, on notions such as 'Zones of Peace' than on the International Law of the Sea. There is little doubt that major maritime nations will maintain that they have such rights and, as the law at present appears to be tending, they will have it on their side.

Finally we return to the impact of the law concerning armed conflict and the use of force, as it has evolved since 1945. This is, of course, linked to the conduct of operations in maintenance of claim – such as the Cod Wars – described above. If the only justification for the use of force is self-defence, then the political and legal premium on not firing the first shot is very high. Analysis of operations since 1945 suggests that most parties to conflicts at sea have, at one time or another, employed stringent rules of engagement and have sought to limit the amount of force to be used. This circumspection has been particularly noticeable in the nations of northwest Europe where – especially in fishing disputes – the use of firearms has been shunned, to the extent where ingenious devices such as trawlcutters have actually been invented to avoid resort to the gun. Other parts of the world have not been so squeamish, but in general the use of heavy weapons – including over-the-horizon missiles and torpedoes – has been minimal. There is, in fact, only one recorded instance of a torpedo warshot being fired since 1945.

It goes without saying that in regulating affairs round their shores, too, coastal states have been reasonably restrained. This may not persist; it is possible to envisage circumstances where a coastal state, incensed about (say) pollution of its shores, would think world opinion on its side in taking draconian measures against merchant ships. But this has not happened yet.

The effect of international law – both as a source and as a regulator of conflict – has probably not been sufficiently taken into account by those responsible for designing and organising maritime forces. If the brief analysis above is correct, states need at least some ships with such qualities as highly discriminatory weapon systems, excellent data acquisition and communications, structural strength and seakeeping: ships optimised, in fact, to operations in support of the law or in maintenance of claims under the law, rather than to war-fighting at the higher levels of operation. The evidence is that there is too much concentration on the latter role. This may apply particularly to the medium maritime powers.

(c) The new technology

With the end of the Second World War, there began, wrote Admiral Gorshkov, 'the start of a military-technical revolution which in scope and depth transcended all the reforms and transformations which had previously occurred in the armies and fleets of the world'. It had been an era of constant and bewildering change, making for 'a radical transformation of the armed forces'. So much so, in fact, that those with the responsibility for managing fleets have had to adopt new methods. Once, this 'was based only on the analysis of the current possibilities of science and technology and their development in the near future. Now, into this sphere has come scientific forecasting based on estimated lines of weapon development, electronic technology, power, shipbuilding theory and a number of non-military sciences.'[1] The rate of change has made it an unsettling period for the navies of the world.

All that can be done here is to sketch in some of the more important technological shifts in the pattern of maritime operations. The revolution in weaponry stands out most obviously. This in itself is not new. 'The unresisting progress of mankind causes continual change in the weapons,' wrote Mahan, 'and with that must come a continual change in the manner of fighting.' Some of these changes were developments of existing weaponry which simply called for the adaptation of existing methods (like the invention of Director Firing for main guns); others, though, led to wholesale reformations of theory and practice – such as the advent of the naval cannon. Many recent changes in weaponry have come into this last more drastic category.

Chief among these has been the development of nuclear weapons. The response to this was initially limited: they were thought of as just another, admittedly rather nastier, kind of big bomb. There was developed, mainly by the leading armies and navies of the world, the idea of the 'broken-backed war'. First there would be a nuclear exchange, then a substantial period of conventional warfare in which the traditional services could display their traditional talents, but, when the full potential of nuclear weaponry was made obvious with the development of thermo-nuclear devices in the early 1950s, this idea seemed less than sensible. Nuclear weapons instead moved to the centre of the stage. With the advent of the British and American strategic doctrine of 'Massive Retaliation', nuclear weapons so dominated the military horizon that the traditional services found it necessary to climb on to the air force band-wagon. It became fashionable to think of war between the major powers as being short, sharp and generally cataclysmic, certainly allowing little time for the deliberate and unhurried processes of conventional military operations. If the war would be over by the first lunch-time, who cared about the state of maritime communications?

When, however, it became clear that there might be little difference between winner and loser, the advantages of restraint, possibly even in the midst of conflict, became increasingly manifest. Technology, in the shape of the hidden sea-based deterrent and the other 'secure' forms of nuclear retaliation, came to the rescue and made restraint feasible as well as desirable. Hence was born the notion of 'Flexible Response', in which nuclear weaponry would take up only the upper, more frightening, less reasonable end of the military spectrum and which allowed for sustained conflicts at lower levels of intensity, even between the great powers. Conventional military operations came once more into the sunlight.

But there was a difference. Even if they were not used, nuclear weapons could be expected to cast a long shadow over these conventional operations. The risks of unwanted escalation were so appalling that every effort would need to be exerted to keep limited wars limited. It was simply too dangerous 'to light the blue touch paper and stand clear'. Wars between great powers, if they occurred at all, would surely have to be short and controlled if they were not to become cataclysmic. Since there was a certain chance that even war between a great power and some other country could escalate unbearably, the necessities of restraint applied at least to some degree to them too. Might not the risk of escalation revolutionise the execution of traditional military tasks?

There were other dramatic sources of change as well. The sinking of the Israeli destroyer *Eilat* by the Egyptian navy in 1967 confirmed the age of the naval missile. These new weapons were more lethal, more accurate, apparently capable of infinite development, launchable from the smallest of naval platforms and came in a bewildering variety of ranges and modes of attack. They gave the surface ship more power than ever it had before. With its array of naval missiles one ship could dominate tens of thousands of square miles of ocean although this, in turn, produced problems of identification, control and of finding out what happened to the target when the missile arrived. It also gave the ship more power against the land. Modern striking power, wrote Gorshkov, allowed navies to aim at 'such a strategic objective as devastation of the military-economic potential of an enemy'.[2]

Nevertheless, missilry also made surface naval power seem more vulnerable. By giving the midget a giant's punch, it seemed to make small countries effective even against the navies of the superpowers. There was also the same equalising tendency between ships. The *Eilat* incident indicated that small ships could at last be as effective against large ones as the Jeune Ecole had predicted nearly one hundred years earlier. Michael Howard wrote, 'There will probably not be any capital ships in the future that is any massive units of power that constitute that core of one's fleet and the principal intruments of one's strategy and provide accurate indications of one's naval strength'.[3] Perhaps naval power would be diffused between more, and smaller, units in the future and fleets would tend to disperse. Naval forces, suggested Gorshkov, would not operate 'as a compact structure... but in split-up combat order and even as single ships a very long way apart'.[4] Even so, with modern communications, fleets and task groups would still be fully integrated and could be expected to fight their new area battles with the same cohesion they displayed in the smaller combat zones of the past.

This tendency towards dispersal was even more marked when there was some possibility of nuclear weapons being used at sea. But this, pointed out Admiral Stansfield Turner, would make them much more vulnerable to a conventional attack and so pose awkward choices. 'Thus the sailor's whole familiar world disappears. Navy men are inclined to set aside the possibility of the use of nuclear weapons and stick with familiar tactical assumptions.' Perhaps all this may force the world's navies increasingly under water, as the only means of making the fleet less vulnerable. 'Are we being driven by tradition alone,' Turner felt able to ask, 'when we continue to build our surface ships?'[5]

Making a vessel submersible is a form of passive defence: it helps the vessel dodge hostile fire. Speed, agility and small size also continue to play a role here as they always have. But the tensions between the requirements of defence against the various kinds of attack seem particularly acute. A ship may be secure against nuclear fall-out but vulnerable to bullets. Such is the lethality of modern weapons that sustained battles and the ability to absorb high levels of punishment seem increasingly remote. According to some, the fate of the *Hood* rather than that of the *Bismarck* gives a more accurate indication of likely events in battle.

There still remains, however, active defence – the traditional capacity to protect oneself by destroying the enemy vessel (or aircraft) before it has time to launch its weapons. Increasingly, though, the defender has a second string to his bow: he can hope to destroy these weapons *after* they are launched. This is relatively new; Nelson had no prospect of swatting down cannon balls after the French had fired them but his successors do have some such possibility. The means by which they hope to do it is a continually changing combination of active point and area defence systems. Since the larger ship or the larger concentration of ships can pack more of such systems into one place, they are sometimes said to have better prospects of survival than small ships and small forces.

Traditionally changes in methods of ship propulsion and in the nature of hull design have also had considerable effects on maritime operations. Since 1945, the two main developments in this field have been the gas turbine engine and nuclear propulsion. Both share some advantages (for instance, their more modest demands on ship space and manpower) but nuclear propulsion in particular has so many advantages that the US Navy plans to use it in every major surface combatant of the future. It makes possible the true submarine and may greatly increase its relative importance in the naval service; it makes fleet operations potentially more independent of the land and it solves what Corbett called 'the main problem which lies at the root of all naval history, the problem of reconciling sea endurance with free movement'.[6]

But, whatever their means of propulsion, conventional-hulled vessels have certain unavoidable physical limits, especially in speed. Hence the contemporary interest in such other possibilities as hydrofoils and surface-effect ships. Although present levels of seaworthiness, endurance and expense largely restrict them to coastal work, it is not inconceivable that they might be a standard element in the navies of the future. As part of a balanced fleet, wrote Gorshkov, they increase combat possibilities, allowing navies to solve their tasks more successfully. They might also require new methods of tactical and strategic procedure.[7]

'The means for depicting the situation',[8] have changed enormously too. Information on the whereabouts and intentions of the enemy is now made available from a bewildering range of the devices from surveillance satellites (sometimes dubbed the 'space arm of seapower'), through infra-red detectors of various sorts to towed, dunked, floating or fixed acoustic sensors. Present advances in this field were in some ways well foreshadowed earlier in the century especially with the advent of maritime airpower. Rosinski wrote, 'Air reconnaissance can be described without exaggeration as pernaps the most revolutionary innovation sea power has experienced in the entire course of its more than two-thousand years of recorded history'.[9] But the amount of maritime information currently available seems, by several orders of magnitude, greater than it was even a generation ago.

Since the task of actually finding your enemy on the high seas has always been such a central issue of naval warfare, the importance of this development for the future can hardly be over-emphasised. Admiral Scheer wrote, 'Enterprises at sea are doubtless in a greater measure dependent on chance than those on land, owing largely to the lack of reliable information of the enemy's movements and the rapidity with which a situation changes'.[10] Few people had any real comprehension of the scale of the sailor's problem. Admiral Bacon wrote:

Imagine England and Scotland and Wales rolled flat, all hedges, towns, lakes, rivers removed until it was merely a sandy waste. One single rabbit in that vast area would be relatively the same in size as a submarine in the North Atlantic. Moreover, it would be a rabbit which could disappear under the sand in half a minute without leaving a track behind it.[11]

This was the background of much traditional maritime strategy.

If the enemy position could now be accurately known, then the whole nature of warfare at sea would change. The chances of strategic and tactical surprise would diminish; uncertainty would decline; there would no longer be any need for ceaseless patrols and endless maritime searches. Hardly anything would be the same.

Not all these developments have pointed in the same direction, however: some of them have acted against each other and so muted the impact of modern surveillance procedures on maritime operations. Sometimes, in order not to be detected fleets revert to old practices; ships switch off their radars and run silently; they communicate by lights and flags. So as not to be 'seen' they operate under considerable self-imposed restraints. Although in some ways they may be less effective as warships, they may still find that the benefits of this policy outweigh the costs.

Deception has always been an important component of strategy, since it allows the deceiver to make the best use of his resources and encourages the victim into strategic error. In the electronic age, the possibilities of deception are legion: satellites may be fooled into thinking big ships are small ones, or vice versa; surveillance devices may simply be swamped with false signals. Sometimes the new devices themselves are vulnerable to manipulation or interference: it is even occasionally argued that the first stage of any naval conflict will take place high above the oceans in an obscure competition among the satellites. Although primarily a battle for information, might it not be decisive?

As Gorshkov pointed out, 'a modern fleet needs global communications capable of ensuring the control of forces tens of thousands of kilometres away from the areas of their stationing'.[12] Computers and data-processing techniques grapple with a torrent of information from an expanding range of sensors. The implications of this could be profound. Even at the onset of the telegraph and radio age, Philip Colomb suggested that the new devices would lead to new patterns in the flow of information. Now it would be from the central authority out to the ships more than the other way about as 'was the ordinary practice in wars carried on by sailing ships'.[13]

The centralised direction of the battle of the Atlantic in the Second World War (making full use of radio direction-finding, special intelligence and so forth) seems very likely to be the exemplar of future naval conflict. This, of course, 'raises . . . the question of where command of naval forces should properly reside'. In what circumstances and to what degree, 'can the commander at sea be permitted to exercise his traditional autonomy?'[14] If one side leans too heavily on his communications might this not become a dangerous vulnerability?

The impact of all these developments in surveillance and communications is very hard to assess. By no means all of it is entirely novel, and there are so many cross currents that the upshot may conceivably leave maritime matters pretty much where they were a generation ago. Even so developments in this field are likely to play a particularly important part in determining the character of future naval conflicts.

It is even more difficult to summarise the possible effects of the new technology as a whole on maritime operations. Certainly, many traditional naval practices have been unsettled. So much is currently on offer that choosing between competing technological options and striking an effective balance between old and new become more difficult than ever. There also arises the question of the degree to which old principles will need to be adapted or discarded, and new ones manufactured.

Even the identity of key maritime decision-makers comes into the question. Perhaps only backroom boffins will have the necessary technical expertise to identify trends and even to make specific professional decisions. In a recent lecture, Stansfield Turner emphasised the increasing role of 'knowledgeable civilian groups' in defence decisions. But these groups will perhaps tend to be scientists rather than historians (in or out of uniform) as they were in the past.[15]

Technology now appears to challenge the relevance of history and the usefulness of the views of those who have used it to identify eternal principles of maritime strategy. In the eyes of many, Mahan, Corbett and the rest may be academically interesting; some of their sayings may be pushed about until they fit new conditions; they can even be quoted to provide extra support for views arrived at by independent modern thought. But, the argument goes, they do not and cannot have anything specific to say about situations which were unheard of when they were putting pen to paper. In this case technology challenges history-based teachings either for what it says or what it is silent about. Also it may well be that hard 'scientific' conclusions produced by sophisticated, quantified and repeatable simulation techniques (themselves by no means the least significant of the many technological advances) will be more helpful than tentative and unproven deductions drawn from historical rumination.

8 Old Tasks for New Navies

(a) Navies in the nuclear age

The last chapter briefly sketched in some important areas of change in the environment of maritime strategy. In the past, changes on this scale have started off much controversy about the future of navies and naval roles. If anything, this tendency is even more marked now than it was then. In the nuclear age there appear to be questions not only about how navies would carry out their traditional tasks but also about whether it is any longer important that they should even try to do so. Traditional naval activities seem to be more open to the charge of their being 'irrevelant' than ever before. Even navies themselves seem, in some peoples' eyes, to be less important than they used to be.

Of course, in itself this is no new development. It is often argued that hardly had the ink dried on Mahan's writings than new technological developments (initially the submarine, and then the aircraft) appeared, to discredit his theories.[1]

In the interwar period, advocates of air power made the case most strongly. Sea power was essentially a thing of the past. Strategic air power was a far quicker and a more effective means of bludgeoning the adversary into submission by an assault on his morale and his war-making capacity. Sea power could offer no defence against it; a navy's major instrument of coercion, the blockade, would be impossible to mount and would take too long anyway; unaided sea power could not even defend shipping against air attack, mount operations against the land or offer defence against them, if the enemy had a modern air force. Richmond summarised these heresies into three chief technology-based objections:

1. Sea power is slow acting. Wars in future will be short and sea power will not have time to make its effect felt.
2. New instruments have come into use, principally under water and above water, which deprive sea power of its capacity to control the sea.
3. New means of communication have been developed on land and in the air which enable a nation to receive what it needs from oversea, irrespective of control of the sea.[2]

Richmond's riposte was two-fold. First these arguments exaggerated the effectiveness of the new technology. He said, in 1921, 'Everything of that kind that has come up has had its counter. It is against science that it should not be so . . . the science that develops one weapon will be equally competent to find out its antidote'.[3] So, sea power would come up with an answer to these developments. Secondly, there was a semantic fallacy of monumental proportions in this rigid distinction between air and sea power. By taking aircraft to sea with them, fleets would be able to take on and perhaps even defeat land-based air forces. Air power, in other words, could be part of sea power; it could strengthen it, and increase its reach.

Although this defence of navies in the air age was largely vindicated by the experience of the Second World War, it immediately came under fire once more when that war ended. In the United States there were bitter inter-service wrangles over defence organisation and the relative priority to be accorded strategic bombing, maritime tasks and, especially, the navy's carrier programmes. The air interest, pushing for the B-36 bomber, stressed the decisive nature of the future bombing campaign and downgraded the relative importance of the other two arms of national defence.

For several reasons this campaign was particularly dangerous for the US Navy. Firstly, as Samuel P. Huntington pointed out, there was no other navy for it to compete with. Mahanist theory rested on the assumption of there being 'a multi-sea power world'. In this case, what was the Navy to defend the country against? As one high-ranking Air Force officer put it:

There are no enemies for it to fight except apparently the Army Air Force. In this day and age to talk of fighting the next war on the oceans is a ridiculous assumption. The only reason for us to have a navy is just because someone else has a navy and we certainly do not need to waste money on that.

This simple but fallacious logic had a powerful effect on public opinion – and so on the future of the navy.[4] In this perspective, the burgeoning Soviet Navy was greeted by naval establishments around the world with sighs of relief, not gasps of horror.

More seriously, there was what Gorshkov has called 'a state of shock amongst naval theoreticians' at that time. Even in the major maritime states naval construction ceased and extremist views attracted much support. The cause of all this was the advent of atomic weapons. Gorshkov wrote,

It turned out unfortunately that we had some very influential 'authorities' who considered that with the appearance of atomic weapons the Navy had completely lost its value as a branch of the armed forces. According to their views, all of the basic missions in a future war allegedly could be fully resolved without the participation of the Navy.[5]

The general notion was that nuclear weaponry would have too swift and terrible an effect on the issue to leave room for maritime activities of any real significance.

Indeed, the vulnerability of large surface ships to nuclear and other forms of attack would make navies themselves prime and easy targets. Speaking of the carrier, Edward Teller ('father of the H-bomb') wrote:

> It looked to me like quite a good target. In fact, if I project my mind into a time, when not only we, but also a potential enemy, have plenty of atomic bombs, I would not put so many dollars and so many people into so good a target. Come to think of it, I would not put anything on the surface of the ocean – it's too good a target.[6]

This argument was taken up with differing degrees of enthusiasm by a good many people, including in his own peculiar way, Mr. Khruschev.

It was the culmination of a long scepticism about the future of the Navy's great ships. 'There have been those', commented Fred T. Jane in 1906, 'who have foreseen the advent of explosives so powerful that a single hit will be decisive and from this they have argued that a return to small units is bound to come.'[7] This situation had not arisen simply because of the advent of atomic weapons. Surface ships operated on the interface of the three dimensions of maritime warfare (air, surface and sub-surface) and so were inevitably vulnerable to craft which could specialise in just one. And with their demise, went the popular argument, would also go many of the Navy's traditional functions.

Just as old arguments were advanced once more in the nuclear age, so too were the connected counter-arguments. First there was the view that sea power itself would absorb these new technologies and so be able to defend itself against new threats. The mere fact that navies could deploy nuclear missilry so effectively in itself meant that, in Gorshkov's words 'the absolute and relative significance of combat at sea in the overall course of a war has unquestionably increased'.[8] Even in a nuclear war, then, what navies did would become more, not less, significant.

Finally, there was the point that the potential devastation of a total war in the nuclear age was such that it could deter the superpowers from starting one. The same fear of unwanted escalation might also dissuade them from entering upon a hot war on NATO's central front – the favourite scenario of the short-war school. Paradoxically, might this not lead to consciously limited and local wars elsewhere? 'Reason suggests,' said Admiral Thomas B. Hayward, US Navy, Chief of Naval Operations, recently, 'that a US/Soviet conflict is more probable as an outgrowth of a non-NATO contingency than from a frontal attack by Warsaw Pact forces against the NATO Alliance.'[9] A local war, in fact, seems more likely as the unintended consequence of policies in unsettled parts of the world where lines of interest are drawn so much less definitely than they are in central Europe.

Such wars could easily have a significant maritime dimension of the traditional sort. As the Russian Admiral S. E. Zakharov pointed out:

> Soviet Military doctrine... recognises the possibility of the outbreak of local wars which take place without the use of nuclear weapons. In this [kind of war] Soviet military doctrine allots an important place to armed battle on the sea, which could acquire an enormous strategic significance.[10]

In this context, the notion is occasionally developed that such a war might take place mainly or even exclusively at sea – on the assumption that maritime conflict would be easier to control, with no borders to cross by accident, and few civilians to kill.

Whether exclusive to the sea or not, such a limited war would be quite a novel affair fought to its own esoteric rules, probably by forces in being, under the tightest control and with the object of securing an early and moderately advantageous end. Neither side could afford to win it by too much, lest its adversary feel impelled to raise the stakes in order to avoid an unacceptable defeat. Even if it were conceivable, such a war would require new rules; the old orthodoxies of maritime strategy might have to be discarded because they generally aimed at victory, not an advantageous stalemate.[11]

Observations like this have led many to quarrel with the whole concept of limited war. Such is the interdependence of the modern world that any kind of significant conflict (and especially one involving the superpowers) would contain too many hazards to last for long. Even a limited war fought on some peripheral sea would provide too many opportunities for error and accident and too many risks of inadvertant escalation, to be undertaken for any but the gravest reasons. And if, by this definition, the war was fought for evidently important reasons, how could it be kept reliably limited? If both sides had the self restraint to prevent it escalating, why should they fight it in the first place? So the discourse goes on.

Although maritime strategy in the nuclear age can only be discussed against some vision of what might be happening on land, the analysis very evidently can quickly degenerate into an exercise in competitive war scenario building. The only thing that seems to emerge from this is that the possibilities are legion, the certainties few. Single contingency forces are manifestly vulnerable to outflanking by circumstances or a resourceful foe, probably more now than ever before. Military establishments around the world have responded to this uncertainty with the commonsense but unremarkable device of consciously identifying their working assumptions and of building for as wide a range of reasonable options as their resources permit. And as far as the larger navies are concerned this has meant striking some balance between old tasks and new.

(b) Securing command of the sea

Doubts about the wisdom of whole-heartedly concentrating on the requirements of decisive battle as a means of securing command of the sea have been reinforced, in the eyes of many observers, by recent developments. The probable length of war at sea, they say, would encourage navies to move immediately to the multifarious tasks of exercising command, instead of seeking out their opposite numbers for some preliminary encounter. Technology would also render obsolete the whole idea of a cohesive battle fleet. In such a case the purposeful destruction of the enemy's naval forces would be a difficult task either to encompass or even to imagine. For such reasons one commentator observed recently: 'Most analysts would agree that except for possible conflict along the sea lines of communication, the days of battles on the high seas are gone for ever'.[12]

This, however, does not appear to be the view taken by either of the world's two major navies. Admiral Gorshkov wrote, 'The battle always was and remains the main means of solving tactical tasks'. This view seems amply confirmed by recent Russian naval construction, which, in their new cruisers, and particularly in the new 32 000-ton nuclear-powered battle cruiser *Kirov*, indicates some stress on the capacity for surface action.

American doctrine follows the same traditional lines. Admiral Hayward recently said, 'In a war at sea the most rapid, efficient and sure way to establish the control of essential sea areas is to destroy the opposing forces capable of challenging your control of those seas'. Western analysis, he added, sometimes tended to forget the necessity for offensive action because NATO tended to think in terms of 'scenarios that were essentially defensive and reactive in nature – convoy escort on the North Atlantic SLOCS (sea lines of communication), and that sort of thing'. It was necessary to 'impose maximum attrition early in the war, on the heart of Soviet offensive capability, the ships, aircraft and submarines capable of attacking our own forces and shipping'.[13] Very evidently there is little here to upset the shades of Mahan.

What contemporary critics probably have more in mind is less the fact of battle, than its style. Battle fleets would obviously not proceed in parallel lines pounding each other into oblivion, as occasionally they did in the past. But to assume that this implies that there would be no battles in the future is to repeat the mistakes of some commentators of the interwar period who argued that the putative decline of the battleship somehow meant the decline of battle.

Any future battle at sea would be a particularly diverse affair of sub-surface, air and surface engagements (probably in that order of respective lethality). It would cover a much wider area of sea than before. Competing fleets would not line up to have a shoot-out but would engage in 'carefully orchestrated activities involving widely dispersed, complementary and supportive forces'.[14] While the range of the new weaponry and modern procedures of command and control would restore some semblance of unity to the naval battleground, battle would be a much more diffuse affair. Probably it would be more fleeting too, with much more stress on the first salvo and the first strike. It is also likely to be very intense with high casualty rates, even if tactical nuclear weapons were not used. Admiral Holloway said:

> In a conflict with the Soviets I would expect very heavy losses to our carrier forces if nuclear weapons were used. If nuclear weapons were not used, I would predict about a 30 to 40 per cent attrition of our carriers. We have no figures, statistically, because we have no view into the future with the infinite set of scenarios in which we could go to war.[15]

The anti-carrier stress of many Soviet naval dispositions and their tactical doctrine of the 'close embrace', however, make such predictions fairly secure.

Moreover, Soviet doctrine does not distinguish as clearly between nuclear and conventional weaponry as does the Western; this may imply fewer inhibitions about 'going nuclear'. There is, however, little in the public literature about what the consequences of this for the future of battle at sea might be. But it seems likely to make battle more costly. 'A special feature of the sea battle is that it has nearly always been waged to destroy the enemy', commented Gorshkov. 'The equipping of the forces of the fleets with nuclear weapons is further accentuating this feature.'[16]

Contemporary naval thought seems to pay little attention to the way in which inferior naval forces may conduct modern versions of the kind of fleet-in-being strategies discussed earlier. In the Ameeican case, of course, this mainly reflects a post-war tradition of predominance. The Soviet Navy, on the other hand, has devoted much thought to the conduct of useful naval operations in adverse conditions, but Gorshkov is doubtless aware that too glowing an account of such possibilities is hardly likely to help the construction of a first-class fleet of the kind he clearly wants.

Nevertheless, certain modern techniques do seem to come into this category even though the fleet-in-being label may not be used to cover them. They include deliberate attempts to influence an adversary's military decisions by the conscious manipulation of his perceptions of one's sea-control capabilities. In this sense, alarmist stories about the Soviet navy can give-them more actual military effectiveness than their strength really warrants. Deception is another quite similar technique. Stansfield Turner wrote:

> Assertive sea control objectives do not necessarily demand destruction of the enemy's force. If the enemy can be sufficiently deceived to frustrate his ability to press an attack, we will have achieved our sea control objective. Forces routing, deceptive/imitative devices, and other anti-search techniques can be deployed, often in combination with other tactics. [17]

Modern forms of blockade, however, have been discussed more explicitly – especially in Western naval literature. The necessity for 'denial to enemy forces of access routes to open ocean areas' (now sometimes called 'containment') is a major Western preoccupation. [18] Action in the northern gaps between the Greenland–Iceland–United Kingdom and Svalbad–Norway lines against the possibility of units of the Soviet Northern Fleet attempting to break into the North Atlantic seems a not unlikely contingency for NATO maritime forces to prepare for.

Admiral Stansfield Turner has discussed the idea of 'Sortie Control' – that is of

> bottling up an opponent in his ports or on his bases... today's blockade seeks destruction of individual units as they sortie. If we assume an opponent will be in control of the air near his ports, sortie control tactics must primarily depend on submarines and mines... a most economical means of cutting of a nation's use of the seas or ability to interfere.

A second blockading technique is 'choke point control'. 'Sometimes' wrote Turner, 'the best place to engage the enemy is in a geographical bottleneck through which he must pass.' The advantage of this procedure is that it can use units which would not survive for long in sortie control operations nearer the enemy's bases. [19]

Soviet naval theory has the corresponding mirror image of this problem. The need for Russia to make her 'break through to the sea' [20] so as to defeat encirclement and wield her scattered fleets as a cohesive whole is a constant if implicit theme of Gorshkov's writings. Some observers have detected in Gorshkov's remarks about the way in which the occupation of vital coastal regions in the past has often facilitated the establishment of command in adjacent areas, a suggestion that amphibious operations (against Norway, Svalbad, Iceland?) would be an important part of any Soviet anti-blockade strategy.[21]

The use of new labels for blockade and counter-blockade operations should not conceal the fact that these are traditional activities with familiar aims and problems. Although the mere fact of technological advance means that there would be great differences in execution if not purpose, there seem likely to be similarities too. Modern blockades, like the old, will doubtless involve much work by small units, mines and the like, will have an important surveillance function and will continue (especially in northerly latitudes) to be affected by the weather. Because they, too, are unlikely to be wholly reliable and, in any case, are helpless against enemy units already out, modern fleet commanders would probably face problems well known to their predecessors. Just as the British Admiralty of 1914–18 had to decide whether to put its flotilla craft with the Grand Fleet or into the direct protection of its merchant shipping, so would their successors have to think about the relative proportion of effort to devote to the task of blocking the northern gaps on the one hand, and to that of directly protecting Atlantic communications on the other. New navies seem to have old problems.

(c) Sea control

Most analysts maintain that recent developments have made it more difficult to secure command of the sea. Gorshkov wrote, 'It will be seen that the period of keeping the dominance gained at sea tends to shorten and the struggle for gaining it becomes even tougher'.[22] This partly reflects perceptions of the impact of the new technology on surface naval power. Missiles, torpedoes, mines, land-based aircraft, even in the hands of non-industrial states, can make it noticeably more hazardous for bluewater navies to pass through or operate in sea areas within reach of land. Politico-legal restrictions on the freedom of the maritime powers to use the sea as they wish are also likely to create extra inhibitions and difficulties, although in the absence of coercive power to back them up, they are not likely to be decisive in war time.[23]

For such reasons as these many modern maritime strategists have been uncomfortable about the continued use of the phrase the 'command of the sea', which they think too absolutist in tone. Such a view is plainly behind the following exploration of types of sea control by Admiral Eccles:

TYPES OF CONTROL OF THE SEA BY AREA AND BY TIME[24]

1. *Absolute control (command of the sea)*
   Complete freedom to operate without interruption. Enemy cannot operate at all.
2. *Working control*
   General ability to operate with high degree of freedom. Enemy can only operate with high risk.
3. *Control in dispute*
   Each side operates with considerable risk. This then involves the need to establish working control for limited portions for limited times to conduct specific operations.
4. *Enemy working control*
   Position 2 reversed
5. *Enemy absolute control (command of the sea)*
   Position 1 reversed.

So, 'command of the sea' is now out and 'sea control' is in. According to Stansfield Turner:

> This change in terminology may seem minor but it is a deliberate attempt to acknowledge the limitations on ocean control brought about by the development of the submarine and the airplane. . . . The new term 'Sea Control' is intended to connote more realistic control in limited areas and for limited periods of time . . . it is no longer conceivable, except in the most limited sense, to totally control the seas for one's own use or to totally deny them to an enemy.[25]

It might be reasonably objected that most traditional maritime strategists regarded command of the sea as an essentially relative concept anyway, as we have seen. But the substitution of the new for the old labels may be justified as a useful reminder that the whole thing is more difficult now. It should, though, not be taken to mean that past experience and past reflection on 'command of the sea' are now irrelevant. Far from it. In Gorshkov's view, 'such a category of naval arts as the gaining of dominance at sea retains its topicality and therefore the elaboration of it, in all its aspects relevant to the present, forms one of the most important tasks of naval science'. And the value of historical comparison and illustration for this 'elaboration' is evident throughout Gorshkov's works.[26] He uses history to develop the differences between strategic and tactical dominance and to show how the destruction of enemy forces has led on to other things.

The extent to which the Soviet Navy has accepted the notion of the command of the sea, however, is still a matter of some controversy. In the best traditions of medieval scholasticism, there have been several thorough investigations of what exactly the Russians mean by the various terms they use for this concept.[27] These investigations indicate that they too have broad and narrow variants of 'command of the sea'. But while geographic and other constraints may have forced them to take a markedly limited view of the concept on some occasions in the past, current fleet operations and construction programmes suggest increasingly extensive perspectives on the matter. The whole issue in fact is a useful reminder of the way in which a navy's interpretations of abstract concepts like this inevitably take on a form appropriate to its real world circumstances. But although the form of the concept may change over time (and from one country to another) its essential character will often be found to have remained, as in this case, basically the same.

Sea control evidently has two complementary dimensions; 'sea assertion' or 'sea use' and 'sea denial'. The first has to do with the ability to use the sea for traditional purposes. Stansfield Turner lists four such purposes:

1. To ensure industrial supplies
2. To reinforce/resupply military forces engaged overseas
3. To provide wartime economic/military supplies to allies
4. To provide safety for naval forces in the Projection of Power Ashore role.[28]

These obviously relate specifically to the United States, but similar lists apply to other Western countries. The manifest reliance of NATO on sea supply and reinforcement means it must have a particular interest in sea use.

Gorshkov, however, was at considerable pains to establish that the Soviet Union, as a great maritime nation, also has a legitimate interest in sea use. The very evident Soviet commitment to ocean-going ships with heavy displacement and high endurance, their *Kiev* class carriers and, possibly, the *Kirov* battle cruiser indicate the intention to turn such aspirations into reality. The defensive capacities of such ships also suggest a level of resilience often associated with ambitions for sea use.

If so, this is a relatively new departure, for the Soviet Navy in the past has generally been said to have a strictly 'sea denial' role. Here the objective is not to use the sea oneself, but to prevent the enemy from doing so. Sometimes, in a manner vaguely reminiscent of some variants of the fleet-in-being strategy, the mere presence of naval forces may have useful results in this manner. 'Soviet Navy ships are constantly on the ocean, including the stamping grounds of the NATO strike fleets', wrote Gorshkov in 1970. 'The presence of our ships in these regions ties the Imperialists' hands and deprives them of opportunity freely to interfere in the people's internal affairs.'[29]

More usually, though, 'sea denial' is regarded essentially as

> guerrilla warfare at sea. The denying naval commander strikes at a
> time and place of his choosing to achieve maximum surprise; he does
> not have to stand his ground toe to toe with the enemy but instead
> hits and runs. In this way a markedly inferior force can successfully
> thwart a superior force.[30]

The inventory of 'sea denial' weapons tends to be offensive in character, and its ships of the 'fire and forget' variety.

Several points need to made about the new taxonomy of sea control. First, it does not actually appear to be 'new' in any substantial sense: 'The object of naval warfare must always be directly or indirectly to secure the command of the sea, or to prevent the enemy from securing it', wrote Corbett after all.[31] Accordingly, the problems regarding the concept of command noticed earlier (the degrees of its necessity, relativity and so forth)[32] apply here too. This is particularly true of the vexed matter of the actual sequence of maritime events. While logically control must be secured before it can be exercised, in practice the two processes may often have to be conducted simultaneously as Gorshkov pointed out. This may be particularly true of a short war; although it may be safer for NATO to remove Soviet Naval threats before the reinforcement convoys sail, time and events on the European mainland may not allow such stately procedures.

This fact has reinforced the notion that it may no longer be necessary to strive after sea control anyway: 'since combat activities had become swift and productive', wrote Gorshkov, 'the forces waging a struggle at sea did not need the creation of favourable conditions'.[33] Certainly even in the past it was no means unkown for two sides to use the sea and studiously avoid encountering each other's main forces (such as in the Black Sea during the Second World War). It is not inconceivable that the same might happen again. Even so, it would doubtless be better to have a sea control capacity and find one does not need it, rather than the other way about. Accordingly, a fleet that knows it will have to use the sea should probably be prepared to fight for its control.

A second general observation about 'sea assertion' and 'sea denial' is that these should evidently not be regarded as alternatives, but as complements. Both navies appear to see them in this latter light. The way these two fit together as far as the Soviet Union is concerned has been lucidly explained by Robert Herrick:

> Soviet writers for many years have talked about zones of defense.
> The Soviets hope to command the sea within a couple of hundred
> miles of their coasts. In these zones, they could use all their small fast
> craft, surface ships and PT boats, and even their expensive missile

artillery. Beyond these zones – which would include their peripheral seas – the Barents, the Baltic, the Black, and the Sea of Japan – they have an area in which they hope to contest us in command of the seas. And beyond that, there is what they call the open-ocean zone, where they have to practise sea denial, because they cannot support their submarines with surface forces until they have more carrier-based aircraft. [34]

Evidently this sea assertion–denial spectrum is another way of expressing the fact that command is a matter of degree in time and place. The further the fleet operates from the main source of its strength, or the weaker it is, the less ambitious can be its aspirations for sea use and the more likely it would be to content itself with a sea denial strategy rather than sea assertion.

Finally, it bears repeating that sea control should not be regarded as an end in itself but simply as a means to an end. Sea control, wrote Admiral Crowe, is the 'pre-eminent function of the US Navy because it is a pre-requisite to the successful conduct of other types of naval operations and to the support of US military forces deployed overseas'. [35] But there is nevertheless a tendency in American naval thinking to conflate the many functions of maritime power into four 'missions' (strategic deterrence, sea control, projection and presence) or even simply to two (sea control and projection). This effectively runs together the two logically discrete procedures of securing command and exercising it, the means and ends of maritime strategy respectively. This could be a very dangerous form of intellectual shorthand if it led people to suppose that sea control was an end in itself. Voices have accordingly been raised (from time to time) in warning against this practice. In 1948, for instance, Vice-Admiral R. L. Conolly commented: 'I believe we err in advancing the proposition that "Control of the Sea" is an end in itself. It is the *exploitation* of this control that is important'. [36] His reminder is evidently as useful now as it was then. But, as we have seen, he was by no means the first to make the point.

(d) The defence of sea lines of communication

In Corbett's view, operations directed at securing the control of maritime communications lay at the heart of naval strategy. Nowadays, however, it is sometimes argued that the attack and defence of these 'sea lines of communication' are much less important than they were. Gorshkov argued that the task slipped down the list of American priorities about 1957 because of American perceptions of their own maritime security. [37] Certainly in contemporary American literature the use of maritime communication is normally regarded merely as part and parcel of the sea-control mission. It is hardly mentioned, as such, in Stansfield Turner's celebrated formulation of naval missions. While there are various references to the importance of this and related tasks in Soviet literature, on the other hand they often seem to be largely ritualistic in tone. But a closer look at current thinking suggests that this neglect of one of the great preoccupations of the maritime strategists of the past is more apparent than real.

The importance of military and commercial shipping to the Western Alliance is certainly well recognised. Recently, Admiral Hayward said, 'Our strategic interests span continents and the interconnecting oceans. Virtually all our allies are separated from us by water. Our economic life depends increasingly on access to overseas markets and resources, and our dependence upon the seas is growing, not lessening'.[38]

The vulnerability of the West's seaborne oil supplies in particular is the subject of debate in the naval literature on both sides of what used to be called the iron curtain. In an article entitled 'Petroleum and NATO', one Soviet commentator noted, disinterestedly: 'Western strategies recognise that in the event of war the severing of these communications would be fraught with the most serious consequences for the countries of NATO'.[39]

The extent to which the Soviet Navy has the interruption of NATO's maritime communications as an important priority is a matter of considerable debate.[40] What is clear, however, is that as the Soviet merchant and fishing fleets grow in size and economic importance, there will begin to develop comparable vulnerabilities on the Soviet side, and doubtless a similar defensive mission for their navy. Gorshkov has in fact already presaged such a development. He noted that however ancient this task might be, it retained its importance 'even in present-day conditions'. Moreover, 'with the growth of the economic power of the Soviet Union, its interests on the seas and oceans are expanding to an even greater degree and consequently new requirements are laid on the Navy to defend them from imperialist encroachments'.[41]

Interestingly, it is quite possible to find Soviet echoes of another familiar proposition in current Western naval thinking, that the defence of surface trade required a *surface* navy. 'Certainly, under special conditions, there will be a possibility of protecting sea communications by means of missiles, aircraft and other means [presumably submarines]. Yet a surface fleet cannot be dispensed with.'[42] We have already seen that the need to protect merchant shipping has always been a major part of the navalist argument for the maintenance of an orthodox fighting fleet. The general consensus of opinion in fact still seems to be that so long as cargoes are conveyed on the surface of the oceans, conventional warships will continue to have important advantages over aircraft and submarines in the protection of trade. They can, for instance, stay longer than the former and communicate and concentrate better than the latter.

The trouble with the proposition that maritime communications need protecting, though, is that it assumes sustained conflict of some kind. But if, on the other hand, the war was short and violent, possibly involving the destruction of ports and perhaps the use of nuclear weapons, the protection of commerce would hardly seem an important priority. Major industrial nations have sufficient stockpiles to outlast the longest of 'short' wars. Furthermore, the enemy would probably have more urgent things to do with his forces than hunt merchant ships unlucky or unwise enough to be at sea.

The riposte to this is that the short, intense war is but one of a whole spectrum of possibilities ranging from a general nuclear conflict at one extreme to low-level harassment at the other. As Admiral Gretton has argued, a significant and sustained threat to commerce could be a feature of several of these levels of conflict. One of the most serious would be some kind of trade war fought out beneath a nuclear umbrella. 'Fighting at sea can be isolated from the land. Only combatants [and merchant seamen] need suffer ... [in] ... an undeclared war of some duration being carried on between the escorts of NATO convoys and the attacking communist submarines.'[43] Somewhere below that there might come a particular assault on the shipping of some distant ally possibly not even involving the navies of the superpowers or their immediate allies, for, as the *Mayaguez* incident showed, these options are open to all. Finally there could be general harassment of merchant shipping to prove some political point, spiced with the occasional anonymous or accidental sinking.

There are as well many scales of threat that fall below the level of military harassment, such as the waging of shipping cut-price wars or political pressure on third-world suppliers. But since, however, the naval role in this area seems largely restricted to 'the presence mission', it will be discussed later.

But even the strictly military possibilities are sufficiently diverse to make it seem unwise for navies to plan for the single contingency of a short sharp war and to let trade protection go largely by default. In the universe of military affairs, after all, nothing is more likely to make a thing happen than openly failing to plan for it.

Nevertheless, there has been a marked and surely reasonable tendency in Western naval thinking to concentrate on ensuring the safe and timely arrival of specifically military shipping. In his discussion of the First and Second World Wars, Gorshkov was often at pains to point out how important it was to sever military communications. Also, he showed himself to be well aware of the West's particular vulnerabilities in this respect; not, he remarked, 'The most zealous advocates of military adventures in the West ought to stop and think of their ... greatly extended communication lines'.[44] But fundamental objections are heard about this as well. A NATO European war, it is often said, could easily develop from 'a standing start' and, such are the difficulties of organising convoys, the fighting would probably be over by the time reinforcements or military supplies from the United States could arrive.

The validity of this bleak type of reasoning can only be assessed after some judgement is made of the present military situation on the mainland of Europe. Although this is beyond the scope of the present work, several observations seem worth making. First, most short-war predictions of the past have been wrong; it also does not follow that a sudden collapse of one part of 'the front' would necessarily entail a cessation of hostilities on all others. Secondly, although the reinforcement issue is usually raised in connection with Atlantic communications between the United States and Europe, there may be other such routes as well, particularly on NATO's northern and sourthern flanks.

More generally, we seem to need to think about maritime and continental strategy as a whole and not as two discrete entities. In the latest version of Gorshkov's *Sea Power of the State* there was a new and particular stress on this point. It was implied that the military high command still did not fully appreciate the role the Soviet Navy could play in war, and that this was due to a failure to recognise the 'paramount significance under today's conditions' of a 'unified military strategy'. Russia's defeat in her war with Japan, he wrote, was due to a 'higher military command [which] worked out plans for war separately for the Army and the Navy, ignoring the need to coordinate them'. Because operations against military communications will adversely affect an enemy's capacity in the land battle, Gorshkov declared, they should be seen as a part of the fleet's operations against the shore.[45]

Although it is interesting that Gorshkov evidently felt he still needed to make this point at some length, his proposition that naval and continental strategies *must* be put into the proper relation, was by no means new. It figured in the work of most orthodox maritime strategists and was one of the most important themes addressed by Corbett particularly. The fact that the point seems constantly to need repeating indicates both how important and how difficult it is to put into practice.

The need to do so in a nuclear age is more acute than ever for, as Laurence Martin has observed, 'the new climate of deterrence and limited military operations blurs the traditional lines between service functions'.[46] NATO's 'Atlantic Bridge' of United States reinforcements to Europe is an especially suitable issue to be addressed in this way for the dangers of mismatching air, sea and land strategies, or of thinking only about particular bits of the problem, are very evident.

The second general observation that needs to be made about transatlantic reinforcement is that, just as the maritime dimension should not be addressed in isolation from the continental, so the military dimension as a whole must be considered in relation to the political. The symbolic significance of maritime communications to the Western alliance has long been recognised. In 1953, for instance, the United States Chief of Naval Operations wrote:

> Our entire politico-military philosophy today is based on the concept of collective security, which comprises overseas alliances, overseas bases, and US military forces deployed overseas. The keystone of this entire structure is the confidence felt by our allies that we can and will maintain control of the sea communications in the face of any threat.[47]

As a senior NATO naval officer has recently pointed out, the uncontested growth of the Soviet Navy could lead to a loss of confidence over the reliability of the maritime communications of the West. If an evident difficulty in sending, supplying, reinforcing (or even withdrawing) American troops in Europe led either to a loss of confidence in NATO Europe that they would come, or to a reluctance in the United States to send them in the first place, 'then the United States will progressively become "decoupled" from Europe. Without the guaranteed backing of the United States, Europe would soon fall under the influence of Soviet power.'[48] Since a commitment to the defence of NATO's maritime communications therefore carries a message of mutual reassurance to allies and of deterrence to possible adversaries, it may in that case have a strategic significance quite transcending questions of strict military utility. Indeed, it has been suggested that the Soviet *Okean 75* exercise and other such demonstrations of a substantial interdiction capacity should also be seen primarily in this light.[49] There must evidently be room in any modern theory about the defence of maritime communications for such political considerations as these.

Assuming, though, that there is a continued need for the defence of maritime communications, how far do traditional practice and orthodox wisdom still hold true in the nuclear age? The first and obvious similarity between then and now is that the task continues to require a whole range of complementary activities, as it always has done.

In addition to orthodox procedures of convoy-and-escort, the modern defence of maritime communications would seem likely to involve the attack of enemy units (particularly aircraft and submarines) whenever encountered, and their attrition in defensive barriers across suitable 'chokepoints'. Mines would seem likely to prove a serious threat to merchant shipping as well, therefore requiring substantial counter-measures in coastal waters and harbour approaches. Non-military activities such as the regulation of ports and shipping and the pre-positioning of stocks would also have their place. The arming of merchant ships with aircraft and point defence systems is also entirely conceivable. There is, in sum, no more likelihood of a single solution to the problem now than there was then.

The precise balance to be struck between these various options would depend on narrowly technical and professional matters specific to particular types of war situation. But if the past is any guide, a lively debate about the relative merits of independent routing, convoy, 'offensive methods' and 'protected sea lanes' is on the cards. In the present literature, for instance, it is not at all difficult to find evidence of the view that the increase in the relative power of the submarine would probably create a threat which might 'destroy or drive into port any present-day surface navy or merchant fleet' and would certainly diminish the value of convoy-and-escort.[50]

Even in the world wars, submarines were notably successful, achieving near decisive levels of destruction and occupying the attention of great numbers of defensive craft. Gorshkov wrote:

> Therefore the question of the ratio of submarine to antisubmarine forces is of great interest even under present-day conditions, since if ASW forces, which were so numerous and technically up to date [for that time], possessing a vast superiority, turned out to be capable of only partially limiting the operations of diesel submarines, then what must this superiority be today in order to counter nuclear powered submarines, whose combat capabilities cannot be compared with the capabilities of World War II-era submarines.[51]

No substantial breakthrough in antisubmarine technology seems in prospect either.

Submarines are now faster, much better armed and, with external help, can find their targets far more easily than they could then. These developments have robbed convoys of several of their traditional advantages: modern surveillance devices mean convoys are no longer necessarily a good way of reducing encounter probabilities; the relatively increased lethality and greater speed of submarines (which can now attack and keep up with surface forces) increases the substance in the old 'all the eggs in one basket' objections to convoy. Concentrations of targets are now simply easier to find and to destroy.

If this is the case, then relatively more attention should presumably be paid to such other 'offensive' strategies as mining submarine transit areas, 'forward roving hunter/killer groups and open sea air patrols'.[52] In view of the new technology, old heresies may have become truth: even the idea of clearance groups shuttling up an down 'sanitised sea lanes' seems acceptable to some. The fact that the old objections to convoy were wrong once, it is concluded, does not necessarily mean they are now.

The modern convoy, though, has at least as many defenders as it does detractors. Not only are the old verities still widely held to be true, but faster and more sophisticated merchant ships, better antisubmarine techniques, the potential of submarine against submarine, improved point defence systems and so forth are sometimes thought actually to have improved the situation. One recent study concluded, 'Compared to thirty years ago the submarine v merchant convoy balance has shifted dramatically in favour of the convoy'.[53]

The wide range of possible scenarios of war and the untested quality of modern means of offence and defence make it unreasonable to seek some specific and definitive answer to contemporary speculation about the importance of maritime communications and the methods by which they might be attacked or defended. For this reason alone, it would plainly be unwise to reject the experience of the past as a possible source of guidance.

(e) The projection of power ashore

Both American and Soviet naval thinking deal with the influence that sea power can bring to bear directly against the land. They call it either 'operations of the fleet against the shore', in the Soviet lexicon, or the 'projection of power ashore', in the American. Both categories are notably comprehensive. Stansfield Turner produced a spectrum of projection which ranged from 'nuclear strike' at one extreme to 'preventitive presence' at the other. Intermediate stages were: tactical air, naval bombardment, amphibious assault and reactive presence. Although Gorshkov's version of this is the same in many respects, he largely left out 'presence' roles but instead specifically included operations against or in support of military shipping which, as we have seen, the Americans include in their sea control mission.

For the moment, however, analysis will be restricted to recent developments in ideas associated with

> power projection in conventional warfare [which] connotes the Navy's ability to launch sea-based air and ground attacks against enemy targets onshore. It also involves naval gun bombardment of enemy naval forces at port and installations. It is meant to enhance the efforts of US and Allied land-based forces in achieving their objectives.[54]

It is often argued these days that conventional over-the-beaches operations are faced with especially severe difficulties, both of the political and of the military sort. Rights of passage have been eroded, and the political and economic costs of strikes against the land have increased. One commentator has spoken of 'the rise of nationalism, the Western withdrawal from empire and the diminishing utility of coercive intervention'[55] as limiting the future possibilities of projection. The trials and tribulations of the US Marine Corps indicate that there have been military problems too. Just after the Second World War, there were those who wished to sweep away the Marines on the grounds that 'a small number of atomic bombs could destroy an expeditionary force as now organised, embarked and landed. . . . With an enemy in possession of atomic bombs, I cannot visualise another landing such as was executed at Normandy or Okinawa'.[56] Large concentrations of ships and men were simply too vulnerable for such operations against the nuclear powers or their immediate allies.

The spread of land-based precision guided munitions amongst the smaller states makes operations against them increasingly hazardous too. The growing mechanisation of the world's armies also tends to increase the difficulty of a force which operates on two dimensions (land and sea) when confronted by an adversary that can afford to specialise in one. The exigencies of going by sea discourages marine forces from investing heavily in armour, for instance, and this increasingly puts them at a military disadvantage. Perhaps for fear of otherwise degenerating into an 'undergunned, slow-moving monument to a bygone era in warfare',[57] the US Marines have tended to operate more with the army than the navy – as in the Vietnam War for example.

The assault on Tang Island in the Gulf of Siam during the *Mayaguez* affair, when casualty rates were relatively high and nearly half the helicopters used were destroyed or disabled by ground fire, demonstrated the vulnerability of assaulting forces to quite basic but resolute defence. Scepticism about the future of contested amphibious operations has reached the highest levels. Said James Schlesinger, United States Secretary of Defense in 1975:

> An amphibious assault force . . . has not seen anything more demanding than essentially unopposed landings for over 20 years, and . . . would have grave difficulties in accomplishing the mission of over-the-beach and flanking operations in a high-threat environment.[58]

All this could have serious implications, not only for the future of the projection role, but also for the future of sea power as a whole. The ability to strike at the land from unexpected and/or advantageous directions gives a flexibility which, wrote Liddell-Hart, was 'the greatest strategic asset that a maritime nation can possess'. Without it, the utility of maritime power would seem considerably diminished.

Despite such doubts in the nuclear age, the navies of the world have continued to stress the projection role. Especially in the days before the Soviet Navy posed a threat of real significance, the US Navy tended to regard projection as its main mission. As far as Gorshkov is concerned, the imperialists have accordingly derived enormous strategic benefit from this attribute of sea power in their capacity to wage local wars of intervention. 'Without wide active use of the fleet,' he wrote, 'the interventionists would hardly have escaped military defeat in Korea.' It was the same story in Vietnam. During the 1968 siege of Khesan, for instance, American carrier aircraft made 25 000 sorties in 77 days, dropped 100 000 bombs and fired 700 000 shells. There were, also, Gorshkov remarked, heavy bombardments, operations against the adversary's supply lines and protection of one's own, the imposition of a sea blockade and important activities by 'riverine' forces in Vietnam itself. It may not be entirely fanciful to detect a touch of wistfulness between the lines of this otherwise generally dispassionate survey of the advantages of projection.[59]

In the past, such operations as these have also frequently been an important part of the struggle to secure sea control. The continued validity of this idea was emphasised at great length by Admiral Holloway in 1976:

> the use of carrier aircraft and Marines in the projection of military force can be an absolute requirement in insuring our control, or continued safe use of areas of the high sea essential to our national needs. . . . Marine amphibious forces, supported by carrier air, can seize and hold land areas either to deny them to the enemy for their use in indicting our sea lines of communication, or to permit our own forces to exploit these areas as advance bases to attack enemy forces which would interdict our own. . . . It is interesting to remember that the island hopping campaigns in the Pacific in World War II were not to acquire real estate, but for the sole purpose of seizing advanced bases to gain control of the sea approaches to the recovery of the Philippines and the invasion of Japan.[60]

It follows from all this that the Navy must continue to have an important anti-projection function as well. When Marshall Sokolovsky's *Military Strategy* first appeared in the Soviet Union in 1962 it was widely criticised for failing to give sufficient prominence to the roles that the Navy could perform in defence of the country. Admiral Alafuzov wrote:

> The authors must take into account the specific fact that a navy is capable of cutting off an amphibious landing while it is still at sea,

before it even arrives off the coast. Worse than that, having a powerful navy in opposition, one cannot always take the risk of an amphibious landing.[61]

Discussing the maritime activities of the imperialists in their local wars, Gorshkov made the point that 'they are not very instructive since they were conducted in conditions of an absence on the defending side of real naval forces capable of putting up proper resistence to the aggressor'. In his book, he evidently believed the necessity of offering 'due counteraction' to projection operations was a point important enough to warrant making three times in four pages.[62]

The strategic utility of operations against the shore seems to have persuaded the Soviet Navy to follow along the traditional path taken by the Americans both in terms of theory and practice. Gorshkov showed himself to be well aware of the impact of maritime operations on the land campaign in the Second World War, as we have already seen. Of course in a country as dominated by continental ideas as the Soviet Union this line is a politically persuasive one to take. The case has also subsequently been strengthened by the advent of sea-based nuclear weapons systems. Nevertheless there seems little reason to doubt that the Soviet Navy wholeheartedly accepts that 'the chief goal of a fleet is becoming that of ensuring the fulfilment of all tasks associated with action against enemy ground objectives and the protection of one's territory from the strikes of his fleet'.[63] The commissioning in 1979 of the 13 000-ton amphibious warfare ship *Ivan Rogov* (capable of carrying a battalion of naval infantry with equipment), the inclusion of related activities in many recent naval exercises and, possibly, recent carrier construction policy seem to imply that the Soviet Navy's interest in land-directed operations is growing.[64]

Since the end of the Second World War, there have been, all the same, several periods of uncertainty about the future of amphibious operations. Early doubts about the utility of the function were silenced with the celebrated 1950 Inchon landings in Korea. In the same way doubts about such operations which surfaced in the aftermath of the Vietnam War may yet prove to have been overdrawn. Certainly current United States discussion about the possibility of forming a maritime striking force for use in the Indian Ocean and elsewhere seem to point in this direction.

Anxieties are certainly much less acute about such subsidiary operations as naval gunfire and logistic support and about minor, supportive or unopposed landings. All of these have indeed been relatively common feature of maritime operations since 1945. But, although amphibious forces may have partially coped with new threats by their use of new equipment (VSTOL aircraft and helicopters, for instance) and new techniques (such as 'vertical envelopment'), doubts about the feasibility of major contested landings nevertheless remain.

In the past, these difficult and dramatic operations, anyway, have only taken up part of what is now called the projection mission. Even if they are thought likely to be too costly in the nuclear age (and this is by no means a universal view) the mission as a whole has certainly survived its new environment. And it is at least arguable that there are sufficient continuities in concept between past and present for analyses of the first to help the second.

9 New Tasks for New Navies

The new environment has not only modified the execution of traditional maritime functions but has also produced new tasks for navies to perform. Sometimes these tasks are new in entire conception (such as those to do with the operation of the nuclear deterrent at sea) or new in their dimensions, demands and perceived importance (such as naval diplomacy and the protection of the offshore estate). To a greater or lesser extent these new tasks compete with the older ones for naval resources. To a greater or lesser extent also, naval policy makers will find little in the established literature of maritime strategy to help them make their choices.

(a) The protection of the offshore estate

Off the shores of many countries, over the past generation or so, there has appeared a new complex of technological, political and economic interests which the British like to call, somewhat whimsically, the 'offshore tapestry'. It represents important new sources of food, energy and raw materials; it makes the sea more, not less, important than it used to be; it forces countries with coastlines to consider how best to manage their new estates. Even the maritime states have found their existing bureaucracies (whose responsibilities to date have been fundamentally territorial) unequal to the task; the United States has some forty overlapping agencies concerned with the offshore estate, the British over twenty. Very evidently, old patterns do not fit the new realities, which demand instead a co-ordinated maritime policy and new patterns of administration. Equally obviously, each new resource and interest needs recognition, understanding and effective management.

These days it is hard not to be aware of the importance of the sea and the sea bed as sources of energy (coal, oil, gas, even wave and tidal power) and of vital raw materials. Gorshkov produced an apparently endless list of chemical and mineral resources to be found at sea, everything in fact from thorium to gravel, and already explorations are underway of the ocean beds beyond the continental shelf where yet more of these assets doubtless lie in rich profusion. Their efficient extraction will certainly require an agreed and equitable ocean regime and protection against nature, accident and hostile act.

As Gorshkov wrote, people have been taking fish from the oceans since time immemorial, but there has been a radical transformation of even this industry since 1945. The world catch, at something like seventy million tons, is now four times what it was a generation ago. It is a vital component of the economies of many countries, Japan and Russia particularly. Inevitable problems have arisen. Some species, like the Atlantic herring and the Arctic cod, have been over-fished to the point of extinction. There have been endless disputes over what is the maximum sustainable yield for these and other types of fish, over its allocation, and over who has the jurisdiction to make the ultimate decision. Tensions have run high between local fishing communities and the high technology fleets which have appeared on their grounds and, with a vacuum cleaner action, sucked up their livelihoods. There promises to be much difficulty in the exploitation of new food sources, such as the huge quantities of krill known to be in the waters between Antarctica, South America and the Falklands, and estimated by Lord Shackleton's 1976 report as likely to produce an annual catch far exceeding the rest of the world fish catch put together.

The management of all this obviously requires international agreement, equitable and effective regulation and the means to ensure that fishing vessels comply with relevant fishery protection and conservation rules. Countries with seaboards will doubtless tend to increase the areas of their maritime jurisdiction as time goes by. Within these areas they will have to identify, plot and monitor the activities of all trawlers, national and foreign, ensuring that individuals are not breaking the rules by using the wrong size mesh on their nets or catching the wrong kind of fish. The even more exacting task of ensuring that foreign fishing fleets are not exceeding their agreed quota will also need to be carried out.

The way in which various forms of sea use interweave is demonstrated by the effects on fishing (and for that matter on recreation) of pollution, often the unintended by-product of other marine activities. In 1971 Jacques Cousteau told the Council of Europe that intensity of life in the world's seas had declined by between 30 and 50 per cent during the previous twenty years. The main causes of the trouble are marine disposal, (either by coastal discharge or ocean dumping) ocean spillage, navigational accident and sea bed operations of various kinds. The vulnerability of the sea lies in the interdependence of its attributes. It has been said, 'All marine life is joined in a complex web of food chains and the relationship between living things, and between living things and their surroundings is so delicately balanced in the sea that a disturbance in one part can have a deleterious effect on the whole system'.[1] The control of pollution clearly requires sea use to be supervised and regulated much more than was the custom in the past.

It requires, for instance, some kind of sea traffic control. Marine accident and sloppy operational practices are a significant cause of pollution. The danger is aggravated first by the financial pressures on ship operators which encourage such hazardous practices as racing tides, cutting corners, crossing sea lanes and shelving maintenance schedules, and secondly by the increase in the sheer volume of sea transport. The size of the world's shipping fleet has gone up over four times in the last twenty-five years. All this suggests that shipping routes, like air routes, will gradually become more regulated as time goes by. Certainly in focal points, like the English Channel, local states are likely to be increasingly involved in shipping surveillance, traffic separation schemes, the identification, interception and arrest of offenders, in salvage and wreck clearance and so on. The task of search and rescue will also become steadily more demanding as the volume of sea use increases. Around the shores of Britain, for example, the annual rate of life boat launching has gone up from 346 in the inter-war period to 2500 in 1979.[2]

Finally, as coastal states increase the extent of jurisdiction over wider areas of sea, there will be a growing need for the enforcement of civil and international law. Safety, health, welfare, law and order on oil rigs and ships passing in national jurisdiction will remain a preoccupation of the authorities. Action will also continue against the ancient and dishonourable practice of piracy, still a significant hazard in many of the world's seas. The patterns of trade and transport are also more likely to increase than to diminish the need to monitor the passage of goods and people. This is no new requirement, of course. In England, for example, the Customs and Excise Service trace their origins back to one John Page appointed as 'The Searcher' in 1356, whose task it was to prevent the export of wool and gold and the import of cloth from Flanders. There seems little doubt that revenue cutters will continue to board and 'rummage' ships, with such objectives as these, to check against the passage of prohibited goods, animals and people. Equally it seems safe to assume that equivalent but far more sinister activities will go on off the coasts of societies less open than the West.

It now remains to suggest ways in which the growth of these activities will affect the world's navies and, indirectly perhaps, the maritime strategy of present and future. In the first place, the establishment of a global regime for the offshore estate is as yet nowhere near accomplishment. For the time being, disputes over lines of jurisdiction would seem a likely feature of the international diplomatic scene. The stakes are high enough to cause difficulties between friends, such as the 1969–70 dispute between Canada and the United States over the status of the North-West passage, Canada's anti-pollution measures and the escorted passage of the United States tanker *Manhattan*. Where relations are less than cordial, as around the potentially oil rich South China Seas, competition has taken the more dangerous form of pre-emptive occupation of disputed islands and particularly bitter diplomatic exchanges and dangerous naval demonstrations. In 1966, probably more in a spirit of hope than expectation, President Johnson said:

> Under no circumstances, we believe, must we ever allow the prospect of a rich harvest and mineral wealth to create a new form of colonial competition among maritime nations. We must be careful to avoid a race to grab and hold the land under the high seas. We must ensure that the deep seas and the ocean bottoms are, and remain, the legacy of all human beings.[3]

But this as yet remains merely an aspiration. Until it becomes reality, navies can expect to play a part in the process through which lines of jurisdiction are gradually settled.

There have also been disputes over the allocation of the resources of particular sea-areas between particular countries. Although the three Cod Wars between Britain and Iceland command the attention, they are by no means the first, last or only examples of their kind. Disputes over jurisdiction and resource allocation seem, at least in the short run, likely to lead to conflicts in which navies might play a significant part. Indeed, in the Cod Wars and with the Chinese occupation of the Paracels in January 1974, and various other incidents in that area, and elsewhere, they already have to a considerable degree.

The naval role in support of mineral extraction in the offshore estate has been the subject of much discussion, which in Britain has principally focused on the business of oil rig protection. This has involved making choices on the connected issues of the kind of threat to prepare against and at what stage responsibility ought to be principally assumed by the naval authorities. The general conclusion is that navies need to be able to demonstrate a sufficient capacity to react in order to deter such military threats at the lower end of the scale as hijackings and limited harrassment. More substantial threats would presumably be catered for by the navy's general war-fighting capacities.

This kind of direct but limited protection seems best afforded by area rather than point defence, not least because the rigs themselves are only a part of the system that needs defending. Aerial surveillance is necessary for the swift reaction of the kind promised by the Royal Marines Special Boat Section established in Arbroath in May 1980. The ships themselves need to be able to respond proportionately to the threat or situation and simple, visible weaponry, high speed, good sea-keeping and loiter characteristics, manoeuvrability and hull strength, are desirable attributes. And so is cheapness, for the area to be covered is a large one, requiring a reasonable number of units.

Much the same can be said of the desirable attributes of naval vessels on fishery protection duties, although their precise mix depends on the particular nature of the task. The protection of deep sea fishing fleets in such hostile waters as those of the Northern Atlantic is obviously an especially demanding task requiring rugged ships and determined crews. Fishery protection is no new task, of course. In Britain, for instance, it began as a formal duty in the eighteenth century, but in scale and in complexity it has grown out of all recognition. In the Icelandic Cod Wars, it developed strategies and tactics that were both distinctive and novel. They were certainly not military activities of the orthodox sort.

This applies even more to the various other auxiliary functions which navies can be expected to perform in the offshore estate. Naval vessels have been commonly employed in pollution control, in law enforcement against errant merchant ships, smugglers and pirates, and in search and rescue – all 'in aid of the civil power'.

Although navies may even maintain units that are specifically dedicated to these specialised tasks (such as search and rescue helicopter flights) they are nevertheless not generally considered to be in the main stream of naval purposes. They often appear either to run counter to or be ignored by most traditional writings on maritime strategy. For instance, the notion that the sea itself is now an area to be defended conflicts with established naval doctrine which, as we have seen, has generally been hostile to the shackling of substantial forces to the defence of fixed positions. Accordingly, the maritime strategists have no advice to offer on this and other matters connected with the protection of the offshore estate.

Since circumstances often seem to require the devotion of highly trained personnel and expensive, complex materiel to the resolution of these simple if arduous tasks, anxieties have also arisen that the protection of the offshore estate may absorb resources better dedicated to the navy's real and main job on the high seas. This has all tended to reinforce the argument that naval forces should not be devoted too readily to a constabulary role, best executed by some non-military organisation like the US Coast Guard.

This solution does however seem to imply some duplication of effort and resource. For this and other reasons the role seems likely to remain one of the principal concerns of most of the world's navies. This will require the performance of tasks that are either *sui generis* (the enforcement of pollution controls) or traditional ones writ small (the physical protection of trawler fleets, anti-piracy operations and the like). Neither are many of these minor naval necessities particularly new. In the last century the Royal Navy, for instance, spent much of its time suppressing piracy and the slave trade and generally maintaining good order at sea. Said one of its Admirals:

> I don't think we thought very much about war with a big W. We looked on the Navy more as a World Police Force than as a warlike institution. We considered that our job was to safeguard law and order throughout the world – safeguard civilisation, put out fires on shore, and act as guide, philosopher and friend to the merchant ships of all nations.[4]

In fact, navies seem always to have had some constabulary role and will certainly continue to do so.

A concern for the offshore estate may have one final effect on the future of the world's navies. The argument is that as one thing leads to another, national jurisdiction will creep steadily out from the shore line, enclosing more and more of the world's high seas: Selden with his notions of the *Mare Clausum* will have his revenge on Grotius. These politico-legal developments will be reinforced by the increasing availability of fast patrol boats and anti-ship missiles like *Gabriel* and *Exocet* which make the forcing of contested passage an increasingly hazardous operation for even the strongest of distant water fleets.

Since the indivisibility and freedom of the sea is central to the philosophy of maritime power, a general decline in the utility of traditional naval functions is therefore to be expected. For instance, an ability to move from one point to another more or less at will would seem to be an essential prerequisite for the military flexibility, so often advanced as a chief benefit conferred by naval power. And yet, as the British carrier *Victorious* and the American *Enterprise* found in 1964 and 1971 respectively, when transiting various Indonesian straits, this freedom may be considerably curtailed as states assert their authority in local waters.

The maritime powers have certainly expressed anxieties about such developments. Thus Gorshkov wrote: 'A highly alarming symptom is the practice of the extension by certain states of the limits of their territorial sea up to 200 miles, which is nothing other than an attempt to seize great expanses of the ocean'.[5]

It seems unlikely, however, that a proposal to which the great powers take such strong exception will progress either as far or as rapidly as has sometimes been suggested. Moreover, it does not follow that simply because coastal states could refuse passage, they automatically would.[6] In sum, although the new technical–legal–political environment will certainly produce new complexities into maritime operations, it would seem premature to write traditional naval power off merely on that account.

(b) Naval diplomacy

Naval diplomacy is a relatively new phrase covering maritime activities at the less dangerous end of the spectrum of procedures which one country may use to influence the behaviour of another. The full spectrum ranges from uninhibited military attack at one extreme to routine diplomatic persuasion at the other, and it has no discontinuities; diplomatic activities merge imperceptibly into threats and acts of war. Although in naval diplomacy, power is exploited rather than force expended, particular occasions may be thought to warrant acts of physical coercion.

Such naval activities can be seen as instruments of foreign policy, not only in peacetime but also in war, often serving the same purpose in different ways. In peace, for instance, navies may try to guarantee the acquisition of strategic materials by exerting political influence on suppliers, but in war they may try to do the same thing by measures of trade protection. Military objectives for which navies may fight (the protection of trade, the conquest of territory and so forth) are of course ultimately political in nature, for war itself, as von Maltzahn reminded his readers, is a political act.[7] Sometimes, in the midst of conflict, navies are used as diplomatic instruments even more directly than this. They may exert leverage over neutrals; or they may be preserved as a bargaining counter for end-of-war negotiations.[8]

But the relationship between naval activities and the political background is more complex than this would suggest. For a start, maritime war, like any other, tends to develop its own momentum and to produce its own imperatives and unintended political consequences. The evolution of the German U-boat war between 1914 and 1918 and its impact on American opinion is a case in point. Furthermore navies themselves, their size and use, are often a consequence (rather than a cause) of political processes either on the domestic or the international scene. So, in all these ways, as Mahan observed: 'Diplomatic conditions affect military action, and military considerations diplomatic measures.... They are inseparable parts of a whole; and as such those responsible for military measures should understand the diplomatic factors, and vice versa'.[9]

All the maritime strategists argued in their various ways that, to quote John Stuart Mill 'our diplomacy stands for nothing when we have not a fleet to back it'.[10] As far as Corbett was concerned, the first function of the fleet was 'to support or obstruct diplomatic effort' (the other two being to protect or destroy commerce and to further or hinder military operations ashore).[11] Mahan argued, too, that the possession of sea power increased a country's prestige, security and influence: it was necessary for great powers to be strong at sea. Although not entirely approvingly, Mahan quoted Nelson as saying: 'I hate your pen-and-ink men; a fleet of British ships of war are the best negotiators in Europe'.[12] Conversely, weakness at sea led inevitably to political and strategic danger both at home and abroad – as Richmond showed on countless occasions.

Orthodox opinion also emphasised, almost laboured, the point that maritime strategy and the use of naval forces should be fitted in with the overall national strategy and should be appropriate to the political purposes the country's leaders hoped to achieve. Although this applied both in peace as well as in war, the bulk of their attention was nevertheless directed at the wartime uses of navies. Apart from recommending that navies should prepare efficiently and visibly for war, the maritime strategists had little advice to offer about naval activities in peacetime. Richmond indeed went the other way and condemned the peacetime display of large navies and large ships for mere purposes of prestige.

This lack of attention, however, no longer applies. Doubtless because of the greater costs and risks of applying force in the nuclear age, there has been a 'shift towards civilian bands of the political spectrum, or at least to lower levels of violence'.[13] This has been accompanied by a correspondingly increased interest in what Admiral Stansfield Turner called the 'Naval Presence mission . . . the use of naval forces, short of war, to achieve political objectives'. Turner discussed 'preventive deployments' (where the appearance of naval forces prevents a problem from becoming a crisis) and 'reactive deployments' (where naval forces respond to a crisis). Deployments, threatened or actual, need to be appropriate to the situation, pose a credible threat to the opposition and must suggest the capacity to engage in any of five basic actions; amphibious assault, air attack, bombardment, blockade, or exposure through reconnaissance.[14]

Although Gorshkov dealt with the matter less explicitly, the peacetime functions of navies are a major preoccupation of his writings as well. He wrote, 'It would be difficult to find an area of our planet where US leaders have not used their pet instrument of foreign policy – the Navy – against the progressive forces of the people of various countries'. But this need not be the prerogative of the Imperialists. The Soviet Navy could be 'the instrument of a policy and friendship of peoples, a deterrent to military activities, and a resolute opposition to the threats to the security of peace-loving peoples on the part of imperialist powers'.[15]

Ship visits to third world states, Gorshkov argued, could be useful for spreading the ideas of the 'Leninist peaceloving policy of the Communist party' and for increasing the influence and prestige of the Soviet Union. Navies could

> demonstrate graphically the real fighting power of one's state. ... Demonstrative actions by the navy in many cases have made it possible to achieve political ends without resorting to armed struggle, merely by putting on pressure with one's own potential might and threatening to start military operations. Thus ... the navy has always been an instrument of the policy of states, an important aid to diplomacy in peacetime.[16]

Although the activity itself is not new, the degree of attention paid to it certainly is. Naval diplomacy for the first time has become a significant preoccupation of maritime strategists, an important declared function of navies and justification for having them. No longer is it merely a kind of bonus, something one does with navies when they have no wars to fight. The elevation of this activity to one of the principal missions of modern navies is not the least important of the changes brought about by the new environment in which they operate.

Even so, as Stansfield Turner admitted, the Naval Presence mission remains the least understood of all. Although modern strategists have identified the importance of the function, their discussion of how it works and what political purposes it can serve has remained fairly rudimentary.

These questions have largely been left to a number of modern civilian analysts. Their work has been in many ways an outgrowth of the burgeoning literature on the diplomacy of force associated with such writers as Thomas Schelling, Oran Young and Coral Bell, to name but a few.[17] Early works in the field were Laurence Martin's *The Sea in Modern Strategy* which dealt extensively with less-than-absolute types of maritime conflict and the seminal *Gunboat Diplomacy* produced by James Cable. Ideas were further refined in Edward Luttwak's *The Political Uses of Sea Power* and Ken Booth's very thorough *Navies and Foreign Policy*. Surveys of this kind are inevitably quite general and so need to be complemented by more specialised works. These include studies of particular episodes in naval diplomacy such as Jonathan T. Howe's *Multicrises* and the growing literature on the activities of the Soviet and American navies in the Mediterranean. More recently still Bradford Dismukes and James McConnell of the Center for Naval Analyses have produced the detailed study *Soviet Naval Diplomacy*.

These analysts produced their own varying taxonomies of the purposes and methods of naval diplomacy. Cable distinguished between four kinds of naval force: the definitive (where it is used to produce a *fait accompli* as in the case of the seizure of the US spy-ship *Pueblo* by the North Koreans); the purposeful (to persuade other nations to change their policy – the object of the British naval deployment to Kuwait in 1961); the catalytic (such as the sending of the *Enterprise* to the Bay of Bengal in 1971, to influence events); the expressive (merely to emphasise attitudes, with no other object necessarily in view). Luttwak discussed what he called 'naval suasion' which was either 'latent' (routine and undirected deployments) or 'active' (by conscious design). Such actions could either support an ally, deter an adversary or compel him to change his policy.

Booth dealt with naval diplomacy less from the point of view of the desired political result than as a function of navies. He produced a triangle of naval tasks – on one side the policing or coastguard role, on another the military (including peacetime deterrence) and on the third the diplomatic role where navies are used to change the political calculations of interested parties. Like Luttwak, he argued that the tactics of naval diplomacy were largely concerned with the desired manipulation of the size, composition, locality, readiness and activity of deployed naval forces but he added to the list naval aid (help in training and arms supply), operational calls and specific good-will visits.

Evidently, navies can be used in many ways to convey messages and influence events. The sending of a dominant force, likely to prevail, for example, will whittle away the adversary's options, demonstrate commitment and may make the desired outcome more likely. A weak force, on the other hand, may be interposed between two competing parties to cool a situation. Forces can be left uncommitted or even sent in the opposite direction to indicate a determination not to get involved. The fact that the more dramatic and forceful manifestations of naval diplomacy command the attention should not conceal the moderating role it often has.

Although there is space here for no more than a tantalisingly brief summary of these important studies, it is clear that naval action can have as wide a range of effects as any other instrument of diplomacy.[18] Like the alternatives, it will sometimes succeed and sometimes fail. Nevertheless naval diplomacy would appear to have certain advantages over the alternatives – especially in the nuclear age. Navies have inherent mobility, tactical flexibility and a wide geographic reach. Individual warships are versatile and controllable, and can still make their way about the world's oceans with relative freedom. They have impressive staying power, can project their power ashore (in a literal or figurative sense) and are important symbols of the countries they serve.[19] Even the sea itself seems a good place for nations to go a-jousting, apparently insulated as it is from the dangers and sensitivities of conflict or menacing manoeuvre on land.[20]

But this view is challenged by those who maintain that the progressive enclosure of the oceans, the risk of escalation intrinsic to the mildest display of military might, the increasing weight of world opinion (which allows the weak to bully the strong), and the new technology of maritime warfare (which increases the relative power of the presumptious local) will all make naval diplomacy less universal, pervasive and useful than once it was. Its utility will decline; it will become, in the words of one leading protagonist of the school 'a mere folkloristic manifestation to be performed only in the territorial waters of already friendly and aligned states'.[21]

Although there is certainly something to be said for this view it can be overdrawn. A (very possibly temporary) decline in Western propensities to use naval diplomacy should not automatically be taken to imply a decline in the function as a whole. In fact, though, as one recent study has shown: 'The Navy has been the foremost instrument for the United States' political uses of armed force: at all times, in all places, and regardless of the specifics of the situation'. The US Navy shared in 177 of the 215 international incidents involving United States forces between 1945 and 1975.[22] Recent events and decisions in the Indian Ocean area seem to suggest that the American disenchantment with things military in the aftermath of the Vietnam war may be more moribund than their willingness to use naval power for such purposes. Neither does the Soviet Union display many apparent doubts about the utility of naval diplomacy.

The principal agents of naval diplomacy seem likely to remain surface ships, which have many obvious advantages over aircraft or submarines in this role. There also obviously needs to be especially good communications between participating ships and their political controllers. Flexibility and the capacity to operate significantly at many different levels of violence are particularly desirable attributes of individual ships; they have to be able to respond to any threat in due proportion and, it is generally agreed, they ought to be able to give a reasonable account of themselves against the adversary's forces. They need to be fast and numerous enough actually to appear where the action is for the *local* 'relations of forces' often decides the outcome. But, probably above all, they need to be appropriate for the particular tasks in hand.

Thus naval diplomacy in the waters of nineteenth-century China required not 'Line of Battle ships [which] are not adapted to the Chinese coasts', but light-draught gunboats which could carry, support, supply and withdraw troops, take on forts and impress with a generally imposing air, '32 pounders . . . [being] . . . more efficacious than other arguments'. They needed to be commanded by men who knew the political realities of their station, who could navigate skilfully and cope with severe winters 'muddy and shallow waters, full of unseen dangers, violent tides, eddies and ripplings'.[23]

The idea that naval diplomacy required specialised forces and procedures of this kind has been much reinforced in recent times. The celebrated squabble between Secretary of Defense Robert MacNamara and his Chief of Naval Operations during the Cuba Missile crisis of 1962 indicated the way in which political realities required considerable revamping of traditional skills and practices. MacNamara said, 'There is no longer any such thing as strategy only crisis management'. [24] It did not matter what John Paul Jones had written long ago about how to operate a blockade; the US Navy's Cuba quarantine was strictly *sui generis* and the navy would have to break its own established rules if necessary. Normal procedures would have to be modified to make them appropriate to the political situation. The task might even need a new kind of navy.

Tensions between the naval requirements of war-fighting and diplomacy are not new. Admiral Fisher demonstrated the fact of competition between these two roles in the early 1900s when he redisposed squadrons and struck nearly 150 ships off the Navy List which were too weak to fight or too slow to run away. He wanted to concentrate his naval resources on the coming war against Germany, not dissipate them on political functions in distant stations. Again, naval commanders have always feared that too many cocktail parties might mean not enough exercises – and continue to do so. In modern times, naval diplomacy might seem to call for large surface ships, but war, for stealthy submarines. Political considerations might require the Sixth Fleet to be 'split up . . . [and sent] . . . to a lot of ports to influence a lot of people', whereas war readiness demands that it be kept in tight and mutually supportive groups. [25]

This task may not appeal to naval warriors trained to the last degree for the pursuit of victory in some high technology encounter on the open oceans. Very possibly, therefore, insufficient attention will be paid to the role and its naval requirements, despite the fact that there is 'a 95 per cent probability that the most likely future use of naval forces will be in the Presence role'. [26] So severe is the resources squeeze on even the largest of the world's navies that it seems unlikely that forces, ships or weaponry will be produced with diplomatic purposes exclusively in mind.

Nevertheless, there are sufficient incompatibilities between the two roles for choices to have to be made. It has been pointed out 'In the opinion of many people the size and configuration of the US Navy should be determined on the basis of scenarios for the most likely intervention or crisis management rather than the worst-case threat of general war'. [27] It may well be, on the other hand, that one needs to be able to survive the worst kind of threat in order to prevail against the most probable.

Deciding on such matters and making policy choices about mission priorities very evidently requires a full and proper understanding of what naval diplomacy is, exactly how it works and what its requirements are. Such an understanding would also be a valuable corrective to that advocacy of naval presence which pays too little attention to its difficulties, failures and occasionally counter-productive results. It should also guard against the tendency to deploy naval forces unthinkingly simply because they are often the first that come to hand. But formulations of the strategy of naval diplomacy have as yet some way to go before these things can be achieved. Sometimes, as Stansfield Turner recently remarked:

> I think that we who exercise naval presence do not know enough about how to fit the action to the situation: how to be sure that the force we bring to bear, when told to help in some situation, is in fact the one most appropriate to the circumstances.[28]

(c) Strategic deterrence

Naval writers have usually argued that strength at sea, as elsewhere, is the best preserver of peace and guarantee of national security. Mahan wrote, 'The surest way to maintain peace is to occupy a position of menace'. Such a principle lay beneath the Pax Britannica of the nineteenth century when the naval majesty of the empire deterred potential aggressors. The thirty miles of home based ships present at the Diamond Jubilee Fleet Review of 1897 were the particular instruments of this form of maritime deterrence. One American visitor commented, 'I guess, Sir, this makes for peace'.[29]

Strength and the general capacity to prevail, or at least to give a sufficient account of oneself, is the main constituent of deterrence, maritime or otherwise. While it is doubtless true that 'the greatest deterrent will be provided by the enemy's knowledge that if he hits you, you can hit back a bloody sight harder',[30] it does not follow that an adversary need think himself outgunned or faced with the prospect of actual defeat in order to be deterred. It may be enough if he is confronted by a maritime force of sufficient strength to make the probable costs of his course of action liable to outweigh the possible benefits. Just such a principle bolstered Admiral Tirpitz's celebrated 'Risk Theory', discussed earlier.

An estimate of the level of the adversary's determination will obviously be a necessary part of the calculation. Since the attributes of deterrence are distinguished only by their ambiguity, they will doubtless need constantly to be identified and explored in times of tension and less than perfect peace. When one side resorts, therefore, to tactics of intrusion and harassment by buzzing the other's ships with his aircraft or sailing ostentatiously through his exercises (or playing even more sinister games beneath the surface) he is effectively demonstrating both his strength and his resolve. Such actions are an important part of the international discourse between adversaries, and between allies. Although the form they take may be new, the concept of such actions is quite traditional. The desire to influence the perceptions of possible adversaries, after all, has always been one of the main reasons why states have navies in peacetime.

The exact requirements of this form of non-verbal communication depend, of course, on the particular occasion, but an evident ability to 'give a good account of oneself' over a wide range of circumstances is an obvious asset in the business of maritime deterrence. The nearer a navy can approach to the ideal of being able to respond against any level or type of threat anywhere, anytime, the better the deterrence it offers. Also, many analysts often refer to the 'seamless web' of deterrence, arguing that the appearance of discontinuities in the spectrum should be avoided since gaps might be a dangerous source of vulnerability, if exploited by a resourceful or misguided enemy. Like a chain, deterrence can only serve its purpose if all its links are securely connected. For both these reasons, deterrence seems to call for 'balanced' forces catering for as wide a range of contingencies as possible.

The seamless web covers wartime operations as well as peacetime ones. In the last war, for instance, submarines were deterred from attacking convoys by the position, number and perceived efficiency of the escorts that guarded them. Deterrence, in other words, does not stop when the fighting starts: not does its essential pattern necessarily change.

Some analysts suggest that Soviet military philosophy has some advantage over its western equivalents in its readiness to recognise this fact. Soviet literature puts the stress not simply on the prevention of war, but also on the war-fighting and war-winning 'if deterrence fails'. The Soviet version of deterrence will only, in fact, have failed if a war breaks out after all – and they do not go on to win it. They do not regard deterrence as separate in any conceptual way from the business of fighting wars and see no incompatibility between wanting to avoid war on the one hand and to win it on the other.[31] Presumably, however, the danger is that by emphasising war prevention at the expense of war fighting, the West may undermine the effectiveness of its means of achieving either.

Maritime deterrence, therefore, is not *sui generis*, a discrete component of maritime strategy with its own specific requirements. Instead it comes merely as a preventative variant of the traditional maritime functions which the ships which exercise it are actually designed to carry out. It is perhaps worth emphasising that ships cannot be 'designed for deterrence': a general deterrent effect on potential adversaries can only be conferred by an evident ability to perform conventional maritime tasks efficiently. Concentrating on the combative function, in other words, will take care of the deterrent variant too.[32]

This is not so evident when it comes to the nuclear end of the spectrum of maritime deterrence. The sheer destructive power of the weapons concerned makes their operation seem a task quite distinct from the rest of a navy's activities. Other factors reinforce this conclusion. The operating style of the forces that carry out the role (these days, mainly ballistic missile firing submarines (SSBNs)), is quite dissimilar from other naval forces. Their military objectives are exclusively land targets: they do not directly affect the war at sea, protect or attack maritime communications or operate against each other. Wherever possible they even try to avoid contact with all other vessels. A study made in 1974 concluded:

> The Polaris ships themselves are a curious element in Western navies. . . . Clearly they have no naval function in terms of classical naval theory. The object of a fleet is to meet and destroy the opposing fleet of the enemy. The Polaris ships have no part in this: they are fighting another war.[33]

The calculations made about their use could equally well be, and in fact usually are, made by the authorities responsible also for land-based bombers and missiles. How then could they be said to serve a naval function? 'Polaris submarines', concluded Admiral Gretton, 'do not represent sea power in its traditional sense – they represent deterrence.'[34]

Such a view contributed to the reluctance of many in the world's leading navies to take on this task – especially as it was so profligate in scarce resources. Though the task was not really naval, it absorbed so much skilled manpower, money and research effort that it made the execution of the more obviously naval tasks more difficult. For this reason, responsibility for the creation of sea-based deterrent forces was often given to people and agencies outside the usual naval bureaucracy.

On the other hand, it is not necessary to resort to dismissive arguments that strategic deterrence is simply a somewhat elevated form of shore bombardment to show that this perception of the uniqueness of maritime strategic deterrence is partly based on two fallacies, one a matter of high principle, the other of operational practice. The attempt to divide the continuum of deterrence into autonomous sections is likely to be fraught, first of all, with semantic and conceptual difficulty. Where, for example, would nuclear capable aircraft operating from strike carriers fit into the picture, or, for that matter, orthodox warships equipped among other things with nuclear cruise missiles? Even if it could be done, the successful isolation of 'strategic deterrence' would bring new difficulties in its train, for the whole burden of contemporary analysis is that discontinuities in the spectrum are conceptually unsound and potentially dangerous, as we have seen.

Secondly, it is usually argued that strategic deterrence at sea is so contingent upon orthodox naval activities that it is better regarded as a part of them. The function is usually subsumed within that mission (variously labelled as 'power projection' or 'operations against the shore') which covers 'a broad spectrum of offensive actions from strategic nuclear response by fleet ballistic missile submarines to surgical air strikes mounted by carrier-based aircraft'.[35]

Moreover, its operations are usually considered to require at least a measure of sea control. The vessels firing the missiles or launching the aircraft would need to use the sea to approach their targets and would have to be protected against the adversary's maritime defences. Gorshkov made a particular point of stressing the importance of the conventional navy in providing the maritime conditions in which the strategic deterrence task could be performed: he wrote:

> Surface ships remain the basic and often sole combat means of ensuring deployment of the main strike force – submarines. The First and Second World Wars showed the fallacy of the view that the submarine by virtue of its concealment after emerging from its base can itself ensure its own invulnerability.[36]

Supportive naval forces can be expected to help SSBNs accomplish their task by 'sanitising' their exit points and disposing of trailing submarines, or ASW groups. These activities are novel in no more than name and it is by no means inconceivable that the observations of orthodox naval theory about methods of securing command of the sea may have a bearing on this preliminary phase of the strategic deterrence mission. In short, even if the mission does seem quite novel in some particulars, it is much less so in others; in any case, it 'presupposes sea power and provides it with a distinctive purpose and rationale'.[37]

The advantages of putting the instruments of strategic deterrence at sea were listed by Gorshkov. This method provides greater reach, allows attacks to be made from many different directions and reduces the enemy's incentive to launch disarming strikes against the homeland. Because SSBNs are so hard to find and destroy, 'a considerable part of the nuclear missile power of the enemy would be dissipated fruitlessly'. As a result of all this, he declared, the navy has become 'a most important factor deterring his nuclear attack'.[38] According to some analysts the operation of the strategic deterrent has now become the first and principal task of the Soviet Navy.[39]

Some of the detail of the task becomes a little clearer when American naval thinking on the matter is examined. Stansfield Turner argued that the strategic deterrent had three main functions:

> to deter all-out attack on the United States or its allies; to face any

potential aggressor contemplating less than all-out attack with unacceptable costs; and to maintain a stable political environment within which the threat of aggression or coercion against the United States or its allies is minimised.

He also identified four 'force preparedness objectives' or 'tactics', the last two of which were concerned with the image the United States presented to the world:

A third objective is to *deter third powers* from attacking the United States with nuclear weapons. Because of the great disparity between any third country's nuclear arsenal and ours, the same forces deterring the Soviet Union should deter others.

Finally, we maintain sufficient strategic forces so that we do not appear to be at a disadvantage to the Soviet Union or any other power. If we were to allow the opinion to develop that the Soviet strategic position is markedly superior to ours we would find that political decisions were being adversely influenced. Thus we must always keep in mind the *balance of power image* that our forces portray to the non-Soviet world. In part, this image affects what and how much we buy for strategic deterrence. In part, it affects how we talk about our comparative strength and how we criticise ourselves.

The first two tactics, however, are to dissuade the Soviet Union from launching an all-out or partial attack on the United States, and, here by implication, on any of her allies:

The first is to maintain an *assured second strike* capability in the hope of deterring an all-out strategic nuclear attack on the United States. Today that means dissuading the Soviets from starting a nuclear war. We hope to achieve this by maintaining a strategic attack force capable of inflicting unacceptable damage on any enemy even after he has attacked us. The Navy's Polaris/Poseidon/Trident forces are fundamental to this deterrence because of their high nuclear survival probability.

A second tactic is to design our forces to ensure that the United States is not placed in an unacceptable position by a partial nuclear attack. If the Soviets attacked only a portion of our strategic forces, would it then make sense for the United States to retaliate by striking Soviet cities, knowing that the Soviets still possessed adequate forces to strike our cities? This means making our strategic strike forces quickly responsive to change in targeting and capable of accurate delivery. SSBN forces can be well tailored to these requirements.

The question of exactly how these aims might be accomplished bears largely on esoteric matters of targeting and general strategic deterrence doctrine, which are obviously beyond the scope of the present enquiry. Nevertheless, two points need to be made. The first is that there is contained within American thinking on the matter a clear intention to make discrimination possible. Secretary of Defense James Schlesinger declared, 'The emphasis is to provide a number of options, selectivity and flexibility, so that our response is appropriate rather than disproportionate to the provocation'.[41] Secondly, a close reading of Soviet strategic literature has led some analysts to argue that at least some of the Soviet Navy's SSBNs might be kept in reserve for purposes of intrawar deterrence; to compel an already weakened enemy to accept their terms; to reduce further damage; to have the last word, if necessary; or to deter third parties (particularly China).[42] So it would seem that both the world's major navies envisage some form of 'withholding strategy'. This means that the maritime forces of strategic deterrence will need a capacity for sustained, considered and controllable operation even after nuclear war has begun. The *prolonged* operational survivability of the SSBN must therefore become a major preoccupation of modern maritime strategy.

The capacity to limit the survivability of the other side's deterrent platforms before they launch their aircraft or missiles has become a correspondingly important naval function. As far as the US Navy is concerned, this task is contained within, but not readily distinguished from, their general anti-submarine warfare (ASW) capacity. The effort devoted to ASW is extensive but only a proportion of it can be brought to bear against the Soviet SSBN fleet. This would apply particularly to such area defence operations as those aimed at controlling SSBN access points and so forth.

There is much controversy about the equivalent priority given this defensive task by the Soviet Navy. Some experts point out that the defence of the homeland against Western strike carriers operating in the waters of the high north was an early but sustained preoccupation of the Soviet fleet. Moreover, the tradition has carried on into the age of the Polaris SSBN, and beyond. It has resulted in a considerable stress on nuclear-powered fleet submarines (SSNs) and in a marked emphasis on ASW in the configuration of their air and surface forces. While the potentialities of the new US Navy Trident SSBNs enormously increase the difficulty, one such study concludes, 'all the evidence, including Gorshkov's own statements, indicate that the Soviet Union is striving to meet this demanding operational requirement'.[43]

Other analysts challenge such findings, arguing that the practical difficulty of this kind of strategic defence has recently forced the Soviet Navy to downgrade the task's priority. Although there was indeed a concentration on the defeat of strike carriers and SSBNs up to the mid 1960s, 'contrary to a widespread but unfounded impression, it has not been its primary task since then'.[44] They argue that Soviet ASW efforts are aimed instead against those Western SSNs which might otherwise threaten their SSBNs. In other words, their intention is to guard the Soviet strategic deterrent, not attack the West's.

Certainly, given the greatly increased range of submarine launched ballistic missiles, and the improbability of an imminent breakthrough in the technology of submarine detection, it seems unlikely for the forseeable future that maritime action will be able to do more than affect some slight reduction in the efficiency of the other side's deterrent forces. But such would be the horrific consequences of an uninhibited nuclear attack that any reduction in the damage threatened might nevertheless be considered worthwhile. This view would accord especially well with Soviet perspectives on deterrence.

In some ways, however, the stability of mutual deterrence rests on both sides feeling confident that they could inflict unacceptable damage on the other even after having absorbed a nuclear attack. If strategic ASW reached a level of efficiency which threatened the present balance of menace, it would be dangerously destabilising. This is why some experts view advances in strategic ASW with misgiving and urge that this function should be a primary target of maritime arms control.

The difficulty of such a solution lies in being able to distinguish unambiguously between the variety of ASW aimed essentially against SSBNs and the traditional version designed to help protect maritime communications. As elsewhere in contemporary maritime strategy, the new seems inextricably entangled with the old.

(d) Maritime strategy: Past, present and future

The last two chapters have identified some contemporary maritime activities which are wholly new, some of which are quite traditional and many which are a mixture of the two. But even where the activity is familiar and long-standing, new conditions have created much uncertainty about their performance these days. For such reasons, such generalised thought as there is, appears tentative in the extreme and the focus is on narrow matters of operational technique. Finally the contemporary value of established thought is regarded with some scepticism for even in the case of familiar naval functions, the observations of classical naval theorists will have to be modified to an important if unknown degree. When the activity is new, it is by no means easy to see the relevance of such thought at all.

For all these reasons, it is perhaps understandable that seamen and those interested in their activities should feel that theorising about the nature of contemporary maritime strategy is too difficult, probably unnecessary and would not in any case derive much practical guidance from the experience of the past.

But this agnosticism springs at least to a degree from a misapprehension about the role of maritime theory. Theory really represents an attempt to advance beyond the particular to the general; to understand the trees by considering the wood as a whole. It does not necessarily aim at providing a series of answers, or commandments engraved on tablets of stone, brought down from the top floor of the world's naval ministries. It is no more and no less than a conceptual framework, to help sailors and scholars make some sense of an otherwise confused jumble of disconnected naval events. Theory, in short, is simply an aid to thought.

The logical analysis of naval activities, past, present or future, in fact demands a theory and is impossible without one. Such a theory may be open and obvious as it is in the work of the maritime strategists discussed in this book. More often it is implicit, unconscious and unarticulated.

As far as naval histories are concerned, this is revealed, to take Donald Macintyre's classic *The Battle of the Atlantic* as a quite random example, by the author's initial choice of topic, by an opening chapter on the convoy system and by countless judgements and generalised observations afterwards. As Macintyre wrote, for instance, 'The strange thing is that the American Admiral should still... call the operations of Doenitz's U-boats...\ "astonishing": whereas it was his failure to use his forces as convoy escorts, however meagre, that was astonishing'.[45] It is manifestly impossible to write good interpretative history without forming judgements; it is impossible to do this without having some generalised view of what should or should not be done; and it is impossible to have this kind of view without a theory. To understand maritime events, in other words, people need a theory, implicit or explicit.

The same goes for naval policy makers. Their theories may be openly revealed in posture-statements, books, lectures or articles, or released in confidential batches for the edification of successive generations of Staff College students. There again, more commonly, they lie hidden in the assumptions that guide such things as training and construction programmes, tactical manoeuvres, ship design and so on.

Naval theory does not need expounding on every conceivable occasion, of course. No one would suggest fleet commanders should immediately arrange a seminar on the nature of trade protection in the nuclear age when a division of hostile cruisers appears, puffing smoke, over the horizon. Nevertheless, the occasional articulation and exploration of fundamental assumptions about maritime strategy would seem a wise precaution against inertial guidance and cumulative error.

When Admiral Stansfield Turner first put pen to paper, to redefine the US Navy's roles, his objective was:

'to force the Navy to think in terms of output rather than

input. . . . By measuring the value of output in terms of national objectives, the country can rationally decide what resources it should allocate to the Navy. Input categories such as manpower, ships, aircraft, and training, are of little help in trying to determine why we need a Navy or, if we do need one, how big it should be and what it should be prepared to do.

Focusing on missions in this way would, he thought, also help tactical commanders keep objectives in mind, establish priorities for the allocation of resources, make selection between competing systems easier and ensure that members of the organisation put vested interests in proper perspective.[46] While the success of this particular endeavour might be a matter of some debate, there can be little doubting the desirability of making the attempt.

Assuming that theory is in fact a useful tool for those either operating or attempting to understand modern navies, how helpful in creating such a theory are historical experience and the conclusions of the classical maritime strategists? The two come together naturally on this question for writers like Mahan, Corbett and the rest have processed history for us. They have used it as a reservoir of past experience, which yields ideas about the nature and conduct of warfare at sea and provides opportunities for those ideas to be tested.

Certainly history, even as moderated by the maritime strategists, is not an infallible guide. It is often ethnocentric, particular rather than general, has a tendency to over-concentrate on battles and excitement, and sometimes begs to be misused. All too often it is not especially good at helping us understand the past, let alone the present or the future. And of course history as a source of prophecy has the difficulty of changed conditions to cope with.

For such reasons as these, it is often implicitly assumed and sometimes explicitly stated that the past has little to offer in the way of guidance to nuclear-age seamen or those interested in their ways. Instead an awareness of the past serves only a series of secondary functions. Naval history (usually of the hagiographic kind) may help socialise new entrants to the profession with desirable attitudes and values. References to the past or to the immortal sayings of some defunct authority occasionally may add style to the arid prose of modern policy-papers, or add a certain something to after dinner speeches, but they are often approached more in the spirit of finding 'something which fits', rather than something which helps us understand. Historical features add interest to a landscape of otherwise unrelieved modernity, but could be done without if necessary.

Despite these doubts, there is enough of relevance in past experience and reflection to make their consultation a worthwhile activity for those interested in modern naval theory and practice. History makes men wiser, if not wise. Even the business of trying to make comparisons between then and now raises aspects of the case that might not otherwise occur. An endeavour to compare and contrast trade protection now and in the First World War could lead us to discover more about both cases. The critical use of the past, in other words, is an aid to naval thinking.

Because, with the advantage of hindsight, it is easier to put some particular species of maritime endeavour into its overall strategic context, this approach also tends to encourage reflection on naval purposes. As such it provides a valuable alternative to the tendency to think about naval operations mainly from the technical and procedural points of view. Given the importance of these matters and the bewildering range of possible war scenarios, it is natural that thought should be concentrated on things like anti-submarine warfare (ASW). anti-carrier warfare (ACW), anti-air warfare (AAW) and the like. Proficiency in such techniques can be turned to good account, after all, in a wide range of possible contingencies. But since response is partially determined by purpose, an over-concentration on means rather than ends could easily distort conclusions in peacetime and lead to misconceived practice in war.

Such distortions have certainly happened in the past. Despite widespread allegations to the contrary, the Royal Navy of the interwar period, for instance, did devote considerable thought to the problem of air attack on ships. For the most part, though, this was treated as a technical problem of AA gunfire accuracy, bomb-lethality, armour strength and so forth. Hardly any thought was devoted to the possible effects on all this of the specific situations in which the problem might be encountered. Consequently, when the war came, the particular difficulties of dealing with enemy aircraft in the context of amphibious operations, for example, were largely unknown, and the learning process in the waters off Norway was very painful.[47] In this case a failure to think seriously about amphibious warfare (a role or function) had significant effects on AAW practices (a means).

This kind of observation is often used as evidence of the proposition that if we knew what happened last time then we will be better placed to predict what will happen next. As the celebrated saying goes, those who ignore history are condemned to relive it. This does not mean that history repeats itself or that it produces lessons universal in time and space, because as a general rule it does not. After all, Corbett wrote, 'the value of history in the art of war is not only to elucidate the resemblance of past and present but also their essential differences'. In fact, the chief utility of history for the analysis of present and future lies in its ability, not to point out lessons, but to isolate things that need thinking about. It is of value chiefly to what the Russians call 'naval science' (the process of thinking) rather than 'naval doctrine' (laid–down conclusions). History provides insights and questions, not answers.

The last functional justification for an acquaintance with past theory and practice is that as yet it has no serious rival as a background for present thinking. As Trotsky observed, we cannot spin strategy out of our fingers: strategists need some kind of starter. Fortunately, the world's navies have few wars to practise in: and the most realistic of exercises is still basically unrealistic. Simulation techniques are usually about means not ends, and are often only as good as the assumptions fed into the computer. The deficiencies of modern naval theory are widely recognised too. One recent study[48] calls it under–intellectualised, practically ignored by outside strategists and the world's navies (with the exception of one or two academic admirals) and beset with semantic obscurity.

Certainly modern naval thought can appear tentative, insubstantial and lacking the intellectual stature of previous thought. In the absence of an attractive replacement, therefore, past experiences and reflection must remain an aid to naval thinking, at least on such established and traditional concerns as the command of the sea, trade protection and so forth. But this is obviously much less true of activities that are essentially new in character, or old ones largely ignored by the maritime strategists of the past.

10 A Survey of Present Practice

All that remains now is to see how well ancient theory suits modern practice. How have the world's navies actually conducted themselves, and are their procedures consistent with traditional thinking? Unfortunately, space precludes anything more than a preliminary reconnaissance; for breadth it will rely on a naval review of 1979, and for depth on a brief survey of the naval aspects of the Arab–Israeli war of 1973 and the Falklands campaign of 1982.

(a) 1979: A maritime review

Although this brief review of maritime events in 1979 will concentrate on the particular and the newsworthy,[1] the world's navies all continued in an unremarked and often unremarkable fashion to rehearse those capabilities which they might one day need 'for real'. As a result, building programmes, training and exercises continued apace throughout the year, providing a constant backdrop to the specific maritime incidents shortly to be considered. The possible range and extent of these routine activities can be gauged by a brief look at the Soviet Navy in 1979.[2]

The devotion of considerable resources to naval development and the second printing of Admiral Gorshkov's *The Sea Power of the State* both indicated the Soviet Union's continued faith in the importance of maritime power. The Soviet Union's carrier programme attracted much comment throughout the year. The 35 000 ton *Minsk* finally joined the *Kiev* at sea in March, leaving a slightly larger third ship of the class, the *Kharkov*, still building. Reportedly a much larger 50–60 000-ton, nuclear-powered carrier was nearing completion together with a large battle cruiser. This building programme and the appearance of a second 13 000 ton amphibious warfare ship of the *Ivan Rogov* class demonstrated ambitions for high-seas fleet operations of the traditional sort, an impression confirmed by a survey of their exercises. In the spring, anti-submarine and anti-carrier warfare techniques were tried out in a sequence of exercises in the Norwegian Sea, which included one of the traditional 'defence of the homeland' operations against a hostile carrier force approaching the Soviet Union from that direction. In

March the two carriers *Kiev* and *Minsk* exercised together for the first time in an impressive way in the Mediterranean. In addition, the Soviet fleet maintained a significant standing presence in the north west quadrant of the Indian Ocean, in the South Atlantic off West Africa and was a frequent visitor to the South China Sea. As well, Soviet units continued to monitor maritime deployments of the Western allies and exercises in all three areas.

As for less traditional activities, the Soviet Navy continued to modernise its SSBN force and deployed about ten *Yankees* and *Deltas* on the strategic deterrence mission at any one time.[3] The *Yankees* adopted forward positions in the Atlantic and Pacific so they could target the United States, while the longer range *Deltas* stayed further back. In addition, *Golf* SSBNs deployed into the Baltic, covering Western Europe. Precisely the same missions were, of course, executed by the US Navy in a year which saw the launching of the first *Ohio* class SSBN and the first operational deployment of the *Francis Scott Key* armed with sixteen Trident I missiles. In Britain also the press reported that the Government was coming closer to a decision to replace the Royal Navy's *Polaris* system with the *Trident*.

While this particular mission was a preoccupation exclusive to a handful of the world's navies, far more had to deal with tasks connected with the offshore estate. The hazardous waters around the British Isles provide a good example of what needed to be done. Stormy weather aggravated the usual crop of maritime disasters. In the last two months of the year, for instance, the nuclear-waste coaster *Pool Fisher*, the Greek tanker *Skopelossky*, the Spanish tanker *Butaseis* and an oil rig barge all came to grief and needed naval help. Worst of all, terrible storms in mid-August caused havoc amongst the 303 yachts competing in the Fastnet Race: fifteen people were drowned and 136 rescued; twenty-four yachts were abandoned or sank and only eighty-five completed the race. A massive rescue operation was mounted which included the British and Irish coast guards and life boat services, innumerable fishing and merchant vessels, the Dutch destroyer *Overijssel*, the British frigates *Broadsword* and *Scylla*, the patrol boat *Anglesey* (among others) and maritime aircraft from the Fleet Air Arm, the Irish Air Corps and the Royal Air Force: over seventy people were rescued by helicopter alone.

Against this example of international co-operation in British waters has to be set abiding European disputes over fishing. At the end and the beginning of the year there was controversy over mackerel fishing to the south west, mainly involving local fishermen, large factory ships from Eastern Europe and deep water trawlers from Scotland and the East Coast. In October, there was dissension between the Danish fishing fleet, mainly from Esbjerg, and the British over conservation measures in the so-called 40 000 square mile 'Norwegian Pout Box'. At the same time there was something of a shrimp war between the British and the French, with the former arresting the latter's trawlers and the latter threatening to harass tanker routes into the oil terminal at Milford Haven. On top of this, there was constant activity to enforce the ban on taking of herring from the North Sea. As would be expected, all this considerably involved the ships flying the yellow and blue pennant of the fishery protection service, though many other ships were involved as well. Despite the fact that this survey has focused on British experience, such activities have been common to most nations with sea coasts and significant maritime interests. Throughout the world, the importance of the offshore task appears to grow yearly.

A brief tour of the world's main seas should give a final impression of the diversity of contemporary maritime tasks and preoccupations in 1979. In the Middle East, both Israel and the Palestinians based in the Lebanon used the sea to mount raids against each other. A particularly bitter exchange was sparked off by a Palestinian raid on the resort of Nahariya in April. The Palestinian forces used small rubber boats to slip through Israeli naval defences and came ashore for an operation which left six people dead. The Israelis responded with a sequence of raids on the Lebanon in April, May and later, in which shore positions were bombarded by Israeli gunboats, small commando forces were landed and several freighters were sunk near Tyre and Sidon. Although described as pre-emptive strikes rather than simple reprisals, they had all the appearance of what Colomb called 'cross-ravaging' operations. On 2 April and 4 June, however, the Israeli Navy claimed to have intercepted and sunk small Palestinian vessels at sea, in the latter instance a speed boat and raft armed with *Katyusha* rockets for shore bombardment – a method of naval defence of which Colomb would doubtless have approved far more.

The Israeli Navy was also used to convey more comforting messages to other actors in the Middle Eastern drama. On 29 May, three Israeli landing craft loaded with lorries from the Sinai (the *Achziv, Ashdod* and *Ashkelon*) became the first Israeli warships to transit the Suez Canal – an important signal of the continuance of the Camp David peace process. In September the Israeli and US Navies guarded President Sadat during a visit to Israel he made on his yacht *al-Huriyah*. A few weeks later, the nuclear carrier *Nimitz* (81 600 tons) and the guided missile cruiser *Texas* visited Alexandria, in a gesture of American support for the Egyptian leader. These events all demonstrated the way in which naval activities can convey sentiments of fraternity.

Much of the Egyptian Navy meanwhile was busy in the Red Sea. Making considerable use of Port Sudan, Egyptian warships patrolled to stop the smuggling of arms and subversives into the Sudan, and monitored Soviet and Ethiopian naval activity around Massawa and the Dahlak archipelago, harassing and being harassed.

Along the North African coast, there was controversy between Morocco and Spain, with Moroccan gunboats taking action against – and in one case shooting at – Spanish fishing boats operating out of Cadiz and Huelva. In the summer, there was aerial jousting between Libyan aircraft and US P3 Orion maritime aircraft and fighters flying from the carrier *Independence* (59 600 tons). Libya quarrelled with Malta and Tunisia over her maritime borders and in February 1980 this led to French warships patrolling part of the disputed area. All these incidents arose out of the complex issue of the defining of maritime borders and the allocation of maritime resources.

More in the tradition of great-power naval diplomacy and deterrence, both Soviet and NATO maritime forces exercised and patrolled the Mediterranean area. The Libyan Government offered the Soviet fleet use of facilities at Tripoli, Benghazi and Tobruk, a move which threatened to upset the naval balance in the central Mediterranean. To some extent NATO's maritime position in that sea was weakened by two further developments that year: the British left Malta for the last time on 31 March, led by the destroyer *London*, and in September the Greek Government offered the Soviet fleet conditional use of some of its shipyards for repairs. Furthermore, Greece also withdrew from a major NATO air–sea exercise called 'Display Determination'; this was all seen as a symptom of Greece's long-standing dispute with Turkey. In August, the Soviet Union demonstrated its sensitivity over the Black Sea by simulating missile attacks on two US Navy destroyers exercising in the area, the *Farragut* and *Caron*.

Nevertheless, the main focus of maritime interest in 1979 was probably the Persian Gulf and the Indian Ocean. Several interwoven elements could be discerned in the maritime activity in this area. First there was the general question of maritime order and the security of oil supplies to the industrial world, in an area which had become something of a vacuum with the withdrawl of the British and the fall of the Shah of Iran. The British and French both continued to maintain a political and maritime interest in the area, however, with the supply of equipment, training and some personnel. Saudi Arabia and the Gulf States discussed naval measures for the protection of the Straits of Hormuz, exercised their forces and contemplated their expansion. The Iraqis were reported to be planning to double the size of their navy, with the acquisition of frigates, patrol craft and ten *Nanuchka* guided missile corvettes, whose 150-mile SS-N-9 missiles would probably make the Iraqi navy the strongest in the Gulf, apart from that of Iran. To correct any impression that internal events had compromised the efficiency of the Iranian Navy, Admiral Ahmad Madani organised an extensive exercise off Bandar Abbas, involving about twenty destroyers, frigates, fast patrol boats and 800 marine commandos in a defensive operation around the country's oil installations.

The second theme for naval activity in the area was the United States' reaction to the unfolding of events inside Iran. In January three destroyers (the *Hoel*, *Decatur* and *Kinkaid*) and the 37 360 ton auxiliary ship *Kansas City* increased the United States presence in the area. On 21 February these ships and others, including the command ship *La Salle*, evacuated 440 people from the Iranian ports of Bandar Abbas and Char Bahar. Shortly afterwards the carrier *Constellation* (60 000 tons) arrived. A high level of maritime activity continued for the next few months.

In early November, the United States Embassy in Tehran and the occupants were seized by Iranian revolutionaries. This led to an unprecedented expansion of United States naval power in the area. In the second week of November, when it began to seem that no early release of the American hostages was contemplated, the carrier *Midway* (51 000 tons) and other ships were ordered to close the Straits of Hormuz, and were soon reinforced by the carrier *Kitty Hawk* (60 000 tons). There was much discussion about possible military options ranging from the launching of a rescue bid, through carrier air strikes on Iran's oil and military installations to the bombing of the city of Qom. The Iranian navy at Bandar Abbas was put on full alert and the whole situation was described by Dr Kurt Waldheim, the UN Secretary General as 'the most serious threat to peace since the Cuban missile crisis'. But however superficially impressive this display of naval power, its actual influence on events is hard to gauge: it certainly did not secure any noticeable improvement in the American position, though the display may have prevented deterioration in the situation. The whole operation indicated that in practice the projection of power is considerably more complicated, militarily and politically, than once it was.

The third element in the maritime activity in this area was that it was the scene for increased tension between the super powers. The Soviet Union was an active participant in these affairs. The contemporary importance of naval bases and the particular strategic attraction of Aden was demonstrated by the Soviet solicitude for the well being and good opinion of South Yemen. Military and other equipment was shipped in and during early June the Soviet carrier *Minsk* and the amphibious warfare ship *Ivan Rogov* and other warships anchored in the area and treated the locals to an impressive display of military might: Soviet naval aircraft flew up and down the Persian Gulf, the Red Sea and, reportedly, into the Mediterranean; the *Ivan Rogov* demonstrated a burgeoning Soviet capacity for intervention. Soviet vessels were also active in the Red Sea, supporting the Ethiopian government against the Eritrean Liberation Front and monitoring Egyptian and Israeli naval movements in the area. Soviet vessels moved into the Persian Gulf area too, one destroyer apparently being involved in a successful attempt to rescue a party of Iraqi communists from inside that country.

Needless to say, the United States did not regard this with complaisance. In the 1960s a proposal that the United States should consciously develop more of an interventionist capacity with fast deployment logistics ships and C5 Galaxy aircraft was turned down by Congress, partly on the basis that 'if it is easy for us to go anywhere and do anything, we will always be going somewhere and doing something'. However, by early 1979 this mood had changed. In the Spring, there was much talk in Washington of the forming of a Fifth Fleet for the Indian Ocean, and of the importance of securing the West's oil supplies.

More immediate attempts to build a maritime alliance between the Gulf States and the United States did not prosper, however. Soviet activities in the South Yemen were, reportedly, one reason for the arrival of the carrier *Constellation* in the area, and for the maintenance of a substantial naval presence in the Indian Ocean, even before the seizing of the United States Embassy in Teheran. In November a British task force, led by the guided missile destroyer *Norfolk*, accompanied by five frigates and Royal Fleet Auxiliaries, arrived and joined in the exercises with the *Midway* task group. Shortly afterwards the decision to form a Rapid Deployment Force was announced in Washington. The scheme included a proposal to build fifteen multi-purpose cargo ships with strengthened decks to be prepositioned around the world. An expansion of naval facilities at Diego Garcia was also envisaged.

An explosion in the central telecommunications station in Kabul on the night of 27 December apparently signalled the start of the Soviet take-over of Afghanistan. The invasion reinforced apprehensions that the security of the oil areas was at risk and awakened age-old fears that the Soviet Union might be after a warm-water port in the Indian Ocean – presumably Gwadar in Pakistan. Although neither as yet appears to be a very likely contingency, the move certainly increased widespread concern about the security of the area, as the reported offer of base facilities by Oman, Somalia and Kenya would seem to indicate. Although the results of all this activity in the Indian Ocean area may be hard to estimate, it does at least indicate an abiding attachment to the importance of maritime strength, and of the capacity to control the seas to some extent so as to be able to project power ashore and protect maritime communications.

The many conflicts in Africa were largely territorial in nature but the generally supportive role of maritime power was well demonstrated throughout the year. The forces involved in these conflicts constantly needed fresh arms and reinforcements, and these generally came by sea. Although the activities of the Cubans and other revolutionaries may command the attention, the use of the Belgian mine countermeasures support ship *Zinnia* to back up a small force of Belgian paratroopers in Zaire should perhaps remind us that this activity was not exclusive to the Soviet Union and her allies. The visit of the Soviet aircraft carrier *Minsk* to Mozambique and the Angolan port of Luanda indicated Soviet support for these regimes and other forces in the area. There was, reportedly, some low level maritime involvement in the coup in Equatorial Guinea, in early August. All this demonstrates the continued capacity of maritime power to influence political events ashore.

Across the Caribbean, dissensions continued. Anxiety about Cuban activities and general maritime disorders prompted several Caribbean states to discuss the formation of a regional maritime force; to ask for British help; to seek the supply of patrol boats; to welcome visits by friendly warships, such as that of the British frigate *Scylla* to Barbados in January and the destroyer *Fife* to Dominica – the latter also providing disaster relief after the passage of Hurricane David.

The main concern was undoubtedly the expansion of Soviet – Cuban military co-operation. The routine arrival and early departure of a Soviet *Kresta*-class cruiser and a *Krivak* destroyer caused little alarm, but the apparent handing-over of a *Foxtrot* submarine and expansion of naval facilities at Cienfuegos awakened considerable apprehension that the Soviet Union and Cuba meant to create a submarine base within reach of United States facilities at New London, Connecticutt and Charleston, S Carolina and of one terminal of United States maritime supply lines to Western Europe. The reported presence of 3000 Soviet combat troops also caused much anxiety for the Carter administration.

Protests and warnings were reinforced by the formation of a new maritime command for the Caribbean based at Key West, an acceleration of the rapid deployment force programme and, on 17 October, a symbolic invasion of the United States base at Guantanamo on Cuba. That morning 2200 US marines came ashore from the amphibious assault ship *Nassau* and two large landing ships, the *Plymouth Rock* and *Spartanburg County*: most flew ashore through driving rain in helicopters, but about one quarter 'hit the beach' in classic style.

Navies were more active still in the Pacific. There was a very significant maritime dimension to relations between Japan and the Soviet Union throughout the year. One of the main points at issue was the fate of four of the South Kuril Islands near Japan, which were seized by the Soviet Union in 1945. Recently several thousand troops had been stationed on the islands of Shikoran, Etorufu and Kunashiri, supported by tanks, surface-to-air missiles, assault helicopters and naval facilities capable of dealing with ships of up to 20 000 tons. The Japanese authorities also took exception to the continual harassment of fishing boats in the sea of Okhotsk and to the deployment of SS-20 surface-to-surface missiles in the Shilka valley west of Manchuria which could be used against targets in the Sea of Japan.

Soviet objectives in all this have been presumed to be the securing of relatively unimpeded access to the high seas and the continued control of the Sea of Okhotsk where they deploy their *Delta* SSBNs. If so, the effects appear to have been somewhat counter-productive. In October 1978, for the first time, the Japanese Maritime Defence Force broke out of the 600-mile circle around Japan to which it had hitherto confined itself, in order to conduct a large scale exercise in the protection of maritime communications. The reported Soviet use of naval facilities at Cam Ranh bay in the summer of 1979 reinforced anxieties about the vulnerability of Japan to attack on her sea-borne supplies, and doubtless contributed to the decision announced in the autumn of increased maritime co-operation with Western navies. In February 1980, again for the first time, a Japanese naval task force deployed into the central-southern Pacific to join United States, Canadian, Australian and New Zealand naval forces in *Exercise Rimpac*. The fact that all of this has so obviously strengthened the position of Japanese hawks indicated once more that coercive naval diplomacy can frequently have the opposite effect to that intended.

In South Korea there was anxiety about the declared United States policy of partial military withdrawal. Coinciding with attempts to persuade President Carter to change his mind about this, the South Korean navy intercepted a small North Korean spy-ship off the south-east coast and sank it after a two-hour battle with rockets and machine guns. Plans for the American departure were delayed and a further gesture of support for South Korea was made at the end of October and thereafter when the carrier *Kitty Hawk* accompanied by several cruisers, destroyers and other vessels sailed into the area shortly after the assassination of the Korean president. There were further visits subsequently, including one by the carrier *Coral Sea*.

Probably the main maritime event of the year, however, in Pacific waters was the continuing tragedy of the Boat People, rather more than 300 000 of whom fled Vietnam from 1978, an exodus which reached a peak in the summer of 1979. The naval response to this quite unprecedented problem was varied. Most local navies made some attempt to keep the refugee boats out of their waters, the Philippine navy for instance reportedly putting a kind of reverse blockade around Manila Bay. Others took tougher measures: the Malaysian Navy, for example, started firing near refugee boats and towing them out to sea again. In early April there was an outcry when 104 refugees were drowned when a boat being towed by the patrol boat *Renchong* capsized. One unexpected result of all this was an increase in the extent of maritime co-operation between the ASEAN nations.

Maritime forces also undertook more humanitarian work in connection with the Boat People problem. Several navies took action against local pirates (mainly Thais) who ruthlessly plundered these unfortunate people. The Italian cruisers *Vittorio Veneto* and *Andrea Doria* and the supply ship *Stromboli* visited the area and, picking up one thousand or so refugees, took them back to Italy. President Carter ordered vessels of the Seventh Fleet to rescue foundering refugee boats and large numbers were picked up by the auxiliary ships *White Plains* and *Wabash*, the cruiser *England*, the destroyer *Parsons* and the frigates *Lang* and *Robert E. Peary*, among others. Paradoxically, this apparently praiseworthy gesture was widely criticised by those who believed it would entice more refugees out to sea and who thought it might endanger a new and precarious agreement with the government of Vietnam. Throughout the year, in addition, the British Navy was engaged in similarly varied efforts against illegal immigrants seeking to enter Hong Kong from China.

Vietnam was also at the centre of the other two main maritime events of the year in this area. On 25 December 1978 Vietnam invaded Kampuchea with 120 000 men, supported with tanks and aircraft, having the declared object of overthrowing the Pol Pot regime. Although obviously mainly a land war, there was a significant maritime dimension. Vietnamese and Kampuchean gunboats reportedly fought each other off the disputed island of Phu Quoc. Vietnamese vessels supported troops fighting in and around the port of Kompong Song and from 17 January 1979 there was a thirty-six hour battle for the island of Koh Kong. After a prolonged bombardment by gunboats and aircraft operating from Bien Hoa, a marine assault force went ashore from a twenty-two ship Vietnamese task force.

After the first stage of the invasion, both sides settled down to a prolonged war of attrition. Soviet and Vietnamese freighters shuttled between the Vietnamese coast and the port of Kompong Som on extensive missions of supply. With the loss of this port – the only deep water port in Kampuchea – Pol Pot's Khmer Rouge relied on external supplies coming covertly via Thailand, but in early March Chinese vessels apparently made use of the island of Koh Kong, bringing them equipment which was transferred from freighters into flat-bottomed boats appropriate for the river estuaries of south west Kampuchea. The extent of this activity indicated the continued importance of maritime communications, even between two neighbouring land powers.

The Vietnamese invasion of Kampuchea was one reason for the Chinese assault on Vietnam in February 1979, but others included a long-standing dispute over the maritime border in the South China Seas and the ownership of the Paracel and Spratly Islands, important for their proximity to oil-rich parts of the Gulf of Tonking. These disputes had already led to several minor clashes in the area and the pre-emptive occupation of several of the islands in question. Relations deteriorated further with the Vietnamese mistreatment of the Boat People, many of whom were of Chinese extraction.

There was no direct naval dimension to the short war which

followed, although the Soviet Union continued to send in supplies and augmented her naval forces in the area, which soon grew to include two cruisers (a *Sverdlov* and *Kresta* II) together with destroyers, intelligence gathering ships, support ships and aircraft operating from the former United States air base at Da Nang. Although there was some discussion in the Western press that the Soviet fleet might support some diversionary moves against Chinese landings in the disputed islands, their function seems to have been to monitor Chinese moves, to dissuade them from too provocative a campaign and to demonstrate support for the Government of Vietnam; certainly, there was no discernible Chinese naval response to these deployments.

There was, however, an international response to the Soviet use of former United States naval facilities at Cam Rahn Bay, which became increasingly obvious from February onwards. The strategic benefits to the Soviet Pacific Fleet of a real base in this vital area could hardly be exaggerated. The Japanese concern about this putative threat to shipping in the South China Sea was expressed most forcefully. The United States protested too, and moved more units of the Seventh Fleet into the area. The Soviet Government, however, denied that it intended to turn Cam Ranh Bay into a major fleet base and, reportedly, turned the carrier *Minsk* away as a deliberate signal of reassurance.

This maritime *tour d'horizon* leaves an immediate impression of the continued diversity and importance of modern sea power. But before its general implications are assessed, we must consider a little more deeply the naval side of a recent war.

(b) Naval aspects of the Arab–Israeli War of 1973

The Arab–Israeli War of 1973 provided several instances of would-be decisive battles between the Israeli, Syrian and Egyptian navies in the first week of the war, and subsequently there were important engagements of Latakia and Tartus in Syria and Damietta in Egypt. Some of these engagements appear to have been pure 'search and destroy' missions: others had some associated objective, such as an attack on the enemy's shore line or port installations. Either way, they confirmed both the place of decisive battle in modern maritime warfare and the continued possible diversity of its immediate purpose.

The style of these battles, however, was quite novel. They were 'the first sea-to-sea missile engagements in history',[4] with the contestants making use of missiles like the *Styx* and the *Gabriel* and various forms of fast patrol boat (FPBs). In the early 1960s, both sides realised that large obsolescent conventionally armed vessels could not adequately meet their purposes and so deliberately concentrated on using technology to create new navies for small, but intense wars in local waters. The battles of October 1973 were the result of this policy and many countries seem likely to follow this lead.

Although both time and sea-room were insufficient for a formal fleet-in-being strategy, there were certainly analogous activities. Reportedly, two old ex-Russian *Kotlin* class destroyers were ordered by the Egyptian naval command to ports on the North African coast. Here they periodically engaged in ostentatious activity indicative of imminent departure, and so occupied the attention of a large number of Israeli FPBs.[5] This conscious use of inferior forces to secure important strategic benefits accords well with traditional fleet-in-being theories. And so, in a more general way, does the war as a whole. Even an inferior fleet implied a threat to the enemy's shore line and coastal cities sufficient to oblige him to keep forces back to guard against such attacks: all the belligerents were conscious of this requirement, and made their dispositions accordingly.

The limited range of both sides' navies and the geographical circumstances seem largely to have ruled out any formal military blockade. However, between 13 and 18 October, Soviet warships deployed into an active war zone for the first time since 1945. They took up positions between the eastern tip of Cyprus and the northern part of Lebanon. If their purpose was, as seems likely, to prevent Israeli naval units interfering with Soviet–Syrian supply lines,[6] then this could probably be regarded as a form of blockade.

The ultimate purpose of these three activities was, as it always has been, to secure some degree of command of the sea. Neither side had anything like absolute command; simple geography was against it and their forces were in any case too limited in number to enforce it. Moreover, the contestants had common land frontiers and the sea was unlikely to assume the kind of strategic significance it would have had if they had been physically separated by water. Consequently, neither side needed to aspire to ambitious levels of command, especially knowing as they did that there were much larger navies around to help them if necessary. Nevertheless, none of the contestants were interested simply in sea denial; they all wanted to use the sea positively. The degree of command actually achieved was sufficient to allow both sides to be reasonably active – though, as time went on, the Israelis appear to have made more positive use of their maritime opportunities.

The ability to use the sea as a means of transportation was probably the most important benefit conferred by maritime power in this war. Military supplies were consumed at an alarming rate and the survival of both sides depended on the prompt arrival of replacements. Hence both were supported by reactive and competitive resupply operations. Some supplies were sent by air, but even these very often required naval support. The dispositions of the United States Sixth Fleet for much of the war reflected the need to buttress the air bridge between the Azores and Israel. Three carriers and other ships were strung out along the length of the Mediterranean, offering navigational support, search-and-rescue facilities and defence against possible interference. Aircraft could be refuelled in flight and A4 Skyhawks were able to make a necessary stop-over on the carrier *Franklin D. Roosevelt* on their way to Israel.

Although some items could be sent by air, most of the resupplies had to go by sea. Tens-of-thousands of tons of military equipment reached the belligerents during the course of the conflict and ensuring their safe and timely arrival was, as always, a vital maritime task. However, the belief that any war in the area would be short meant that for many years the Israeli Navy gave little priority to the protection of shipping. The 1969–70 war of attrition caused some revision of this policy, a change likely to be confirmed by the experience of 1973. The then Commander-in-Chief of the Israeli Navy, Admiral Benjamin Telem, declared, 'The Yom Kippur War has proved to us as well as to the Arabs the great importance of open sea lanes in any all-out conflict'. Significantly, he went on to warn against relying too much for this on friendly naval powers, who might be politically handicapped or unwilling actually to exercise their capabilities.[7]

Although neither side directly challenged the military shipping of the opposition's large ally, the attack and defence of maritime communications involved them in a wide range of diverse activities – as in fact is usually the case. Defensively, the protagonists sought to protect their trade either by sinking the ships that might threaten it (such as the Israeli destruction at Ghardala on the Red Sea of an Egyptian *Komar* boat, which had disrupted Israeli shipping) or by providing direct 'cover'. Merchant ships proceeding to Israel through the Eastern Mediterranean were afforded protection, sometimes by close escort if particular vessels were especially important.

Methods of attack were equally varied. Declaration of military and blockade zones, the existence of ruse minefields and pressure on Liberian flag-ships (even if American owned) not to trade with Israel[8] had important deterrent effects. The commerce blockade established by the Egyptian Navy at Bab-el-Mandeb from 11 October to 13 December 1973 was a more pointed message to the same end. Merchant ships were stopped and searched; some were turned back and several shot at or sunk, one apparently by an Egyptian submarine. The United States merchantman *La Salle* was among those shot at and had the French not delayed the sailing of the US Navy's guided missile destroyer *Charles F. Adams*, from Djibouti, there might have been an interesting exploration of the current legal status of neutral rights.[9] The effects of this blockade were backed up by a minefield near the Straits of Tiran which reportedly sank an Israeli tanker.

This blockade appears to have cut off Israeli trade through the Red

Sea for the duration of the war, though the volume and importance of that trade in war-time was unlikely to have been great in any case. For obvious reasons, it was much more difficult to blockade the enemy's Mediterranean supply lines. Both sides, nevertheless, did their best. The Israeli attacked the Egyptian fishing fleet, and on several occasions installations and shipping at such ports as Tartus and Latakia. The loss of a Soviet merchantman in one of these raids doubtless prompted the Soviet Navy to take up the preventative dispositions described earlier.

Finally, the sea was important as an avenue of amphibious assault of various kinds. Several months before the fighting started the Soviet Navy convoyed two Moroccan brigades into the war zone in a significant display of sea lift capacity. Once the war started, both sides were vulnerable to sea-based interference behind the lines. There were consequently many small-scale operations to mount or defeat such attacks. They usually involved small forces taken in by FPBs for commando raids of various sorts, or shore bombardments. The vulnerability of Haifa and Tel Aviv to such attacks makes their defeat a particularly high priority for the Israeli Navy one of whose principal tasks is 'to deny the enemy any possibility of turning Israel's coastline into another battleground in the event of war'.[10]

As always there were two competing ways of meeting this threat; defensive interception near the threatened coast, or the maintenance of command and preemptive strikes. As Admiral Telem has subsequently written, the Israeli conception was:

> We must not wait to intercept the enemy off our own coast, but go to meet him out wherever he may be, thereby depriving him of the initiative. This is the best starting point for the defence of our own coastline and keeps the potential threat in enemy coastal waters.[11]

One feels that Drake, Colomb and the rest would have approved of this.

The Soviet and American fleets were also very active throughout the war; both greatly augmented their forces in the area as the conflict progressed, the Soviet total reaching ninety-six ships, an all-time record. Their purpose was to offer support to local allies and to transmit important messages to each other. Both wished to demonstrate their interest in the area, to prevent the other superpower dominating the situation and to guard against the military extinction of their proteges. Messages were transmitted by the careful control of movements and fleet composition. A move away from the war-zone, the granting of shore leave and visible relaxation of states of readiness were all indications of restraint.

Conversely, some occasions seemed to warrant both superpowers adopting the posture of gladiators. To accompany their declaration of a

Defence Condition III nuclear alert, the Americans concentrated their three carriers into an area to the south of Crete from 25–30 October. Accordingly, the Soviet Navy deployed their forces into three carrier-directed surface attack groups, and a fourth which threatened the sixth Fleet's amphibious assault helicopter carrier *Iwo Jima*, the Americans' major instrument of intervention. When the crisis receded, these menacing dispositions accordingly dispersed, mission presumably accomplished.

(c) The Falklands Campaign of 1982

Shortly after the first edition of this book appeared, many of the people whose views were so helpful to my colleagues and me in writing it sailed off to fight in the world's most serious naval war for nearly forty years. The Falklands Campaign of 1982 was a very public war. It produced a flood of books, newspaper and magazine articles and much radio and television coverage which as yet shows little sign of slackening. The results of all this attention have educated the public into a familiarity with the concepts and arcane acronyms of maritime warfare in the 1980s which would gladden the heart of any maritime strategist were it not for the human suffering the conflict caused as well. Naturally, there was and is much argument about the lessons of the campaign. Indeed there were many who argued that the whole thing was so unique, so unrepeatable, that there was more danger in paying it too much attention than too little. Such was plainly the view of the British Secretary for Defence of the time.[12]

Whatever the particular conclusions that people come to, it is quite clear that no one writing or thinking about maritime strategy for the rest of this century will be able safely to ignore the implications of this campaign. Accordingly, it seems right to conclude this edition of the book with a few tentative pages on them. What follows is not simply another battle account of the campaign; it is instead an attempt to see the extent to which the various ideas put forward in this book are illustrated by the events experienced in the chilly waters of the South Atlantic.

(i) Navies and Diplomacy

The manoeuvring which preceded the conflict saw both sides using their naval forces as a way of expressing their national interests in the dispute over the Falklands. During the past few years, Argentina has frequently employed its navy as a way of signalling dissatisfaction with the existing situation, such as in the incident of February 1976 when the destroyer *Almirante Storni* fired across the bows of the unarmed British research ship *Shackleton*. Indeed the Argentine Navy itself has always led the hunt to take the islands over and in March 1982 used the scrap merchants affair in South Georgia as a way of putting pressure on the

British Government. Admiral Anaya neatly deterred the British from attempting to reverse the situation here by deploying two powerful frigates between South Georgia and the Falklands. The presence of these ships dissuaded the British Government from attempting to remove Argentine personnel from 'Leith by force. As Mrs Thatcher commented subsequently: 'We know there was a threat that if we took them off by force *Endurance* might well have been stopped and there were ships about which could do the stopping.'[13] Encouraged by its evident success in this regard, the Argentine Government seems to have considered this an example of what James Cable has called the application of definitive force, that is the determined attempt to short circuit the normal processes of diplomacy by presenting the adversary with something close to a *fait accompli*. As Dr Costa Mendez told the British Ambassador in Buenos Aires on 1 April: 'I judge pointless the despatch of a person to examine the events in the Georgias since Argentina considers this incident resolved.'[14]

The Argentine Government however appears to have believed that it could repeat this success on a larger scale. The size of the forces involved in *Operation Rosario*, the hardness of Argentine diplomacy thereafter and the immediate attempt to change the inhabitants' way of life suggest that the invasion of the Falklands was not simply a symbolic affair designed to improve Argentina's negotiating position: it was instead a method of permanently effecting radical change in the situation. But as events turned out, this was an example of definitive force which failed to define the situation in the way its initiator would have wished.

For their part the British had for several years maintained the ice patrol ship HMS *Endurance* and a small symbolic garrison of Royal Marines on the islands as a means of dealing with small scale incidents and of deterring large and official enterprises by Argentina itself. As it turned out, this level of force proved to be too low to achieve either objective. In the wake of the failure of British deterrence, contrasts were drawn between the 1982 situation and an earlier one in 1977 when the previous Government had despatched two frigates and a nuclear propelled submarine into the area to 'buttress our negotiating position.' The presence of this mini task force was not known to Argentina but the expectation was that, 'If the talks broke down we could then reveal the force was there and this might discourage Argentina from taking action.'[15] Whether such a display of deterrent force would have done the trick either in 1977 or in 1982 is of course a matter for speculation. The difficulty of coming to any very firm conclusion about this, even with the advantage of hindsight shows how demanding is the task of deciding how much deterrent force is sufficient for particular circumstances. Underestimating the level may encourage the adversary to take the risk; overestimating it may provoke him into actions he would not otherwise have considered. This last danger played a part in dissuading the British Government from despatching surface warships into the disputed area earlier.[16]

Another problem for the British was the geographic divide which separated them from the disputed area and their adversary. The time it would take to cross that divide forced them into the difficult position of deciding their response before they knew what they were responding to. The only alternative to this was to maintain a force in the area capable of dealing with all possible contingencies. This would have made, in the circumstances then prevailing, a harmonious political solution to the Falklands issue much more difficult and would have been militarily very expensive.

That naval diplomacy is a difficult and imprecise art also emerged from the Argentine failure to predict the British reaction to *Operation Rosario*. The senior Argentine officer interviewed by Eduardo Aliverti and Nestor Montenegro in their book *Los Nombres de la Derrota* (widely believed to be General Galtieri himself) stated: 'Perhaps the most important error was not to have considered as probable the real magnitude of the British military reaction.' One of the reasons for this miscalculation was the declared intention of the British Government to scrap HMS *Endurance* for reasons of economy. This was wrongly seen in Buenos Aires as an indication of a slackening of British resolve to defend the Falkland Islands and the Franks Report showed that there were many people who feared this might be the case even at the time.[17]

Another point worth bearing in mind is that the British themselves were surprised at their own reaction. The resolution of the British press for instance was much clearer in retrospect than it was at the time. Two days after the invasion the leader in *The Observer* asked: 'So what can the Government do now? If it rules out an attempt to recover the Falklands and drive out the invaders – as it surely must – what other courses are open to it?' Opinion polls at the time also showed heavy majorities against the shedding of British blood in any bid to recover the islands. Opinion changed of course as perceptions of Argentine intransigence grew but its initial character may well have helped decide the Argentine Government to call what it thought was the British bluff even after the Task Force sailed.

A final reason for the Argentine miscalculation was a clear underestimate of the fighting effectiveness of the British Task Force itself. Shortly after the Task Force left Britain, the news agency *Noticias Argentinas* reported the Government's view that it would not have the necessary embarked manpower to drive the Argentine garrison off the islands, that it comprised ships designed and equipped to conduct quite different operations in a NATO context and had insufficient organic airpower to deal with Argentine air forces. The news agency reported that Britain would eventually have to accept broadly what the junta offered. General Galtieri thought it 'inconceivable' that the British would mount an amphibious assault in such circumstances, still less that they should succeed. Admiral Anaya was even more confident about this.[18] Nor was the Argentine Government alone in this view. In April 1982, for instance, the American press contained many reports from military and naval figures expressing scepticism about Britain's chances of success. A US Navy Admiral was quoted by the *Washington Post*, for example, as concluding: 'The British made the decision to structure their navy to only certain NATO tasks and have lost their ability to conduct independent operations in the process.'[19]

British military figures did believe they would prevail in the end but few of them thought it would be anything but 'a long and bloody campaign' with 'no simple short quick military solution' if the junta refused to budge. As Admiral John Fieldhouse, the Task Force's overall commander said at Ascension: 'I hope that people realise that this is the most difficult thing we have attempted since the Second World War.'[20] Given the prevalence of such attitudes it is perhaps not surprising that the Argentine Government should have decided that the British would probably not respond militarily and that Argentina would be able to hold its own even if they did.

The conclusion that emerges from this brief survey of the way that both sides attempted to use their naval forces as a near bloodless instrument of diplomacy is that it was an immensely complex process in which many things could go wrong and most of them did. Naval diplomacy of this type is a difficult and dangerous business in which misjudgements and misperceptions naturally abound. Its prime justification of course is that it might succeed in helping resolve a situation short of conflict; in the case of the Falkland Islands dispute of 1982 though, it did not. The British failed to deter; Argentina failed to redefine the situation to its own satisfaction. For that reason, the crisis began to slide into war.

But it was a very special kind of war. It was not, as Michael Howard pointed out '. . . a total war . . . between adversaries each bent on the complete defeat of the other without regard to loss of blood and treasure.' Instead it was a limited war, with limited means, for limited objectives analogous to '. . . the wars fought between Britain and . . . Spain for the possession of islands in the Caribbean 200 or 300 years ago.'[21] It was a conflict which clearly confirmed those advantages of sea power in conducting wars of limited liability enunciated by maritime strategists like Sir Francis Bacon and Sir Julian Corbett.[22] The moderation of this conflict contrasted strongly with the more normal pattern being demonstrated at the same time in the Lebanon principally by the Israelis and the Palestinians. 'If the Falklands lay on a contiguous frontier between the two countries' Michael Howard added, 'the dangers of escalation would be extreme.' As it was they did not and the dangers could be contained but only by the strictest observance of the arcane rules of limited war. Amongst these were 'a clear identification of the political objective. Skill in waging . . . (limited wars) . . . lies in exactly matching the available means to the attainable ends.' It was also necessary to accept that 'the safety of our forces cannot be considered paramount It is important but must be carefully weighed against other factors no less important.'[23] Above all, perhaps, it demands the rejection of the notion that peace and war are like night and day in that one cannot have both at the same time; instead both belligerents found themselves operating in a kind of perpetual twilight where the political logic of events was at least as important as the military.

In these circumstances, the maritime activities of each side were intended to convey a political signal to the adversary as well as to accomplish some military purpose. A good example of the way in which force can be used as a symbol of a country's point of view was provided by the resistance of the tiny party of Royal Marines on South Georgia led by the 22-year-old Lt Keith Mills RM. His objective was not to defend the island, a task plainly beyond his capacity, but to oblige Argentina to take it by force, exemplifying thereby the British proposition that their titles to the Falklands (whose garrison had already surrendered) and to the dependencies were different Having shot down a Puma helicopter and badly damaged the 1000 ton corvette *Guerrico* with Carl Gustav anti-tank rockets and small arms fire, Lt Mills judged that he had made his point and so surrendered. Afterwards he reported, 'We made sure that the Falklands and South Georgia were two separate issues.'[24]

The sailing of the Royal Navy Task Force and the whole of its subsequent operation can also be seen as a controlled demonstration of competitive resolve. The evident disinclination of the Argentine Government to compromise was answered by the British increasing the pressure. First came the departure of the Task Force. The publicity which attended its sailing (although this could in truth hardly be concealed) and the composition of the force itself both signalled messages of determination to Buenos Aires. Even so most in the Task Force believed they were part of a gigantic bluff which would not be called and doubted whether they would need to go into action. Then came the declaration of exclusion zones (of increasing scope and extent) and the key decision to proceed south of Ascension on 18 April. The seizure of South Georgia followed a week later but was not intended to imply that negotiations were at an end – indeed rather the reverse; the operation was at least partly meant to increase Argentine flexibility and thus make more possible the prospects of an acceptable compromise outcome.[25] The subsequent shooting down of Argentine aircraft, air attacks on Stanley airfield, the raid on Pebble Island, the landings and the subsequent progress of operations ashore were military steps which certainly made sense in their own right but which can also be represented as increasingly persuasive moves in a deadly type of diplomacy. In the event, a negotiated settlement was found to be impossible and the British resorted to a display of definitive force to restore the *status quo ante bellum*.

Concluding this brief survey of the naval-diplomatic side of the Falklands conflict, the lessons (if such they can be called) appear to be that naval forces gave both sides a much wider range of political options than they would have had otherwise. The isolated and sparsely populated nature of the theatre of operations combined with the particular controllability of naval and air forces in such an environment to help politicians contain the war and keep its effects limited. Nevertheless, the dangers of misperception and misjudgement remained. So far from increasing the possibility of compromise, success on the field of battle sometimes reduced it. According to *Los Nombres de la Derrota* for example, General Galtieri wanted to negotiate his way out of a losing situation but was dissuaded by the hard-line arguments of Admiral Anaya that the Argentine people, having expected and suffered so much, would not stand for it. Rather than making an adversary more amenable to reason, defeat may freeze him into a state of fatalistic apathy where nothing can be done but to wait for the unthinkable end. Still worse, the exercise of military forces may sometimes lead to inadvertent escalation. The need for close political control in the form of careful rules of engagement was accordingly underlined, although it should not be assumed that the dogs of war were always straining at the leash while the politicians held them back; indeed some say the reverse to have sometimes been the case.[26] Finally for both belligerents, it was far from being a cost-free exercise militarily, politically and economically. It also proved hard for either side to predict exactly what these costs would be. In the event Argentina found them far worse than expected; the British significantly less.

(ii) Sources and Elements of Sea Power

Turning now to the exclusively military aspects of the campaign, the contribution of the traditional sources and elements of sea power to the eventual outcome was amply demonstrated. The Falklands campaign showed, for example, the importance of national resources and styles of government in determining the character of maritime power and of influencing the way it is employed in war. It is generally accepted that after an uncertain start the British established a war management machinery which worked extremely well on the whole.[27] This strongly contrasted with the situation in Buenos Aires where the running of the campaign was gravely compromised by the chaotic state of government and acute inter-service rivalry which in turn reflected a country approaching political and economic collapse. In particular, the leading role of Admiral Jorge Anaya and his *Armada Republica Argentina* demonstrated the military as well as the political dangers of a navy which sees itself as the originator of policy rather than simply as its instrument.

From the British side, a principal difficulty lay in the conduct of a sharp and possibly prolonged conflict in a most inhospitable area 8000 miles from home. The island base of Ascension was therefore invaluable in reducing the enormous logistical challenge to anything like manageable proportions. This tiny volcanic island became an indispensable staging post for the reorganisation, restowing and supply of equipment. Wideawake lived up to its name and for a while became the world's busiest airport. Ascension was valuable as a communications centre, as an exercise area and as a military airbase for the operation of air defence aircraft, long-range reconnaissance aircraft and Vulcan bombers. On the other hand, the original loss of South Georgia and the Falkland Islands reminds us that such distant possessions can be a source of strategic weakness if they are not defended to the necessary extent.

Maritime geography of a more general sort also did much to determine the character of the conflict. Had the islands been 150 miles nearer to Argentina, or further away, the nature of the conflict would have been very different. The outcome of operations also depended quite critically on the weather. With all the aids of modern technology, ship's captains at sea and air force commanders on land scanned the morning skies as anxiously as ever did their forefathers.

The continued contribution of the merchant marine to a country's sea power was also most convincingly demonstrated. Three large passenger liners, fifteen tankers, eight Ro-Ro general cargo ships, one container ship, one cable ship, five trawlers, four passenger cargo ships, six general cargo ships, four offshore support vessels and four tugs were pressed into service in a whole variety of indispensable roles. Many of these ships had to be fitted for war service with helicopter pads, replenishment at sea facilities and so forth. That so many ships were thus converted in a few days and virtually without notice was a considerable tribute to the residual versatility of Britain's ship-building and repair yards. With the ships sailed some 330 officers and 1170 men of the merchant navy, often into positions of great danger. The Task Force was also supported by twenty-one ships of the Royal Fleet Auxiliary service (mainly tankers, replenishment ships and logistic landing ships) although this was for them a more familiar function. At the end of the conflict, Jim Slater, leader of the Seamen's Union summed up the situation quite concisely: 'Quite simply, if it wasn't for the back up force provided by the Merchant Navy, the Royal Navy vessels might as well have stayed in port'.[28]

The Falklands campaign demonstrated in sum that the traditional strengths of a maritime community were as decisive for success in war now as they were at the time when Mahan and the rest were busy first identifying them. The technological, political and economic changes that have followed do not seem to have substantially reduced the value of such assets – at least in this kind of war. During and after the campaign, spokesmen for Britain's maritime community were at pains to point out the implications of this for the future. 'If that capability is allowed to disperse,' argued Robert Atkinson, Chairman of British Shipbuilders, for instance, 'then it will be lost to the nation and therefore unavailable in times of national emergency. Ship-building, like shipping, is a strategic industry.'[29]

On a smaller scale the same was equally true for Argentina. Naval auxiliaries (tugs, transports and landing ships) and supply ships played an important role in the initial seizure of the Falklands and South Georgia and in the subsequent costly attempts to support the garrisons newly established ashore. Turning to the fighting instruments of sea power, the *Armada Republica Argentina* was a balanced, relatively modern and efficient regional force, comprising one carrier, one cruiser, nine destroyers, five frigates and four submarines, plus auxiliaries. The older ships had been updated with the fitting of modern missiles and radars. The air force, and naval air force, comprised some 250 modern combat aircraft whose equipment and training (supplied in the main by the United States, Israel and France) were clearly more than adequate.

Two points can be made about the Argentine Navy and its strategic relationship with its British adversary. In the first place, the two navies operated much common equipment – Sea King helicopters, Exocet missiles and Type 42 destroyers. The British had to paint their own Type 42s with identification marks to lessen possible confusions. The British also knew these ships were efficiently run, since they had trained some of the Argentine crews. Only a few months before the conflict for instance, the Type 42 *Santisima Trinidad* had carried out missile firing trials at the Ministry of Defence range off Aberporth in Wales. The Royal Navy, trained for action against one adversary with completely different concepts and equipment, found itself instead most unexpectedly posed against a navy that worked to the same principles and often with the same equipment that it did. As Captain Jeremy Black of HMS *Invincible* is said to have remarked: 'Exocet v. Exocet. Hmmm. That's not nice.'[30]

The second point is that the balance between the two navies (and their supporting maritime air power) was a dynamic one whose trend was strongly in Argentina's favour. Firstly, the conflict took place shortly after there had been a much remarked shift in Britain's defence priorities which worked particularly to the disadvantage of the surface fleet. The irony of such a maritime effort being required so soon after this revision in Britain's policy was not lost on the newspapers, who were quick to point out that the Task Force was prepared in dockyards facing closure and run-down, was led by two carriers (HM Ships *Hermes* and *Invincible*) due for premature disposal, and manned by sailors hundreds of whom had notices of redundancy in their back pockets. Indeed the intended de-commissioning of HMS *Endurance* which played a part in precipitating the crisis in the first place was part of this process. The *Armada Republica Argentina* on the other hand was engaged on a significant programme of renewal (though it too had rather oddly de-commissioned its major amphibious warfare ship the *Candido de Lasala* six months before). Recent and anticipated acquisitions included four fast frigates built in Germany together with six effective Type 209 submarines, a number of *Meko* class corvettes, more aircraft and more missiles. That the Argentine junta did not bide its time until the strategic balance moved even more strongly in its direction, strongly suggests that it was not fully in command of events.

Despite the relative decline in its maritime fortunes since 1945, Britain was in the event able to construct a formidable Task Force of thirty-three major combatants, eleven lesser units supported by over seventy auxiliary vessels of various kinds. Its capacity to respond so quickly to a quite unexpected situation reflected the strengths of the Royal Navy's supply and support infrastructure and the inherent flexibility of naval forces. Though the Royal Navy had been configured for operations in a NATO context it had not yet become so specialised that it could do nothing else. Ships designed essentially for anti-submarine activities like HMS *Invincible* and the Type 22 frigates like HMS *Brilliant* still had the residual versatility to perform quite different roles, that of a mini strike carrier and an air defence 'goal-keeper' respectively.

The capital ships of the Task Force were the two carriers whose air component was vital. The other leading elements of the force were the two recently reprieved assault ships HMS *Fearless* and HMS *Intrepid* whose presence was indispensable, and the small but equally essential submarine force which comprised up to five nuclear propelled submarines and one diesel submarine. These units were supported by a combined destroyer and frigate force which involved some twenty-three ships during the campaign. In the press at the time and subsequently, there was a good deal of ill-informed and exaggerated comment about the vulnerability of surface ships in general and British surface ships in particular. Apparently stimulated by the curious notion that even major wars can reasonably be expected to involve casualties only to the other side, these ideas were nourished by the dramatic imagery of ships in distress as conveyed by press photographers. The mythology thus produced obscured the real question, which is not whether ships are vulnerable (which of course they are, and particularly so in the circumstances prevailing in the Falklands), but whether they are so vulnerable that they cannot perform their tasks, and, clearly, they were not. The whole argument about surface ships in the Falklands campaign in fact was a fascinating re-appearance in amended form of the arguments associated with the *Jeune Ecole*, the submarine enthusiasts of the First World War, airpower theorists of the interwar period and such idiosyncratic maritime thinkers of the nuclear age as Mr Khruschev.[31]

The apparent disparity between the two navies needs however to be offset by a number of factors in a way which reminds us of the dangers of the number-crunching approach to maritime strategy noted earlier.[32] In the first place, Britain had other maritime duties which had still to be performed the Falklands campaign notwithstanding, and so found it impossible to concentrate her maritime capabilities on this issue to the same extent as Argentina. Argentina's geographic proximity to the theatre of operations and its quantitative air superiority also did much to even up the balance. Finally there is the point that the Argentine Navy was able to use its reported exercises with the Uruguayan Navy as cover for a surprise assault on the Falklands that gave little warning of its intention and which, once achieved, greatly improved its strategic position *vis-à-vis* its nominally superior adversary. The whole operation in fact reminds us of the remaining feasibility and the all-too-evident military advantage of strategic surprise.

(iii) The Conduct of the Campaign

It was always clear that a contested landing in the Falklands would be a hazardous operation. Such operations are always difficult, but those conducted in the presence of strong enemy air and naval forces are especially dangerous. For this reason, the Royal Navy Task Force seems to have decided to make a serious challenge to its adversary before attempting to mount a large scale amphibious operation. As has been remarked above, it seems logical to secure a working command of the sea, *before* attempting to exercise it.[33] If the Task Force could defeat or neutralise the Argentine Navy and/or Air Force first, it would then be able to conduct its amphibious operation in much greater security. For this reason, the British battle group led by the two carriers sailed south of Ascension on 18 April, leaving the bulk of the amphibious force behind.

By the time the main part of the battle group entered the Falklands exclusion zone, a small element of it had already secured South Georgia without loss. The main part of the challenge to Argentine forces was posed on 1 May, however, when operations against Argentine forces on the islands themselves began. The Argentine Navy appears at least partially to have taken up this challenge. A small force (Task Group 79.3) comprising the cruiser *General Belgrano* plus two destroyers took up a position south of the islands while a much larger one (split into the two Task Groups 79.1 and .2) took station to the north and west. These three groups actively probed British defences and were considered to be a significant threat. Accordingly the *General Belgrano* was sunk on 2 May. The *25 de Mayo* group stayed in the area for a further two days and there are indications that the Argentine carrier attempted to launch an air strike on the British battle group.[34] On 4 May, however, *25 de Mayo* and her escorts were ordered to return to port. For the rest of the campaign no major Argentine warship attempted to leave territorial waters. The British had inflicted a cost-free (for them) defeat on the Argentine Navy and effectively neutralised it for the remainder of the campaign – though of course, this was not absolutely clear at the time.

The Argentine Air Force (supplemented by the naval air force which subsequently included the *25 de Mayo*'s air group) did not make its major challenge at this time though. Some aircraft (including two Mirages and two Canberras) were shot down and the destroyer HMS *Sheffield* was sunk in this period, but the bulk of Argentina's air force stayed at home presumably judging that a naval/air battle on the open sea before the invasion started would not be to its best advantage. In effect the main engagement was postponed. This meant that the neat and tidy method of first securing a working command and then exercising it by some positive and strategic use of the sea proved impossible. As Admiral Gorshkov has reminded us this is now in fact usually the case.[35]

For this reason, the adversaries conducted their battle for naval/air supremacy while the major amphibious operation of the campaign was under way. The Task Force had simultaneously therefore to deal with the Argentine Air Force and protect the vulnerable ships engaged in the landing. This meant it had to divide its forces and deploy some of its warships in particularly exposed positions. For its part the Argentine Air Force knew more or less exactly where its targets were and that most of them would be virtually stationary. The additional problems all this posed for the British explains why the Task Force would have preferred to do the two things in sequence and why the Argentine Air Force instead made it to do them simultaneously.

This is not the place for a detailed analysis of the tactical and technological methods by which both sides conducted their struggle for maritime supremacy. Nevertheless, a few general points can be made, first of all about the naval/air battle. The Task Force almost naturally fell into a complex air defence system very analogous to the formations adopted by equivalent fleets in the closing stages of the Pacific War 1944–5. The paucity of British naval assets and the requirement to protect the San Carlos bridgehead, support the ground forces ashore and protect the carriers all at the same time meant that not all the elements of the system were present at any one time. But at least notionally the system consisted of a whole series of concentric arcs.

The outer arc represented the best method of dealing with an enemy air force, namely catching it on the ground. Although the option of bombing Argentina's airbases was put on one side, the Task Force made every effort to destroy hostile aircraft in their Falklands bases, such as by the very, successful special attack on Pebble Island and by the suppression raids on Stanley airfield conducted by Task Force Harriers and Vulcan bombers from Ascension. The latter were the longest range bombing raids in aviation history; the fact that they were mounted at all was a considerable achievement. Their object was the limited one of denying the airfield to Mirage, Skyhawks or Super Etendards. Little more could realistically have been expected with the armaments then available. The British Pacific Fleet's arduous operations against the Sakashima Gunto in 1945 shows how hard it is to put airfields totally out of commission.

The Argentine version of this was their attempts to attack the British carriers. In a small way, the potential benefits of success were shown by the destruction of the *Atlantic Conveyor* and the consequential loss of the helicopters carried aboard. The Task Force carriers had to keep their distance since the operational benefits of coming in closer were completely outweighed by the extra risks entailed. Keeping the flight decks safe in fact was 'the classic carrier way of operating.'[36]

The second arc of the defence was the timely identification of the course and nature of incoming flights by submarines and surface radar pickets given the absence of airborne early warning aircraft in the British inventory. Active defence then began with the Task Force Harriers on combat air patrol and with ships acting as missile traps. The Sea Harriers shot down 23 aircraft[37] and established a complete ascendancy over the Argentine Air Force. A big advantage of this for the British was the increasing deterrent effect the prospect of Harrier interception had on Argentine attacks. According to Argentine sources, only 302 of the 445 attack sorties that set out actually arrived at their destination. Thus Lieutenant Ricardo Lucero: 'I was shot down on my fourth attempt to attack your beachhead. Three previous attempts were aborted when your Harriers intercepted us over the sea. We dropped our weapon loads into the water and turned for home to escape them.'[38] The Harriers often acted in conjunction with surface ships whose superior radars made it possible and desirable to control air interceptions. For their own part, the ships themselves were sometimes able to form themselves into what became known as the '22–42 Combo', that is joint action groups of pairs of Type 22 frigates and Type 42 destroyers whose missile systems usefully complemented one another. Until overwhelmed on 25 May, HMS *Coventry* was particularly effective in this role when acting with HMS *Broadsword*.

The next arc in the system was provided by the self-defence

capacities of the ships themselves. Off the San Carlos bridgehead, three to four ships formed themselves into a 'gun line' just inside the entrance to the Falkland Sound. Their function was to protect the amphibious warfare shipping (which included such highly vulnerable ships as the huge cruise liner SS *Canberra* and ships loaded with ammunition and fuel) by shooting down as many aircraft as they could and by physically interposing themselves between the attackers and their real targets. This was a hazardous and bloody business – as such operations always are unless the force conducting the landing or evacuation has near complete air superiority. The point is made by a comparison of the losses suffered off Norway and Dunkirk in 1940 and Crete in 1941 with those off Normandy in 1944. On the first day alone the Argentine Air Force, which had saved itself up for this occasion, launched twelve separate attacks involving 72 aircraft on the San Carlos bridgehead.

The British missile system forced the Argentine pilots to fly low and drop their bombs at the wrong angle. This often prevented the bombs from fusing themselves and caused them to ricochet along the surface of the water, damaging their mechanisms and often bouncing relatively harmlessly over the ships under attack. This forced method of attack also restricted the pilots' tactical choice. They tended to attack the first ship they saw, those on the gunline, rather than the vulnerable ships in the anchorage. But, not surprisingly, losses were high on both sides.

Since the landings proceeded it was clear that the Argentine Air Force had nevertheless failed in its strategic objective. When the bridgehead's own defences came into play (the anti-aircraft weapons of the ships in the anchorage and the Rapier and other systems deployed ashore – which formed the centre of the Task Force's whole air defence system), the tide turned decisively against the Argentine Air Force, losses became prohibitive and the rate of attack dwindled markedly. The air force did however make one last major effort on 8 June when HMS *Plymouth* was badly damaged at San Carlos and the landing ships *Sir Galahad* and *Sir Tristram* were attacked at Bluff Cove. The latter incident in particular indicates what might well have happened more generally if the British air defence system (which for various reasons was not fully in place at Bluff Cove) had not been so successful.

At sea, the escorts goalkeeping for the carriers were the equivalent of the San Carlos gun-line. Here the threat was not generally from conventional bombs but from air-launched Exocet missiles such as the one which had already sunk HMS *Sheffield* in an earlier stage of the campaign. The Argentine naval air force made two more such attacks, one on the 25 May and another five days later. The Task Force defended itself against these attacks by seducing the missiles with chaff and other deception techniques and by attempting to shoot them down. One Exocet was destroyed by the 4.5-inch gun on HMS *Avenger*. The launching Super Etendard aircraft were nearly caught by Sea Harriers, and accompanying Skyhawks (which had to come closer) were shot down by the ships under attack. However on 25 May the individually defenceless *Atlantic Conveyor* was hit and eventually lost. The final Exocet missile was fired by a shore battery in the vicinity of Port Stanley at HMS *Glamorgan* which had just completed a spell of shore bombardment. Despite the damage and loss of life the ship retained her speed and steerage and was operational shortly afterwards.

The inactivity of the Argentine Navy made the battle for naval/air supremacy primarily one between Argentine aircraft and British ships, but not entirely so. A number of smaller Argentine warships and auxiliaries were active around the islands and British aircraft sank or damaged a large proportion of these including the surfaced submarine *Santa Fe*, the spy trawler *Narwhal*, an armed tug, several patrol ships and a number of supply and support ships.

Turning briefly to the subsurface aspect of the battle for maritime supremacy off the Falkland Islands takes us into a hidden world whose certainties are particularly few, especially in the South Atlantic where the conditions for anti-submarine operations are so bad. There are some reports that the Argentine Navy sought to attack the Task Force with the *San Luis*, one of its new, quiet Type 209 submarines on 5 May and spent a harrowing three days on the ocean floor being hunted by British warships after its torpedoes failed. Whether that was so or not, the Royal Navy's traditional expertise in ASW operations had to be much employed throughout the campaign.

But the main feature of this dimension of the war was the attack by HMS *Conqueror* on the *General Belgrano*, the operational circumstances of which have already been described. Further details have subsequently emerged about the nature of the attack which show that it was nothing like the easy or risk-free enterprise for the attacking submarine it was at first thought to have been.[40] Submarines, even nuclear-propelled ones, are no more wonder weapons capable of solving all problems than other earlier products of what Captain Roskill has so aptly called the fallacy of the single weapon.

Nevertheless, the effects of this attack were to confine the Argentine fleet into harbour for the remainder of the campaign. The message was reinforced by a British declaration on 7 May, shortly after the loss of HMS *Sheffield*, that Argentine warships and aircraft proceeding outside Argentina's twelve-mile limit would be liable to attack. This was in fact a close blockade, novel only in that it was largely enforced by submarine. It was the culmination of a long series of British declarations which sought to inhibit the Argentine Navy and Air Force from moving about the South Atlantic at will.

These declarations were of two sorts because they had two distinct purposes. The first captured the public attention; declarations of this type were designed to blockade the Argentine forces on the Falkland

Islands themselves by establishing and attempting to enforce to the greatest possible extent a two-hundred-mile exclusion zone around the islands. At one stage, the possibility of restricting British naval activity to the enforcement of such a blockade was canvassed in London but was rejected on the grounds that the time it would take to be effective would make the Task Force too vulnerable to attrition through weather and enemy attack and would undermine the political momentum of the campaign.[41]

The second type of blockading declarations were designed to increase the security of the British Task Force itself. There were a number of them (and several did not attract the public attention they warranted). Of particular importance was the declaration of 23 April, which said among other things that, under Article 51 of the UN Charter, Britain wished to make it clear that '... any approach on the part of Argentine warships ... which could amount to a threat to interfere with the mission of British Forces in the South Atlantic will encounter the appropriate response.' The attack carried out on the *General Belgrano* nine days later came within the scope of this declaration. As a result of all this the Argentine Navy was effectively neutralised and its surface fleet ceased to have any significant effect on the outcome of the campaign. British submarines remained on station, though, in order to keep it that way.

There were those who believed that the Argentine Navy accepted its imprisonment too passively. When the campaign was over, the Argentine Air Force journal *Aerospacio* declared: 'The number of English submarines in the theatre of operations was too small to maintain an efficient vigilance of the enormous sea area which they had to cover.'[42] On the basis of such ideas, some have suggested that the Argentine Navy could have gone in for a more active fleet-in-being strategy which might at the least have put the Task Force's command of the sea under more strain, perhaps especially in the critical period of 21 to 25 May, when it was already dealing with the Argentine Air Force and protecting the landings at San Carlos.[43] Failing that, all the Argentine Navy could do was to keep its forces in being in the most passive way so that they could be a factor for the British to consider when the campaign was over.

It only remains now to look at the degree of command the British won for themselves and what they did with it. The campaign illustrates two things about command of the sea in such conflicts: firstly, how necessary it was. Sea denial was not enough for either side. For the British the military point of the exercise (given the decision not to proceed with a lengthy blockade) was to land troops ashore and keep them supplied. This was a positive use of the sea which required the capacity to control events taking place on it. Until the day when we have underwater aircraft carriers and supply vessels or conduct invasions solely by air, the exercise of sea power by positive use quite clearly demands the employment of surface ships. This being so, the occasionally heard claim that surface ships have had their day effectively means that sea power as generally understood has had it too. The British knew this, braced themselves against the inevitable risks and consoled themselves with the reflection that this was likely to be a short campaign one way or another, so a high rate of loss would not last long. Interestingly, exactly the same considerations applied to Argentina too. To get to the Falklands and to stay there for a prolonged period required the capacity to control the sea. Argentine operations against the British Task Force were not simply ones of sea denial. The Argentine Navy knew that unless it eventually won for itself the freedom to keep the garrison on the islands supplied by sea and air its position would ultimately prove untenable. In short this campaign provides an emphatic reminder that aspirations for command of the sea are not the exclusive preserve of the major maritime powers.

The campaign also shows that command of the sea is a relative not an absolute thing. The British obviously had most of it but by no means all; this was particularly the case in the naval/air side of the campaign. The Task Force simply did not have the assets to aim for air supremacy; all it could aspire to was local air superiority for limited periods of time. Nor could it hope to enforce the exclusion zones absolutely. Its operations were like those of the Customs Service. The British prosecuted the offenders they caught and hoped that this would deter others, but knew that some would always slip through. Their blockade of the Falklands garrison was not and, in the circumstances then prevailing, could not be completely impermeable. Their command of the sea, in other words, was not absolute; nor did they or anyone else familiar with the situation expect it to be.

It was though of a degree sufficient for them to use the sea in the traditional ways described earlier in this book – for the transport and supply of men and material and for operations against the shore. British supply lines were quite extraordinarily long and in theory vulnerable to Argentine attack. A communiqué issued in Buenos Aires on 11 May stated that any vessel flying the Red Ensign 'headed towards the operations area or which presumably constituted a threat to Argentine security is to be considered hostile and subject to consequences'.[44] Perhaps fortunately for the Task Force the Argentine Navy had decided against buying British submarines of the Oberon class and the capacity of their Type 209 submarines for maritime interdiction was limited.[45] The British took this threat seriously however. Otherwise Argentine efforts in this direction were restricted to an improvised and ineffective air attack on the tanker British Wye on 29 May 350 miles north of South Georgia and a mistaken attack on the empty Liberian tanker Hercules on 8 June. The British were able to use the sea as a means of transport virtually with impunity. At the same time, their command of the sea made it difficult for Argentina to do the same for its beleaguered garrison on the Falklands.

The British decided against trying to enforce a commercial blockade of Argentina as a whole, concluding that this would be militarily impracticable and politically foolish, though the declaration by Lloyds, the insurers, that war risk policies would not apply to a large area of the South Atlantic did disrupt shipping going in and out of the River Plate. Instead the Task Force contented itself with cutting supply lines between the Falklands and Argentina. HMS *Alacrity* sank the storeship *Cabo de los Estados* in the Falkland Sound on the night of 11 May and British aircraft sank or damaged several other freighters and supply ships attempting to run the blockade. The British also attempted to interdict air supply operations into the islands. According to *Aeroespacio* Argentine Air Force transports flew 33 sorties into Port Stanley between 1 May and 14 June carrying in 450 tons of cargo and evacuating 264 wounded,[46] clearly a much lower figure than the garrison needed or which would have been the case if Falklands air space had not been contested.

Turning now to operations against the shore, *Operation Rosario*, the original Argentine invasion of South Georgia and the Falklands, was a maximum effort by the Navy involving their carrier, *25 de Mayo*, plus six destroyers, two corvettes, one submarine, one landing ship and two transports carrying the 2nd Marine Battalion and auxiliaries. All went according to plan and some 2500 men plus equipment were put ashore. The landings themselves were not contested in the Falklands but the resistance of the Royal Marine garrison at Leith on South Georgia was a reminder of how difficult opposed landings can be.

The eventual British counter-invasion was on a much larger scale and faced immensely greater military and logistical difficulties. The seizure of South Georgia was not the surgically exact operation it was first thought to have been and usefully reminded the British how things can easily go wrong in so hazardous an enterprise. It probably put paid to any lingering ideas about a full-scale Normandy-type assault on Port Stanley itself. Instead the British prepared themselves for the long haul.

The Task Force methodically went through all the normal stages of a large-scale amphibious operation, complicated mainly by its great range. Everything the Task Force needed had to be taken with it, transported and packed in battle order, with due allowance made for losses and enemy action. Reconnaissance of possible landing sites was conducted by helicopter, submarine and by small detachments of special forces put ashore for the purpose. Every effort was made to distract and confuse the garrison by feints and diversionary raids, something that was doubly necessary given the fact that this was a very public war. The British could not hope for strategic surprise but merely for the tactical variety. The landings began on 21 May and the bridgehead had to be protected in the desperately dangerous way already described.

Once the ground forces had landed, the Task Force moved into the second phase of its operation against the shore, namely close support. This was initially provided by naval gunfire support which again emerged from clouds of post-war scepticism as an important and sometimes decisive contribution to the land battle. Naval gunfire support proved to be quite extraordinarily accurate and provided invaluable covering fire for many of the operations, not least by sometimes demoralising enemy forces into submission, as for example on South Georgia. The Task Force also provided air cover for the troops ashore, shooting down enemy aircraft, bombing and rocketing enemy strong-points ashore and so forth. The contrast between this and the largely ineffective attempts by the Argentine Air Force to do likewise led to both General Menendez and General Americo Daher (former commander of the Argentine ground forces on the Falklands) bitterly complaining of lack of air support, the reputation of the Pucara anti-insurgency aircraft notwithstanding.[47] Given the extreme difficulty of moving men and military supplies overland, Task Force helicopters did a great deal to improve the ground forces' mobility and hitting power, although there were never enough of them. Finally the Task Force was able to support the troops ashore by supplementary landing operations such as the costly but ultimately effective landing at Bluff Cove on 7 to 8 June and the diversionary raid on the eastern end of Wireless Ridge on 12 June.[48] The Falklands campaign in short provides what was an almost copy-book example of amphibious warfare of the traditional sort.

(d) Conclusions

This survey of recent maritime events supports three tentative conclusions about contemporary maritime strategy. First their range and extent confirm rather than deny traditional ideas about the importance of the sea to the security and prosperity of most countries. The economic importance of the sea in peace-time is growing and will continue to grow. The extent to which this is the case has been particularly well demonstrated by Phillipe Masson in his *Marines et Oceans* (Paris: Imprimerie Nationale, 1982), a book which has appeared since the first edition of this one. It follows obviously, that the need to protect and police the exploitation of these benefits will grow as well. Given the prevailing and entirely laudable preference of most countries for the avoidance of the actual use of force, the sea seems set to remain an important arena for political activity in peace-time too – as must emerge from any attentive reading of a maritime record of 1979 to take the random example given above. The contrast between the Falklands campaign and the war going on in the Lebanon at the same time reinforces, moreover, the notion that events at sea remain much easier to control in the politico-military twilight of limited war than do their counterparts on land.

The events of the last decade or so have also convincingly shown that the sea is as important to the conduct of war as ever it was. In the case of those situations where the adversaries are divided by great stretches of water as was the case in the Falklands campaign and would be the case in any East/West conflict, this point is perhaps hardly surprising. But the Arab–Israeli War of 1973 and Vietnam's various wars of 1979 show that this is even true of neighbouring countries engaged in limited territorial conflict. In these cases, sea power may serve ancillary and subordinate purposes. Their navies may do little more than cancel each other out. But at the very least such countries will need to practice sea denial: they will need to be sure that their adversaries cannot use the sea with impunity. A moment's reflection about what might have been the consequence in 1973, if the Syrian and Egyptian navies had been able to operate at will in the sea whose waves washed the beaches of Tel Aviv and Haifa, will show that this negative function can easily be of extreme strategic importance. All experience suggests moreover that sea denial must at least partially be conducted by forces that are naval in character. But in wars like that of 1973, sea power is not in fact restricted simply to such negative functions in any case. There is in short little evidence to support the contention that the general idea of maritime strategy or of sea power itself are moribund matters of interest only to historians. On the contrary, maritime capacity remains at least as important as ever it was: complicated but not excluded by land/air power, it is often still fundamental to the outcome of wars on land.

Secondly, both past theory and present practice indicate that neither sea power nor the ability to command the sea are absolute but merely relative questions of degree. Accordingly, countries with coasts and significant interests in the sea (a group more likely to expand than diminish) tend to share similar maritime preoccupations, being divided mainly by scale. For this reason, general conceptions of sea power and maritime strategy are not and should not be regarded as the exclusive preserve of states with blue-water navies or established traditions of sea-faring. Recent experience confirms that few countries can afford to restrict their activities simply and solely to negative operations of sea denial. To a greater or lesser extent, at some time or other, most of them will want the capacity to use the sea in some way and its corollary – the ability to protect that capacity. It follows then that most countries with serious maritime aspirations, whether these are at the global, regional or local level will continue to need significant surface ships for the foreseeable future and the corresponding capacity to operate positively in what the jargon would now call a multi-threat environment. Most will therefore continue to need a fleet offering a variety of means and capabilities, because this assures flexibility whereas (over-) specialisation simply invites tactical or technical outflanking. Admiral Gorshkov put the matter like this:

> The balance of a fleet consists in the fact that all the elements making up its fighting power and their protection are constantly in the most advantageous combination, in which the fleet can completely realise the quality of universality it has, that is the ability to fulfil different tasks in conditions both of a nuclear and any possible war.[49]

Of course, Admiral Gorshkov was here addressing the possibilities for a Superpower but the same message holds fundamentally true for any sea power of whatever scale.

Whether minor maritime powers (or major ones, come to that) can afford the balanced fleet they may think they need is of course another matter. The question throws up complex issues about the best mix between high quality and low numbers and vice-versa and between air, surface and sub-surface assets. Particular solutions depend largely on particular sets of circumstances but the sheer expense even of getting the balance right (let alone the chilling hazards of getting it wrong) make it imperative for planners, designers, analysts, users and the humble majorities who pay for it all to have the best guidance available.

This takes us to the third conclusion to be drawn from this survey, namely that worthwhile parallels can still be drawn between past and present experience. Perhaps not surprisingly there are considerable similarities between the purposes of sea power then and now; rather less expectedly useful analogies can often be drawn between its methods too. The Falklands campaign may for example have seen a new and deadly duel between missile and counter-missile defences, but it also saw a task force perform many of the same evolutions as predecessors in the Pacific nearly forty years before. The novelties should not blind us to the familiar.

For this reason, those interested in contemporary maritime strategy would be unwise to ignore such previous thinkers as Mahan, Corbett and the rest, whose works may help us to understand the present as well as the past. Their counsel is of abiding value not so much for the answers they supply, for these were often conflicting or afterwards found to be in error, but because they help to identify the questions that need asking. Given the importance and the complexity of many of the issues involved, this is no mean contribution to make to our understanding of maritime strategy in the nuclear age.

References

I have used a short form of reference in which the author's surname is followed by the year of publication in brackets and the page number(s). Full details of the books and articles cited can be found in the bibliography in the section 'Books and articles cited in the references'.

Preface

1. Brown (1964) p. 107.

Chapter 1: An Introduction

1. Quoted in Sprout (1943) pp. 442–3.
2. de Lanessan (1903).
3. Gorshkov (1979) pp. 59, 66, 68, 152–5.
4. Ibid. p. 2.
5. Quoted in Jane (1906) p. 179.
6. Corbett (1918) p. 49.
7. Spear (1970) p. 62 ff.
8. de Lanessan (1903).
9. Mahan (1890) pp. 63–7.
10. Mahan (1899) p. 272.
11. Roskill (1954) p. 1.
12. Richmond (1934) pp. 17 ff.
13. Graham (1978) pp. 408–9.
14. Puleston (1939) p. 110.
15. Graham (1965) pp. 26–7.
16. Ibid. pp. 8–9.
17. Corbett vol. 1 (1907) p. 5.
18. Bridge (1907) p. viii.
19. Quoted in Schurman (1965) p. 190.
20. Richmond (1939).
21. Quoted in Marder (1952) p. 296.
22. Puleston (1939) p. 150.
23. Ibid. p. 200; Taylor (1920) p. 28.
24. Clarke and Thursfield (1897) pp. 246–7.
25. Richmond (1939).
26. Quoted in Richmond (1953) p. 205.

27. Mahan (1911) p. 114.
28. Booth (1976) p. 6.
29. Herrick (1968); also Woodward (1965) p. 207 and MccGwire (1978).
30. Dewar (1904).
31. Mahan (1911) p. 114.
32. Roskill (1954) p. 4.
33. Mahan (1890) p. 88.
34. Keegan (1961) pp. 71–2.
35. Quoted in Mahan (1899) p. 192.
36. Air Staff Memo of 12 Feb 1936, in Air 9/2, Public Record Office, London.
37. Mahan (1911) p. 2.
38. For these arguments see Lanchester (1916); Waddington (1947).
39. Mahan (1911) p. 2, pp. 299–301; also Corbett vol. 1 (1907) pp. 332–3.
40. Mahan (1899) p. 200.
41. Brodie (1965) p. 115.
42. Gretton (1965) p. 21.
43. Quoted in George (1978) p. 86.
44. Castex vol. 1 (1929) p. 9.
45. Respectively, Mahan (1890) pp. 25–59; Richmond (1946) p. x; Roskill (1954) pp. 6–7; James (1948) p. 395; Wegener (1975) pp. 2–4.
46. Quoted in Taylor (1920) p. 42.
47. Jane (1906) p. 21.
48. Richmond (1943) p. 8.
49. Richmond (1934) p. 252.
50. Wegener (1975) p. 4.
51. Richmond (1934) p. 258.
52. Respectively Reitzel (1977) p. 95; Wegener (1975) p. 74.
53. Diodorus Siculus, quoted in Rodgers (1937) pp. 188–9.
54. Jowett (1900) book viii, lines 27 and 29.
55. Ibid. book vii, line 7.
56. Ibid. book v, line 97.
57. Ibid. book v, line 110.
58. Ibid. book vi, line 22.
59. Ibid. book vii, line 24.
60. Ibid. book vi, line 47.

Chapter 2: A Review of the Literature

1. Custance (1918) pp. 67, 109.
2. Puleston (1939) pp. 83–4.
3. Corbett (1905) pp. 3–13.
4. Quoted in Richmond (1953) pp. 30–1.
5. Quoted in Clarke and Thursfield (1897) p. 120.
6. Sutcliffe (1593).
7. Quoted in Colomb, P. (1899) pp. 22–3; Clarke (1897) p. 1.
8. Sir William Monson quoted in Colomb, P. (1899) p. 22.
9. Quoted in Richmond (1953) pp. 30–1.
10. Corbett vol. 2 (1898) p. 129.

11. Father Paul Hoste quoted in Bridge (1873).
12. Admiral Stephen B. Luce quoted in Hayes and Hattendorf (1975) p. 84.
13. This is the verdict of Laughton (1874) but this is disputed by Corbett (1905). The matter is discussed further in Chapter 4.
14. Bridge (1873).
15. Quoted in Colomb, P. (1896) p. 134.
16. Cobden (1862).
17. Colomb, P. (1896) p. vi; (1899) p. v.
18. Colomb, P. (1896) p. 197; the highwayman analogy is suggested in Schurman (1965) p. 55.
19. Colomb, P. (1899) p. 452.
20. Quoted in d'Egville (1913) p. 69; Colomb, Sir John (1880) pp. 54–5.
21. Colomb, P. (1896) pp. 194–229.
22. Marder (1940) p. 70.
23. Quoted in Gretton (1965) p. 8.
24. Colomb, Sir John (1880) p. 41.
25. Colomb, P. (1896) pp. 230–58.
26. Lord Carnarvon, quoted in Schurman (1965) p. 32.
27. Bridge (1873) p. 227; Custance (1907) preface.
28. Quoted in Schurman (1965) p. 52.
29. Sprout (1943) p. 415.
30. See for example the important article Seager (1953) which states that the 'broad theory of naval expansion was clearly enunciated... before Admiral Mahan published his famous book' and that Mahan's contribution was that of 'summing up' rather than innovation. p. 493.
31. Report of the Naval Advisory Board, 47th Congress, 1st session, House Report No. 653.
32. Annual Report of the Secretary of the Navy, 1899, 51st Congress, 1st Session, House Executive Document No. 1, Part III. It is possible, though uncertain, that Mahan helped influence Tracy's report. This is claimed by Harold and Margaret Sprout, *Rise of American Naval Power* (Princeton University Press, 1939) p. 207. They are on firmer ground when they write that Mahan 'provided an ideological basis' for Tracy's report.
33. On Mahan's early life, see Seager (1977).
34. Mahan (1907) pp. 276–7.
35. Mahan (1890) pp. 25–57.
36. Ibid. pp. 72–6.
37. US Congress, *The Annals of Congress*, 5th Congress, 3rd Session, p. 2837.
38. Mahan (1890) p. 76.
39. I am indebted to Lt Cmdr Ph. M. Bosscher R Neth N for this information.
40. Gorshkov (1979) p. 230; Admiral Stepan Makarov, *Considering Questions of Naval Tactics* was another important source.
41. Peattie (1977).
42. I am indebted to Professor Keith W. Bird for his help on this matter.
43. Von Maltzahn (1908) p. 109; also pp. 79, 82.
44. Ibid. p. 130.
45. Ibid. p. 70, 137.
46. Ibid. p. 39, 51, 121.
47. Extract from 'La Marine Aujourdhui' *Journal of RUSI* (1874).

48. Daveluy vol. 1 (1902) p. 8.
49. Jane (1906).
50. Vice Admiral Baron Jean Grivel, *De La Marine Militaire* (Paris, 1837).
51. Grivel (1869) p. 50.
52. Quoted in Richmond (1953) p. 43.
53. Quoted in Marder (1940) p. 87.
54. Extract from Admiral Reveillere, 'France and the Marine', in *Journal of RUSI* (1893) Feb.
55. Brodie (1943) p. 102.
56. de Lanessan (1903).
57. Quoted in Ropp (1937) p. 31.
58. This survey is based on the forthcoming, *Sailor–Scholar: Admiral Sir Herbert Richmond 1871–1946* by Barry Hunt to be published by the Wilfred Laurier University Press.
59. Richmond in a review of Castex vol. IV (1929) *Naval Review* (1933).
60. Castex vol. I (1929) pp. 276–373; vol. II, pp. 277–86.
61. Castex vol. I (1929) pp. 99–105, 114–15.
62. Ibid. pp. 214–15 *et seq*.
63. Ibid. p. 151, 344.
64. Castex vol. II (1929) p. 12; vol. I, pp. 200–2.
65. Castex vol. IV (1929) p. 149–51 *et seq*.
66. Rosinski (1977) p. 64.
67. Vice Admiral A. Meurer quoted in Richmond (1946) p. 298.
68. Von Waldeyer-Hartz, 'Naval Warfare of Tomorrow', *Wissen und Wehr* (1936); Kruse, *Neuzeitliche Seekriegsführung* (Berlin: Mittler, 1938).
69. Quoted in Rosinski (1977) p. 64.
70. I am indebted to Professor Keith W. Bird for this point; see Bird (1979).
71. Both of these reviews are taken from contemporary editions of the *Naval Review*.
72. Roskill (1954) p. 1.
73. Ibid. p. 12.
74. Brodie (1965) p. 75.
75. Ibid. p. 167.
76. Ibid. p. 13–14.
77. Nimitz (1947).
78. Barjot (1956); Gretton (1965); Wegener (1972, 1975). Edward Wegener is the son of Wolfgang Wegener, noted earlier in text.
79. Gretton (1965) p. 194.
80. Wegener (1972) p. 192.
81. Ibid. p. 193.
82. Ibid. pp. 199–200; Gretton (1965) p. 180.
83. Wegener (1972) pp. 204–5.
84. Gretton (1965) p. 180.
85. I would like to thank the following for their advice in the preparation of this essay. My conclusions are entirely my own, but I could not have written this essay without considering their viewpoints: Dr D. C. Allard; Adm. Arleigh Burke; Rear Adm. Henry E. Eccles; Dr John Gaddis; Adm. Isaac C. Kidd, Jr.; Dr Edward N. Luttwak; Dr J. K. McDonald; D. A. Rosenberg; Brig. Gen. E. H. Simmons; Dr B. M. Simpson, III; Dr C. L.

Symonds; Adm. Harry D. Train, II; Admiral Stansfield Turner; Frank Uhlig; F. J. West; Rear Adm. E. F. Welch, Jr.; Adm. Elmo Zumwalt.
86. Cottrell and Moorer (1977) p. 6.
87. Sprout (1943, 1946).
88. Brodie's book went through several revisions before eventually appearing in its 1965 form.
89. Reitzel (1977); Rosinski (1977); also Captain R. A. Bowling 'The Negative Influence of Mahan on Anti-Submarine Warfare', *Journal of the RUSI* (1977) Dec.
90. Martin (1967) p. 10.
91. Reynolds (1974) pp. 12–15.
92. Hayes (1953) p. 193.
93. Stansfield Turner (1977) p. 348.
94. Zumwalt (1976) p. 60.
95. Stansfield Turner (1974).
96. Brown (1949) p. 16.
97. Rosinski (1977) p. 64.
98. Ballantine (1949) pp. 1–3.
99. Wylie (1967) p. 91.
100. Crowl (1978) p. 11.
101. Morgenstern (1959) p. 90.
102. Enthoven (1969) p. 82.
103. Wylie (1967) p. 80.
104. Stockdale (1978) p. 1.
105. Naval War College Archives, R G 8, Series II, XWAG: Enclosure B: 'Reassessment of the Fields and Value of Three Elements of Land, Sea and Air Power,' in President, Naval War College. Letter to Chairman, General Board, 30 Apr. 1948.
106. Stansfield Turner (1976a).
107. Scharfen and Wilcox (1979) p. 36.
108. Foreword to Luttwak (1974) p. vi.

Chapter 3: Sources and Elements

1. Potter and Nimitz (1960) p. vii.
2. Quoted in Richmond (1934) p. 38.
3. Mahan (1890) p. 23.
4. Clarke (1967) p. 163.
5. Quoted in Herrick (1968) p. 82.
6. Quoted in MccGwire (1973) pp. 280–1.
7. Quoted in Gorshkov (1972) Art. 10.
8. See generally Roskill (1968, 1976); Till (1979) pp. 187–201. Also Kennedy (1976).
9. Letters of 2 April 1745 and 14 Mar 1745/6 in Julian Gwyn (ed.), *The Royal Navy and North America* (London: Naval Records Society, 1973) p. 71, 223.
10. Mahan (1890) p. 58.
11. Mahan (1911) p. 447.

12. Captain Mark Kerr quoted in Marder (1940) pp. 401–2.
13. Mahan vol. 1 (1892) p. 67.
14. de Lanessan (1903).
15. Corbett vol. 2 (1907) p. 206.
16. Mahan's views on all this are conveniently summarised in Westcott (1919) pp. 21–48.
17. Graham (1965) p. 45.
18. Quoted in Colomb, P. (1899) p. 142.
19. For instance see Dr Walther Ströbe, 'Forecasting for the Escape of the *Scharnhorst* and *Gneisenau*', *Meteorological Magazine*, (1976) Nov. p. 322.
20. Quoted in Marder (1940) p. 473; also Colomb (1896) p. 67.
21. Gorshkov (1972) Art. 2.
22. Mackinder (1919).
23. Strausz-Hupe (1942) p. 261.
24. Richmond (1946) p. 28.
25. Kennan (1966) p. 65.
26. Castex (1929) vol. v p. 557.
27. Quoted Strausz-Hupe (1942) p. 146.
28. Richmond (1954) p. 7.
29. Earl Macartney, Governor of the Cape, 1797. Quoted in Graham (1965) p. 47.
30. Gorshkov (1972) Art. 2.
31. For a convenient summary see Brodie (1965) pp. 178–88.
32. Roskill (1952) p. 432.
33. Mahan (1890) p. 81.
34. Colomb, P. (1899) Appendix pp. xii–xiii.
35. For British experience see Till (1979) esp. Chapter 2.
36. Richmond (1934) p. 117.
37. For an example of the genre see 'NATO navies outgun Russia' the London *Observer*, 30 Mar. 1980.
38. Acworth (1935) p. 234 *et seq*.
39. Dr John Foster, Director of Defense Research and Engineering, 12 March 1970. Quoted in J. Ronald Fox, *Arming America* (Harvard University Press, 1974) p. 464.
40. Quoted in Marder (1952) p. 296.
41. The *Edinburgh Review* (1894), quoted in Marder (1940) p. 205.
42. Medina Sidonia quoted in Clarke and Thursfield (1897) p. 166.

Chapter 4: The Decisive Battle

1. Richmond, Evidence to the Cabinet Sub-Committee on Ship-building 5 January 1921, Cab 16/37 Public Record Office, London.
2. Battle description from 'An Authentic Narrative' quoted in Woodward (1965) p. 52; also Gorshkov (1979) p. 75.
3. Tunstall (1936) p. 173.
4. Jane (1906) pp. 149–50.
5. Quoted in Rodgers (1937) p. 241.
6. Corbett (1918) pp. 104, 154–5.

7. Quoted in Richmond (1946) pp. 30–1.
8. These passages owe much to Wilson (1957).
9. Ramatuelle quoted in Rosinski (1977) p. xiii.
10. Richmond, book review, *Naval Review* (1933).
11. de Lanessan (1903).
12. Such is the argument of Laughton (1875) p. 524.
13. Lewis (1948) pp. 455–536.
14. Quoted in Puleston (1939) p. 295.
15. Custance (1907) p. 123–4.
16. Mahan quoted and discussed in Corbett (1918) pp. 114–136; (1910) p. 250.
17. Richmond (1946) p. 67.
18. Mahan (1911) p. 422.
19. Mahan quoted in Westcott (1919) p. 156.
20. Ibid. pp. 128–9; Mahan quoted in Puleston (1939) p. 294.
21. Nelson quoted in Mahan (1899) p. 695; Mahan quoted in Taylor (1920) pp. 234–5.
22. Quoted in Mahan vol. I (1892) p. 284.
23. Quoted in Bacon (1936) p. 247.
24. Bridge (1907) p. 218.
25. Letter of 17 June 1916, in author's possession.
26. Gorshkov (1979) pp. 98–9.
27. Grenfell (1937) pp. 137, 175 *et seq.*
28. Custance (1907) p. 113.
29. In my view there is such a misjudgement in the excellent Schurman (1965) p. 142.
30. Richmond (1946) p. 67.
31. Acworth (1935) p. 116.
32. Corbett vol. I (1920) p. 2.
33. Quoted Sydenham (1931).
34. Gorshkov (1979) p. 11.
35. Corbett (1918) p. 143.
36. Corbett vol. I (1907) pp. 3–4.
37. Ibid. p. 289.
38. Corbett (1918) p. 153.
39. Corbett (1910) p. 94.

Chapter 5: Alternative Routes and Command of the Sea

1. Castex vol. IV (1929) p. 137.
2. Jowett (1900) book vi, lines 33–4; Custance (1924) p. 68; Mahan (1911) pp. 226 *et seq.*
3. Quoted in Colomb, P. (1899) pp. 115, 122.
4. Colomb, P. (1899) preface to 2nd edition p. ix; (1896) p. 173.
5. Corbett (1918) pp. 191–5; Richmond (1953) pp. 214–19.
6. Corbett vol. I (1907) pp. 329, 475; vol. II, pp. 373–5.
7. Corbett (1918) pp. 199, 191.
8. Corbett vol. I (1907) p. 128.
9. Castex vol. IV (1929) pp. 149–54, 164–6.

10. Mahan (1911) pp. 243–4, 295–6.
11. Richmond (1953) 217.
12. Mahan (1890) pp. 529–35.
13. Colomb, P. (1899) preface to 2nd edition and Spanish War section p. xxxi.
14. Castex vol. IV (1929) p. 146.
15. Quoted Steinberg (1965) p. 165.
16. Scheer (1920) pp. 25, 68.
17. German Naval War Order, 4 Aug. 1939.
18. Churchill, Aug. 1941 quoted in G. Frere-Cook, *The Attacks on the* Tirpitz (London: Ian Allan, 1973) p. 12.
19. Bacon (1936) pp. 194–5.
20. Acworth (1930) p. 12.
21. Castex vol. IV (1929) p. 164.
22. Mahan vol. I (1892) p. 340; (1911) p. 183.
23. Colomb, P. (1896) p. 196.
24. Roskill (1962) pp. 48–9.
25. Colomb, P. (1896) p. 196.
26. Richmond (1934) p. 163.
27. Corbett vol. II (1907) p. 34.
28. Colomb, P. (1896) p. 195.
29. Corbett vol. II (1907) pp. 234–5.
30. Mahan vol. II (1892) p. 126; vol. I, p. 339.
31. Mahan vol. II (1892) pp. 118–19.
32. Colomb, P. (1899) p. 51.
33. Richmond (1930) p. 40.
34. Pollen (1918) p. 287.
35. Callender (1924) p. 253–4.
36. Corbett vol. I (1907) p. 308; Bridge (1910) p. 84.
37. Corbett vol. II (1907) pp. 20–1.
38. Brodie (1965) p. 75.
39. Clarke and Thursfield (1897) pp. 126–7; Rosinski (1977) p. 4.
40. Comment by G. S. Graham, quoted in Reynolds (1974) p. 211.
41. Mahan (1911) pp. 260–1.
42. Brodie (1965) p. 108.
43. Mahan (1980) p. 14.
44. Bacon (1936) p. 192.
45. Castex vol. I (1929) pp. 99–101; Roskill (1962) p. 184.
46. Corbett vol. II (1907) p. 5.
47. Brodie (1965) p. 74.
48. Arthur Pollen in letter to Richmond 11 Nov. 1936: Richmond Papers, RIC/7/4, National Maritime Museum, quoted by Permission of the Trustees. See also Chapter 4, section d and, on Mahan's role, Custance (1924) pp. 95–8.
49. Gorshkov (1979) p. 215.
50. Brodie (1965) pp. 91, 112.
51. Corbett vol. I (1907) p. 6.
52. Colomb, P. (1891) p. 173.
53. MccGwire (1975) p. 624.
54. Richmond (1946) pp. 326–36.

55. Corbett (1918) p. 211.
56. Gorshkov (1979) pp. 122, 217, 233.
57. A major theme of Ruge (1979).
58. Colomb, P. (1899) p. 24.
59. Ibid. p. 129.
60. Mahan (1911) p. 218, emphasis added.
61. Corbett (1918) p, 89.
62. Raeder, report to the Führer, 9 Mar. 1940, Führer Naval Conferences.
63. Corbett (1910) p. 41.
64. Clarke and Thursfield (1897) p. 54.
65. Colomb, P. (1891) pp. 32–3, 212, 256–7.
66. Roskill (1962) p. 34.
67. Mahan (1890) p. 138.
68. de Lanessan (1903).

Chapter 6: The Exercise of Command

1. Gorshkov (1979) p. 214; Brodie (1965) p. 153.
2. Kennedy (1976) p. 114.
3. Richmond (1934) p. 173.
4. Gorshkov (1979) p. 3.
5. Quoted by Rear Adm. T. Byam Martin in dispatch to Lord Keith, 21 Sep. 1813. Naval Records Society, vol. XII, p. 409.
6. Corbett (1918) p. 51.
7. Corbett vol. I (1907) pp. 207–8.
8. Ibid. p. 228.
9. Quoted in Brodie (1965) p. 155–6.
10. Quoted in Richmond (1946) pp. 338–9.
11. Brodie (1965) p. 155.
12. Richmond (1946) p. 340.
13. Quoted in ibid. p. 117.
14. Corbett vol. I (1907) pp. 269–70.
15. Roskill (1954) p. 11.
16. Grenfell (1937) pp. 28–9.
17. Corbett (1918) p. 269.
18. Richmond (1941b).
19. Corbett vol. I (1907) pp. 218–19.
20. Mahan (1911) pp. 200, 205.
21. Richmond (1941b).
22. Brodie (1965) p. 157.
23. Ruge (1979) p. 77.
24. Nimitz (1947).
25. See Chapter 2, Section c.
26. Quoted in Marder (1940) p. 65.
27. Quoted in Grenfell (1937) p. 43.
28. Quoted in Custance (1907) p. 302.
29. Quoted in Woodward (1965) pp. 206–7.
30. Quoted in Bridge (1910) p. 269.

31. Mahan (1911) pp. 151, 293.
32. Corbett vol. i (1907) pp. 93–4.
33. Corbett (1918) p. 256.
34. Quoted in Richmond (1930) p. 74.
35. Ibid. p. 24.
36. MccGwire (1976) p. 15.
37. Corbett (1918) p. 236.
38. Jane (1906) p. 145; Hipper quoted in Philbin (1977) p. 77.
39. Symcox (1974) pp. 221–33; Richmond (1953) pp. 352–3.
40. Corbett (1898) pp. 129, 335; Mahan (1890) pp. 132–3; Castex vol. iv (1939) pp. 113–14, 285–344; Gorshkov (1979) p. 120.
41. de Lanessan (1903).
42. Mahan (1890) p. 539; Corbett vol. ii (1907) pp. 375–6.
43. Mahan (1890) p. 138.
44. Mahan vol. ii (1892) p. 184.
45. Richmond (1930) p. 56.
46. Corbett (1918) p. 166.
47. Acworth (1930) p. 56.
48. Grenfell (1937) p. 45.
49. Corbett (1918) p. 87.
50. de Lanessan (1903).
51. Westcott (1919) pp. 16, 18; but see also Mahan (1911) p. 355–6.
52. Respectively, Waters (1957) pp. 7–8; Schurman (1965) pp. 135–7; Grenfell (1937) p. 91.
53. Richmond, evidence to Bonar Law Enquiry, 5 Jan. 1921, Cab. 16/37, Public Record Office, London; Rosinski (1977) p. 13; also Castex vol. i (1929) p. 147.
54. Jane (1906) p. 174.
55. Colomb quoted in Waters (1957) p. 57; Richmond (1953) p. 116.
56. Gretton (1965) p. 22.
57. Bridge (1907) p. 123; Sir John Fisher, quoted in Marder (1940) p. 95.
58. Roskill (1954) pp. 10ff; (1962) pp. 158, 179.
59. Gretton (1965) p. 22.
60. Mahan (1890) p. 25.
61. Waters (1957).
62. Quoted in Mahan (1899) p. 28.
63. Corbett (1918) p. 245.
64. Roskill vol. iii, Pt. I (1954) p. 348.
65. Quoted in Waters (1957) p. 21.
66. Grenfell (1937) p. 54.
67. Mahan vol. ii (1892) p. 217.
68. Richmond (1930) p. 65.

Chapter 7: A New Environment for Navies?

1. Gorshkov (1979) pp. 157, 187.
2. Ibid. p. 224.
3. Michael Howard in 'Power at Sea', *Adelphi* (1976).

4. Gorshkov (1979) p. 210.
5. Stansfield Turner (1976a) pp. 2, 10.
6. Corbett vol. 1 (1898) p. 3.
7. Gorshkov (1979) p. 199.
8. Gorshkov (1972) Art. 2.
9. Rosinski (1977) p. 48.
10. Scheer (1920) p. 87.
11. Bacon (1936) p. 349.
12. Gorshkov (1979) p. 209.
13. Colomb, P. (1899) Appendix p. xxi.
14. Stansfield Turner (1976) p. 2.
15. Ibid.

Chapter 8: Old Tasks for New Navies

1. Graham (1965) pp. 29–30, 124–5.
2. Richmond (1934) pp. 100–3, 112–17, 249; also Till (1979).
3. Richmond evidence to Bonar Law Enquiry 5 Jan. 1921. Cab. 16/37, Public Record Office, London.
4. Huntington (1954).
5. Quoted in Herrick (1968) p. 68.
6. Edward Teller quoted by Norman Polmar in George (1978) p. 212.
7. Jane (1906) p. 306.
8. Gorshkov (1972) Art. 11.
9. Adm. Thomas B. Hayward, before the Sea power sub-committee of House Armed Services Committee, 20 Dec. 1979.
10. Adm. S. E. Zakharov quoted in MccGwire (1978) p. 254.
11. See Martin (1967) pp. 46–99.
12. George (1978) p. 93.
13. Adm. Thomas B. Hayward, Statement before Sea power sub-committee of House Armed Services Committee, 20 Dec. 1979.
14. Jungius (1979).
15. Adm. James L. Holloway, Chief of Naval Operations, quoted in George (1978) p. 302.
16. Gorshkov (1979) pp. 225–6.
17. Stansfield Turner (1974).
18. Adm. William Crowe, US Navy quoted in George (1978) p. 22.
19. Stansfield Turner (1974).
20. Gorshkov (1972) Art. 1.
21. For instance Gorshkov (1972) Art. 3; (1979) pp. 234–4. Also MccGwire (1978).
22. Gorshkov (1979) p. 233.
23. Booth (1978).
24. Rear Adm. Henry E. Eccles, US Navy, notes 20 Jan. 1972. I am indebted to Rear Adm. Eccles and Dr John Hattendorf for this.
25. Stansfield Turner (1974).
26. Gorshkov (1979) p. 234.
27. For instance Vigor (1975); MccGwire (1975).

28. Stansfield Turner (1974).
29. Gorshkov quoted in MccGwire (1973) p. 255.
30. Stansfield Turner (1977).
31. Corbett (1918) p. 87.
32. See Chapter 5, Sections f and h.
33. Gorshkov (1979) p. 232.
34. Robert W. Herrick in George (1978) p. 84.
35. Adm. William Crowe, US Navy in ibid. p. 69.
36. In a comment on a formulation by Adm. Raymond A. Spruance, in Eccles Papers, Naval Historical Collection, Naval War College, Rhode Island.
37. Gorshkov (1979) pp. 162, 177.
38. Adm. Thomas Hayward to Sea Power sub-committee of House Armed Services Committee, 20 Dec. 1979.
39. A. Lagovskii quoted in Herrick (1968) p. 95.
40. For instance see the sceptical McConnell (1978) esp pp. 49–51; Hibbits (1978) pp. 8–9; Daniel (1978) pp. 227–8.
41. Gorshkov (1979) p. 276; quoted in MccGwire (1973) p. 350.
42. Adm. Ivan Isakov quoted in Herrick (1968) p. 74.
43. Gretton (1964) p. 27; (1965) pp. 87 et seq.
44. Gorshkov quoted in Herrick (1968) p. 95.
45. For these points and extracts from the original Russian version of Gorshkov's work I am indebted to Prof. Donald C. Daniel.
46. Martin (1967) p. 166.
47. Memo by CNO for the Joint Chiefs of Staff on Military Strategy and Posture, 7 Dec. 1953, Ser: 0001250P30. I am indebted to Dr John Hattendorf for this.
48. Mariner (1979) p. 719.
49. Daniel (1978) pp. 227–8.
50. Cohen (1971) p. 331.
51. Gorshkov (1972) Art. 9.
52. Letter by Capt W. J. Ruhe, US Navy to Proceedings of the USNI, (1961) Dec.
53. Karber and Lellenberg (1977) p. 50. This subject has been extensively researched in Nitze (1979) pp. 312–18, 337–82.
54. Washington Planning US General Purpose Forces: The Navy. Congressional Budget Office, Dec 1976, p. 1.
55. MccGwire (1977) p. 11.
56. Lt Gen. Roy S. Geiger, USMC, 21 Aug. 1946, after observing the atomic bomb test at Bikini Lagoon. I am indebted to Dr John Hattendorf for this.
57. Lind and Record (1978) p. 39 and their important study of 1976.
58. Dr James Schlesinger quoted and discussed in Nathan and Oliver (1979) p. 48.
59. Gorshkov (1979) pp. 240 et seq.
60. Quoted in Lt Col. Michael K. Sheridan, 'The Power Projection of Marines is an Essential Part of Sea Control', Marine Corps Gazette, (1977) Sep.
61. Adm. Alafuzov quoted in Herrick (1968) p. 105.
62. Gorshkov (1979) pp. 242, 243, 245.
63. Ibid. p. 217.
64. Daniel (1979) p. 6.

Chapter 9: New Tasks for New Navies

1. Reed (1972) p. 26.
2. I am indebted to Mr Ray Kipling of the Royal National Lifeboat Institution for this and much other information.
3. Quoted in Mann (1972) p. 240.
4. Vice Adm. Humphrey Smith quoted in Marder (1940) p. 15.
5. Gorshkov (1972) Art. 11.
6. See Booth (1978).
7. von Maltzahn (1908) p. 1.
8. Gorshkov discussed this in (1972) Art. 4.
9. Quoted in Puleston (1919) p. 273.
10. Quoted in Graham (1978) p. 415.
11. Corbett vol. ı (1907) p. 6.
12. Mahan (1899) p. 463; Richmond (1946) pp. 141–2.
13. L. F. Duchene in Martin (1979) p. 33.
14. Stansfield Turner (1974).
15. Gorshkov (1972) Art. 10.
16. Ibid. and (1979) pp. 247–8.
17. See T. C. Schelling, *The Strategy of Conflict* (Harvard University Press, 1960); *Arms and Influence* (Yale University Press, 1966); Oran Young, *The Politics of Force* (Princeton University Press, 1968); C. Bell, *The Conventions of Crisis* (Oxford: Clarendon Press, 1971). Also Barry M. Blechman and Stephen S. Kaplan, *Force Without War* (Washington: Brookings Institution, 1978).
18. Booth (1977) p. 47.
19. Ibid. pp. 33–5.
20. O'Connell (1975) p. 8.
21. Young (1974) p. 267.
22. Barry M. Blechman and Stephen S. Kaplan op. cit. p. IV–3.
23. Quotations from various officers on the China Station in Graham (1978) pp. 58, 135 *et seq.*
24. Quoted in Martin (1979) p. 168.
25. Adm. Gene La Roque in George (1978) p. 197.
26. Adm. Elmo Zumwalt quoted in McNulty (1974).
27. Rear Adm. C. A. H. Trost in George (1978) p. 331; also Cable (1971) p. 166.
28. Stansfield Turner quoted in Nathan and Oliver (1979) pp. 72–3.
29. Quoted in Marder (1940) p. 17.
30. Eberle (1976) p. 30.
31. Discussed in MccGwire (1978).
32. Stansfield Turner (1976b) p. 25.
33. Walters (1974) p. 131.
34. Gretton (1965) p. 180.
35. Crowe (1978) p. 22.
36. Gorshkov (1979) pp. 196–7.
37. Bull (1976) p. 2.
38. Gorshkov (1979) pp. 167–8.
39. McConnell (1978) pp. 37 *et seq.*

40. Stansfield Turner (1974).
41. James Schlesinger 1974, quoted in Nathan and Oliver (1979) p. 45.
42. For example McConnel (1978) pp. 45–6.
43. MccGwire (1978) pp. 40–1.
44. McConnell (1978) p. 47.
45. Macintyre (1961) p. 147.
46. Stansfield Turner (1974).
47. Till (1979) pp. 11–28.
48. The reference is to an early draft of Ken Booth's important *The Study of Naval Strategy*, currently under preparation for the Harvester Press.

Chapter 10: A Review of Present Practice

1. Although the incidents which follow have not been individually documented, information about them is derived from contemporary reports in *The Times*, the *Guardian* and the *Daily Telegraph*, supplemented by such news magazines as *The Economist* and *Time*. Supplementary material comes from the International Institute for Strategic Studies, *Strategic Survey* (1979) and the survey *Naval and Maritime Events 1979* published in the *Proceedings of the USNI* (1980) May. This review is intended to be representative rather than wholly comprehensive.
2. Daniel (1979).
3. Ibid. The figure is extrapolated from statements made in 1978 by the Chairman of the US Joint Chiefs of Staff and the Secretary of Defense before Congress.
4. Heikal (1975) p. 165.
5. Adm. Sir James Eberle in Veldman and Olivier (1980) p. 113.
6. Weinland (1979) p. 81.
7. Telem (1975) p. 237.
8. Daniel K. Inouye in George (1978) p. 357.
9. O'Connell (1975) pp. 101–3.
10. *Israeli Navy a Short History – A Proud Record*, by the IDF Spokesman's Office, p. 1.
11. Telem (1980) p. 26.
12. John Nott, 'After the Falklands Let's Not Go Overboard on Navy Spending!', *The Times*, 27 July 1982.
13. *Telegraph*, 7 May 1982. See also *Falkland Islands Review*. A Report of a committee of Privy Counsellors (London: HMSO, 1983) (hereinafter called The Franks Report) paras 192, 193, 199.
14. The Franks Report, para. 244.
15. Cabinet minutes read to the Franks Committee by the Right Hon. James Callaghan MP, *The Times*, 20 Jan. 1983, and statement by Chief of the Defence Staff, Adm. Sir Terence Lewin, *Guardian*, 31 Jan. 1983.
16. The Franks Report, para. 224.
17. Ibid., paras 114–18, 287 and 288.
18. Interview with Oriana Fallaci, *The Times*, 12 June 1982. Also the Sunday Times Insight Team, *The Falklands War* (London: Andre Deutsch, 1982) p. 138.

REFERENCES 273

19. *The Washington Post*, 4 April 1982, and *The Wall Street Journal*, 27 Apr. 1982.
20. Comment by Admiral Woodward (later Rear-Admiral Sir John Woodward) quoted in the *Guardian*, 29 April 1982, and Admiral Sir John Fieldhouse, quoted in Max Hastings and Simon Jenkins, *The Battle for the Falklands* (London: Michael Joseph, 1983) (hereinafter Hastings & Jenkins) p. 123.
21. M. Howard, 'Invade or Withdraw', *Sunday Times*, 9 May 1982.
22. See above, pp. 21, 41.
23. Howard, op. cit.
24. Quoted in the *Guardian*, 21 April 1982.
25. *Guardian*, 20 May 1982.
26. Thus Admiral Lewin, *Telegraph*, 26 May 1982. Also Hastings and Jenkins, pp. 230, 256, 311.
27. Ibid., pp. 329–30.
28. *Guardian*, 14 May 1982.
29. *Telegraph*, 2 June 1982.
30. Hastings and Jenkins, p. 116.
31. Ibid., pp. 36–7, 176–7, 181–3.
32. Ibid., p. 88.
33. Ibid., p. 135.
34. Capt. C. W. Koburger, 'Argentina in the Falklands. Glory Manque', *Navy International*, May 1983.
35. Ibid., p. 191.
36. Admiral Woodward quoted in the *Telegraph*, 5 July 1982.
37. Confirmed and probables as claimed in *The Falklands Campaign: The Lessons* (London: HMSO, 1982) p. 45.
38. See Gregory R. Copley, 'How Argentina's Air Force Fought in the South Atlantic War', *Defense and Foreign Affairs*, Oct. 1982, and interview with Lt Lucero in the *Telegraph* and other papers, 28 May 1982.
39. *The Times*, 14 Sep. 1982.
40. See particularly, the interview with HMS *Conqueror*'s Commanding Officer Cdr C. Wreford-Brown given in Geoffrey Underwood, *Our Falklands War* (London: Maritime Books, 1983).
41. Hastings and Jenkins, p. 125.
42. *Aerospacio*, Sep. 1982, quoted in *The Times*, 20 Oct. 1982.
43. Koburger, op. cit.
44. *Guardian*, 12 May 1982.
45. *Telegraph*, 22 May 1982.
46. *The Times*, 20 Oct. 1982.
47. Ibid. and 28 Mar. 1983.
48. Described in Hastings and Jenkins, p. 304.
49. Gorshkov (1979) p. 253.

Bibliography

There follows, first, a selective bibliography for the main maritime strategists and then an alphabetical list of books and articles actually cited in the text.

The Colomb Brothers

Both the Colomb brothers were regular attenders at, and contributors to, the Royal United Services Institute, whose journal is full of their articles, lectures and book reviews from the early 1860s onwards. Captain Sir John Colomb's main writings were the pamphlet, *The Protection of Our Commerce and Distribution of Our Naval Forces Considered* (London: Harrison, 1867) and *Colonial Defence* (London, 1873). Many of his articles were gathered together as, *The Defence of Great and Greater Britain* (London: Edward Stanford, 1880). His views have been sympathetically summarised by Howard D'Egville, *Imperial Defence and Closer Union* (London: King, 1913).

Vice Admiral Philip Colomb was even more prolific, but his main writings may be found in, *Essays on Naval Defence* (London: Allen, 1896) and *Naval Warfare*, 3rd ed. (London: Allen, 1899).

D. M. Schurman, *The Education of a Navy* (London: Cassell, 1965) is a useful introduction to the work of both the Colomb brothers. This book in fact is a good introduction to most of the following maritime strategists as well.

Mahan

Mahan was a prolific writer and spent the last 25 years of his life writing for a living. Between 1879 and 1914, Mahan wrote over a dozen books and a total of 137 articles. Throughout all of these run the themes offered in his first 'Sea Power' volume. By far the most important of his works, therefore, is *The Influence of Sea Power Upon History 1660–1783* (Boston: Little, Brown, 1890). The sea power doctrine is carried on chronologically in, *The Influence of Sea Power Upon the French Revolution and Empire*, 2 vols. (Boston: Little, Brown, 1892), and *The Influence of Sea Power Upon the War of 1812*, 2 vols. (Boston: Little, Brown, 1905).

Mahan himself thought his best work was his, *Life of Nelson*, 2 vols. (Boston: Little, Brown, 1897). Less important but still interesting is Mahan's autobiographical, *From Sail to Steam, Recollections of Naval Life* (New York: Harper, 1907).

Almost as much has been written about Mahan. The most recent, thorough, and interesting biography is Robert Seager, II, *Alfred Thayer Mahan, the Man and his Letters* (Annapolis: Naval Institute Press, 1977). Also useful are William D. Puleston, *Mahan: the Life and World of Alfred Thayer Mahan, USN* (Yale University Press, 1939); Charles C. Taylor, *The Life of Admiral Mahan, Naval Philosopher* (London: John Murray, 1920); and William C. Livezey, *Mahan on Sea Power* (University of Oklahoma Press, 1947).

Jeune Ecole

The earliest expression of the views associated with this school is Baron Richard Grivel, *De La Guerre Maritime* (Paris: 1869). Admiral Aube's ideas are best explored in the collection, *A Terre et a Bord, Notes d'un Marin* (Paris: 1884). Another standard text-book of the school was, *Essai de Strategie Navale* (Paris: 1893) by Commander Z and H. Montechant. The best scholarly analysis of their ideas and their influence is the unpublished thesis by T. Ropp, *The Development of a Modern Navy* (Harvard University Press, 1937).

More conventional statements on French maritime strategy are Admiral R. Daveluy, *L'Esprit de la Guerre Navale* (Paris: 1902), and *Strategie Navale* (Paris: 1905). Admiral G. Darrieus' work was translated into English as *War on the Sea: Strategy and Tactics* (Annapolis: USNI Press, 1908). See also J. I. de Lanessan *Le Programme Maritime de 1900–1906* (Paris: 1903) which was translated by the *Journal of the RUSI* (1903) pp. 1024 ff.

For German strategic thinking see Baron Curt von Maltzahn, *Naval Warfare* (London: Longmans, Green, 1908). Carl-Axel Gemzell *Organisation, Conflict and Innovation: A Study of German Naval Strategic Planning 1888–1940* (Scandinavian University Books, 1974) provides an excellent background.

Corbett

Among Sir Julian Corbett's main works were *Some Principles of Maritime Strategy* (London: Longmans, Green, Second Edition 1918); *England in the Seven Years War*, 2 vols. (London: Longmans, Green, 1907); and *The Campaign of Trafalgar* (London: Longmans, Green, 1910). Both these last works are important for their interpretation of the interconnection between land and sea warfare. Bryan Ranft (ed.), *Technical Change and British Naval Strategic Thought, 1867–1914* (London: Hodder & Stoughton, 1977) has an article by the editor, 'The Protection of British Seaborne Trade and the Development of Systematic Planning for War, 1860–1906', which gives the background of Admiralty policy against which Corbett wrote.

Richmond

Richmond's best-remembered and broadest works were his, *Statesmen and Sea Power* (Oxford: Clarendon Press, 1946) and the unfinished, *The Navy as an Instrument of Policy 1558–1727* (Cambridge University Press, 1953) edited by E. A. Hughes. For general surveys of Richmond's life there are Barry Hunt, *Sailor–Scholar: Admiral Sir Herbert Richmond, 1871–1946* to be published shortly by the Wilfred Laurier University Press; Arthur J. Marder *Portrait of an Admiral* (London: Jonathan Cape, 1952); G. M. Trevelyan 'Admiral Sir Herbert Richmond, 1871–1946', *The Proceedings of the British Academy*, XXXII (Reprint 1946) with a naval insight by Rear Adm. H. G. Thursfield; Stephen Roskill, 'The Richmond Lecture', *Naval Review*, (1969) April.

Continental Maritime Strategy

The outstanding work of the interwar period on the continent of Europe was Adm. R. Castex, *Theories Strategiques*, 5 vols. (Paris: Societe d'Editions, 1929–1935). Another important figure was Herbert Rosinski whose essays have been gathered together under the title, *The Development of Naval Thought. Essays by Herbert Rosinski* (B. Mitchell Simpson, ed.) (Newport: Naval War College Press, 1977).

T. Ropp, 'Continental Doctrines of Sea Power', in E. M. Earle (ed.), *Makers of Modern Strategy* (Princeton University Press, 1943) provides an excellent background. R. Grenfell, *The Art of the Admiral* (London: Faber, 1937) is a useful introduction to British thought in this period.

Reactions to Second World War

Captain Roskill's conceptions of maritime strategy are to be found in his, *The Strategy of Sea Power* (London: Collins, 1962) and, succinctly summarised in the first chapter of the first volume of his *The War at Sea 1939–1945*, 5 vols. (London: HMSO, 1954–61). Bernard Brodie's classic work is, *A Guide to Naval Strategy* (New York: Praeger, 1965).

See also Vice Adm. P. Barjot, *Vers La Marine De L'Age Atomique*

(Paris: Amiot Dumont, 1956); Vice Adm. Sir Peter Gretton, *Maritime Strategy* (London: Cassell, 1965); Rear Adm. Edward Wegener, 'Theory of Naval Strategy in the Nuclear Age', *Proceedings of the USNI*, (1972) May, 192–207, and *The Soviet Naval Offensive* (Annapolis: Naval Institute Press, 1975).

Stephen Ambrose, 'Sea Power in World Wars I and II', in B. Mitchell Simpson III (ed.), *War, Strategy and Maritime Power* (Rutgers University Press, 1977) is a short and stimulating survey of the main issues.

American Naval Thinking

The most celebrated text is Adm. Stansfield Turner, 'Missions of the US Navy', *Naval War College Review*, (1974) Mar.–Apr. The best summary of American naval affairs in this period is to be found in the last three chapters of Kenneth J. Hagan (ed.), *In Peace and War: Interpretations of American Naval History 1775–1978* (London: Arcenwood Press, 1978). A general description of the state of thinking at the end of the 1970s may be found in James A. Nathan and James K. Oliver, *The Future of United States Naval Power* (Indiana University Press, 1979).

Gorshkov

The best English language texts are Sergei G. Gorshkov, *The Sea Power of the State* (Oxford: Pergamon, 1979) and his, 'Navies in War and Peace'. This last was the title given to a series of 11 articles which appeared in *Morskoi Sbornik*, (1972–3) and which have been translated as *Red Star Rising at Sea* (Annapolis: Naval Institute Press, 1974). David Fairhall, *Russia Looks to the Sea* (London: Andre Deutsch, 1971); and Norman Polmar (ed.), *The Modern Soviet Navy* (London: Arms and Armour Press, 1979) provide the background.

Other books and articles cited in the references

Acworth, Captain B. (1930) *The Navies of Today and Tomorrow* (London: Eyre & Spottiswoode).
—— (1935) *The Restoration of England's Sea Power* (London: Eyre & Spottiswoode).
Adelphi Paper (1976) *Power at Sea* Nos 122–4 (London: International Institute for Strategic Studies).
Bacon, Admiral Sir Reginald (1936) *The Life of John Rushworth Earl Jellicoe* (London: Cassell).

Ballantine, D. S. (1949) *US Naval Logistics in the Second World War* (Princeton University Press).

Barjot, Vice Admiral P. (1956) *Vers La Marine De L'Age Atomique* (Paris: Amiot Dumont).

Bell, C. (1971) *The Conventions of Crisis* (Oxford: Clarendon Press).

Bertram, C. and Holst, J. J. (eds.) (1977) *New Strategic Factors in the North Atlantic* (Oslo: Universiteitsforlagt).

Bird, K. W. (1979) 'The Origins and Role of the German Naval History in the Interwar Period', *Naval War College Review*, March–April.

Blechman, B. M. and Kaplan, S. S. (1978) *Force Without War* (Washington: Brookings Institute).

Booth, K. (1976) 'Ethnocentrism and the Theory and Practice of Strategy'. A paper prepared for the Annual Convention of the International Studies Association, Toronto, February.

—— (1977) *Navies and Foreign Policy* (London: Croom Helm).

—— (1978) 'The Military Implications of the Changing Law of the Sea'. A paper prepared for the 12th Annual Conference of the Law of the Sea Institute, The Hague, October.

—— (forthcoming) *The Study of Naval Strategy*, in preparation.

Bowling, Captain R. A. (1977) 'The Negative Influence of Mahan of Anti-submarine Warfare', *Journal of the RUSI*, December.

Bridge, Admiral Sir Cyprian (1873) 'Fleet Evolutions and Fleet Tactics', *Journal of the RUSI*.

—— (1907) *The Art of Naval Warfare* (London: Smith, Elder).

—— (1910) *Sea Power and Other Studies* (London: Smith, Elder).

Brodie, B. (1943) *Sea Power in the Machine Age* (Princeton University Press).

—— (1965) *A Guide to Naval Strategy* (New York: Praeger).

Brown, C. R. (1949) 'The Role of the Navy in Future Warfare', *Naval War College Review*, April.

Brown, Neville (1964) *Nuclear War: the Impending Strategic Deadlock* (London: Pall Mall Press).

Cable, Sir James (1971) *Gunboat Diplomacy* (London: Chatto & Windus); 2nd ed. (London: Macmillan, 1981).

Callender, G. (1924) *The Naval Side of British History* (London: Christopher).

Castex, Admiral R. (1929–35) *Theories Strategiques* (Paris: Societe d'Editions) 5 vols.

Clark, G. S. and Thursfield, J. R. (1897) *The Navy and the Nation* (London: John Murray).

Clarke, J. J. (1967) 'Merchant Marine and the Navy', *Journal of RUSI*, May.

Cobden, R. (1862) *The Three Panics* (London).

Cohen, P. (1971) 'The Erosion of Surface Naval Power', *Foreign Affairs*, January.

Colomb, Sir John (1880) *The Defence of Great and Greater Britain* (London: Stanford).

Colomb, P. (1896) *Essays on Naval Defence* (London: Allen).

—— (1899) *Naval Warfare*, 3rd ed. (London: Allen).

Corbett, J. S. (1894) *Sir Francis Drake* (London: Macmillan).

—— (1898) *Drake and the Tudor Navy* (London: Longmans, Green).

—— (ed.) (1905) *Fighting Instructions 1530–1816* (London: Navy Records Soc.).

—— (1907) *England in the Seven Years War* (London: Longmans, Green) 2 vols.

—— (1910) *The Campaign of Trafalgar* (London: Longmans, Green).

—— (1918) *Some Principles of Maritime Strategy* (London: Longmans, Green 2nd edition).

—— (1920–31) *History of the Great War: Naval Operations*, 5 vols. last two by Sir Henry Newbold (London: Longmans, Green).

Cottrell, A. J. and Moorer, T. H. (1977) *US Overseas Bases*, The Washington Papers, vol. 5.

Crowe, Vice Admiral W. (1978) 'Western Strategy and Missions Approaching the Twenty-First Century', in J. L. George (ed.) *Problems of Sea Power as We Approach the Twenty-First Century* (Washington: American Enterprise Institute).

Crowl, P. A. (1978) *The Strategist's Short Catechism* (USAF Academy).

Custance, Admiral Sir Reginald (1907) ('Barfleur') *Naval Policy* (Edinburgh: Blackwood).

—— (1912) *The Ship of the Line in Battle* (Edinburgh: Blackwood).

—— (1918 and 1970) *War at Sea* (London: Conway Maritime Press).

—— (1924) *A Study of War* (London: Constable).

Daniel, D. C. (1978) 'Trends and Patterns in Major Soviet Naval Exercises', in P. J. Murphy (ed.) *Naval Power in Soviet Policy* (US Air Force).

—— (1979) 'Navy', in David Jones (ed.) *Soviet Armed Forces Review Annual*, vol. 3. (Gulf Breeze: Academic International).

Daveluy, Admiral R. (1902) *L'Esprit de la Guerre Navale* (Paris).

Darrieus, Admiral Gabriel (1908) *War on the Sea: Strategy and Tactics* (Annapolis: USNI Press).

Dewar, A. G. (1904) 'Gold Medal Prize Essay', *Journal of RUSI*, April.

Dismukes, B. and McConnell, J. M. (1979) *Soviet Naval Diplomacy* (New York: Pergamon).

Eberle, Admiral J. F. (1976) 'Designing a Modern Navy', in *Adelphi* 123.

Eccles, H. E. (1965) *Military Concepts and Philosophy* (Rutgers University Press).

d'Egville, H. (1913) *Imperial Defence and Closer Union* (London: King).

Enthoven, A. C. and Smith K. W. (1969) 'What Forces for NATO? And From Whom?', *Foreign Affairs*, October.

Fox, J. R. (1974) *Arming America* (Harvard University Press).

Frere-Cooke, G. (1973) *The Attacks on the* Tirpitz (London: Ian Allan).

George, J. L. (ed.) (1978) *Problems of Sea Power as We Approach the Twenty-first Century* (Washington: American Enterprise Institute).

Gorshkov, Sergei G. (1974) *Navies in War and Peace*; published as *Red Star Rising at Sea* (Annapolis: Naval Institute Press).

—— (1979) *The Sea Power of the State* (Oxford: Pergamon).

Graham, G. S. (1965) *The Politics of Naval Supremacy* (Cambridge University Press).

—— (1978) *The China Station* (Oxford: Clarendon Press).

de la Graviere, Admiral Jurien (1874) 'La Marine Aujordhui', *Journal of the RUSI*.

Grenfell, R. (1937) *The Art of the Admiral* (London: Faber).

Gretton, Admiral Sir Peter (1964) 'Threat to Sea Communications As a Means of Limited War', *Brassey's Naval Annual*.

—— (1965) *Maritime Strategy* (London: Cassell).

Grivel, Vice Admiral Baron Jean (1837) *De La Marine Militaire* (Paris).

Grivel, Baron Richard (1869) *De la Guerre Maritime* (Paris).

Gwyn, J. (ed.) (1973) *The Royal Navy and North America* (London: Navy Records Society).

Hayes, J. D. (1953) 'Peripheral Strategy – Mahan's Doctrine Today', *Proceedings of the USNI*, November.

—— and Hattendorf, J. B. (1975) *The Writings of Stephen B. Luce* (Newport: Naval War College).

Heikal, M. (1975) *The Road to Ramadan* (London: Collins).

Herrick, R. W. (1968) *Soviet Naval Strategy* (Annapolis: Naval Institute Press).

Hibbits, J. G. (1978) 'Admiral Gorshkov's Writings', in Murphy (ed.) op. cit.

Howard, M. (1976) 'Power at Sea', *Adelphi*, 123 op. cit.

Howe, J. T. (1971) *Multicrises* (Cambridge: MIT Press).

Hunt, B. (forthcoming) Sailor-Scholar: Admiral Sir Herbert Richmond, 1871–1946 (Wilfred Laurier University Press) to be published.

Huntingdon, S. P. (1954) 'National Policy and the Transoceanic Navy', *Proceedings of the USNI*, May.

James, Admiral Sir William (1948) *The Influence of Sea Power* (Cambridge University Press).

Jane, F. T. (1906) *Heresies of Sea Power* (London: Longmans).

Jowett, B. (1900) *Thucydides Translated into English* (Oxford: Clarendon Press) 2 vols.

Jungius, Admiral Sir James (1979) 'The Balance of Power at Sea', *NATO Review*, December.

Karber P. A. and Lellenberg, J. L. (1977) 'The State and Future of US Naval Forces in the North Atlantic', in Bertram and Holst, (eds.) op. cit.

Kennan, G. (1966) *Realities of American Foreign Policy* (New York: Norton).

Kennedy, P. M. (1976) *The Rise and Fall of British Naval Mastery* (London: Allen Lane).

Kruse, E. (1938) *Neuzeitliche Seekriegsführung* (Berlin: Mitler).

Lanchester, F. W. (1916) *Aircraft in Warfare* (London: Constable).

de Lanessan, J. I. (1903) *Le Programme Maritime de 1900–1906* (Paris).

Laughton, J. K. (1874) 'The Scientific Study of Naval History', *Journal of the RUSI*.

Lewis, M. (1948) *The Navy of Britain* (London: George Allen & Unwin).

Lind, W. S. and Record, J. (1976) *Where Does the Marine Corps Go From Here?* (Washington: Brookings Institute).

—— (1978) 'Twilight for the Corps?', *Proceedings of the USNI* July.

Luttwak, E. (1975) *The Political Uses of Sea Power* (Johns Hopkins University Press).

McConnell, J. (1978) 'Strategy and Missions of the Soviet Navy in the Year 2000', in George (ed.) op. cit.

Macintyre, D. (1961) *The Battle of the Atlantic* (London: Batsford).

Mackinder, Sir Halford (1919) *Democratic Ideals and Reality* (London: Constable).

McNulty, Commander J. F. (1974) 'Naval Presence – the Misunderstood Mission', *Naval War College Review*, September–October.

Mahan, A. T. (1884) *The Gulf and Inland Waters* (New York: Scriveners).

—— (1890) *The Influence of Sea Power Upon History 1660–1783* (Boston: Little, Brown).

—— (1892) *The Influence of Sea Power upon the French Revolution and Empire* (Boston: Little, Brown) 2 vols.

—— (1899) *The Life of Nelson* (London: Sampson, Low).

—— (1907) *From Sail to Steam, Recollections of Naval Life* (New York: Harper).

von Maltzahn, Baron Curt (1908) *Naval Warfare* (London: Longmans, Green).

Mann, B. E. (ed.) (1972) *Pacem in Maribus* (New York: Dodd, Mead & Co.).

Marder, A. J. (1940) *The Anatomy of British Sea Power* (New York).

—— (1952) *Portrait of an Admiral* (London: Jonathan Cape).

'Mariner', (1979) 'Admiral Gorshkov, naval genius or political opportunist?', *International Defence Review* No. 5.

Martin, L. (1967) *The Sea in Modern Strategy* (London: Chatto & Windus).

—— (ed.) (1979) *Strategic Thought in the Nuclear Age* (London: Heinemann).

Masson, P. (1982) *Marines et Oceans* (Paris: Imprimerie National).

McGwire, M. *et al.* (eds.) (1973) *Soviet Naval Developments* (New York: Praeger).
—— (ed.) (1975) *Soviet Naval Policy* (New York: Praeger).
—— (1975) 'Command of the Sea in Soviet Naval Strategy' in ibid.
—— (1976) 'Maritime Strategy and the Superpowers', *Adelphi* 123.
—— (1977) 'Changing Naval Operations and Military Intervention', *Naval War College Review* Spring.
—— (1978) 'Soviet Naval Doctrine', prepared for Seminar on Soviet Military Doctrine at Harvard University, Spring.
Monson, Sir William (1902–14) in M. Oppenheim (ed.), *Naval Tracts* (London: Naval Records Society).
Morgenstern, O. (1959) *The Question of National Defense* (New York: Random House).
Murphy, P. J. (1978) *Naval Power in Soviet Policy* (US Air Force).
Natham, J. A. and Oliver J. K. (1979) *The Future of United States Naval Power* (Indiana University Press).
Nimitz, Fleet Admiral C. W. (1947) Report to Secretary of the Navy, December reprinted in *Brassey's Naval Annual*, 1948.
Nitze, P. H. (1979) *Securing the Seas* (Boulder, Colorado: Westview Press).
O'Connell, D. P. (1975) *The Influence of Law on Sea Power* (Manchester University Press).
Peattie, M. (1977) 'Akiyama Saneyjuki and the Emergence of Modern Japanese Naval Doctrine', *Proceedings of the USNI*, January.
Philbin, T. (1971) 'Admiral Franz Hipper on Naval Warfare', *Naval War College Review*, Fall.
Pollen, A. H. (1918) *The Navy in Battle* (London: Chatto & Windus).
Potter, E. B. and Nimitz, C. (1960) *Sea Power: A Naval History* (New Jersey: Prentice Hall).
Puleston, W. D. (1939) *Mahan: the Life and Works of Alfred Thayer Mahan, USN* (New Haven: Yale University Press).
Reed, L. (1972) *An Ocean of Waste* (London: Conservative Political Centre for Bow Group).
Reitzel, W. (1977) 'Mahan on the Use of the Sea' in B. M. Simpson (ed.) *War Strategy and Maritime Power* (Rutgers University Press).
Reveillere, Admiral E. (1893) 'France and the Marine', *Journal of the RUSI*.
Reynolds, C. G. (1974) *Command of the Sea* (New York: Morrow).
Richmond, H. W. (1930) *Naval Warfare* (London: Ernest Benn).
—— (1934) *Seapower in the Modern World* (London: Bell).
—— (1939) 'The Importance of the Study of Naval History', *Naval Review*.
—— (1941a) 'The Modern Conception of Sea Power', *Naval Review*.
—— (1941b) *Amphibious Warfare in British History* (London: Historical Association).

—— (1943) 'The Objects and Elements of Sea Power in History', *Naval Review*.

—— (1946) *Statesmen and Sea Power* (Oxford: Clarendon Press).

—— (1953) *The Navy as an Instrument of Policy 1558–1727*, ed. by E. A. Hughes (Cambridge University Press).

Rodgers, W. L. (1937) *Greek and Roman Naval Warfare* (Annapolis: Naval Institute Press).

Ropp, T. (1937) *The Development of a Modern Navy* (Harvard University Press).

Rosinski, H. (1977) 'New Thoughts on Strategy' in Simpson (ed.) op. cit.

Roskill, Captain, S. W. (1952) 'Some Strategic Lessons to be drawn from the Second World War', *Naval Review*.

—— (1954) *The War at Sea 1939–1945*, vol. I, (London: HSMO), Chap. 1.

—— (1962) *The Strategy of Sea Power* (London: Collins).

—— (1968, 1976) *Naval Policy Between the Wars* 2 vols. (London: Collins).

Ruge, F. (1979) *The Soviets as Naval Opponents* (Cambridge: Patrick Stephens).

Ruhe, Captain W. J. (1961) Letter, *Proceedings of the USNI*, December.

Scharfen, J. C. and Wilcox K. S. (1979) 'Strategic Metaphors' *Proceedings of the USNI*, September.

Scheer, Admiral R. (1920) *Germany's High Sea Fleet in the World War* (London: Cassell).

Schelling, T. C. (1960) *The Strategy of Conflict* (Harvard University Press).

—— (1966) *Arms and Influence* (Yale University Press).

Schurman, D. M. (1965) *The Education of a Navy* (London: Cassell).

Seager, R. (1953) 'Ten Years Before Mahan', *Mississippi Valley Historical Review*.

—— (1977) *Alfred Thayer Mahan, the Man and his Letters* (Annapolis: Naval Institute Press).

Sheridan, Lieutenant Colonel M. K. (1977) 'The Power Projection of Marines is an Essential Part of Sea Control', *Marine Corps Gazette*, September.

Simpson, B. M. (ed.) (1977) *War Strategy and Maritime Power* (Rutgers University Press).

Sokol, A. E. (1961) *Sea Power in the Nuclear Age* (Washington: Public Affairs Press).

Sokolovsky, Marshal V. D. (1963) *Military Strategy: Soviet Doctrine and Concepts* (New York: Praeger).

Spear, P. (1970) *A History of India*, vol. II (London: Penguin).

Sprout, M. T. (1943) 'Mahan, Evangelist of Sea Power', in E. M. Earle (ed.), *Makers of Modern Strategy* (Princeton University Press).

Sprout, M. T. and H. M. (1939) *Rise of American Naval Power* (Princeton University Press).

—— (1946) *Toward a New Order of Sea Power* (Princeton University Press).

Stansfield Turner, Admiral (1974) 'Missions of the US Navy', *Naval War College Review*, March–April.

—— (1976a) *Navies for Yesterday or Tomorrow?* A special university lecture in war studies, King's College, London, 4 May.

—— (1976b) 'Designing a Modern Navy' in *Adelphi* 123.

—— (1977) 'The Naval Balance: Not Just a Numbers Game' *Foreign Affairs* January.

Steinberg, J. (1965) *Yesterday's Deterrent: Tirpitz and the Birth of the German Battle Fleet* (London: Macdonald).

Stockdale, J. B. (1978) 'Taking Stock', *Naval War College Review*, Spring.

Strausz-Hupe, R. (1942) *Geopolitics: The Struggle for Space and Power* (New York: Putman).

Ströbe, Dr. Walther (1976) 'Forecasting for the Escape of the *Scharnhorst* and *Gneisenau*', *Meterological Magazine*, November.

Sutcliffe, M. (1593) *The Practise, Proceedings and Lawes of Armes* (London).

Sydenham, Lord (1931) 'Sea Heresies' *Naval Review*.

Symcox, G. (1974) *The Crisis of French Sea Power 1688–1697* (The Hague: Martinus Nijhoff).

Taylor, C. C. (1920) *The Life of Admiral Mahan, Naval Philosopher* (London: John Murray).

Telem, Admiral B. (1975) 'Naval Lessons of the Yom Kippur War' in Williams (ed.) *The Military Aspects of the Israeli Arab Conflict* (Tel Aviv: University Publishing Projects).

—— (1980) 'Israel's Guided Missile Fast Attack Craft in the Yom Kippur War', *Naval Forces* vol. 1 no. 2.

Till, G. (1979) *Air Power and the Royal Navy* (London: Jane).

Tunstall, B. (1936) *The Realities of Naval History* (London: George Allen & Unwin).

Veldman, J. H. and Olivier, F. T. (1980) *West-European Navies and the Future* (Den Helder: R. Neth. N. College).

Vigor, P. H. (1975) 'Soviet Understanding of Command of the Sea' in MccGwire (ed.) op. cit.

Waddington, C. H. (1947) *O.R. in World War 2* (London: Elek Science).

von Waldeyer–Hartz (1936) 'Naval Warfare of Tomorrow', *Wissen und Wehr*.

Walters, R. E. (1974) *Sea Power and the Nuclear Fallacy*; published in Britain as *The Nuclear Trap: An Escape Route*, (London: Penguin).

Waters, Lieutenant Commander D. W. (1957) *A Study of the Philosophy and Conduct of Maritime War 1815–1945* (London: Naval Historical Section, Admiralty).

Wegener, Rear Admiral E. (1972) 'Theory of Naval Strategy in the Nuclear Age', *Proceedings of the USNI*, May, 192–207.
—— (1975) *The Soviet Naval Offensive* (Annapolis: Naval Institute Press).
Weinland, R. G. (1979) *Superpower Naval Diplomacy in the October 1973 Arab–Israeli War*, Washington Papers no. 61, Pt. II.
Westcott, A. (ed.) (1919) *Mahan on Naval Warfare* (Boston: Little, Brown).
Williams, L. (1975) *The Military Aspects of the Israeli Arab Conflict* (Tel Aviv: University Publishing Projects).
Wilson, C. (1957) *Profit and Power: A Study of England and the Dutch Wars*. (London: Longmans).
Woodward, D. (1965) *The Russians at Sea* (London: Kimber).
Young, E. (1974) 'New Laws for Old Navies', *Survival*, November–December.
Young, O. (1968) *The Politics of Force* (Princeton University Press).
Zumwalt, Admiral E. (1976) *On Watch* (New York: Quadrangle).

Index

Acworth, Capt. Bernard, 54
  on decisive battle, 104, 120
  on British blockade, 154
  hostility to large battleships, 88
Aircraft
  challenge to navies, 51, 85, 101,
    126, 152, 181–3, 188
  development of naval air power,
    53, 56, 57, 78, 146–7
  part of naval operations, 87–8,
    108–9, 161, 178, 224
Alafuzov, Adm. V. A., 200
Allison, Graham, 67
American Independence, War of, 5,
  41, 78, 114, 115, 116, 122, 141
Anaya, Adm. Jorge, 240, 242, 244, 245
Andre, Jean-Bon St., 80
Arab–Israeli conflict, 228
Arab–Israeli War (1973), 226, 235–
  9
Arginussae, battle of (406 BC), 14–15
Armada Republica Argentina, 239–56
  passim
Armada, the Spanish (1588), 89, 93,
  96, 136, 141, 147
ASDIC, 108
ASW, 220–1, 224
Atlantic, battle of (1939–45), 108,
  160, 179, 222
Aube, Adm. Theophile, 36–7
Austria, 84

Bacc ι, Sir Francis, 20, 21, 131, 242
Bacon, Adm. Sir Reginald, 120, 178
Balanced fleet concept, 74
Balfour, Arthur James, 26
Ballantine, Duncan S., 63
Barjot, Adm. P., 57
Bases, 86–7, 145, 245

Battleship
  importance of, 53, 78, 87, 104
  scepticism about, 47, 54, 91,
    103–4, 109, 156, 183, 186
Beachy Head, battle of (1690), 113,
  114
Beatty, Adm. Earl, 54, 46, 107,
  108
Bell, Coral, 211
Black Sea, 68
  no command of, 191–2
Blockade, 16, 26, 121, 132–3
  in Arab–Israeli war, 236
  in Falklands campaign, 252–3
  commercial blockade, 154–5, 169
  modern versions of, 187–8
  types of, 122–8
Booth, Ken, 62, 211, 212
Boscawen, Adm. Hon. Edward,
  123
Bridge, Adm. Sir Cyprian, 28
  on command, 128–9
  on naval history, 6, 28, 102
Britain
  attitude to Germany, 118
  disinclination to use naval diplo-
    macy, 164–5
  emergence as sea power, 3, 31–2,
    77, 88
  interests in sea, 203, 205, 206,
    207
  maritime activities in 1979, 227
  see also Falklands campaign; Royal
    Navy
Brodie, Bernard, 55–6, 60
  on command, 130, 132–3
  on operations against shore, 140,
    143, 146
  on universality of strategy, 11
Brown, Adm. C. R. (USN), 63